W9-BUI-234

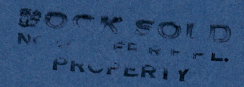

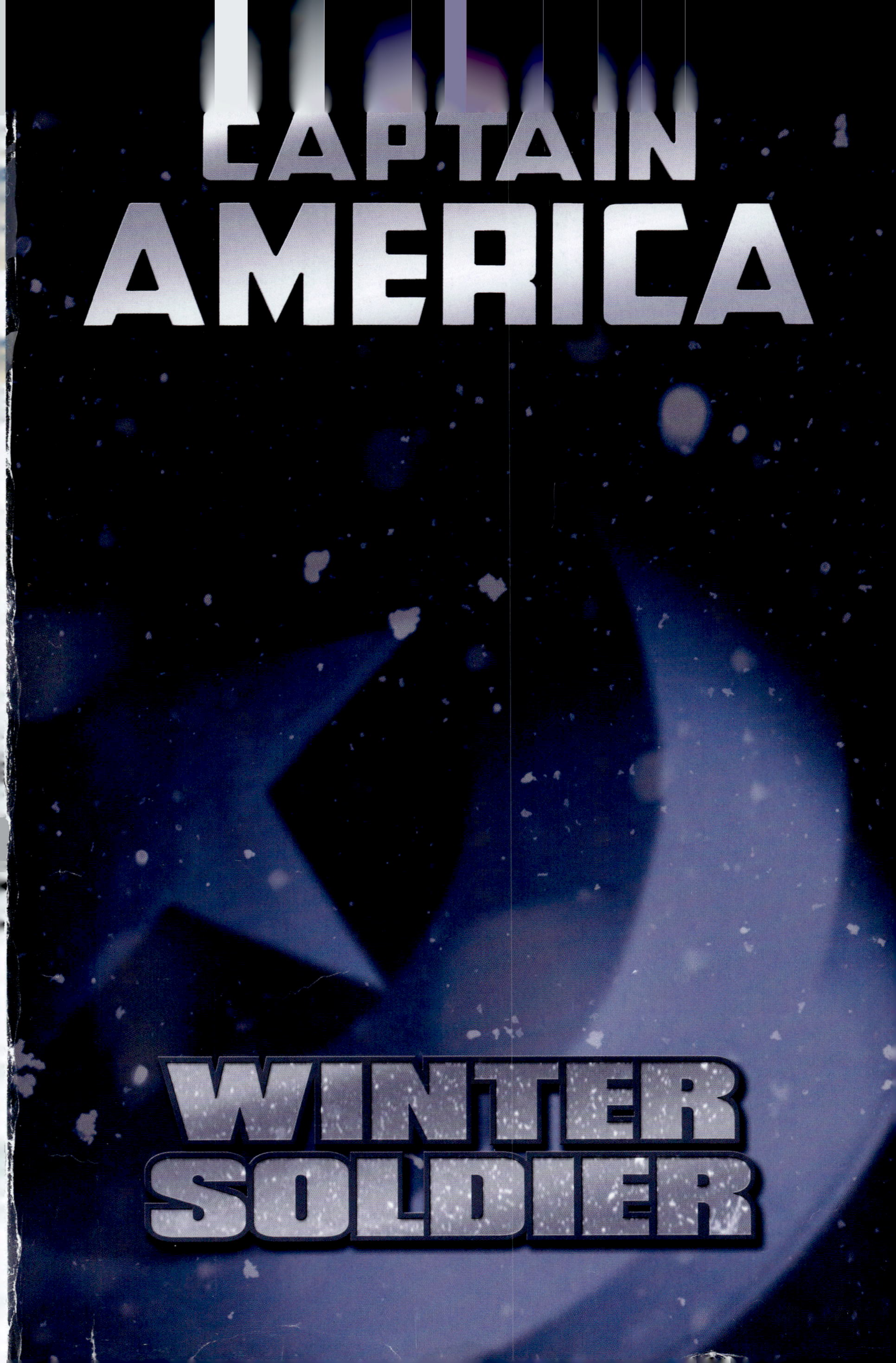
CAPTAIN
AMERICA
WINTER
SOLDIER

CAPTAIN AMERICA
WINTER SOLDIER

WRITER: Ed Brubaker
ARTIST: Steve Epting
Michael Lark (Flashback Art)
John Paul Leon & Tom Palmer (Issue #7)
COLORIST: Frank D'Armata
LETTERS: Virtual Calligraphy's Randy Gentile
ASSISTANT EDITORS: Nicole Wiley, Molly Lazer
& Andy Schmidt
EDITOR: Tom Brevoort

Captain America created by
Joe Simon & Jack Kirby

COLLECTION EDITOR: Jennifer Grünwald
SENIOR EDITOR, SPECIAL PROJECTS: Jeff Youngquist
DIRECTOR OF SALES: David Gabriel
BOOK DESIGNER: Patrick McGrath
CREATIVE DIRECTOR: Tom Marvelli

EDITOR IN CHIEF: Joe Quesada
PUBLISHER: Dan Buckley

CAPTAIN AMERICA: WINTER SOLDIER VOL. 1. Contains material originally published in magazine form as CAPTAIN AMERICA #1-7. First printing 2005. ISBN# 0-7851-1651-6. Published by MARVEL COMICS, a division of MARVEL ENTERTAINMENT GROUP, INC. OFFICE OF PUBLICATION: 10 East 40th Street, New York, NY 10016. Copyright © 2004 and 2005 Marvel Characters. Inc. All rights reserved. $21.99 per copy in the U.S. and $35.25 in Canada (GST #R127032852); Canadian Agreement #40668537. All characters featured in this issue and the distinctive names and likenesses thereof, and all related indicia are trademarks of Marvel Characters, Inc. No similarity between any of the names, characters, persons, and/or institutions in this magazine with those of any living or dead person or institution is intended, and any such similarity which may exist is purely coincidental. Printed in the U.S.A. AVI ARAD, Chief Creative Officer; ALAN FINE, President & CEO of Toy Biz and Marvel Publishing; DAN CARR, Director of Production; ELAINE CALLENDER, Director of Manufacturing; DAVID BOGART, Managing Editor; STAN LEE, Chairman Emeritus. For information regarding advertising in Marvel Comics or on Marvel.com, please contact Joe Maimone, Advertising Director, at jmaimone@marvel.com or 212-576-8534.

10 9 8 7 6 5 4 3 2 1

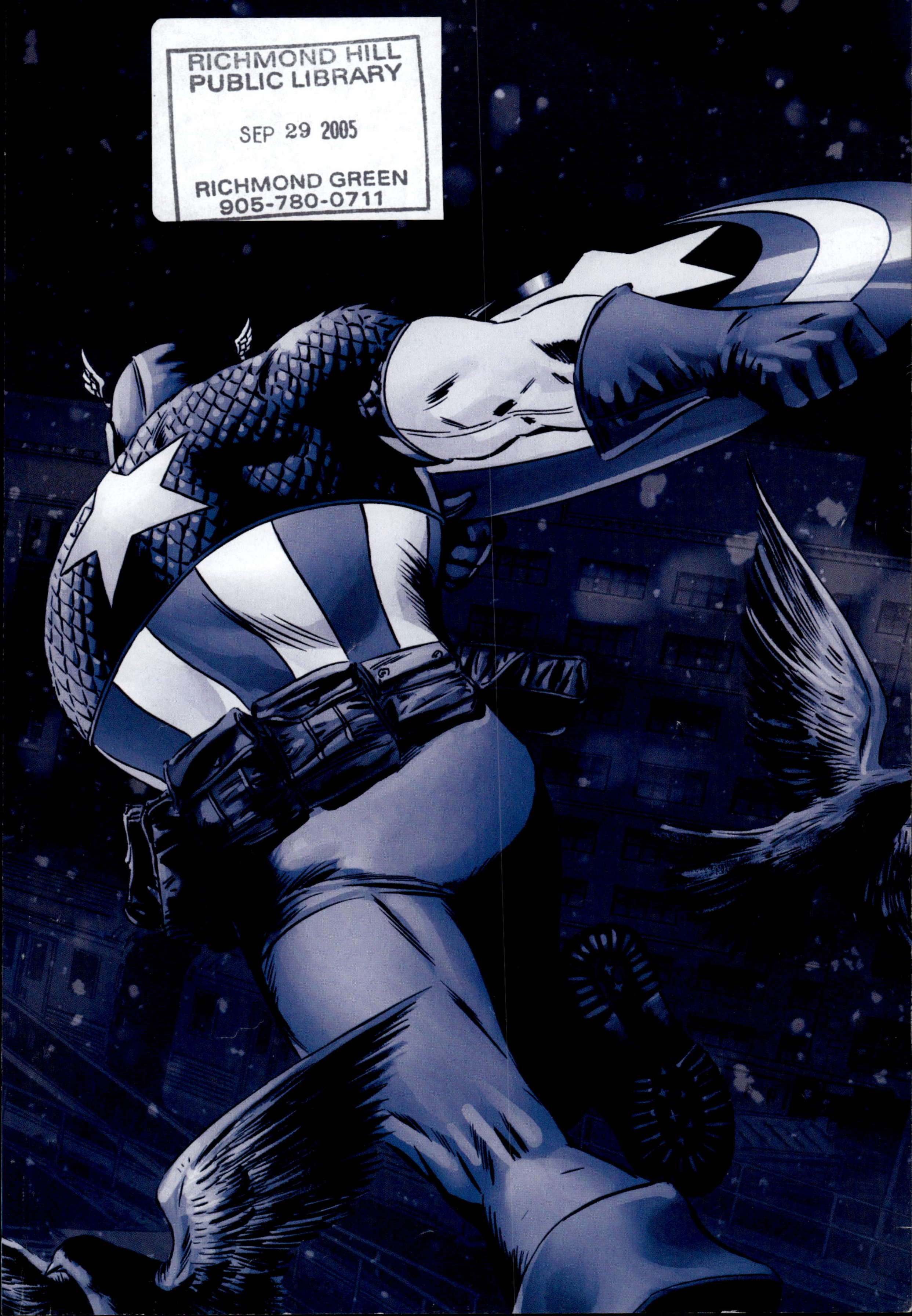

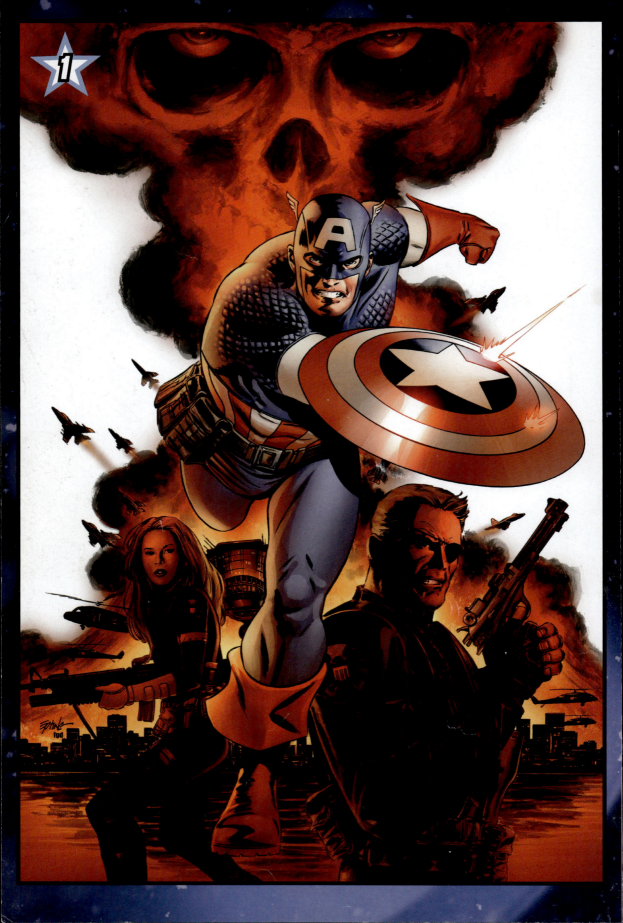

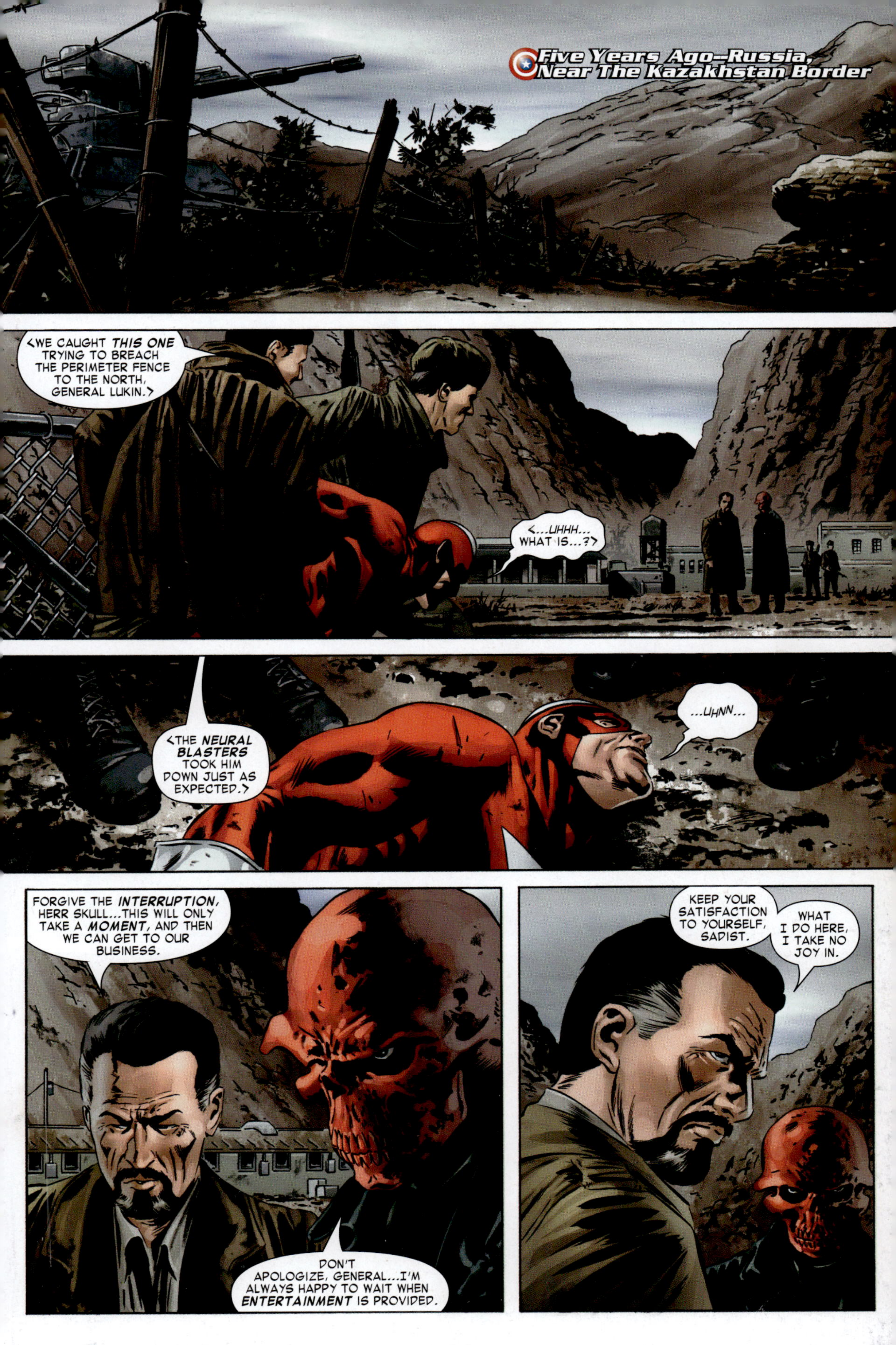
Five Years Ago--Russia, Near The Kazakhstan Border
<WE CAUGHT THIS ONE TRYING TO BREACH THE PERIMETER FENCE TO THE NORTH, GENERAL LUKIN.>
<...UHHH... WHAT IS...?>
<THE NEURAL BLASTERS TOOK HIM DOWN JUST AS EXPECTED.>
...UHNN...
FORGIVE THE INTERRUPTION, HERR SKULL...THIS WILL ONLY TAKE A MOMENT, AND THEN WE CAN GET TO OUR BUSINESS.
DON'T APOLOGIZE, GENERAL...I'M ALWAYS HAPPY TO WAIT WHEN ENTERTAINMENT IS PROVIDED.
KEEP YOUR SATISFACTION TO YOURSELF, SADIST.
WHAT I DO HERE, I TAKE NO JOY IN.

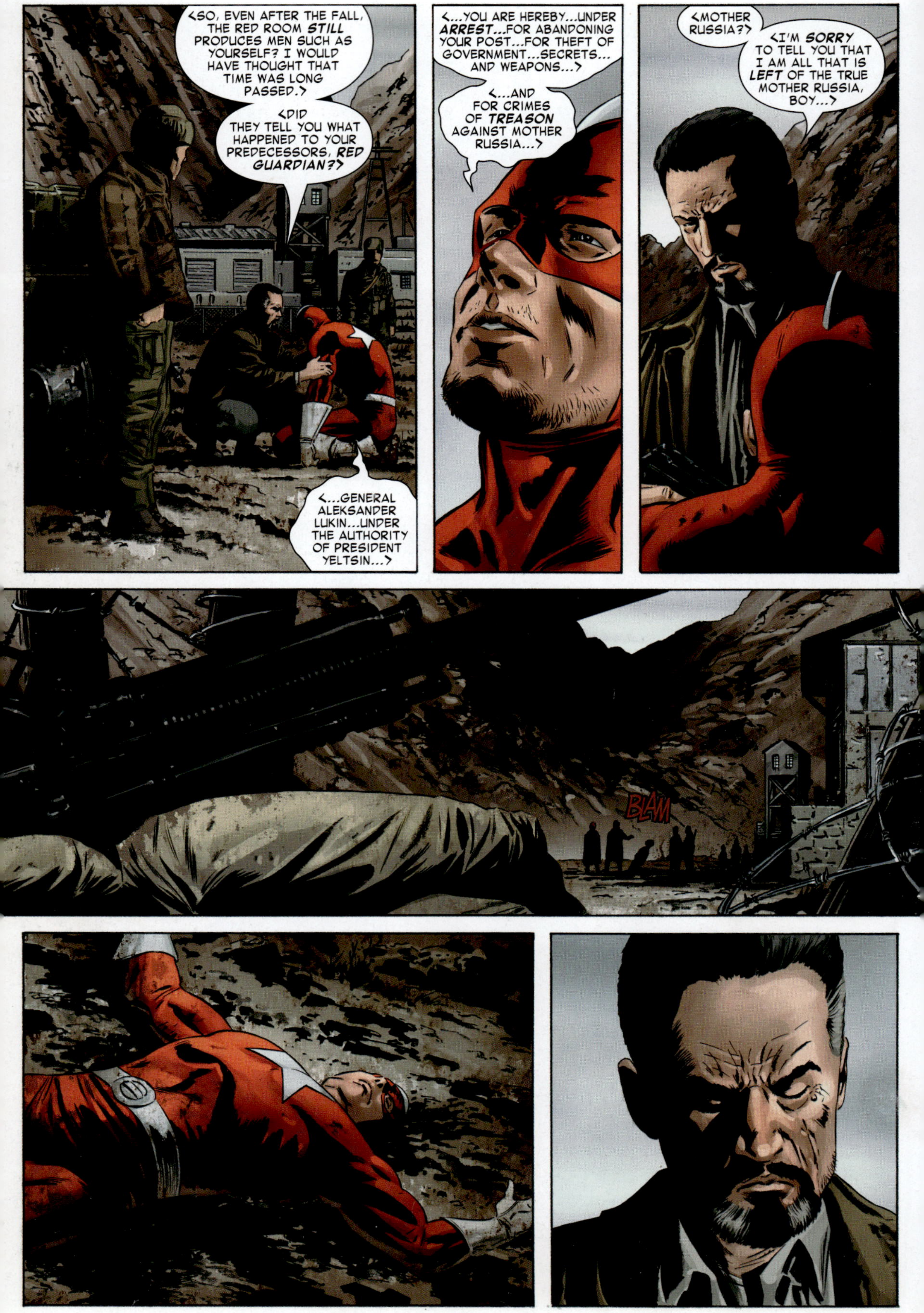

<SO, EVEN AFTER THE FALL, THE RED ROOM STILL PRODUCES MEN SUCH AS YOURSELF? I WOULD HAVE THOUGHT THAT TIME WAS LONG PASSED.>
<DID THEY TELL YOU WHAT HAPPENED TO YOUR PREDECESSORS, RED GUARDIAN?>
<...GENERAL ALEKSANDER LUKIN...UNDER THE AUTHORITY OF PRESIDENT YELTSIN...>
<...YOU ARE HEREBY...UNDER ARREST...FOR ABANDONING YOUR POST...FOR THEFT OF GOVERNMENT...SECRETS...AND WEAPONS...>
<...AND FOR CRIMES OF TREASON AGAINST MOTHER RUSSIA...>
<MOTHER RUSSIA?>
<I'M SORRY TO TELL YOU THAT I AM ALL THAT IS LEFT OF THE TRUE MOTHER RUSSIA, BOY...>
BLAM

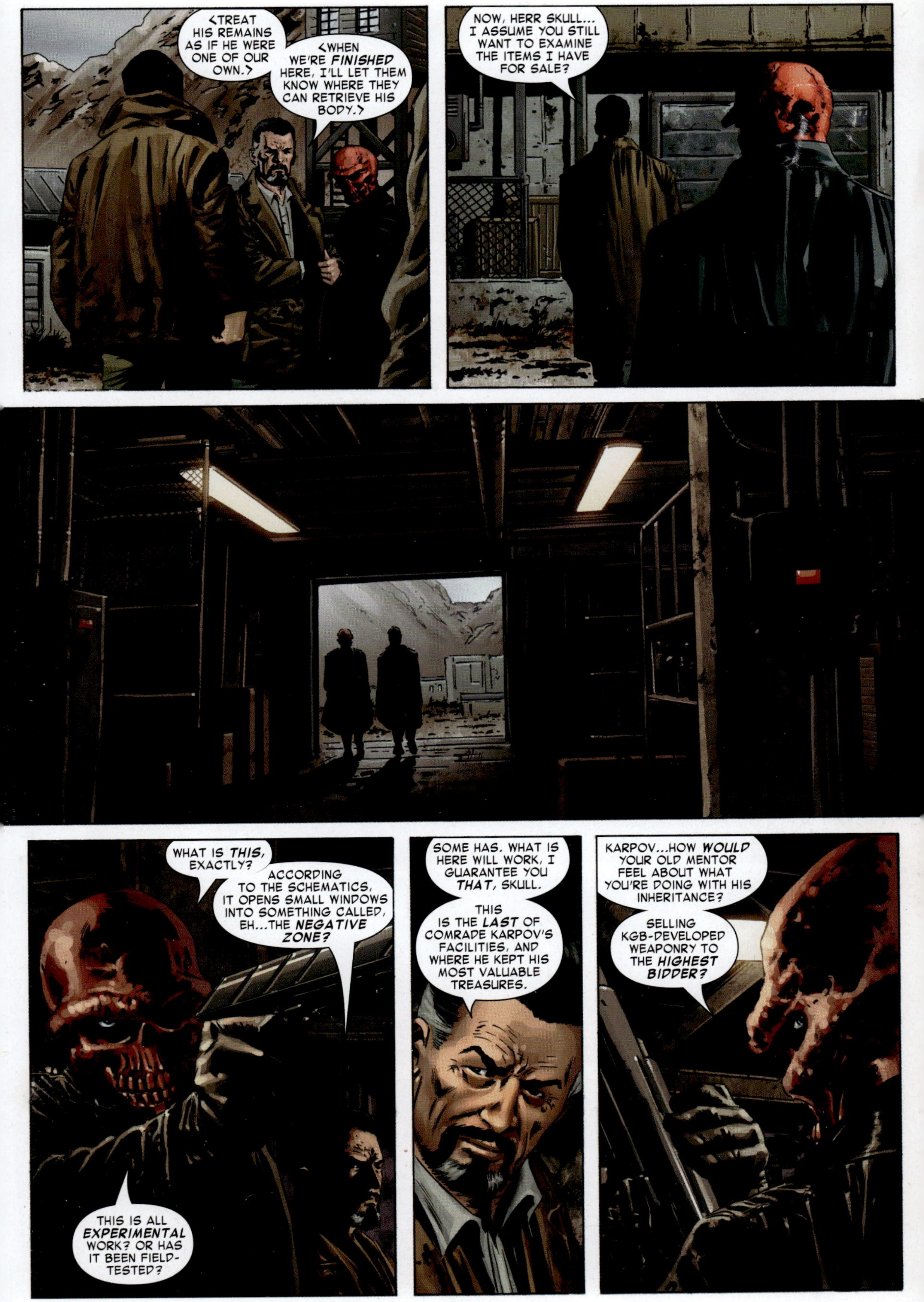

<TREAT HIS REMAINS AS IF HE WERE ONE OF OUR OWN.>
<WHEN WE'RE FINISHED HERE, I'LL LET THEM KNOW WHERE THEY CAN RETRIEVE HIS BODY.>
NOW, HERR SKULL... I ASSUME YOU STILL WANT TO EXAMINE THE ITEMS I HAVE FOR SALE?
WHAT IS THIS, EXACTLY?
ACCORDING TO THE SCHEMATICS, IT OPENS SMALL WINDOWS INTO SOMETHING CALLED, EH...THE NEGATIVE ZONE?
THIS IS ALL EXPERIMENTAL WORK? OR HAS IT BEEN FIELD-TESTED?
SOME HAS. WHAT IS HERE WILL WORK, I GUARANTEE YOU THAT, SKULL.
THIS IS THE LAST OF COMRADE KARPOV'S FACILITIES, AND WHERE HE KEPT HIS MOST VALUABLE TREASURES.
KARPOV...HOW WOULD YOUR OLD MENTOR FEEL ABOUT WHAT YOU'RE DOING WITH HIS INHERITANCE?
SELLING KGB-DEVELOPED WEAPONRY TO THE HIGHEST BIDDER?

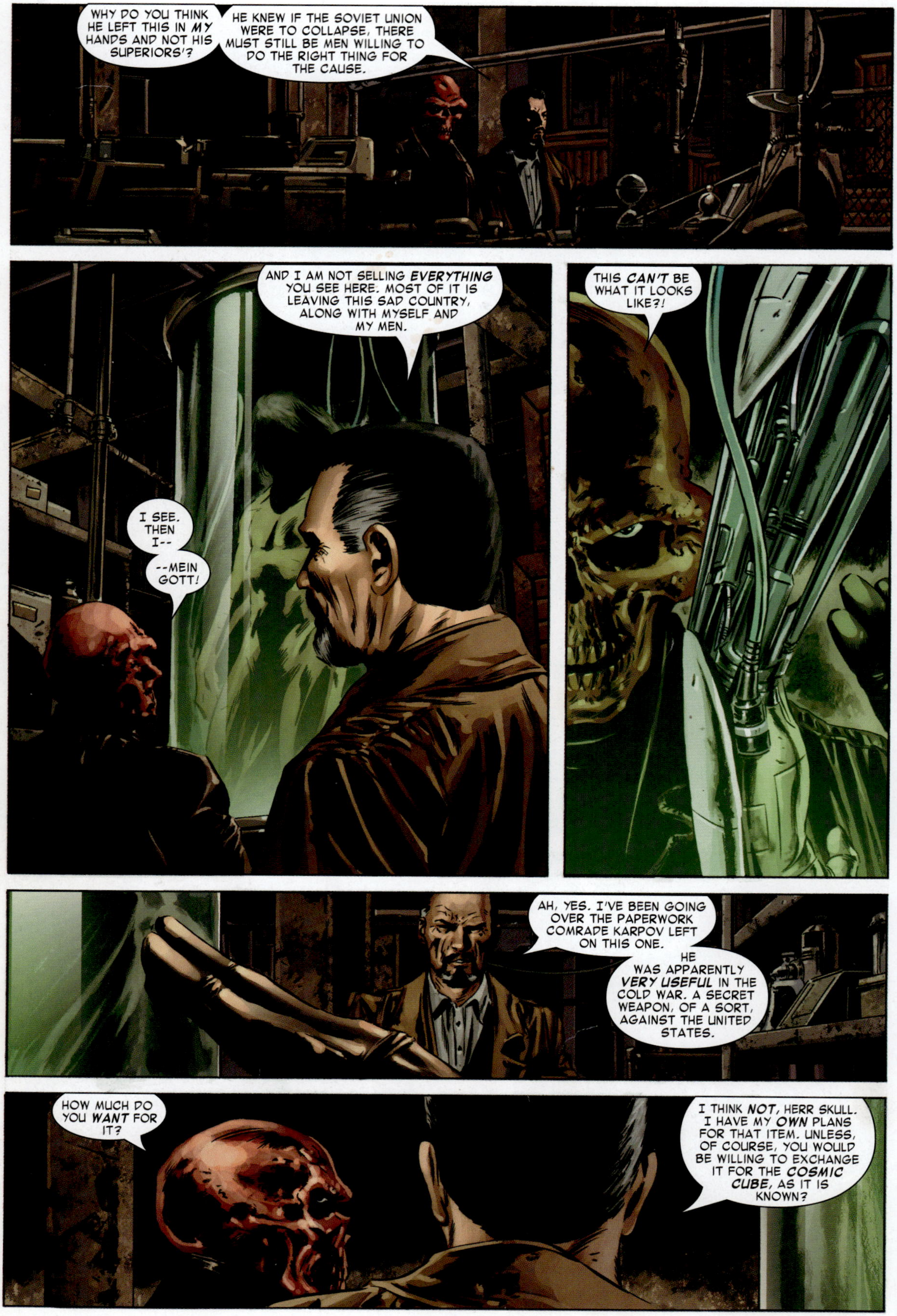
WHY DO YOU THINK HE LEFT THIS IN *MY* HANDS AND NOT HIS SUPERIORS'?
HE KNEW IF THE SOVIET UNION WERE TO COLLAPSE, THERE MUST STILL BE MEN WILLING TO DO THE RIGHT THING FOR THE CAUSE.
AND I AM NOT SELLING *EVERYTHING* YOU SEE HERE. MOST OF IT IS LEAVING THIS SAD COUNTRY, ALONG WITH MYSELF AND MY MEN.
I SEE. THEN I--
--MEIN GOTT!
THIS *CAN'T* BE WHAT IT LOOKS LIKE?!
AH, YES. I'VE BEEN GOING OVER THE PAPERWORK COMRADE KARPOV LEFT ON THIS ONE.
HE WAS APPARENTLY *VERY USEFUL* IN THE COLD WAR. A SECRET WEAPON, OF A SORT, AGAINST THE UNITED STATES.
HOW MUCH DO YOU *WANT* FOR IT?
I THINK *NOT*, HERR SKULL. I HAVE MY *OWN* PLANS FOR THAT ITEM. UNLESS, OF COURSE, YOU WOULD BE WILLING TO EXCHANGE IT FOR THE *COSMIC CUBE*, AS IT IS KNOWN?

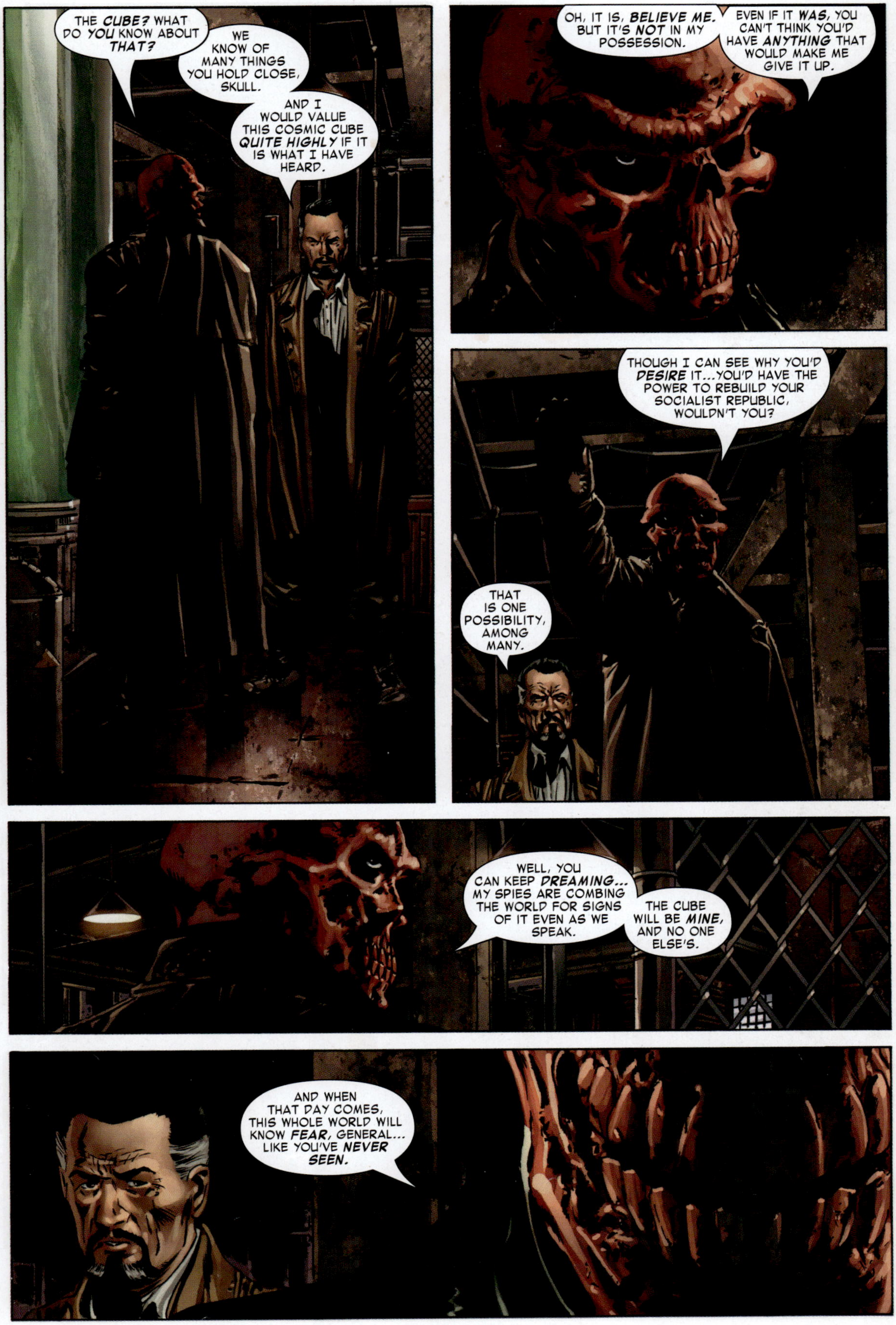
THE CUBE? WHAT DO YOU KNOW ABOUT THAT?
WE KNOW OF MANY THINGS YOU HOLD CLOSE, SKULL.
AND I WOULD VALUE THIS COSMIC CUBE QUITE HIGHLY IF IT IS WHAT I HAVE HEARD.
OH, IT IS, BELIEVE ME. BUT IT'S NOT IN MY POSSESSION.
EVEN IF IT WAS, YOU CAN'T THINK YOU'D HAVE ANYTHING THAT WOULD MAKE ME GIVE IT UP.
THOUGH I CAN SEE WHY YOU'D DESIRE IT...YOU'D HAVE THE POWER TO REBUILD YOUR SOCIALIST REPUBLIC, WOULDN'T YOU?
THAT IS ONE POSSIBILITY, AMONG MANY.
WELL, YOU CAN KEEP DREAMING... MY SPIES ARE COMBING THE WORLD FOR SIGNS OF IT EVEN AS WE SPEAK.
THE CUBE WILL BE MINE, AND NO ONE ELSE'S.
AND WHEN THAT DAY COMES, THIS WHOLE WORLD WILL KNOW FEAR, GENERAL... LIKE YOU'VE NEVER SEEN.

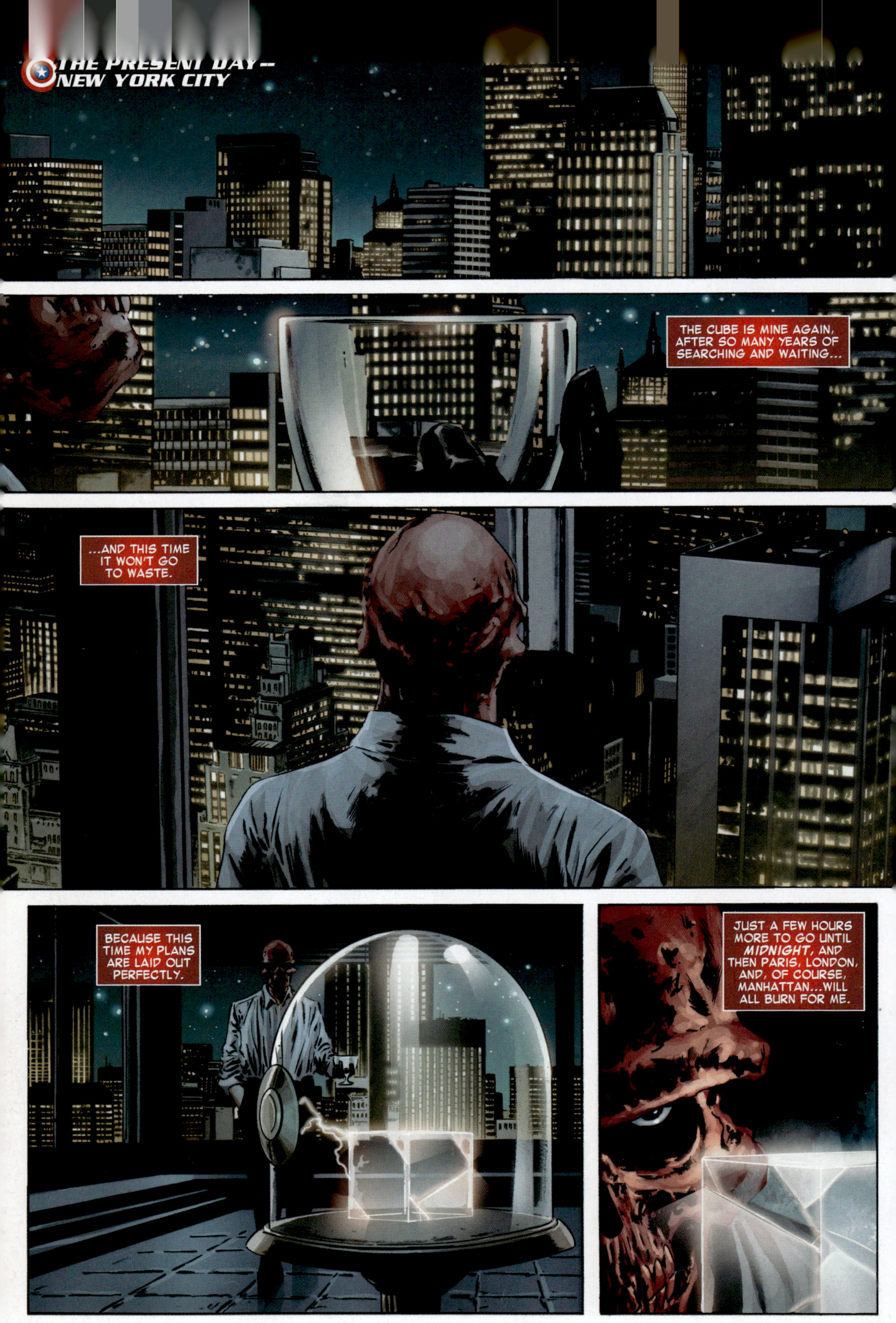
THE PRESENT DAY-- NEW YORK CITY
THE CUBE IS MINE AGAIN, AFTER SO MANY YEARS OF SEARCHING AND WAITING...
...AND THIS TIME IT WON'T GO TO WASTE.
BECAUSE THIS TIME MY PLANS ARE LAID OUT PERFECTLY.
JUST A FEW HOURS MORE TO GO UNTIL *MIDNIGHT*, AND THEN PARIS, LONDON, AND, OF COURSE, MANHATTAN...WILL ALL BURN FOR ME.

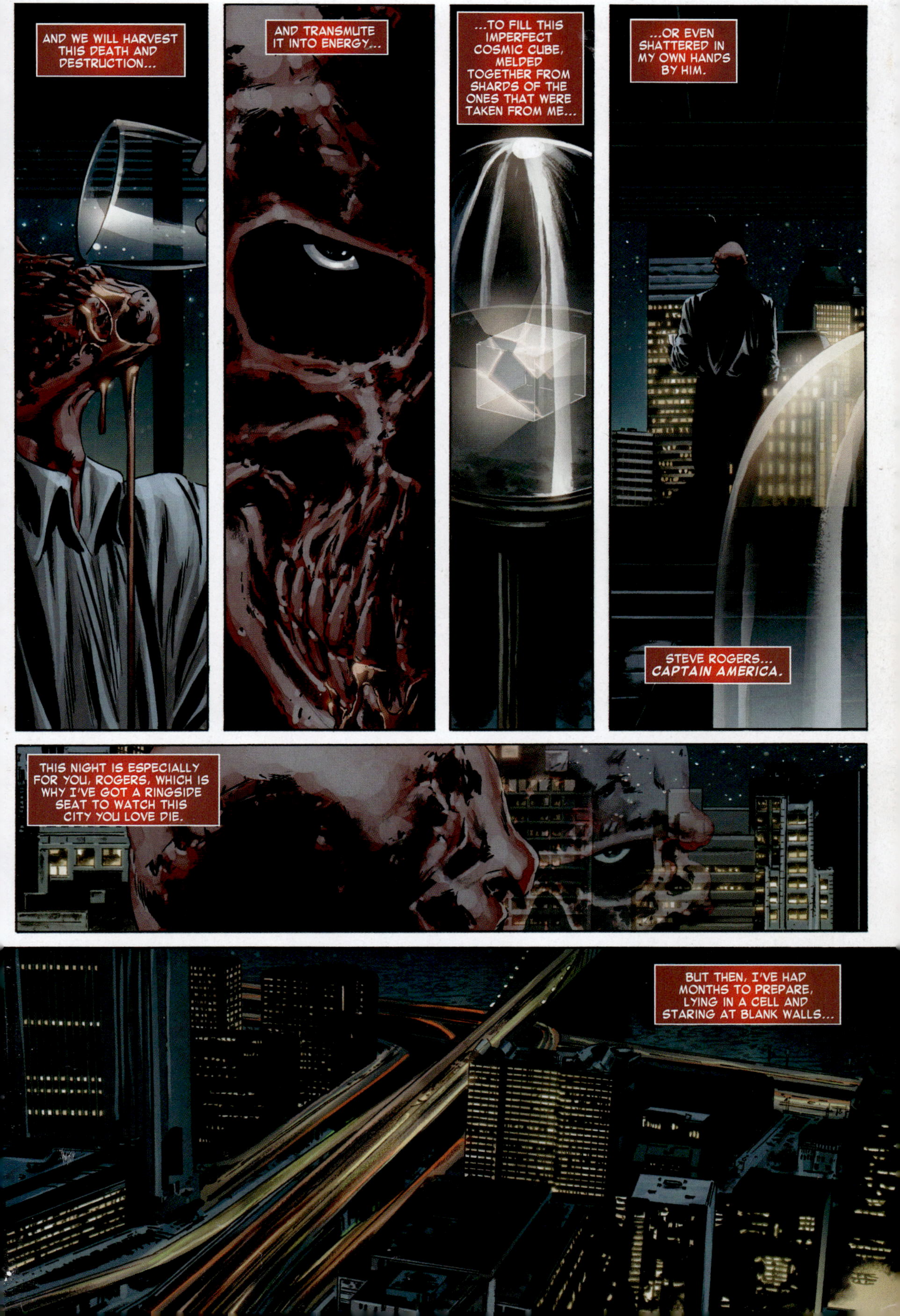
AND WE WILL HARVEST THIS DEATH AND DESTRUCTION...
AND TRANSMUTE IT INTO ENERGY...
...TO FILL THIS IMPERFECT COSMIC CUBE, MELDED TOGETHER FROM SHARDS OF THE ONES THAT WERE TAKEN FROM ME...
...OR EVEN SHATTERED IN MY OWN HANDS BY HIM.
STEVE ROGERS... CAPTAIN AMERICA.
THIS NIGHT IS ESPECIALLY FOR YOU, ROGERS, WHICH IS WHY I'VE GOT A RINGSIDE SEAT TO WATCH THIS CITY YOU LOVE DIE.
BUT THEN, I'VE HAD MONTHS TO PREPARE, LYING IN A CELL AND STARING AT BLANK WALLS...

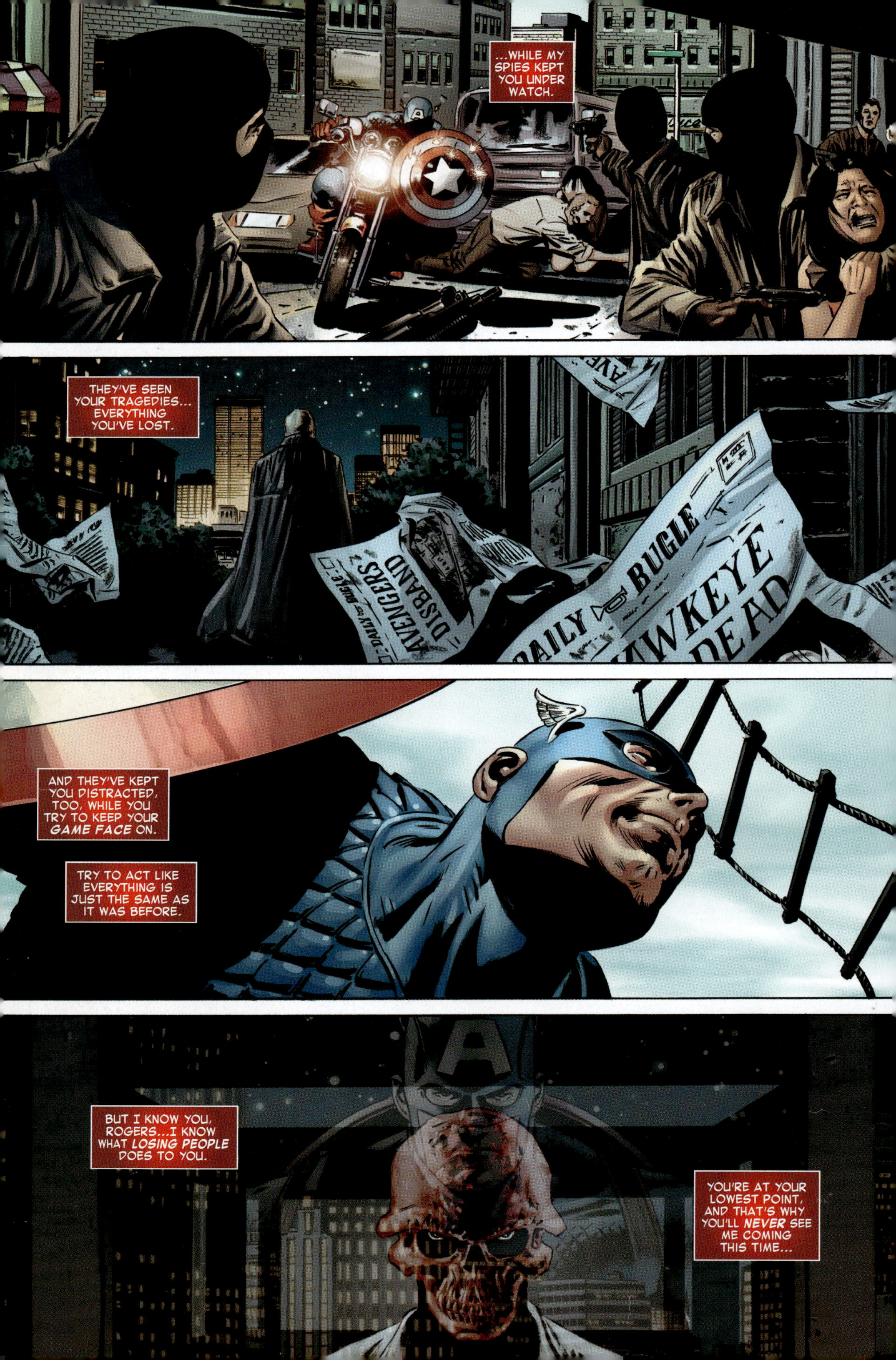
...WHILE MY SPIES KEPT YOU UNDER WATCH.
THEY'VE SEEN YOUR TRAGEDIES... EVERYTHING YOU'VE LOST.
AVENGERS DISBAND
AND THEY'VE KEPT YOU DISTRACTED, TOO, WHILE YOU TRY TO KEEP YOUR *GAME FACE* ON.
TRY TO ACT LIKE EVERYTHING IS JUST THE SAME AS IT WAS BEFORE.
BUT I KNOW YOU, ROGERS...I KNOW WHAT *LOSING PEOPLE* DOES TO YOU.
YOU'RE AT YOUR LOWEST POINT, AND THAT'S WHY YOU'LL *NEVER* SEE ME COMING THIS TIME...

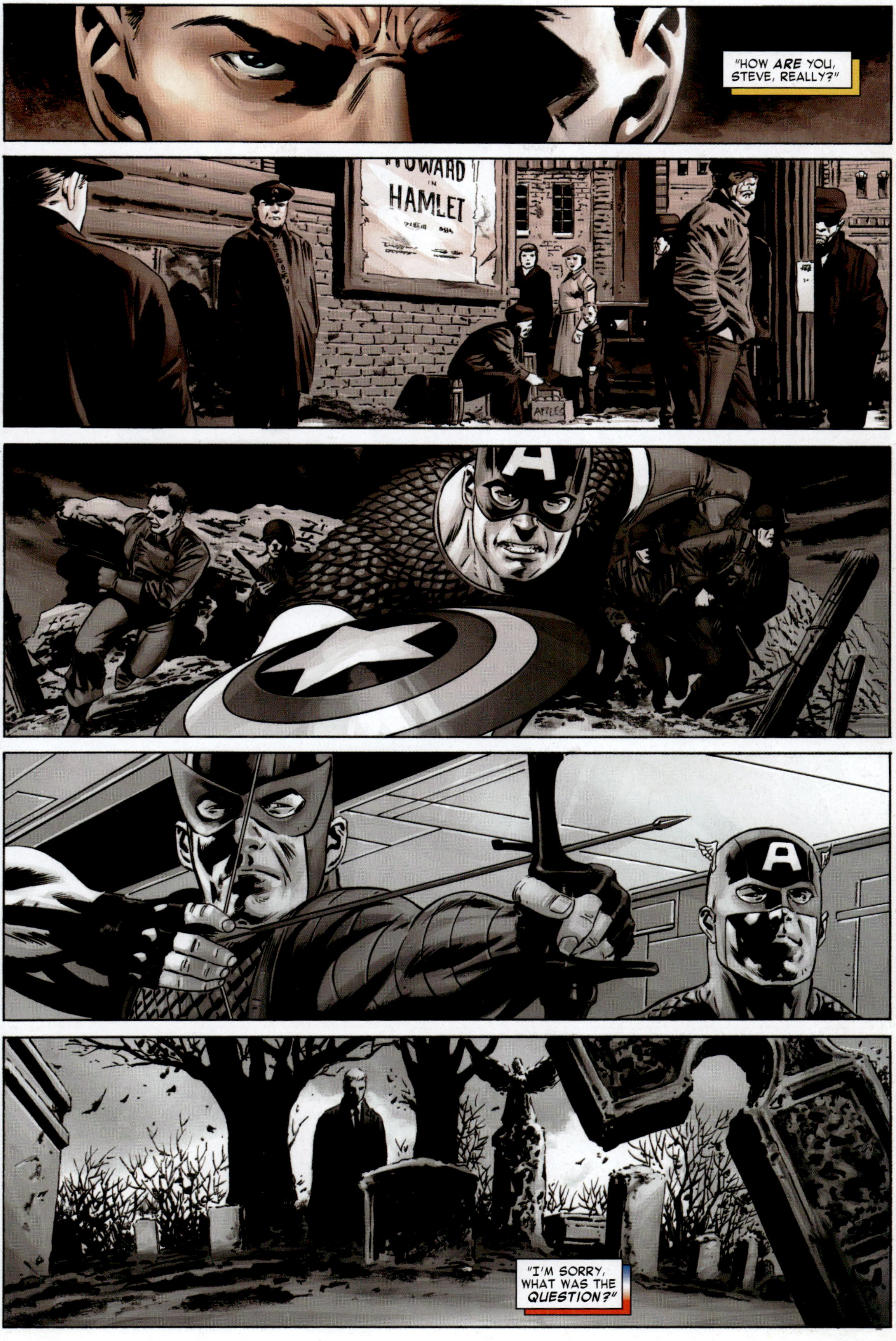
"HOW ARE YOU, STEVE, REALLY?"
HOWARD IN HAMLET
APPLES
"I'M SORRY, WHAT WAS THE QUESTION?"

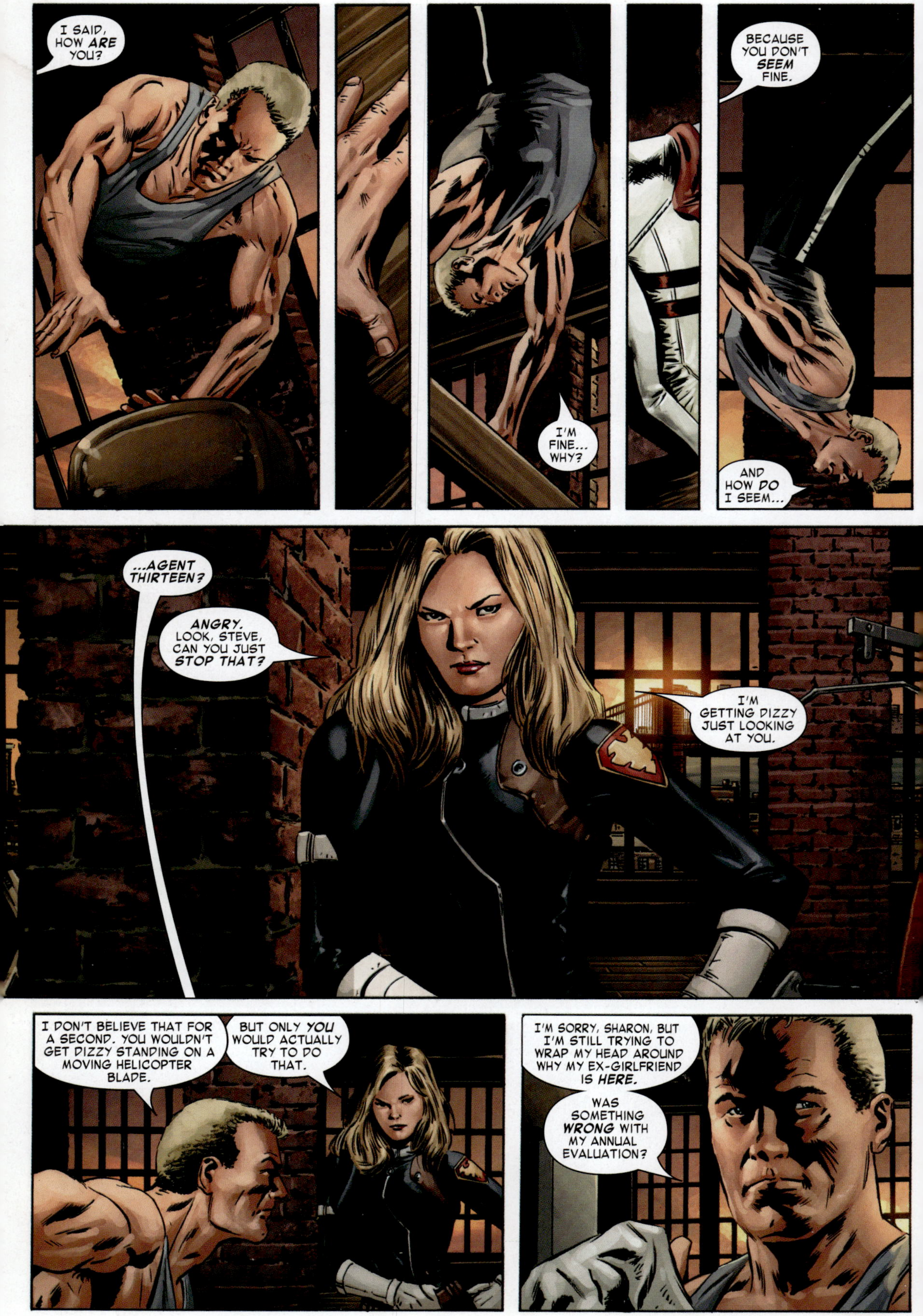
I SAID, HOW ARE YOU?
I'M FINE... WHY?
BECAUSE YOU DON'T SEEM FINE.
AND HOW DO I SEEM...
...AGENT THIRTEEN?
ANGRY. LOOK, STEVE, CAN YOU JUST STOP THAT?
I'M GETTING DIZZY JUST LOOKING AT YOU.
I DON'T BELIEVE THAT FOR A SECOND. YOU WOULDN'T GET DIZZY STANDING ON A MOVING HELICOPTER BLADE.
BUT ONLY YOU WOULD ACTUALLY TRY TO DO THAT.
I'M SORRY, SHARON, BUT I'M STILL TRYING TO WRAP MY HEAD AROUND WHY MY EX-GIRLFRIEND IS HERE.
WAS SOMETHING WRONG WITH MY ANNUAL EVALUATION?

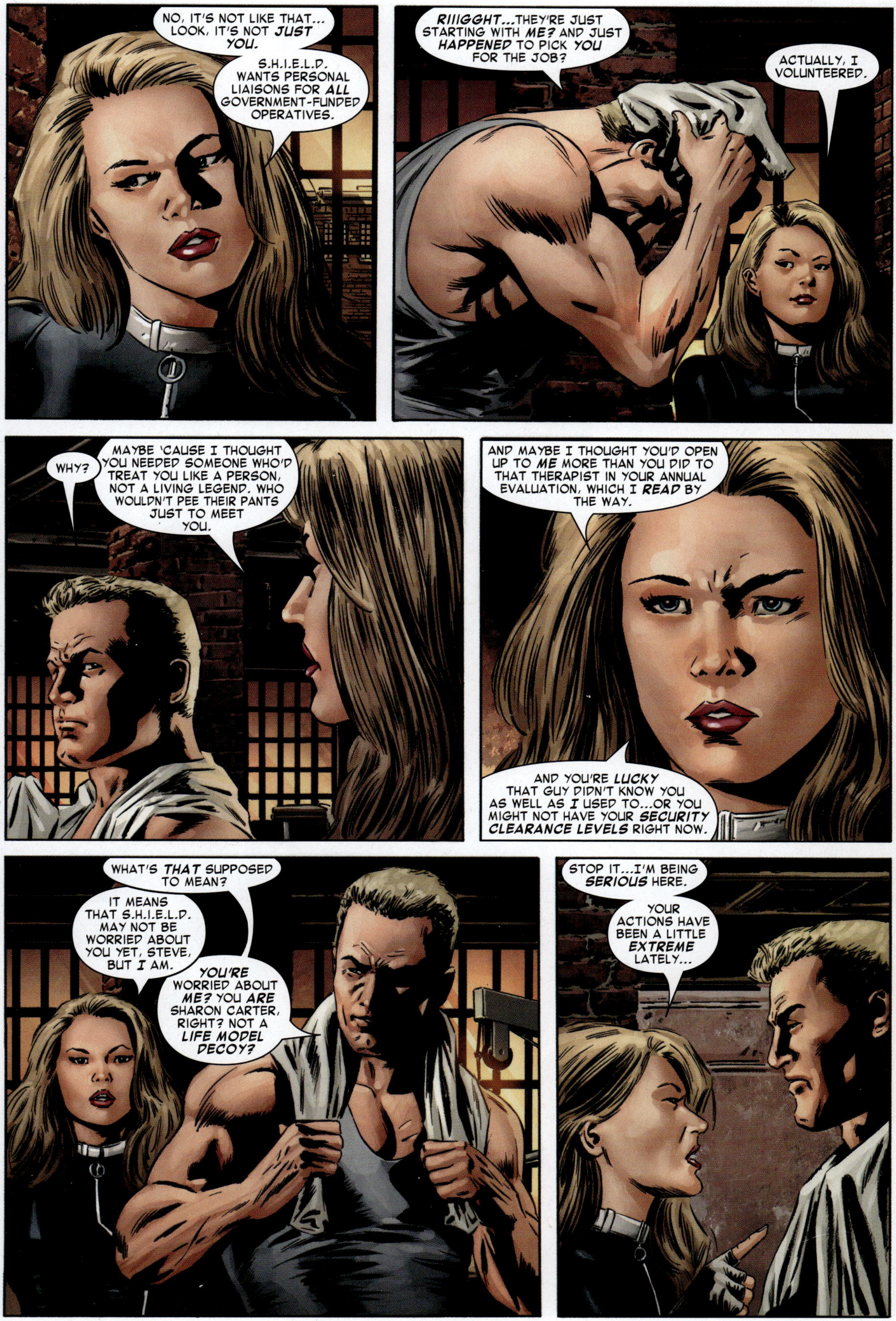

NO, IT'S NOT LIKE THAT... LOOK, IT'S NOT JUST YOU.
S.H.I.E.L.D. WANTS PERSONAL LIAISONS FOR ALL GOVERNMENT-FUNDED OPERATIVES.
RIIIGGHT...THEY'RE JUST STARTING WITH ME? AND JUST HAPPENED TO PICK YOU FOR THE JOB?
ACTUALLY, I VOLUNTEERED.
WHY?
MAYBE 'CAUSE I THOUGHT YOU NEEDED SOMEONE WHO'D TREAT YOU LIKE A PERSON, NOT A LIVING LEGEND. WHO WOULDN'T PEE THEIR PANTS JUST TO MEET YOU.
AND MAYBE I THOUGHT YOU'D OPEN UP TO ME MORE THAN YOU DID TO THAT THERAPIST IN YOUR ANNUAL EVALUATION, WHICH I READ BY THE WAY.
AND YOU'RE LUCKY THAT GUY DIDN'T KNOW YOU AS WELL AS I USED TO...OR YOU MIGHT NOT HAVE YOUR SECURITY CLEARANCE LEVELS RIGHT NOW.
WHAT'S THAT SUPPOSED TO MEAN?
IT MEANS THAT S.H.I.E.L.D. MAY NOT BE WORRIED ABOUT YOU YET, STEVE, BUT I AM.
YOU'RE WORRIED ABOUT ME? YOU ARE SHARON CARTER, RIGHT? NOT A LIFE MODEL DECOY?
STOP IT...I'M BEING SERIOUS HERE.
YOUR ACTIONS HAVE BEEN A LITTLE EXTREME LATELY...

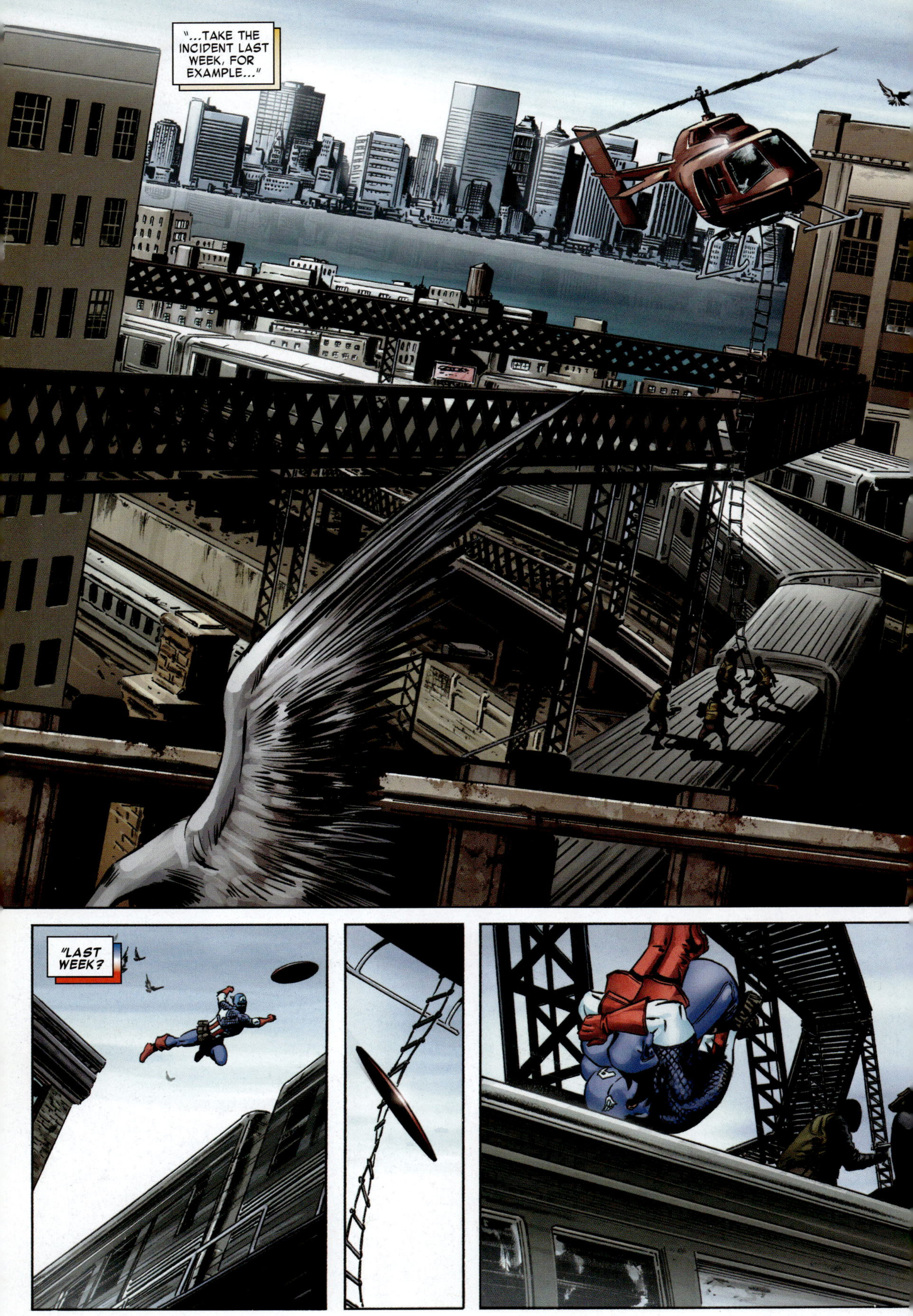
"...TAKE THE INCIDENT LAST WEEK, FOR EXAMPLE..."
"LAST WEEK?

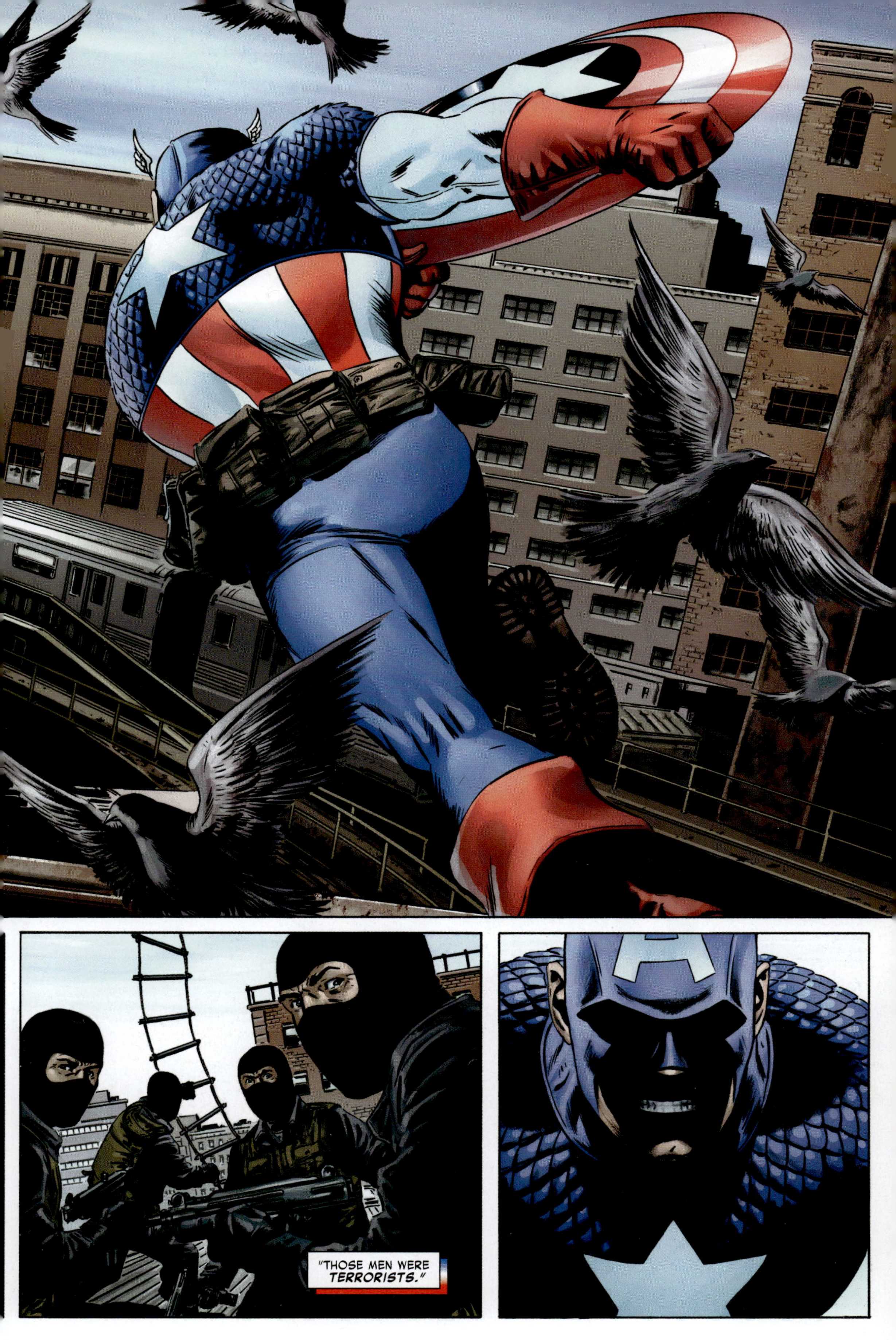
"THOSE MEN WERE TERRORISTS."

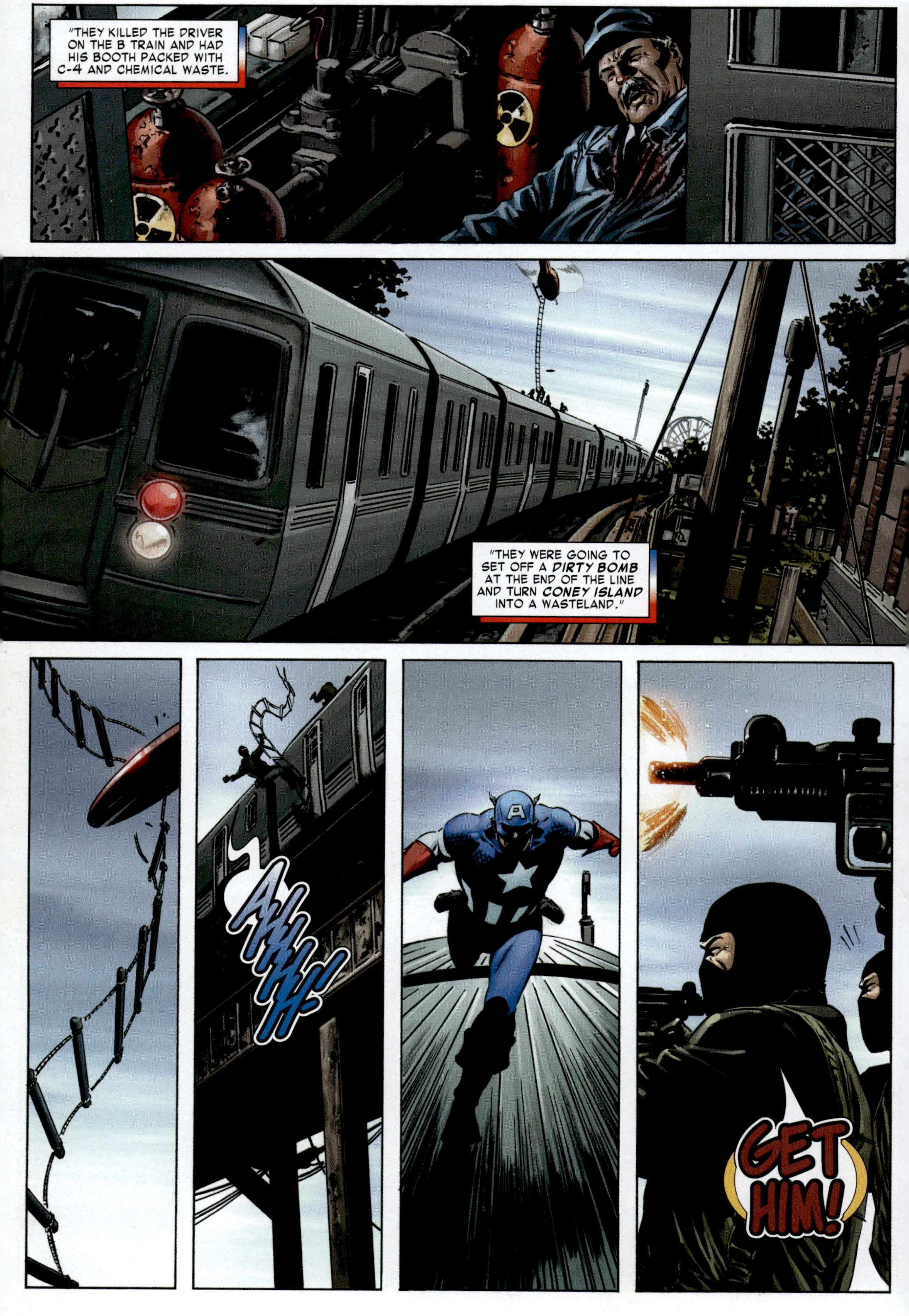
"THEY KILLED THE DRIVER ON THE B TRAIN AND HAD HIS BOOTH PACKED WITH C-4 AND CHEMICAL WASTE.
"THEY WERE GOING TO SET OFF A *DIRTY BOMB* AT THE END OF THE LINE AND TURN *CONEY ISLAND* INTO A WASTELAND."
AHHHH!
GET HIM!

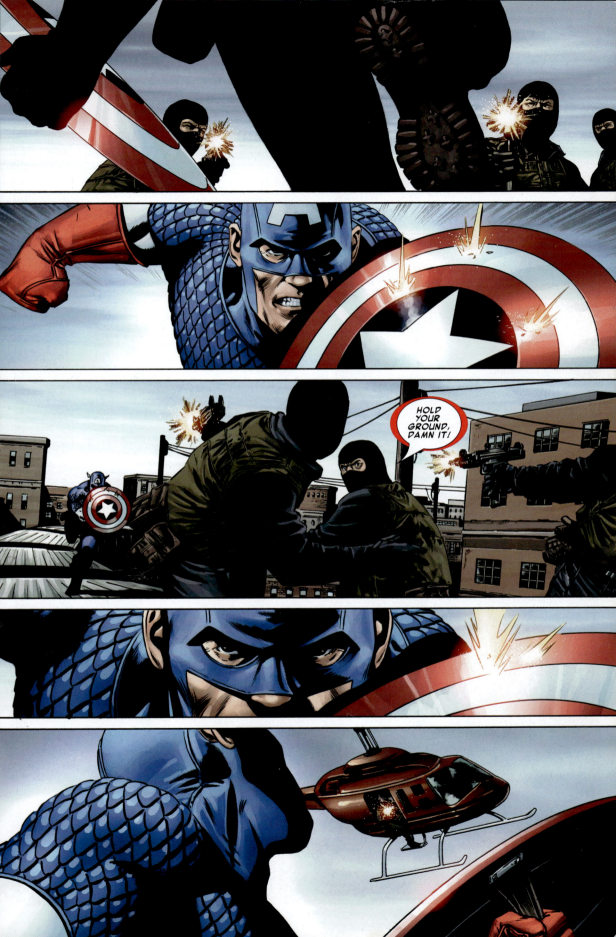

HOLD YOUR GROUND, DAMN IT!

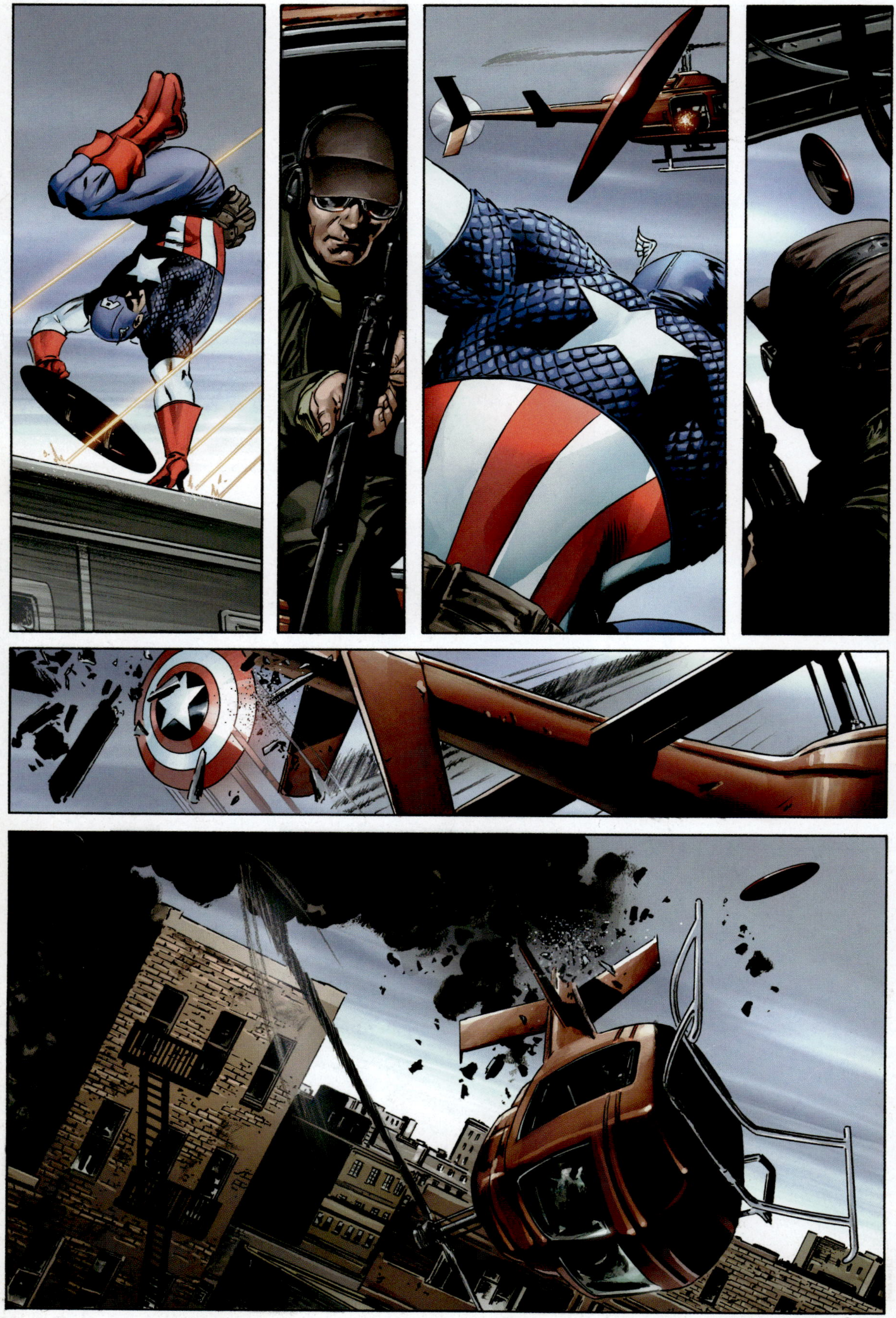

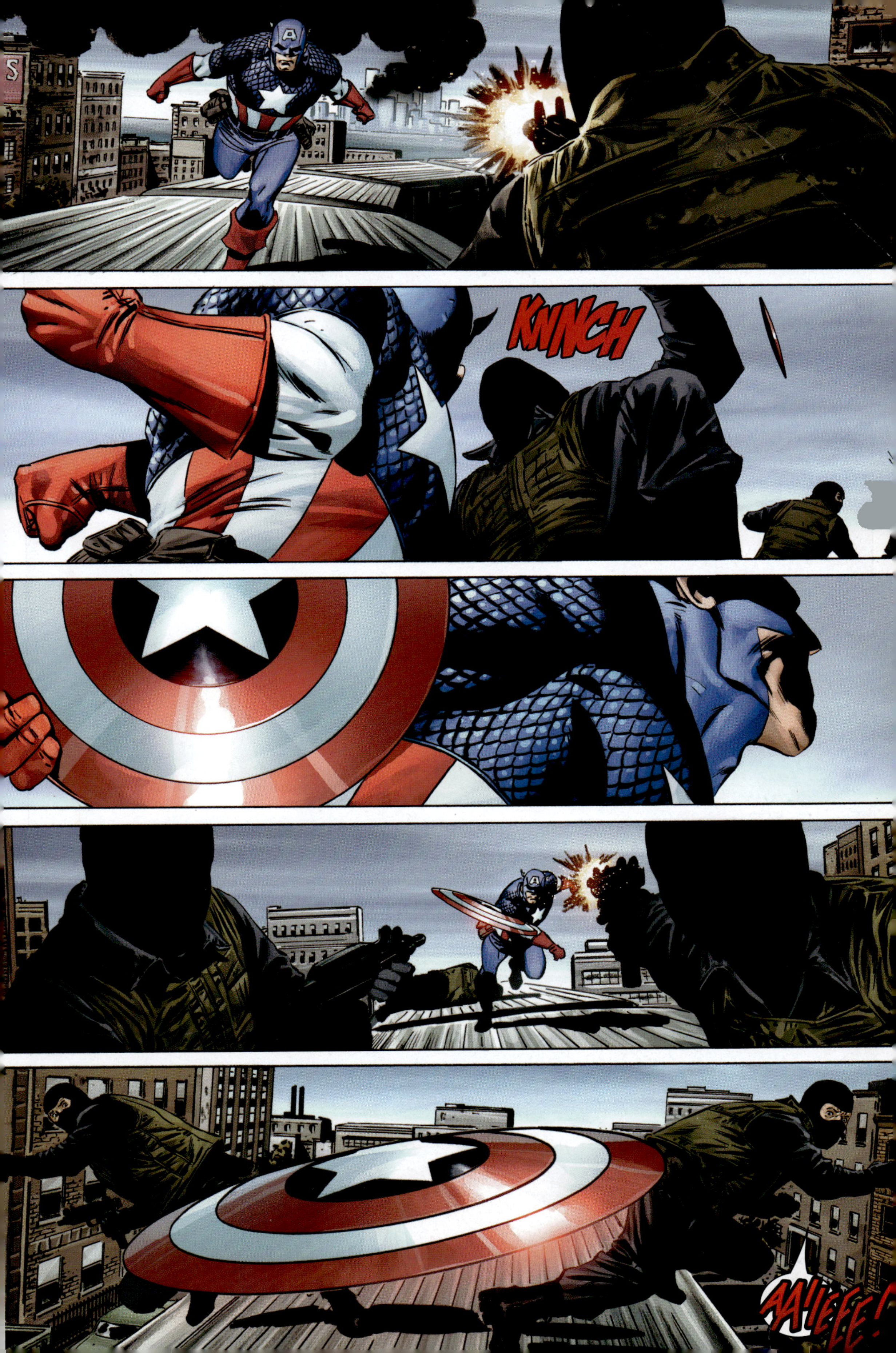
KNNCH
AAIIEEEE!

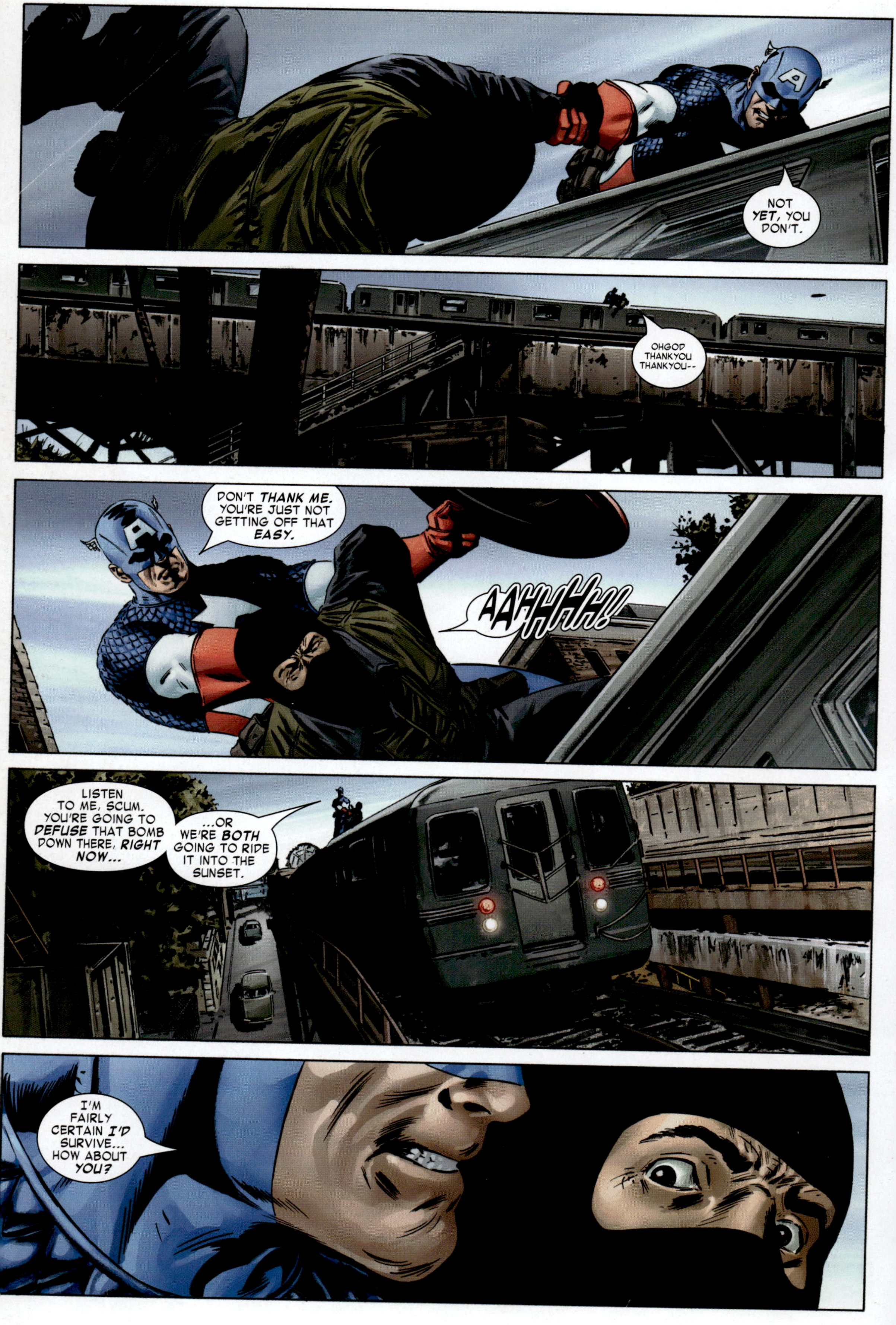
NOT YET, YOU DON'T.
OHGOD THANKYOU THANKYOU--
DON'T THANK ME. YOU'RE JUST NOT GETTING OFF THAT EASY.
AAHHHHH!
LISTEN TO ME, SCUM. YOU'RE GOING TO DEFUSE THAT BOMB DOWN THERE, RIGHT NOW...
...OR WE'RE BOTH GOING TO RIDE IT INTO THE SUNSET.
I'M FAIRLY CERTAIN I'D SURVIVE... HOW ABOUT YOU?

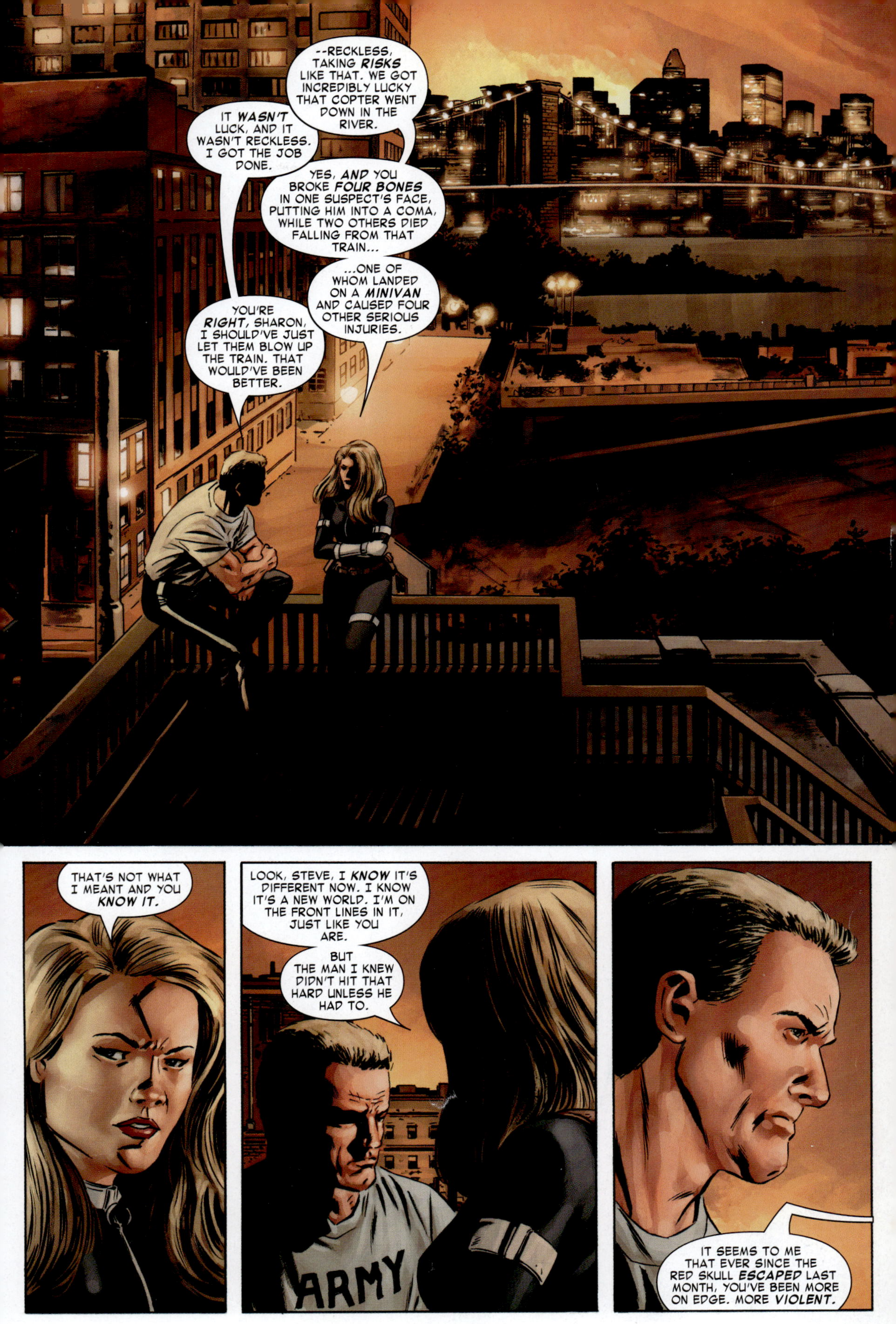
--RECKLESS, TAKING RISKS LIKE THAT. WE GOT INCREDIBLY LUCKY THAT COPTER WENT DOWN IN THE RIVER.
IT WASN'T LUCK, AND IT WASN'T RECKLESS. I GOT THE JOB DONE.
YES, AND YOU BROKE FOUR BONES IN ONE SUSPECT'S FACE, PUTTING HIM INTO A COMA, WHILE TWO OTHERS DIED FALLING FROM THAT TRAIN...
...ONE OF WHOM LANDED ON A MINIVAN AND CAUSED FOUR OTHER SERIOUS INJURIES.
YOU'RE RIGHT, SHARON, I SHOULD'VE JUST LET THEM BLOW UP THE TRAIN. THAT WOULD'VE BEEN BETTER.
THAT'S NOT WHAT I MEANT AND YOU KNOW IT.
LOOK, STEVE, I KNOW IT'S DIFFERENT NOW. I KNOW IT'S A NEW WORLD. I'M ON THE FRONT LINES IN IT, JUST LIKE YOU ARE.
BUT THE MAN I KNEW DIDN'T HIT THAT HARD UNLESS HE HAD TO.
ARMY
IT SEEMS TO ME THAT EVER SINCE THE RED SKULL ESCAPED LAST MONTH, YOU'VE BEEN MORE ON EDGE. MORE VIOLENT.

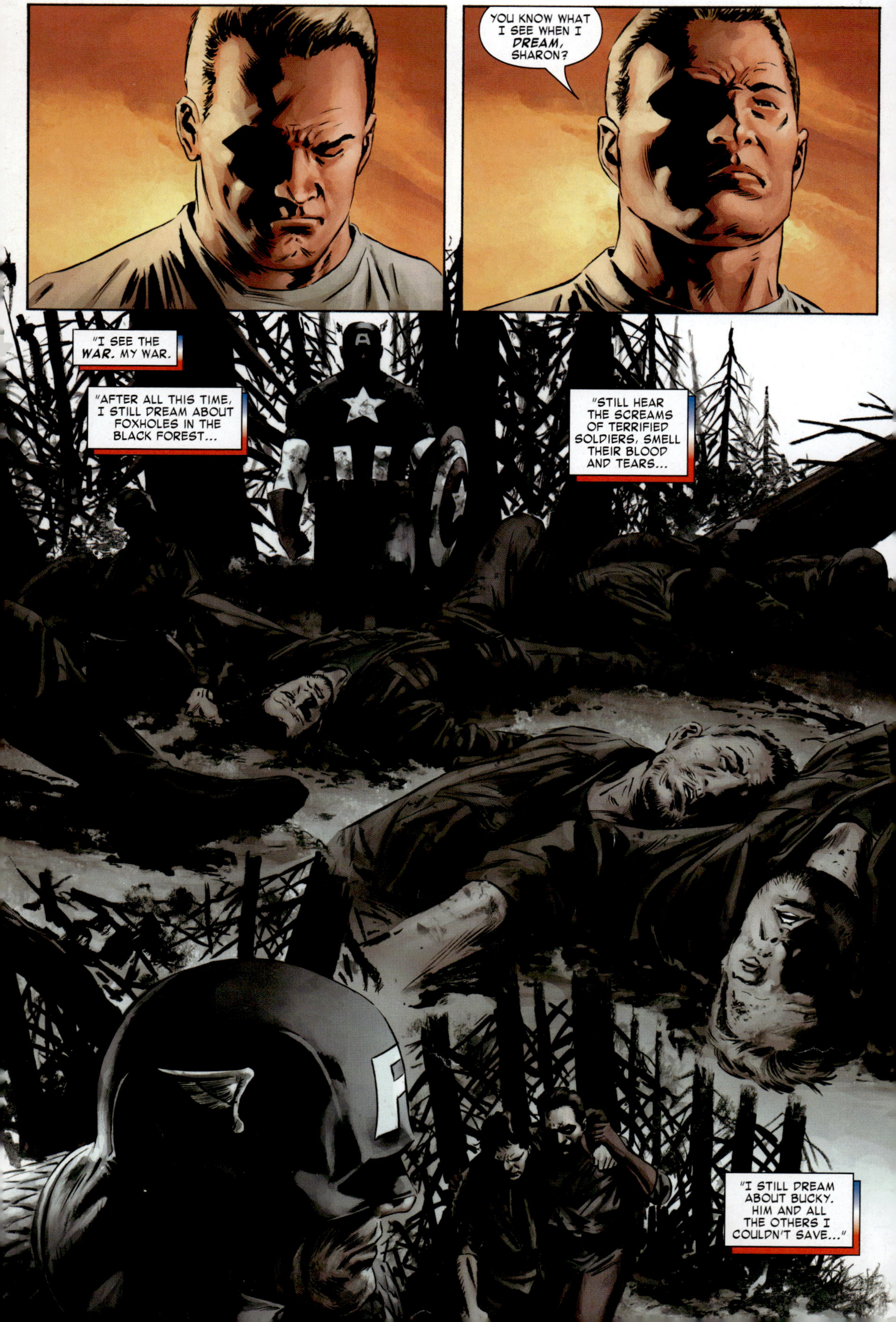
YOU KNOW WHAT I SEE WHEN I DREAM, SHARON?
"I SEE THE WAR. MY WAR.
"AFTER ALL THIS TIME, I STILL DREAM ABOUT FOXHOLES IN THE BLACK FOREST...
"STILL HEAR THE SCREAMS OF TERRIFIED SOLDIERS, SMELL THEIR BLOOD AND TEARS...
"I STILL DREAM ABOUT BUCKY. HIM AND ALL THE OTHERS I COULDN'T SAVE..."

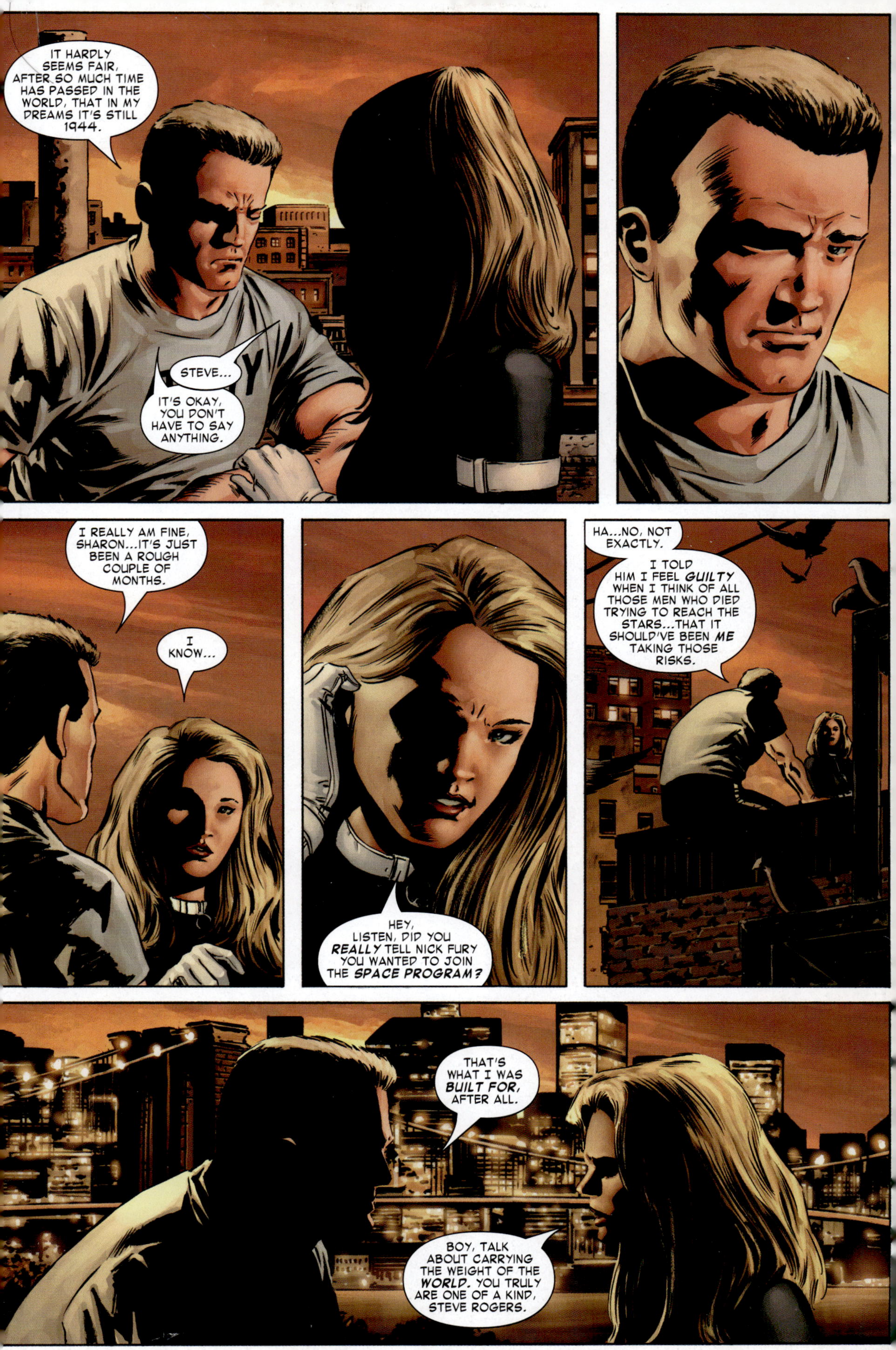
IT HARDLY SEEMS FAIR, AFTER SO MUCH TIME HAS PASSED IN THE WORLD, THAT IN MY DREAMS IT'S STILL 1944.
STEVE...
IT'S OKAY, YOU DON'T HAVE TO SAY ANYTHING.
I REALLY AM FINE, SHARON...IT'S JUST BEEN A ROUGH COUPLE OF MONTHS.
I KNOW...
HEY, LISTEN, DID YOU REALLY TELL NICK FURY YOU WANTED TO JOIN THE SPACE PROGRAM?
HA...NO, NOT EXACTLY.
I TOLD HIM I FEEL GUILTY WHEN I THINK OF ALL THOSE MEN WHO DIED TRYING TO REACH THE STARS...THAT IT SHOULD'VE BEEN ME TAKING THOSE RISKS.
THAT'S WHAT I WAS BUILT FOR, AFTER ALL.
BOY, TALK ABOUT CARRYING THE WEIGHT OF THE WORLD. YOU TRULY ARE ONE OF A KIND, STEVE ROGERS.

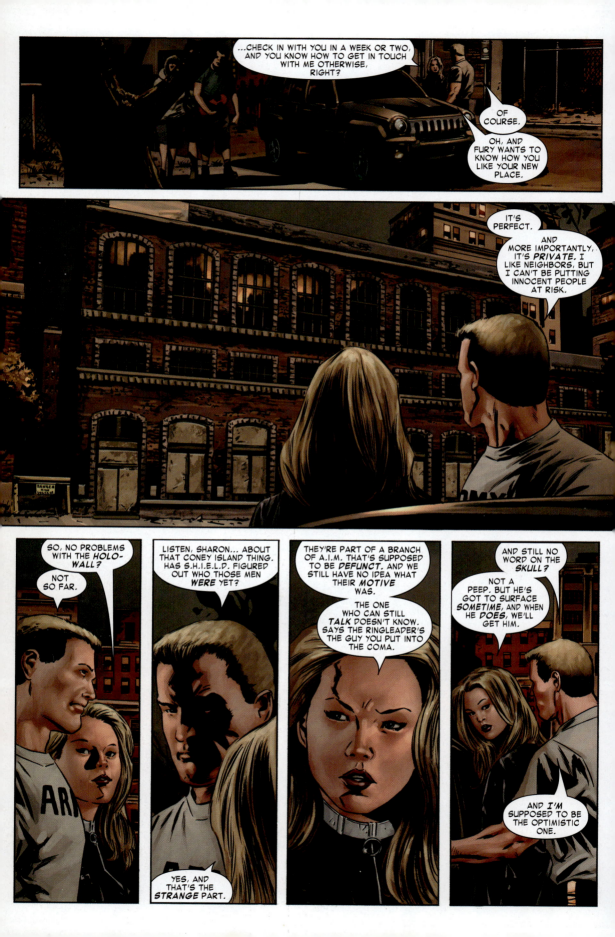

...CHECK IN WITH YOU IN A WEEK OR TWO, AND YOU KNOW HOW TO GET IN TOUCH WITH ME OTHERWISE, RIGHT?

OF COURSE.

OH, AND FURY WANTS TO KNOW HOW YOU LIKE YOUR NEW PLACE.

IT'S. PERFECT.

AND MORE IMPORTANTLY, IT'S *PRIVATE*. I LIKE NEIGHBORS, BUT I CAN'T BE PUTTING INNOCENT PEOPLE AT RISK.

SO, NO PROBLEMS WITH THE *HOLO-WALL*?

NOT SO FAR.

LISTEN, SHARON... ABOUT THAT CONEY ISLAND THING. HAS S.H.I.E.L.D. FIGURED OUT WHO THOSE MEN *WERE* YET?

YES, AND THAT'S THE *STRANGE* PART.

THEY'RE PART OF A BRANCH OF A.I.M. THAT'S SUPPOSED TO BE *DEFUNCT*. AND WE STILL HAVE NO IDEA WHAT THEIR *MOTIVE* WAS.

THE ONE WHO CAN STILL *TALK* DOESN'T KNOW. SAYS THE RINGLEADER'S THE GUY YOU PUT INTO THE COMA.

AND STILL NO WORD ON THE *SKULL*?

NOT A PEEP. BUT HE'S GOT TO SURFACE *SOMETIME*, AND WHEN HE *DOES*, WE'LL GET HIM.

AND *I'M* SUPPOSED TO BE THE OPTIMISTIC ONE.

SAFE TRIP.

SURE, I'LL JUST REMEMBER TO STAY AWAY FROM ELEVATED TRAIN TRACKS.

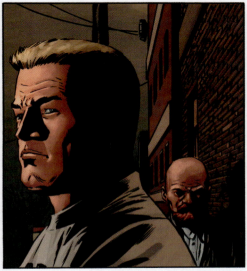

YOU'RE OUT THERE SOMEWHERE, SKULL...AND WHEN I FIND YOU...

DANGER
HIGH VOLTAGE

YOU THINK YOU'RE SAFE IN YOUR NEW SECRET HOME, IN THE SHADOW OF YOUR BROOKLYN BRIDGE?

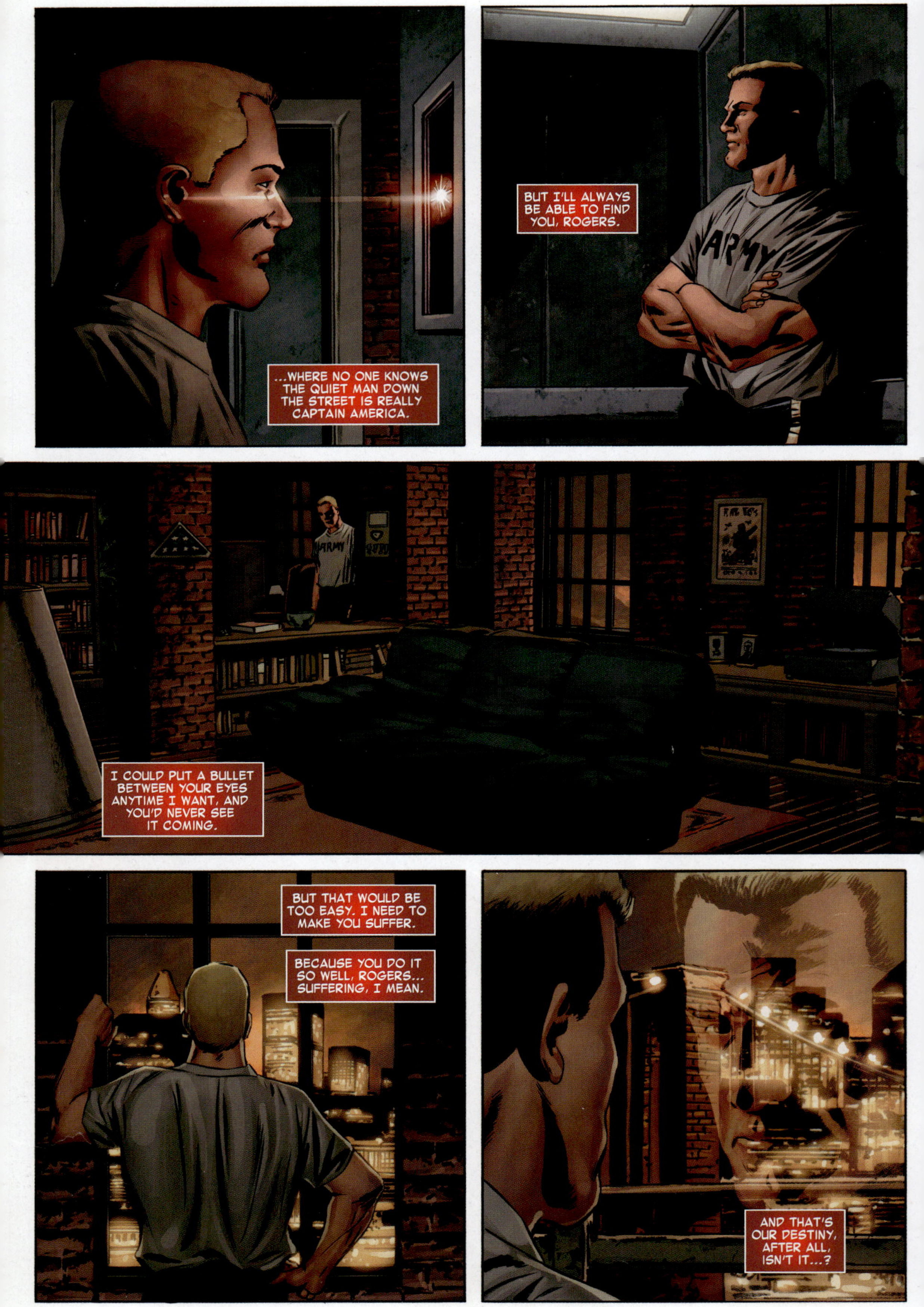
...WHERE NO ONE KNOWS THE QUIET MAN DOWN THE STREET IS REALLY CAPTAIN AMERICA.
BUT I'LL ALWAYS BE ABLE TO FIND YOU, ROGERS.
I COULD PUT A BULLET BETWEEN YOUR EYES ANYTIME I WANT, AND YOU'D NEVER SEE IT COMING.
BUT THAT WOULD BE TOO EASY. I NEED TO MAKE YOU SUFFER.
BECAUSE YOU DO IT SO WELL, ROGERS... SUFFERING, I MEAN.
AND THAT'S OUR DESTINY, AFTER ALL, ISN'T IT...?

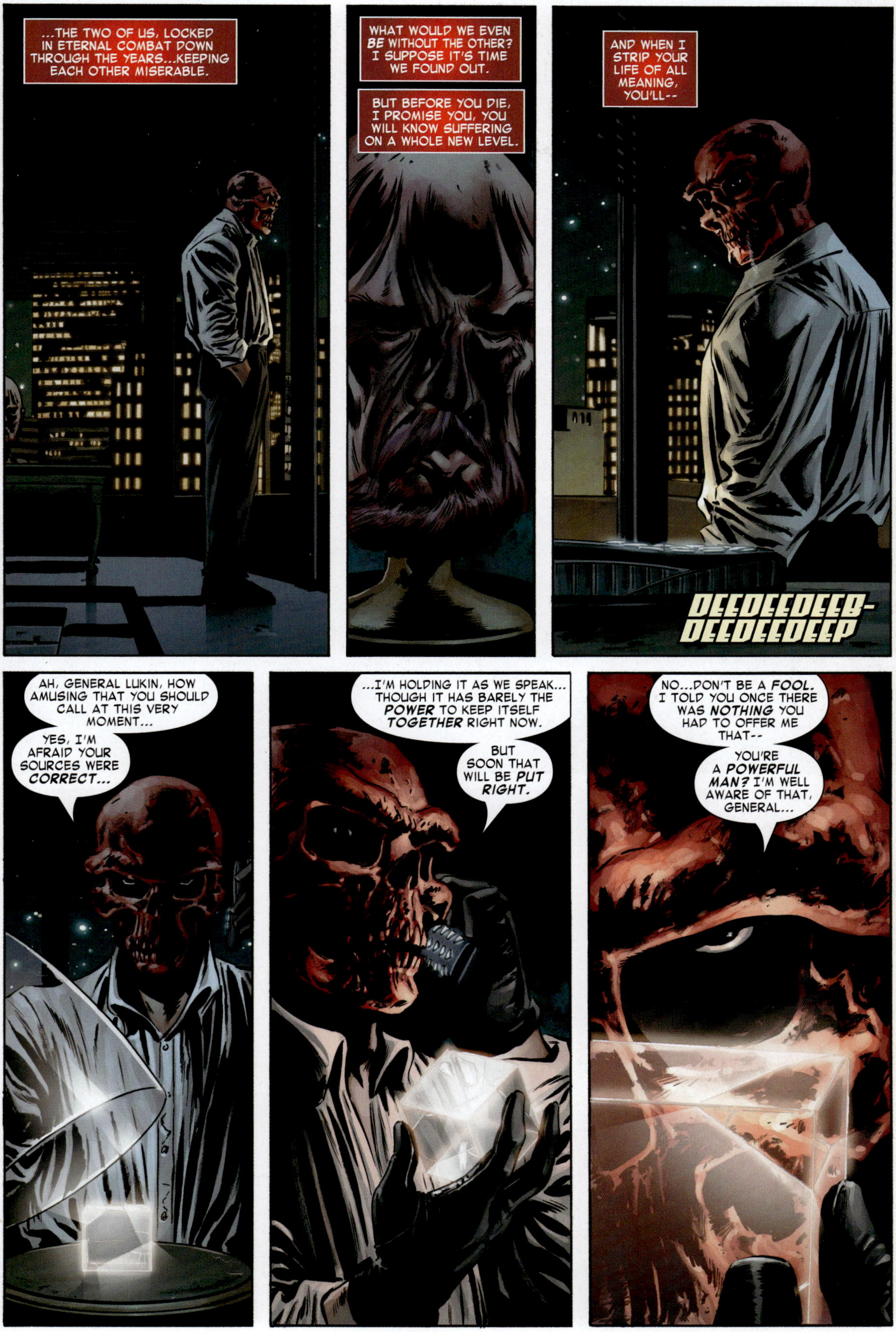
...THE TWO OF US, LOCKED IN ETERNAL COMBAT DOWN THROUGH THE YEARS...KEEPING EACH OTHER MISERABLE.
WHAT WOULD WE EVEN BE WITHOUT THE OTHER? I SUPPOSE IT'S TIME WE FOUND OUT.
BUT BEFORE YOU DIE, I PROMISE YOU, YOU WILL KNOW SUFFERING ON A WHOLE NEW LEVEL.
AND WHEN I STRIP YOUR LIFE OF ALL MEANING, YOU'LL--
DEEDEEDEEB-DEEDEEDEEP
AH, GENERAL LUKIN, HOW AMUSING THAT YOU SHOULD CALL AT THIS VERY MOMENT...
YES, I'M AFRAID YOUR SOURCES WERE CORRECT...
...I'M HOLDING IT AS WE SPEAK... THOUGH IT HAS BARELY THE POWER TO KEEP ITSELF TOGETHER RIGHT NOW.
BUT SOON THAT WILL BE PUT RIGHT.
NO...DON'T BE A FOOL. I TOLD YOU ONCE THERE WAS NOTHING YOU HAD TO OFFER ME THAT--
YOU'RE A POWERFUL MAN? I'M WELL AWARE OF THAT, GENERAL...

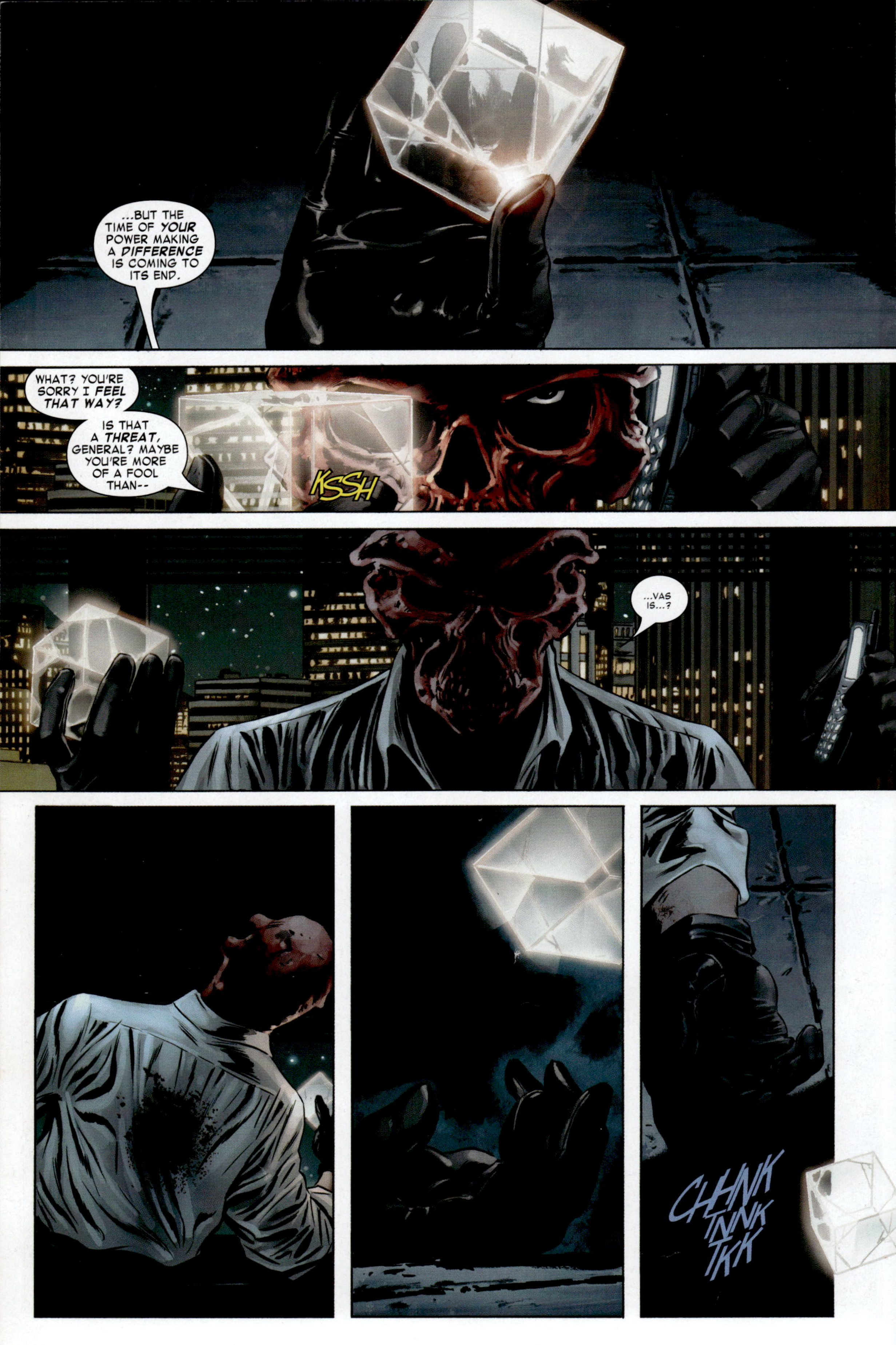
...BUT THE TIME OF *YOUR* POWER MAKING A *DIFFERENCE* IS COMING TO ITS END.
WHAT? YOU'RE SORRY I *FEEL THAT WAY?*
IS THAT A *THREAT*, GENERAL? MAYBE YOU'RE MORE OF A FOOL THAN--
KSSH
...VAS IS...?
CHINK TINNK TKK

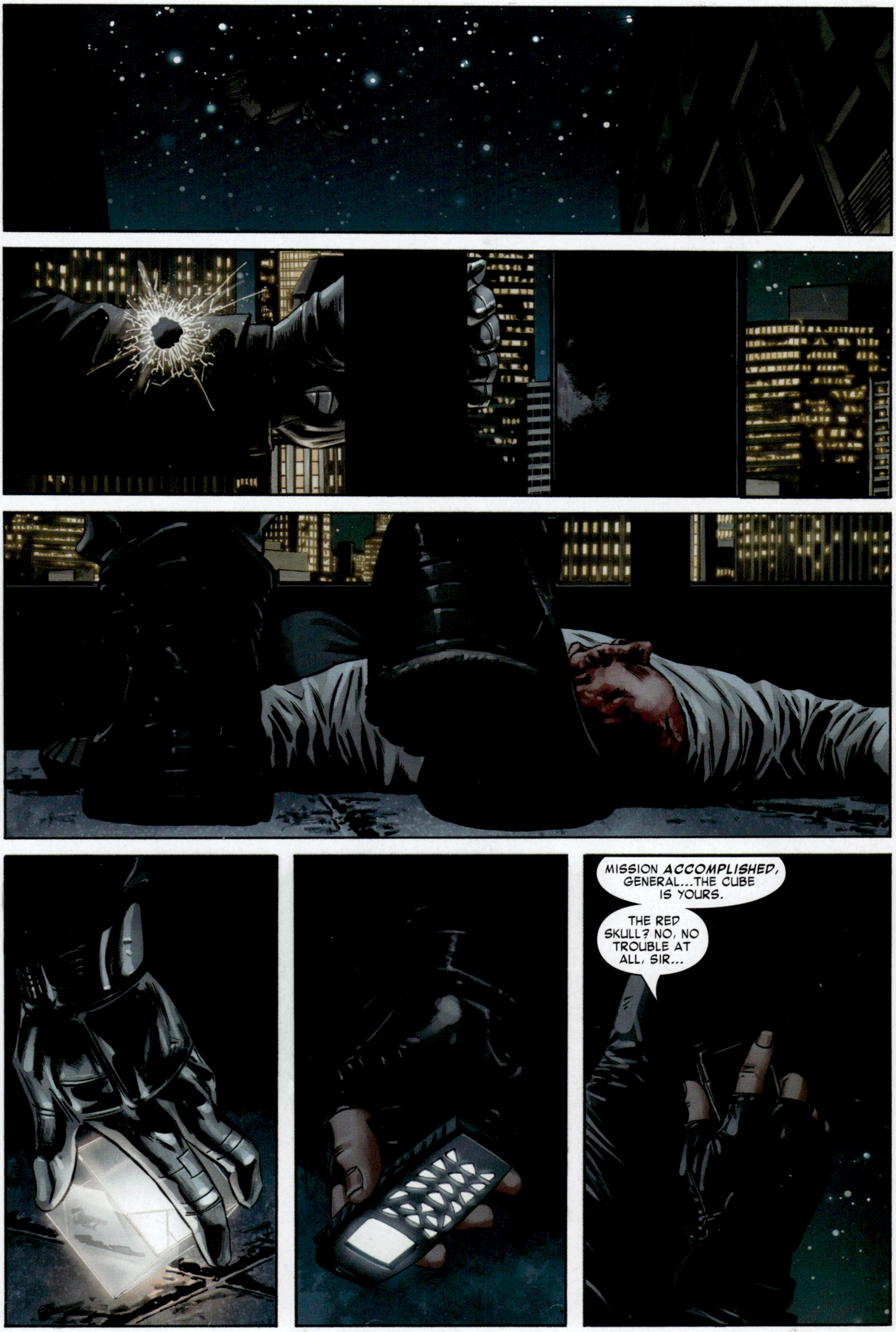
MISSION ACCOMPLISHED, GENERAL...THE CUBE IS YOURS.
THE RED SKULL? NO, NO TROUBLE AT ALL, SIR...

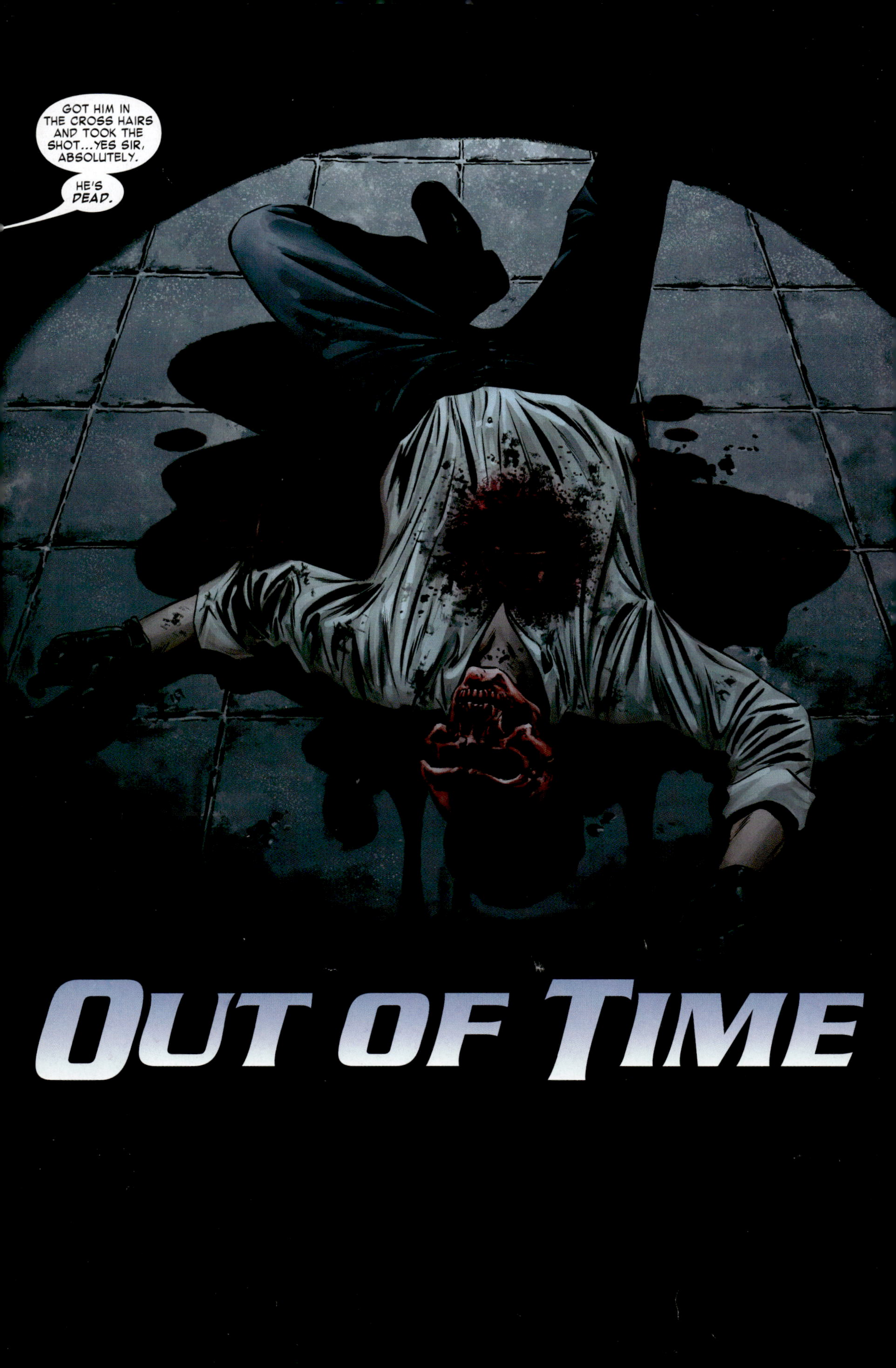
GOT HIM IN THE CROSS HAIRS AND TOOK THE SHOT...YES SIR, ABSOLUTELY.
HE'S DEAD.
OUT OF TIME

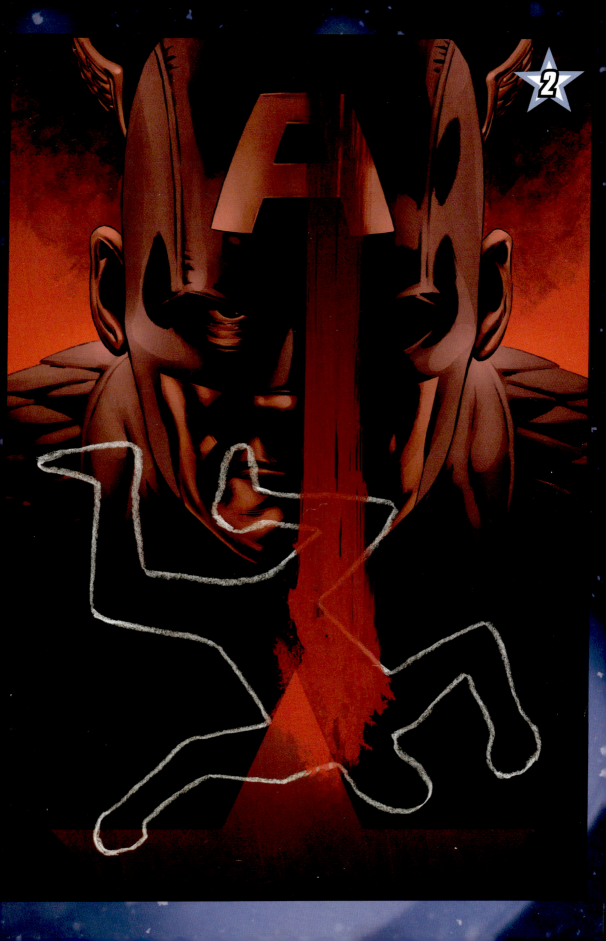

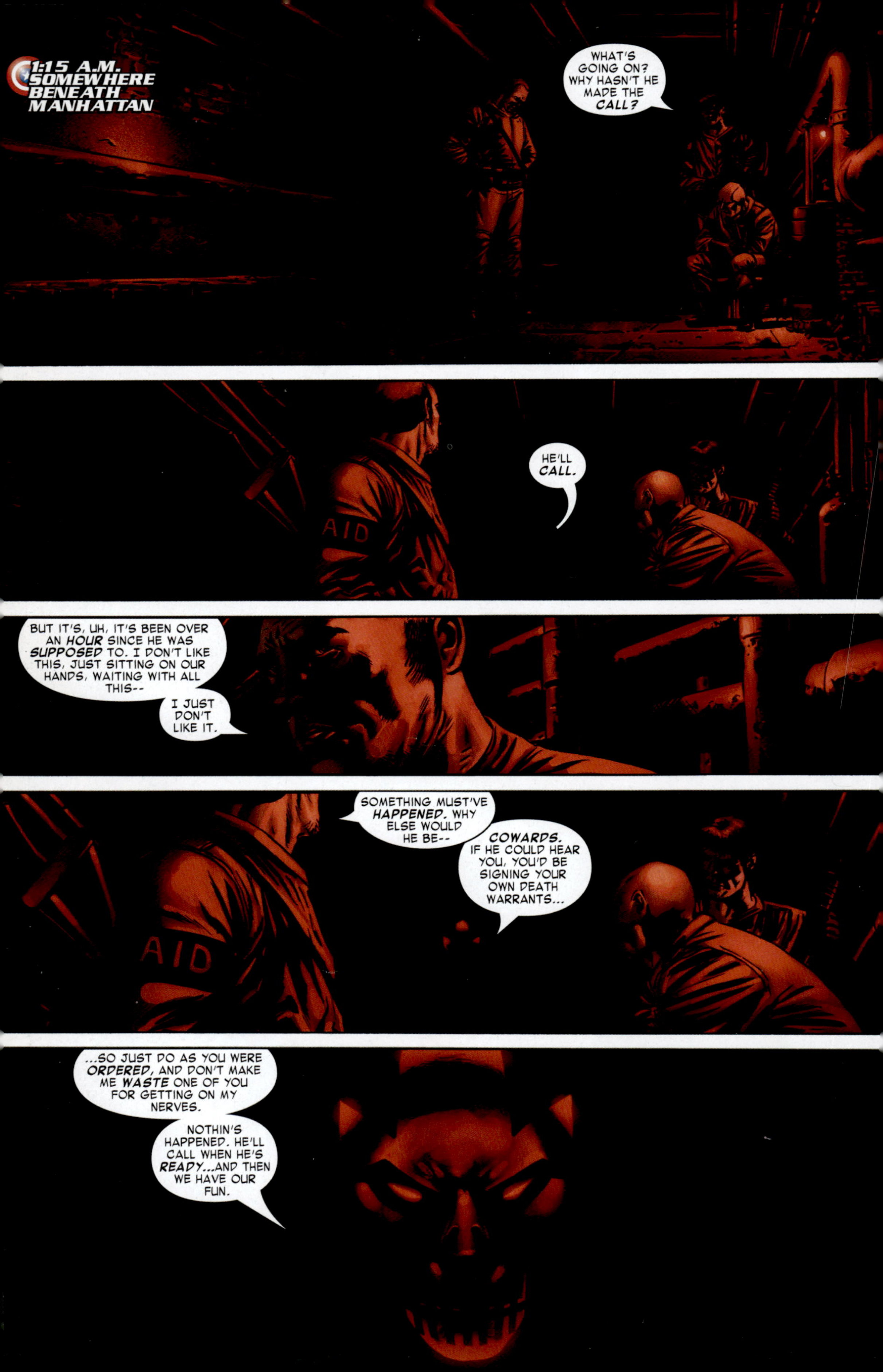
1:15 A.M. SOMEWHERE BENEATH MANHATTAN
WHAT'S GOING ON? WHY HASN'T HE MADE THE CALL?
HE'LL CALL.
AID
BUT IT'S, UH, IT'S BEEN OVER AN HOUR SINCE HE WAS SUPPOSED TO. I DON'T LIKE THIS, JUST SITTING ON OUR HANDS, WAITING WITH ALL THIS--
I JUST DON'T LIKE IT.
SOMETHING MUST'VE HAPPENED. WHY ELSE WOULD HE BE--
COWARDS. IF HE COULD HEAR YOU, YOU'D BE SIGNING YOUR OWN DEATH WARRANTS...
AID
...SO JUST DO AS YOU WERE ORDERED, AND DON'T MAKE ME WASTE ONE OF YOU FOR GETTING ON MY NERVES.
NOTHIN'S HAPPENED. HE'LL CALL WHEN HE'S READY...AND THEN WE HAVE OUR FUN.

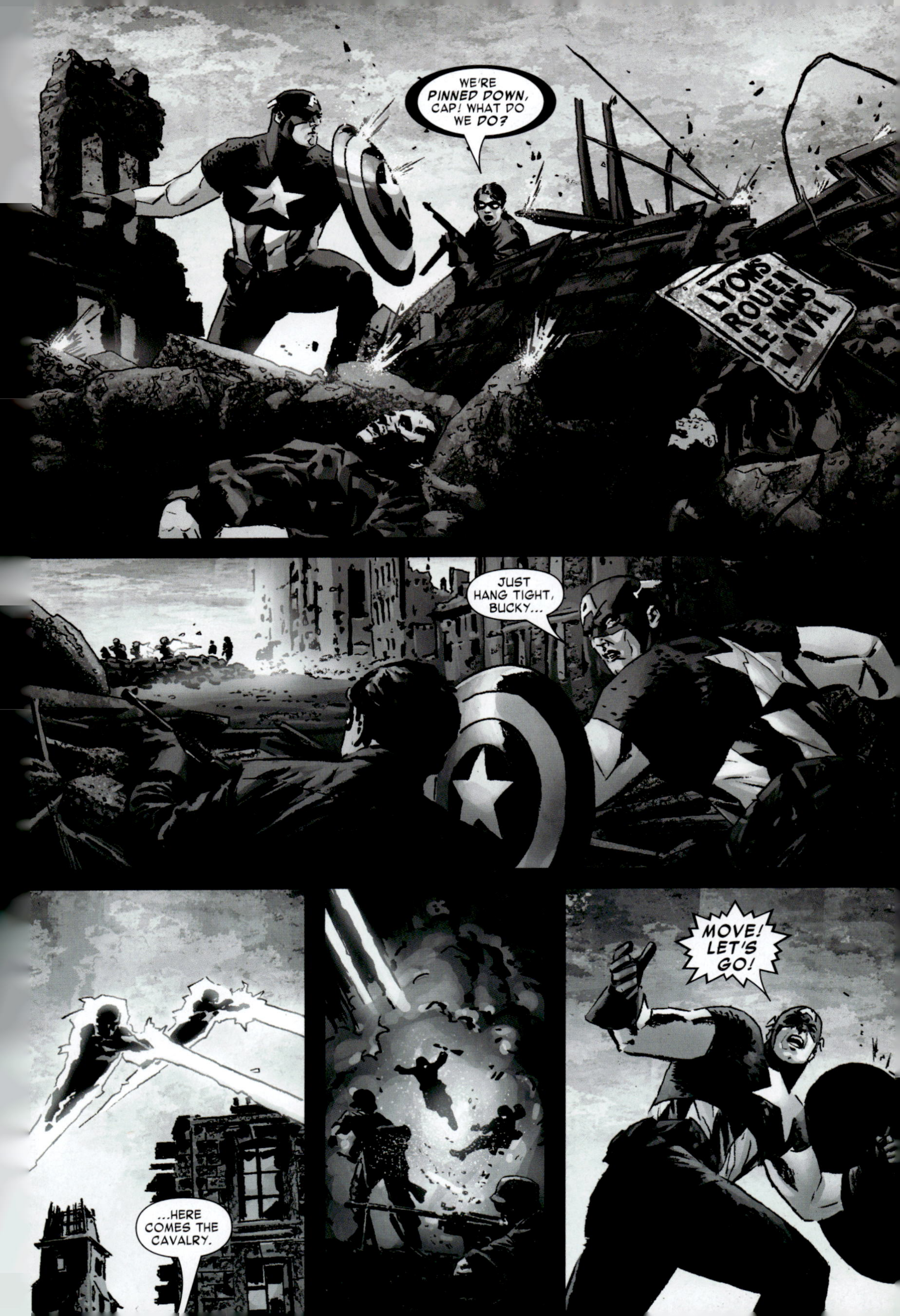
WE'RE PINNED DOWN, CAP! WHAT DO WE DO?
LYONS ROUEN LE MANS LAVAL
JUST HANG TIGHT, BUCKY...
...HERE COMES THE CAVALRY.
MOVE! LET'S GO!

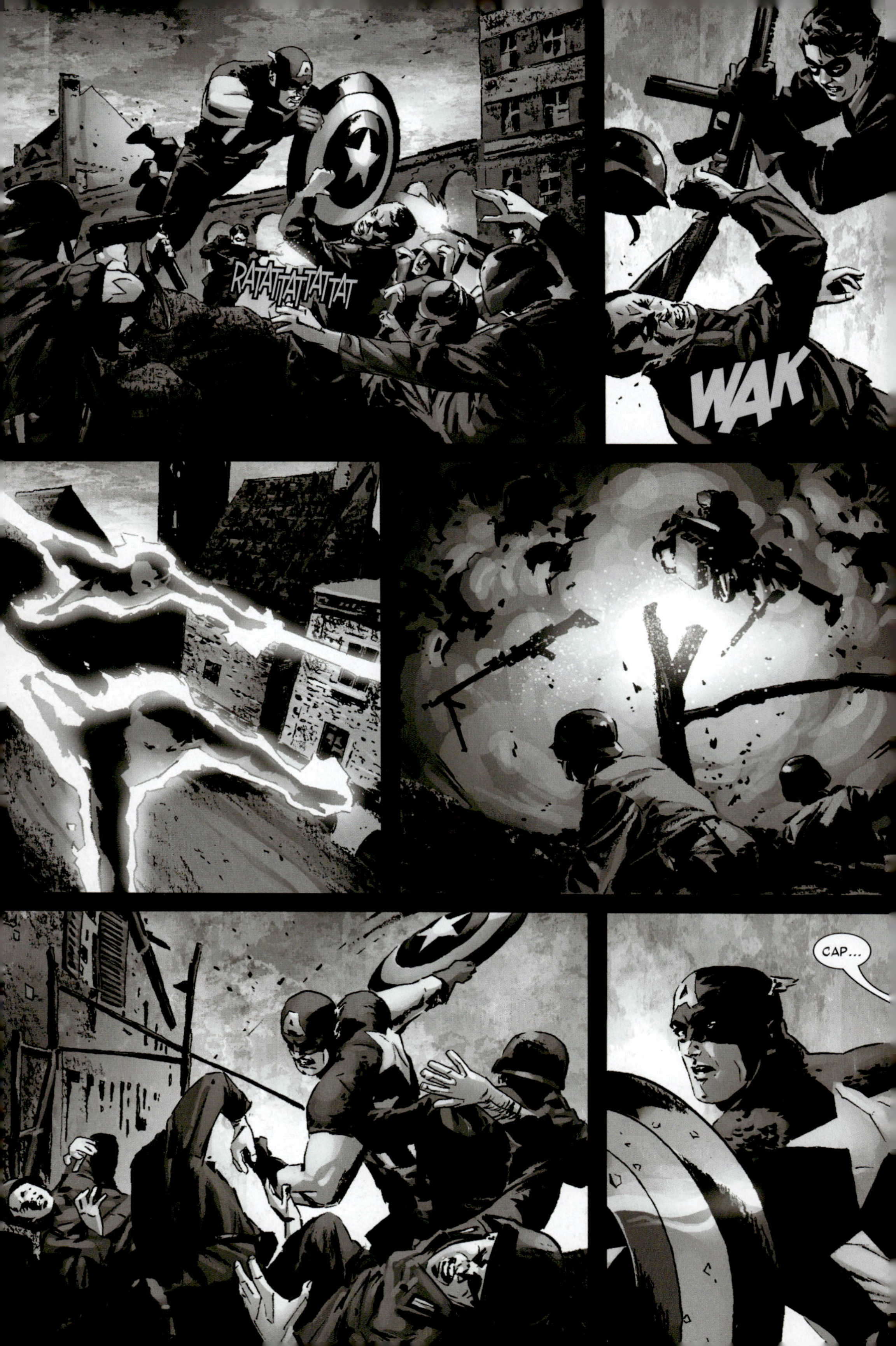
RATATTATTATTAT
WAK
CAP...

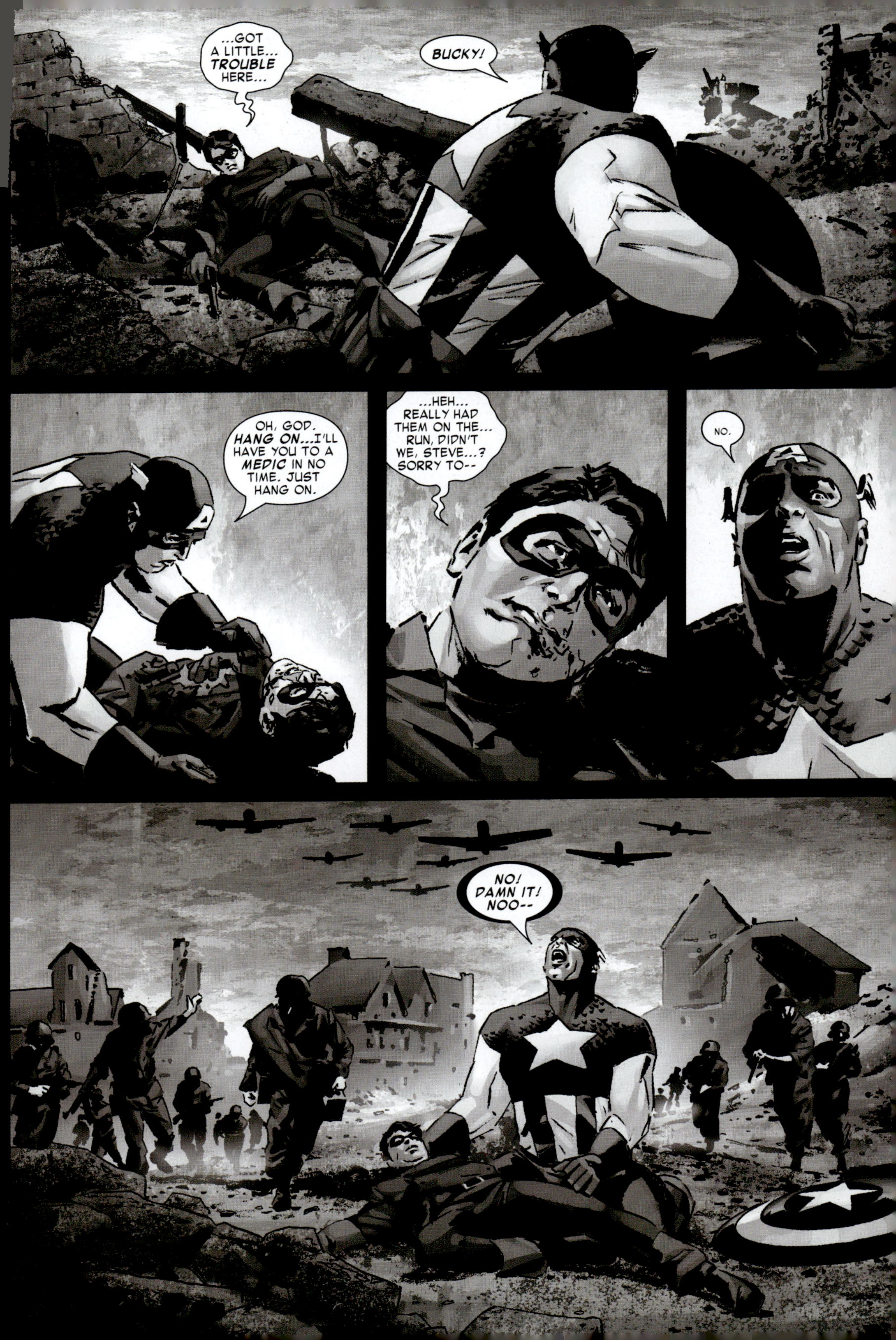
...GOT A LITTLE... TROUBLE HERE...
BUCKY!
OH, GOD. HANG ON...I'LL HAVE YOU TO A MEDIC IN NO TIME. JUST HANG ON.
...HEH... REALLY HAD THEM ON THE... RUN, DIDN'T WE, STEVE...? SORRY TO--
NO.
NO! DAMN IT! NOO--

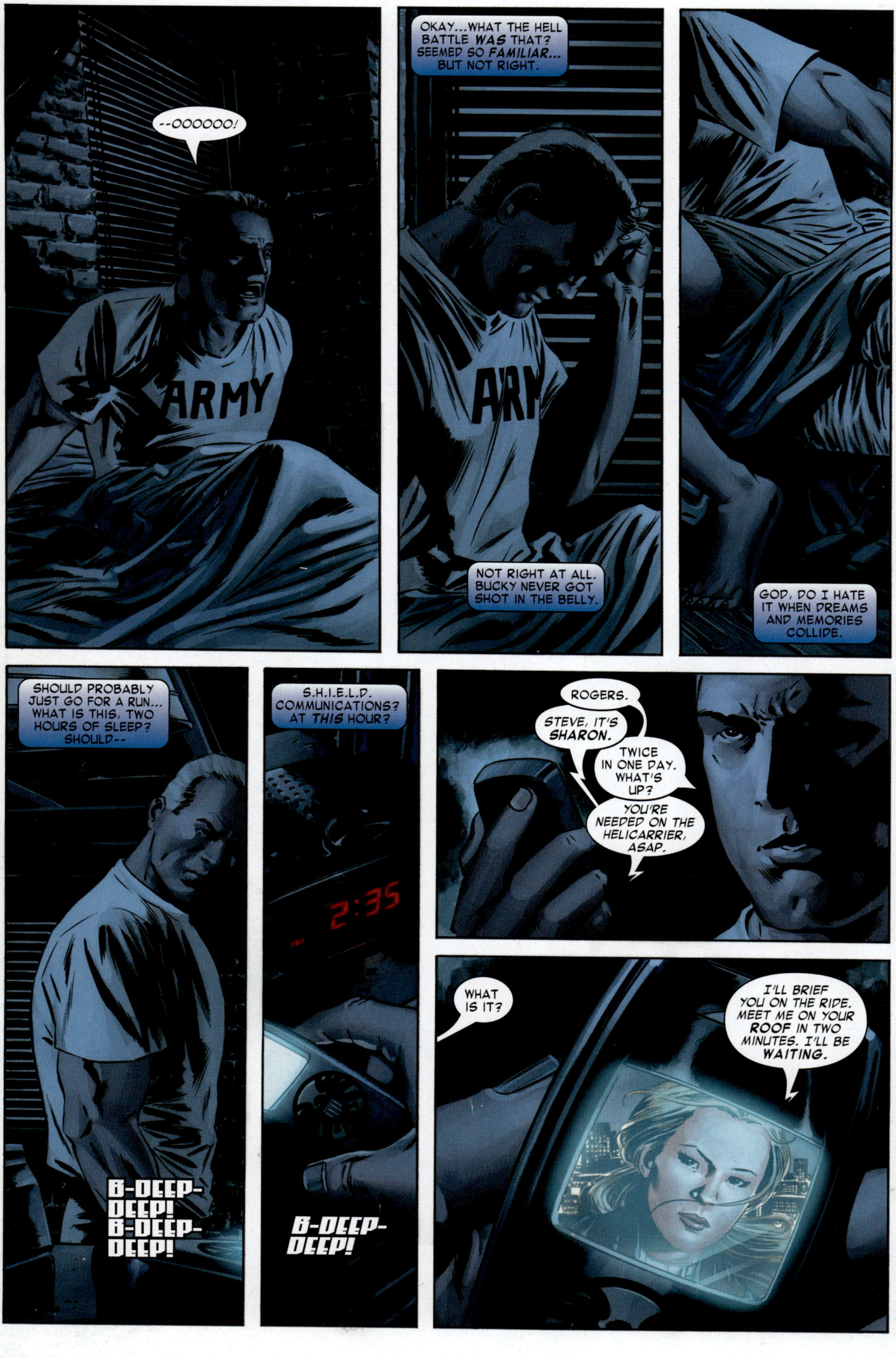
--OOOOOO!
OKAY...WHAT THE HELL BATTLE WAS THAT? SEEMED SO FAMILIAR... BUT NOT RIGHT.
NOT RIGHT AT ALL. BUCKY NEVER GOT SHOT IN THE BELLY.
GOD, DO I HATE IT WHEN DREAMS AND MEMORIES COLLIDE.
SHOULD PROBABLY JUST GO FOR A RUN... WHAT IS THIS, TWO HOURS OF SLEEP? SHOULD--
B-DEEP-DEEP! B-DEEP-DEEP!
S.H.I.E.L.D. COMMUNICATIONS? AT THIS HOUR?
2:35
B-DEEP-DEEP!
ROGERS.
STEVE, IT'S SHARON.
TWICE IN ONE DAY. WHAT'S UP?
YOU'RE NEEDED ON THE HELICARRIER, ASAP.
WHAT IS IT?
I'LL BRIEF YOU ON THE RIDE. MEET ME ON YOUR ROOF IN TWO MINUTES. I'LL BE WAITING.

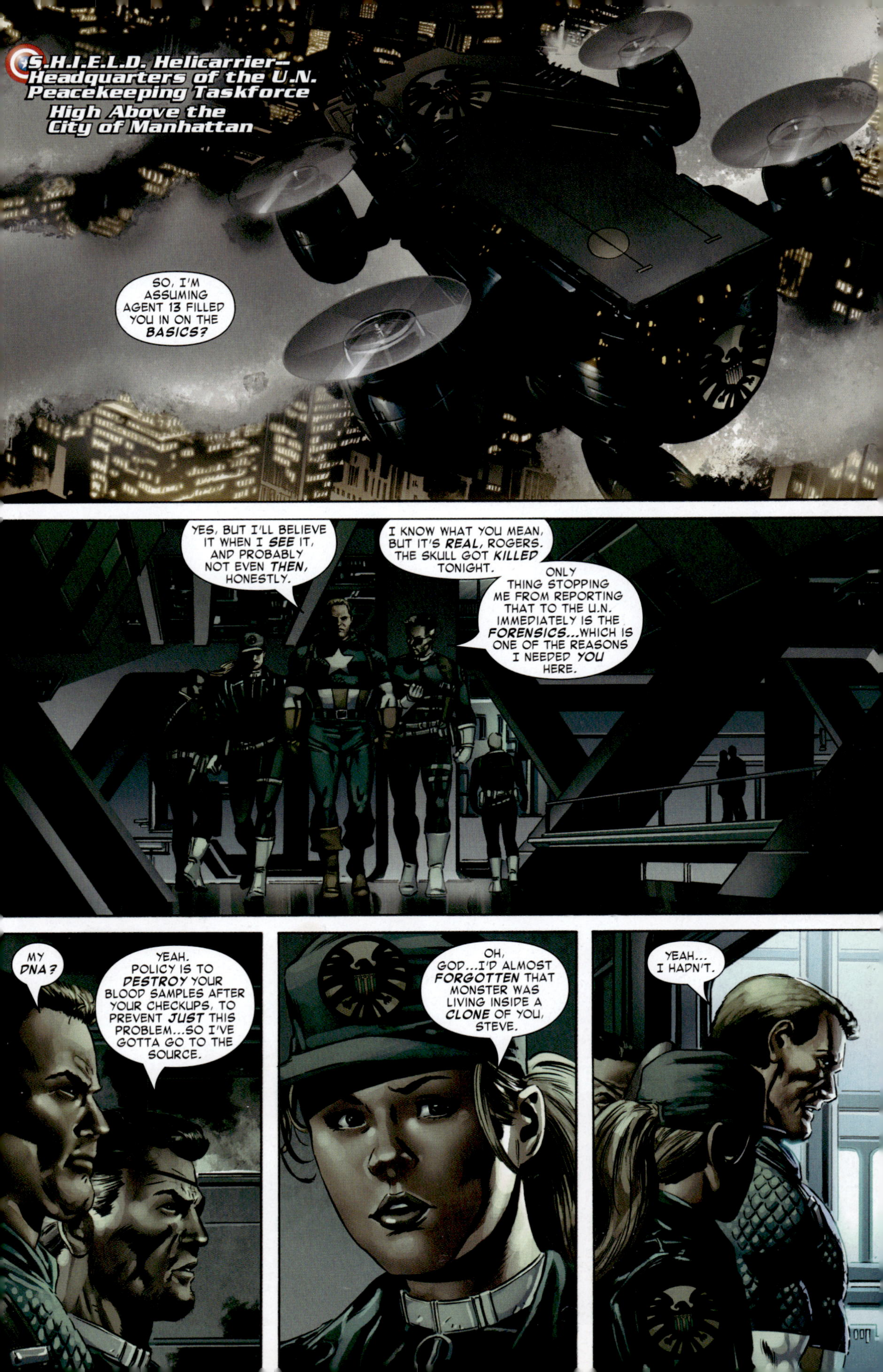
S.H.I.E.L.D. Helicarrier— Headquarters of the U.N. Peacekeeping Taskforce
High Above the City of Manhattan
SO, I'M ASSUMING AGENT 13 FILLED YOU IN ON THE BASICS?
YES, BUT I'LL BELIEVE IT WHEN I SEE IT, AND PROBABLY NOT EVEN THEN, HONESTLY.
I KNOW WHAT YOU MEAN, BUT IT'S REAL, ROGERS. THE SKULL GOT KILLED TONIGHT.
ONLY THING STOPPING ME FROM REPORTING THAT TO THE U.N. IMMEDIATELY IS THE FORENSICS...WHICH IS ONE OF THE REASONS I NEEDED YOU HERE.
MY DNA?
YEAH. POLICY IS TO DESTROY YOUR BLOOD SAMPLES AFTER YOUR CHECKUPS, TO PREVENT JUST THIS PROBLEM...SO I'VE GOTTA GO TO THE SOURCE.
OH, GOD...I'D ALMOST FORGOTTEN THAT MONSTER WAS LIVING INSIDE A CLONE OF YOU, STEVE.
YEAH... I HADN'T.

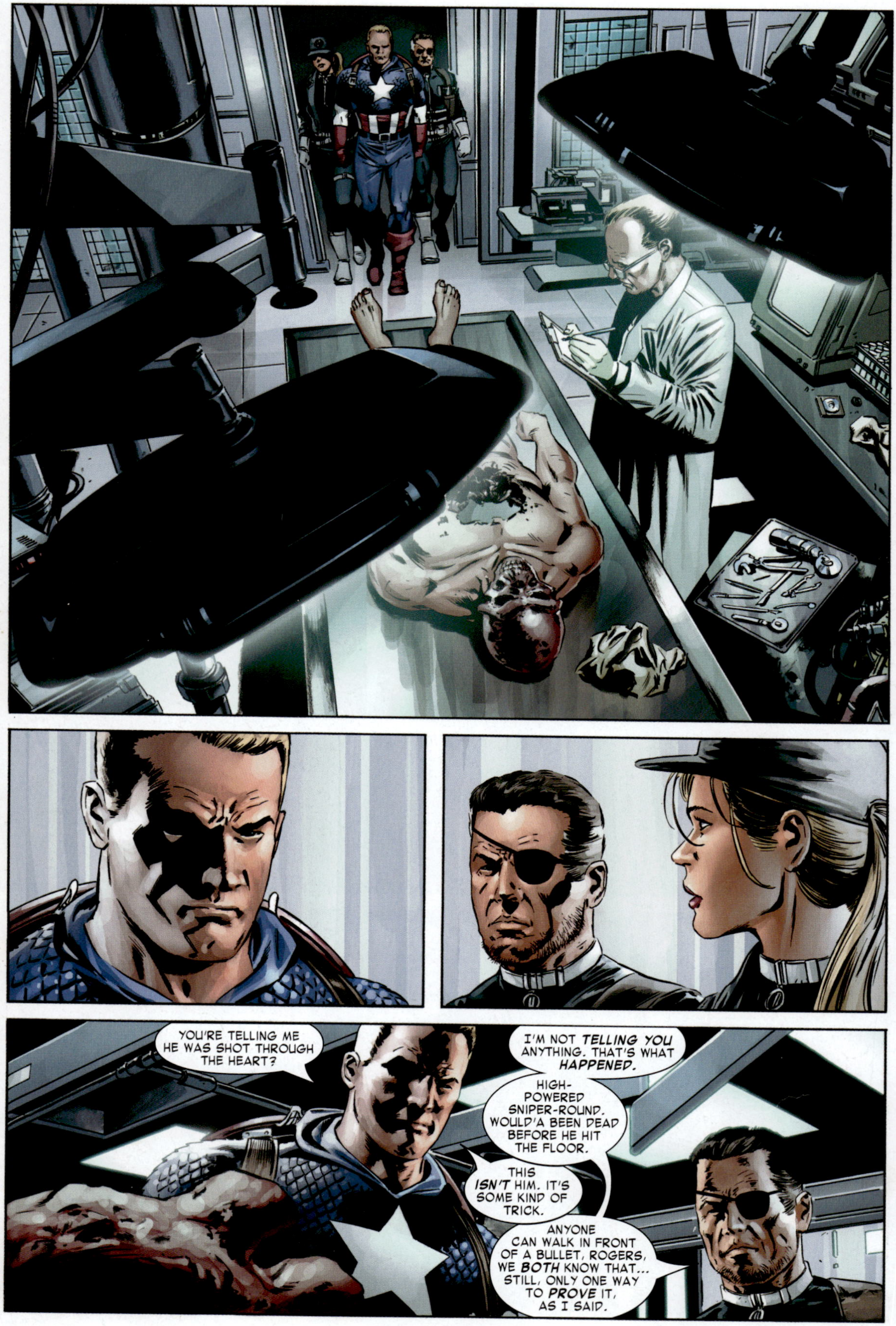
YOU'RE TELLING ME HE WAS SHOT THROUGH THE HEART?
I'M NOT TELLING YOU ANYTHING. THAT'S WHAT HAPPENED.
HIGH-POWERED SNIPER-ROUND. WOULD'A BEEN DEAD BEFORE HE HIT THE FLOOR.
THIS ISN'T HIM. IT'S SOME KIND OF TRICK.
ANYONE CAN WALK IN FRONT OF A BULLET, ROGERS, WE BOTH KNOW THAT... STILL, ONLY ONE WAY TO PROVE IT, AS I SAID.

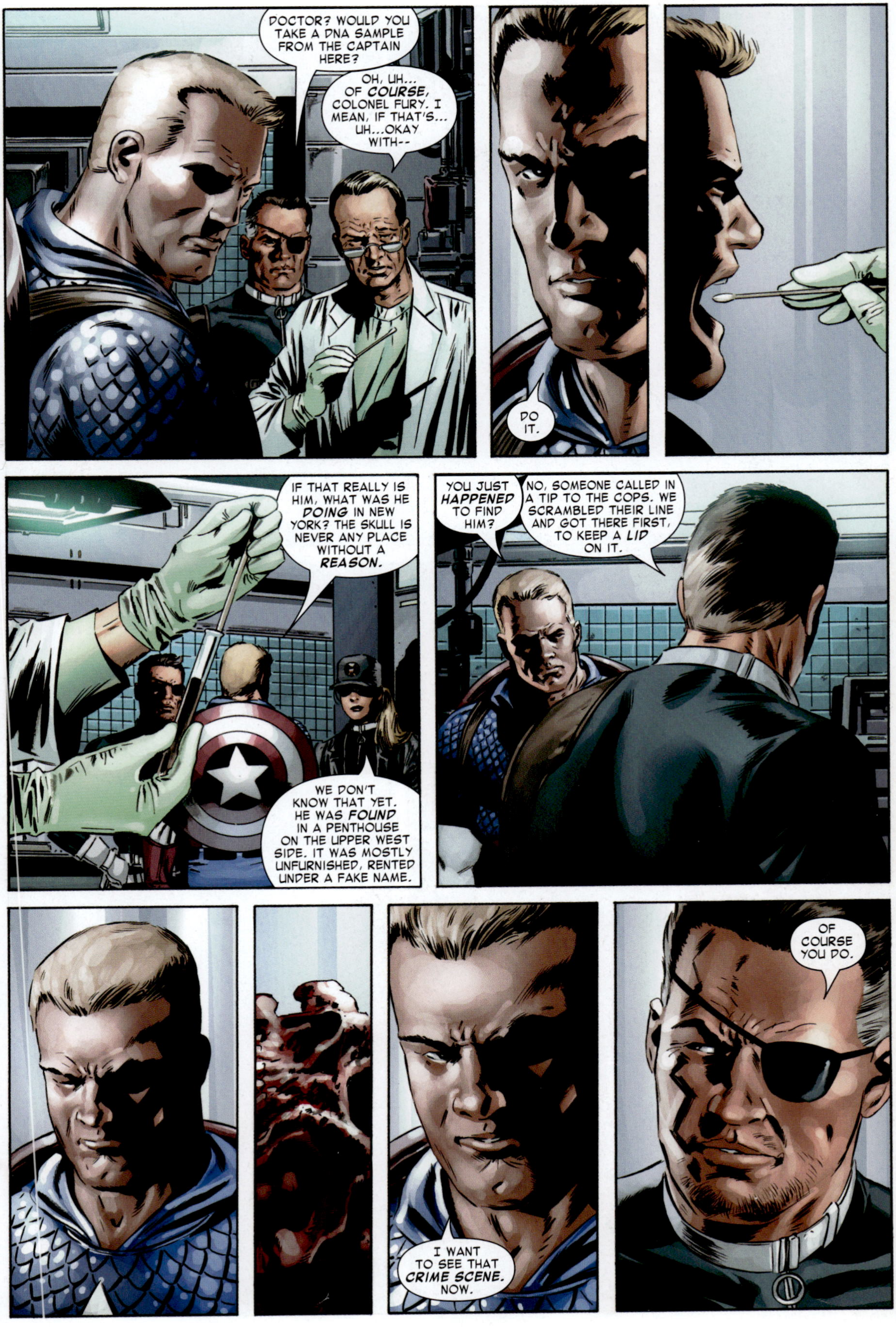
DOCTOR? WOULD YOU TAKE A DNA SAMPLE FROM THE CAPTAIN HERE?
OH, UH... OF COURSE, COLONEL FURY. I MEAN, IF THAT'S... UH...OKAY WITH--
DO IT.
IF THAT REALLY IS HIM, WHAT WAS HE DOING IN NEW YORK? THE SKULL IS NEVER ANY PLACE WITHOUT A REASON.
WE DON'T KNOW THAT YET. HE WAS FOUND IN A PENTHOUSE ON THE UPPER WEST SIDE. IT WAS MOSTLY UNFURNISHED, RENTED UNDER A FAKE NAME.
YOU JUST HAPPENED TO FIND HIM?
NO, SOMEONE CALLED IN A TIP TO THE COPS. WE SCRAMBLED THEIR LINE AND GOT THERE FIRST, TO KEEP A LID ON IT.
I WANT TO SEE THAT CRIME SCENE. NOW.
OF COURSE YOU DO.

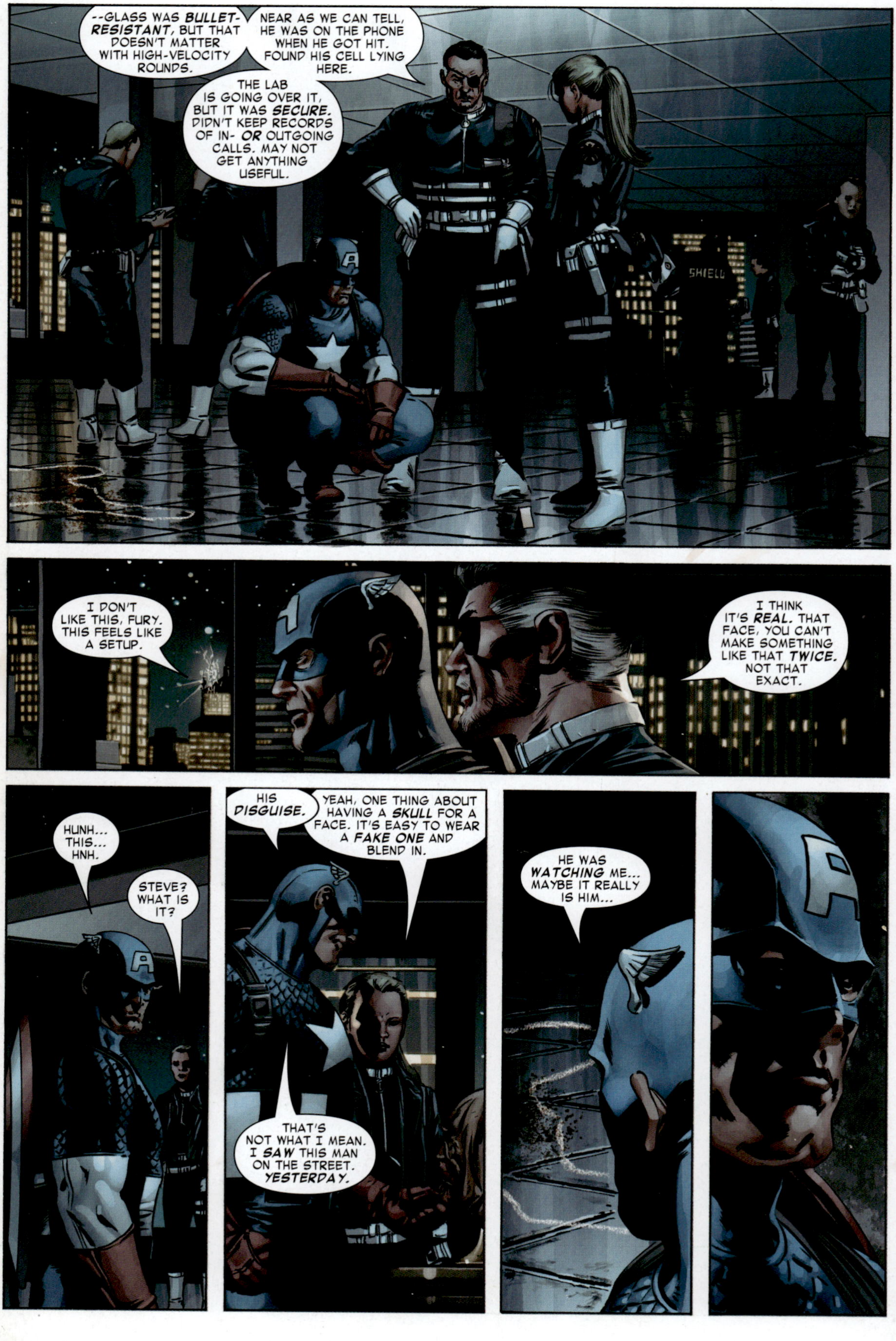
--GLASS WAS BULLET-RESISTANT, BUT THAT DOESN'T MATTER WITH HIGH-VELOCITY ROUNDS.
NEAR AS WE CAN TELL, HE WAS ON THE PHONE WHEN HE GOT HIT. FOUND HIS CELL LYING HERE.
THE LAB IS GOING OVER IT, BUT IT WAS SECURE. DIDN'T KEEP RECORDS OF IN- OR OUTGOING CALLS. MAY NOT GET ANYTHING USEFUL.
SHIELD
I DON'T LIKE THIS, FURY. THIS FEELS LIKE A SETUP.
I THINK IT'S REAL. THAT FACE, YOU CAN'T MAKE SOMETHING LIKE THAT TWICE. NOT THAT EXACT.
HUNH... THIS... HNH.
STEVE? WHAT IS IT?
HIS DISGUISE.
YEAH, ONE THING ABOUT HAVING A SKULL FOR A FACE. IT'S EASY TO WEAR A FAKE ONE AND BLEND IN.
THAT'S NOT WHAT I MEAN. I SAW THIS MAN ON THE STREET. YESTERDAY.
HE WAS WATCHING ME... MAYBE IT REALLY IS HIM...

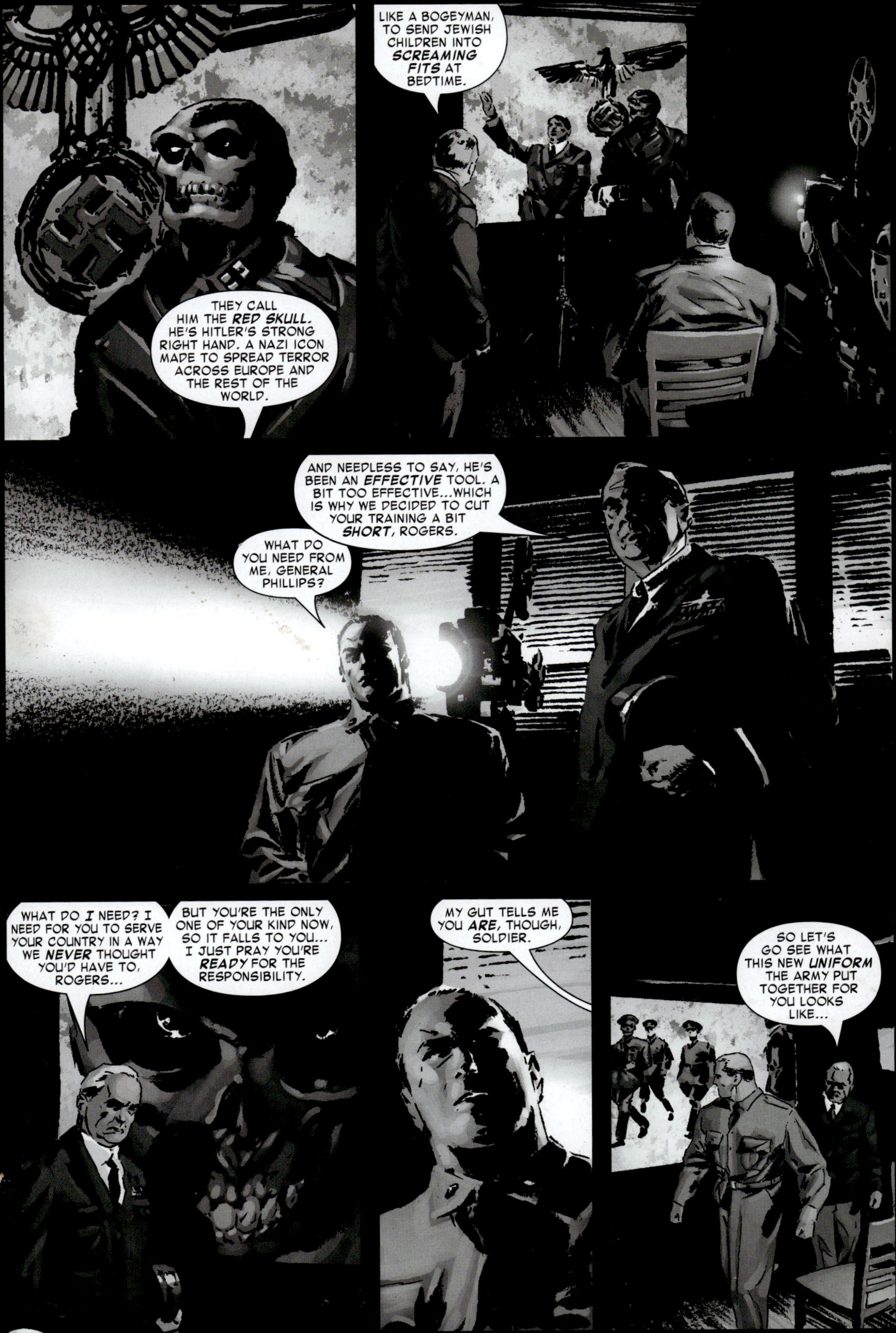
THEY CALL HIM THE RED SKULL. HE'S HITLER'S STRONG RIGHT HAND. A NAZI ICON MADE TO SPREAD TERROR ACROSS EUROPE AND THE REST OF THE WORLD.
LIKE A BOGEYMAN, TO SEND JEWISH CHILDREN INTO SCREAMING FITS AT BEDTIME.
AND NEEDLESS TO SAY, HE'S BEEN AN EFFECTIVE TOOL. A BIT TOO EFFECTIVE...WHICH IS WHY WE DECIDED TO CUT YOUR TRAINING A BIT SHORT, ROGERS.
WHAT DO YOU NEED FROM ME, GENERAL PHILLIPS?
WHAT DO I NEED? I NEED FOR YOU TO SERVE YOUR COUNTRY IN A WAY WE NEVER THOUGHT YOU'D HAVE TO, ROGERS...
BUT YOU'RE THE ONLY ONE OF YOUR KIND NOW, SO IT FALLS TO YOU... I JUST PRAY YOU'RE READY FOR THE RESPONSIBILITY.
MY GUT TELLS ME YOU ARE, THOUGH, SOLDIER.
SO LET'S GO SEE WHAT THIS NEW UNIFORM THE ARMY PUT TOGETHER FOR YOU LOOKS LIKE...

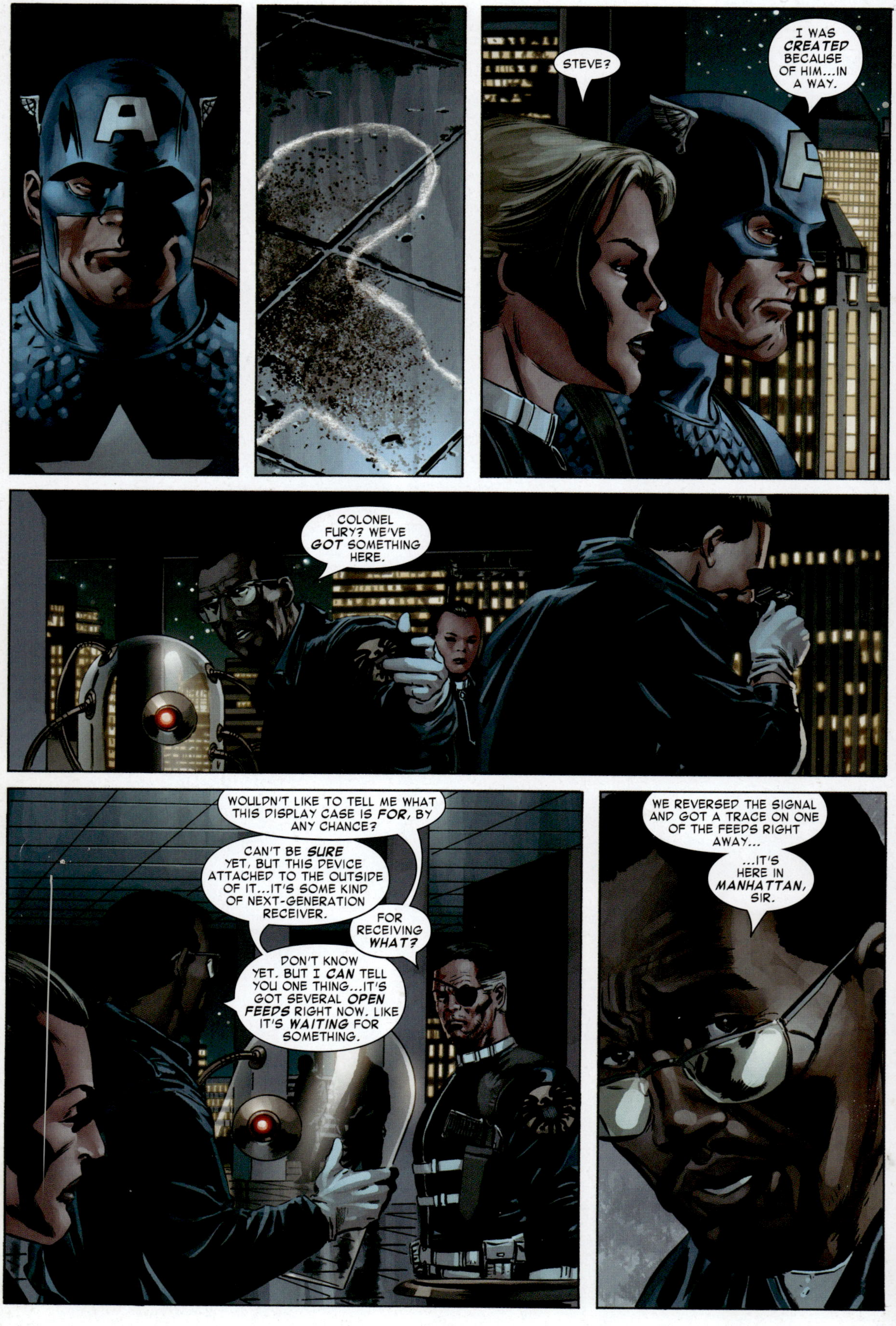
STEVE?
I WAS CREATED BECAUSE OF HIM...IN A WAY.
COLONEL FURY? WE'VE GOT SOMETHING HERE.
WOULDN'T LIKE TO TELL ME WHAT THIS DISPLAY CASE IS FOR, BY ANY CHANCE?
CAN'T BE SURE YET, BUT THIS DEVICE ATTACHED TO THE OUTSIDE OF IT...IT'S SOME KIND OF NEXT-GENERATION RECEIVER.
FOR RECEIVING WHAT?
DON'T KNOW YET. BUT I CAN TELL YOU ONE THING...IT'S GOT SEVERAL OPEN FEEDS RIGHT NOW. LIKE IT'S WAITING FOR SOMETHING.
WE REVERSED THE SIGNAL AND GOT A TRACE ON ONE OF THE FEEDS RIGHT AWAY...
...IT'S HERE IN MANHATTAN, SIR.

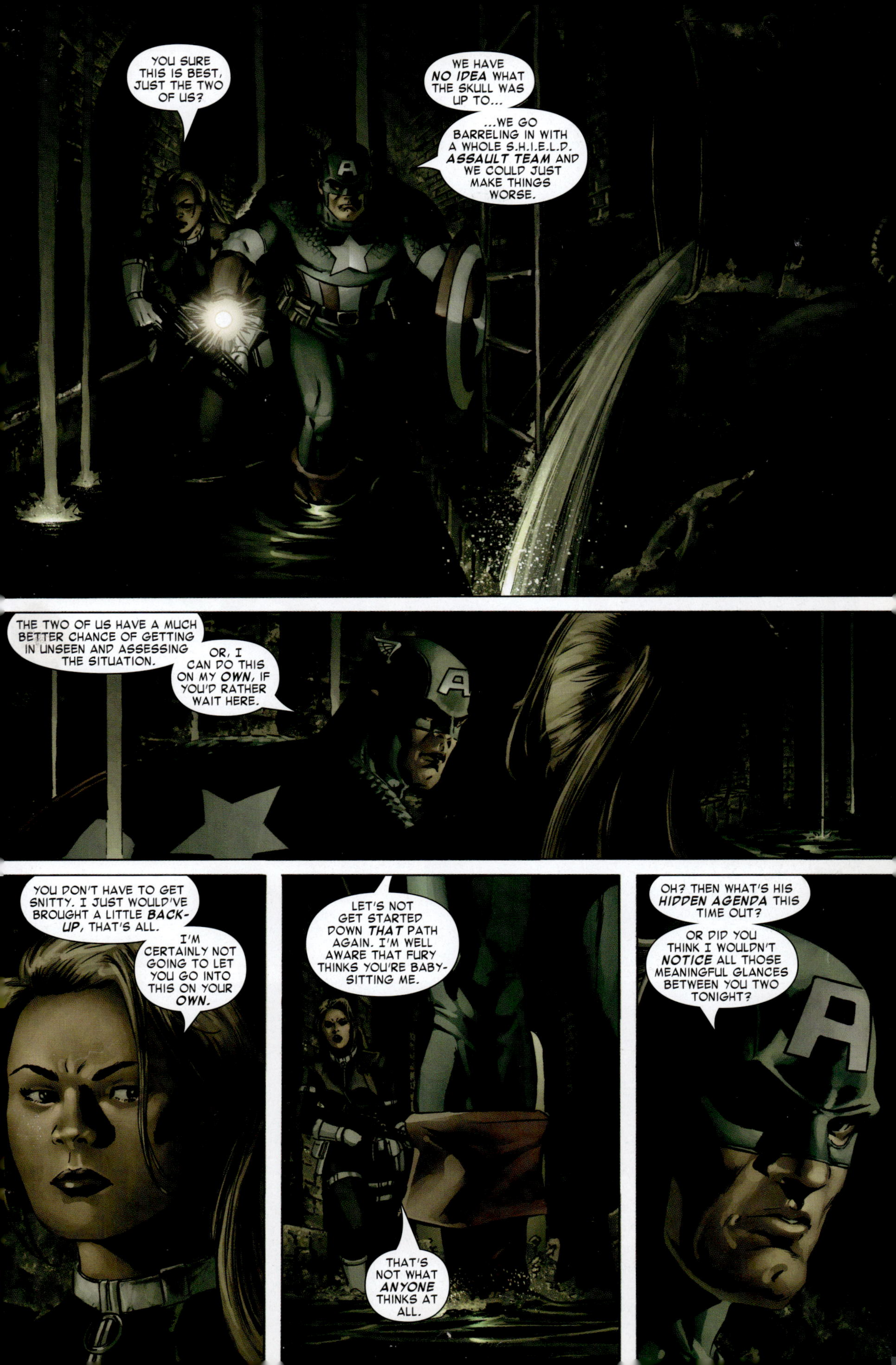
YOU SURE THIS IS BEST, JUST THE TWO OF US?
WE HAVE NO IDEA WHAT THE SKULL WAS UP TO...
...WE GO BARRELING IN WITH A WHOLE S.H.I.E.L.D. ASSAULT TEAM AND WE COULD JUST MAKE THINGS WORSE.
THE TWO OF US HAVE A MUCH BETTER CHANCE OF GETTING IN UNSEEN AND ASSESSING THE SITUATION.
OR, I CAN DO THIS ON MY OWN, IF YOU'D RATHER WAIT HERE.
YOU DON'T HAVE TO GET SNITTY. I JUST WOULD'VE BROUGHT A LITTLE BACK-UP, THAT'S ALL.
I'M CERTAINLY NOT GOING TO LET YOU GO INTO THIS ON YOUR OWN.
LET'S NOT GET STARTED DOWN THAT PATH AGAIN. I'M WELL AWARE THAT FURY THINKS YOU'RE BABY-SITTING ME.
THAT'S NOT WHAT ANYONE THINKS AT ALL.
OH? THEN WHAT'S HIS HIDDEN AGENDA THIS TIME OUT?
OR DID YOU THINK I WOULDN'T NOTICE ALL THOSE MEANINGFUL GLANCES BETWEEN YOU TWO TONIGHT?

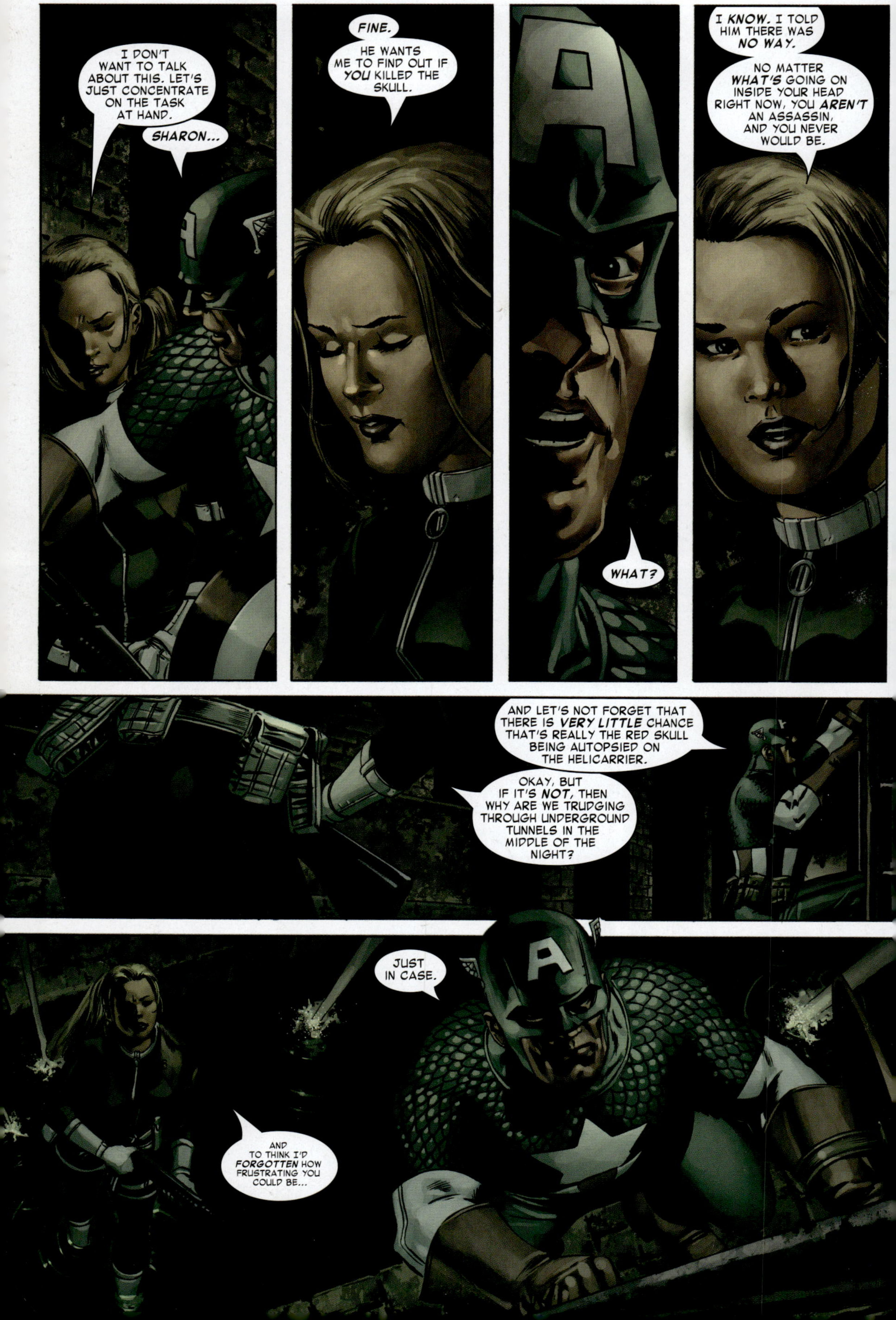
I DON'T WANT TO TALK ABOUT THIS. LET'S JUST CONCENTRATE ON THE TASK AT HAND.
SHARON...
FINE.
HE WANTS ME TO FIND OUT IF YOU KILLED THE SKULL.
WHAT?
I KNOW. I TOLD HIM THERE WAS NO WAY.
NO MATTER WHAT'S GOING ON INSIDE YOUR HEAD RIGHT NOW, YOU AREN'T AN ASSASSIN, AND YOU NEVER WOULD BE.
AND LET'S NOT FORGET THAT THERE IS VERY LITTLE CHANCE THAT'S REALLY THE RED SKULL BEING AUTOPSIED ON THE HELICARRIER.
OKAY, BUT IF IT'S NOT, THEN WHY ARE WE TRUDGING THROUGH UNDERGROUND TUNNELS IN THE MIDDLE OF THE NIGHT?
JUST IN CASE.
AND TO THINK I'D FORGOTTEN HOW FRUSTRATING YOU COULD BE...

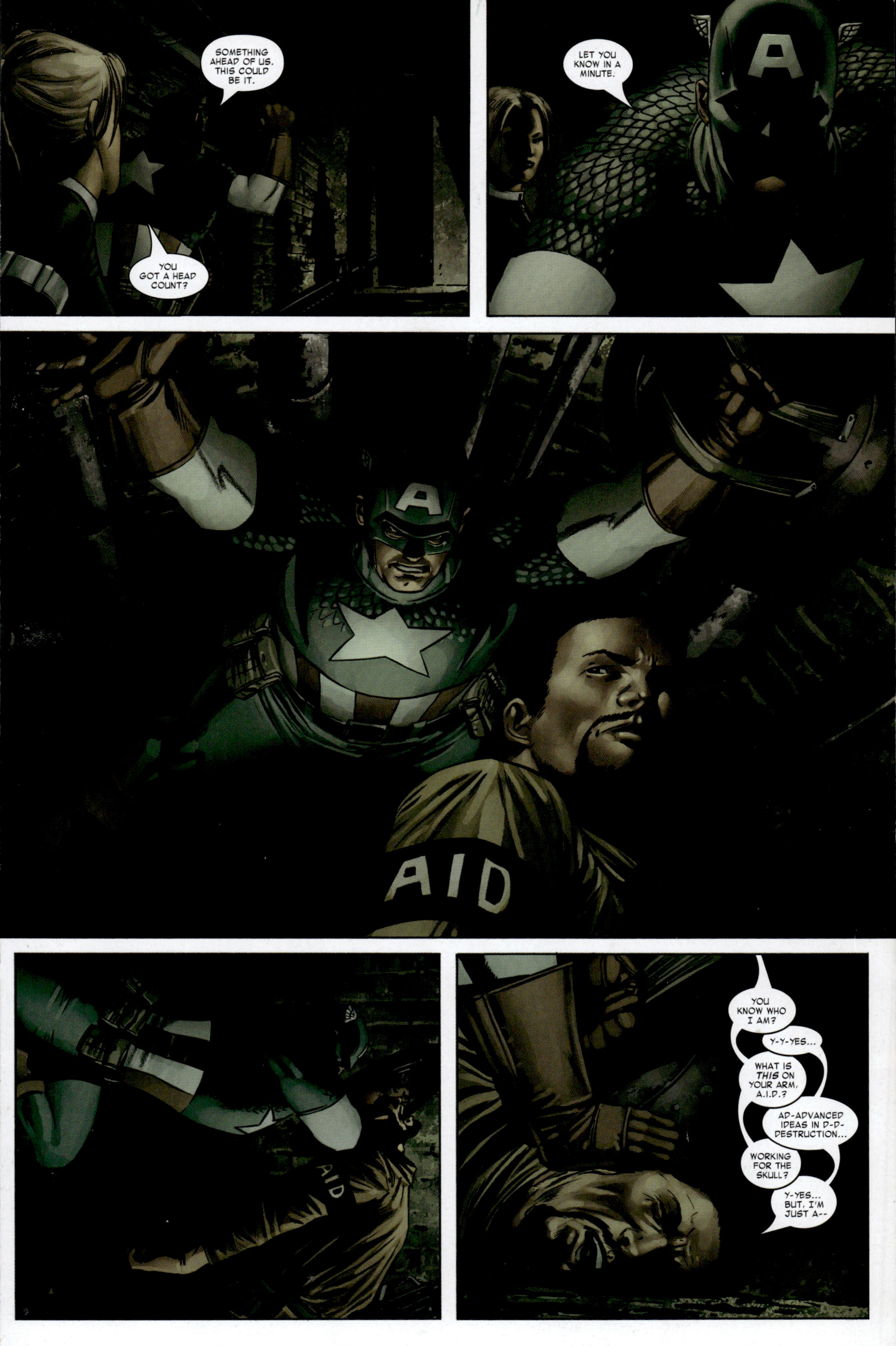
SOMETHING AHEAD OF US. THIS COULD BE IT.
YOU GOT A HEAD COUNT?
LET YOU KNOW IN A MINUTE.
AID
AID
YOU KNOW WHO I AM?
Y-Y-YES...
WHAT IS *THIS* ON YOUR ARM, A.I.D.?
AD-ADVANCED IDEAS IN D-D-DESTRUCTION...
WORKING FOR THE SKULL?
Y-YES... BUT, I'M JUST A--

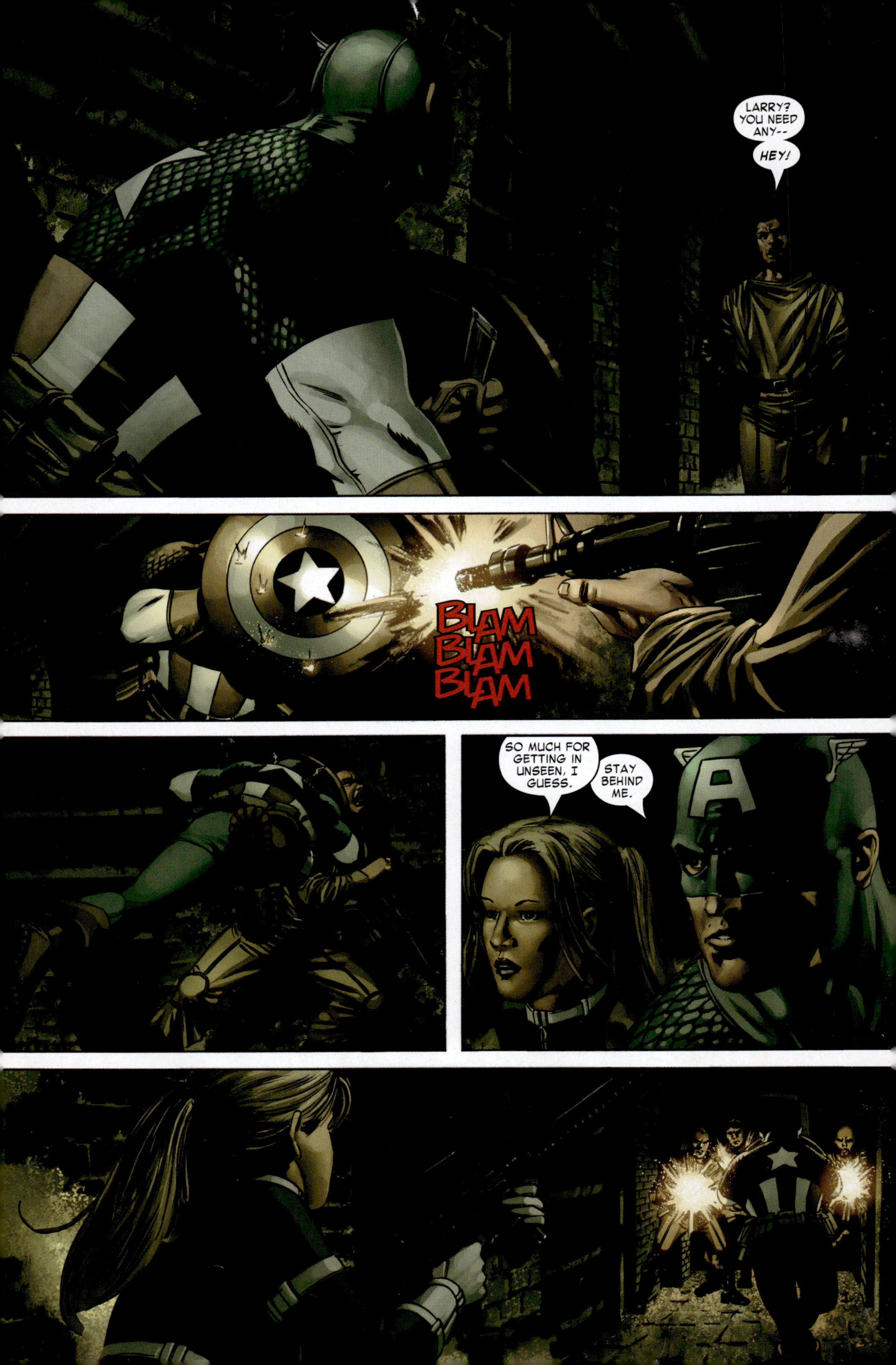
LARRY? YOU NEED ANY--
HEY!
BLAM BLAM BLAM
SO MUCH FOR GETTING IN UNSEEN, I GUESS.
STAY BEHIND ME.

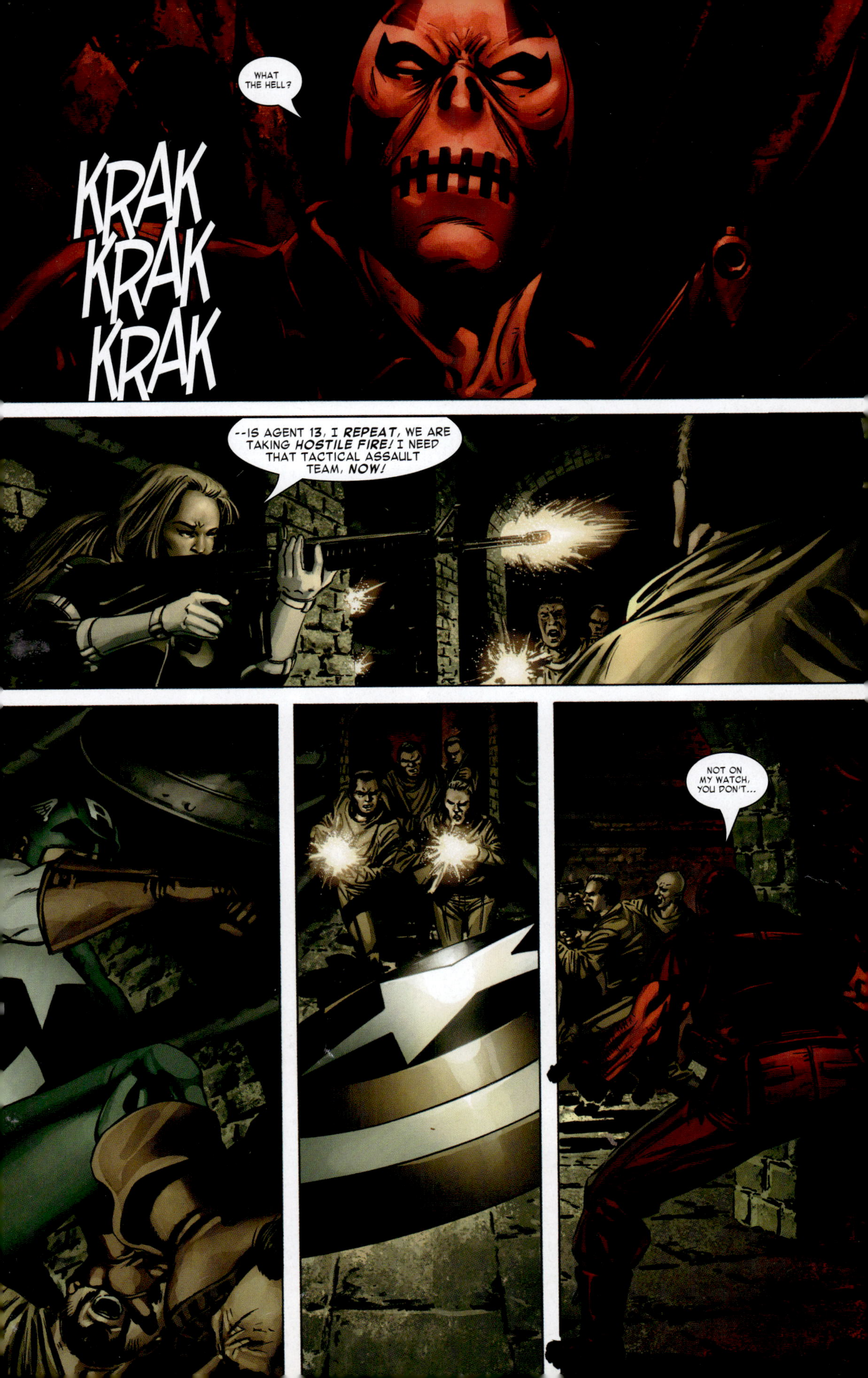
WHAT THE HELL?
KRAK KRAK KRAK
--IS AGENT 13, I REPEAT, WE ARE TAKING HOSTILE FIRE! I NEED THAT TACTICAL ASSAULT TEAM, NOW!
NOT ON MY WATCH, YOU DON'T...

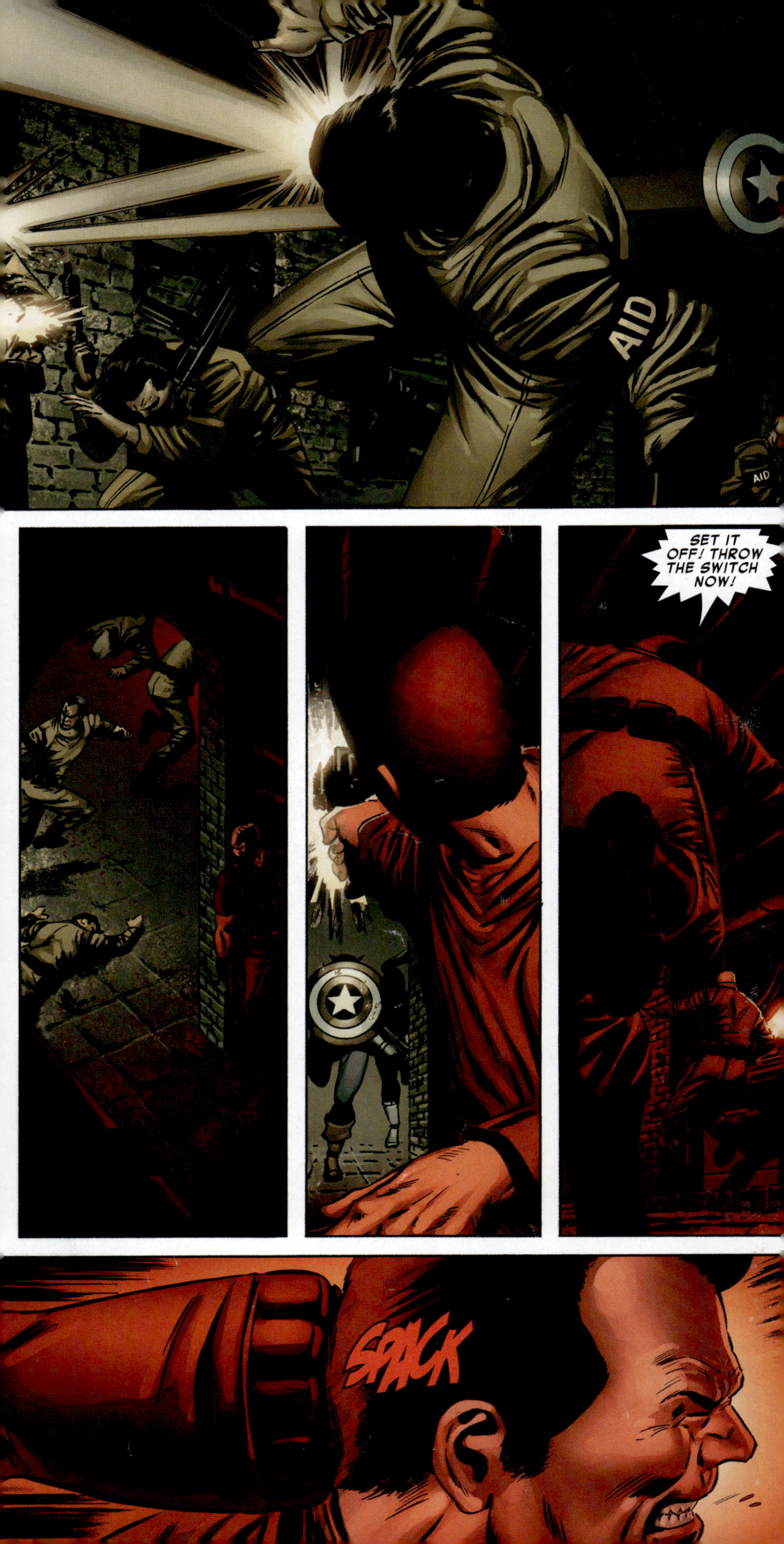
AID
AID
SET IT OFF! THROW THE SWITCH NOW!
SPACK

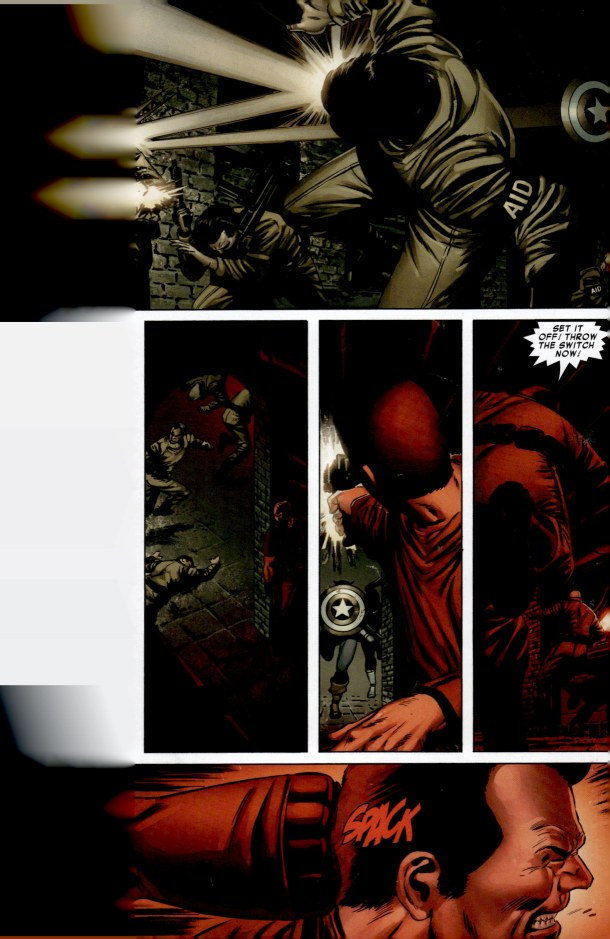

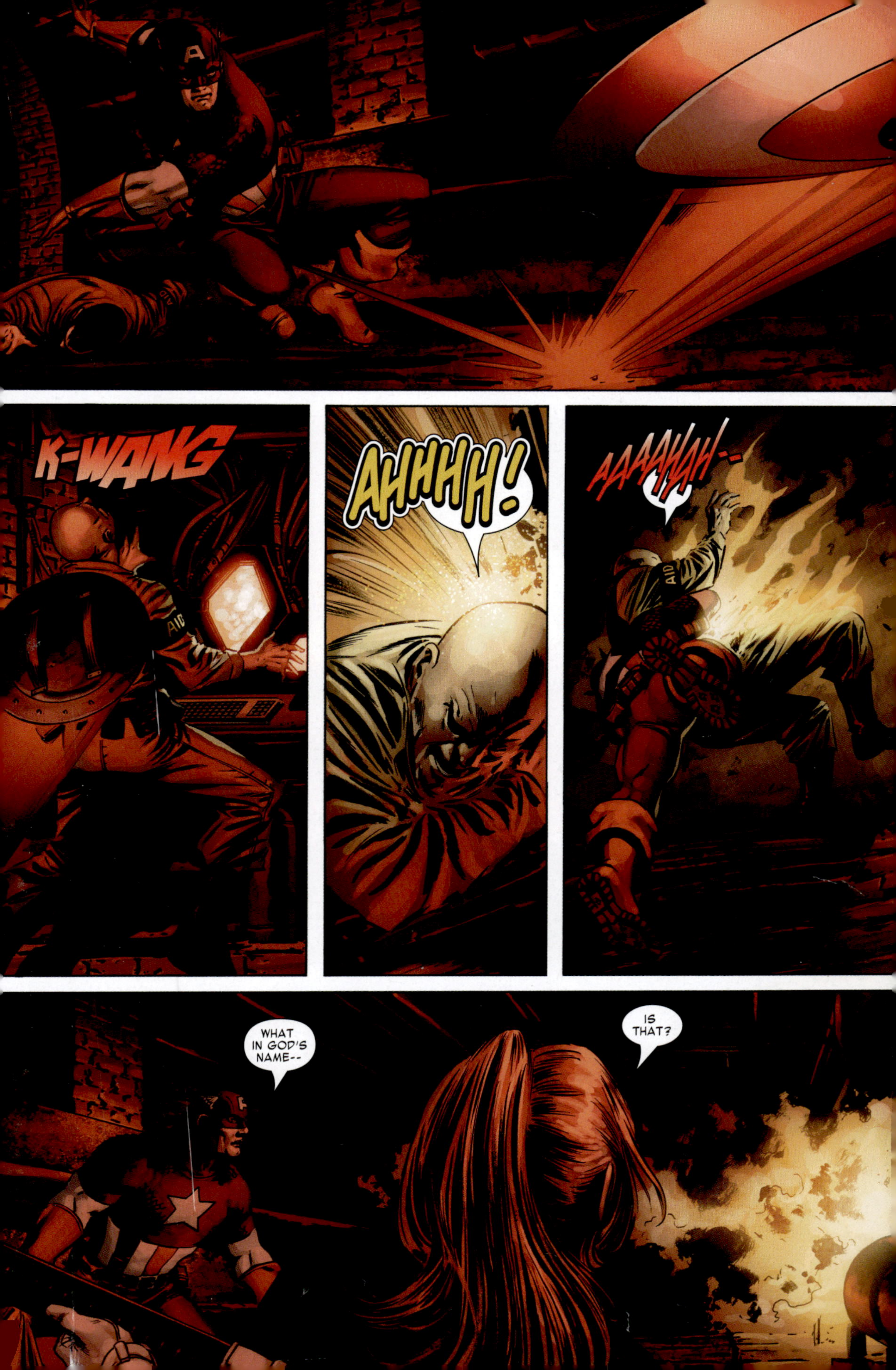
K-WANG
AHHHH!
AAAAHAH--
WHAT IN GOD'S NAME--
IS THAT?

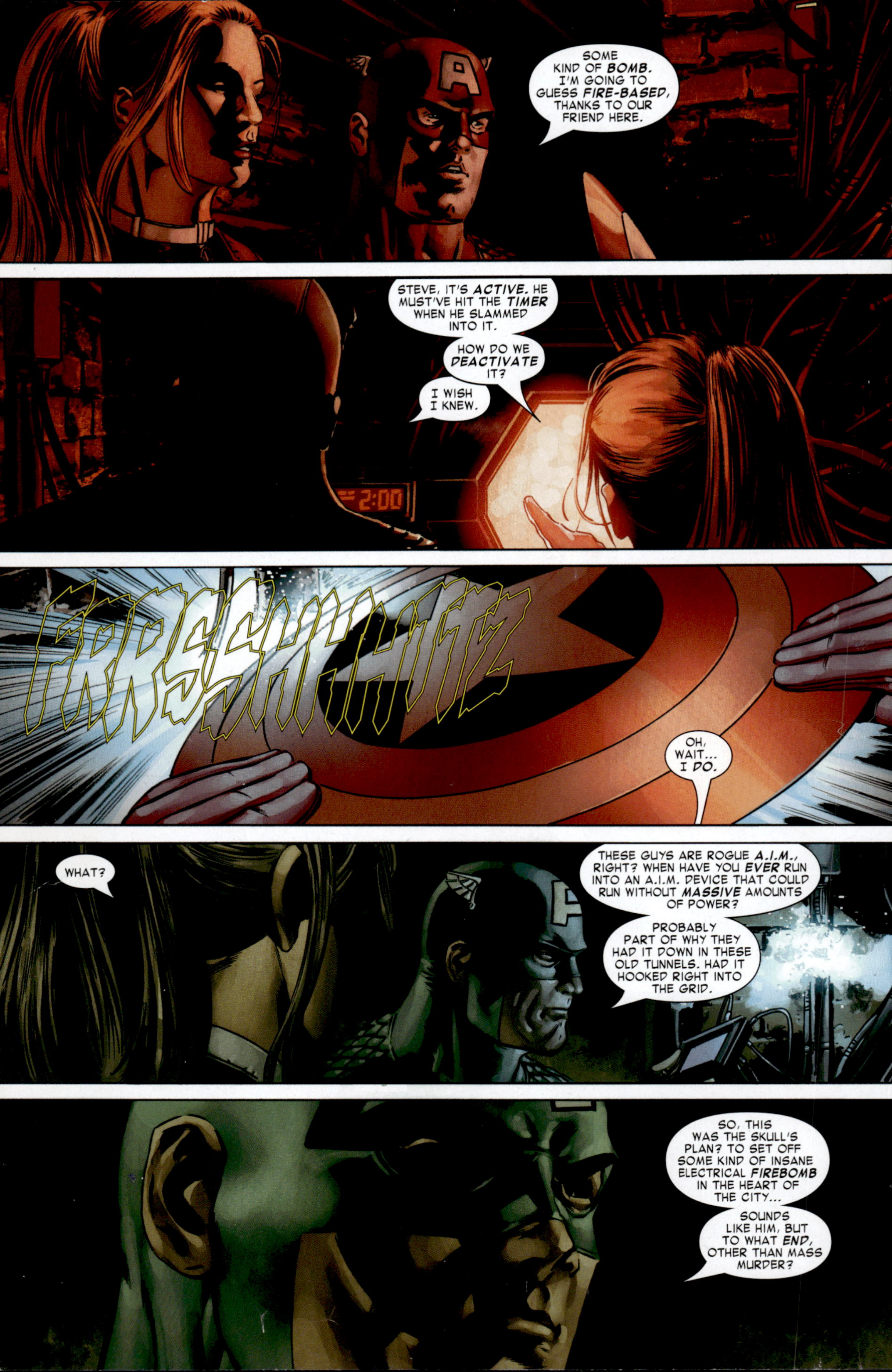
SOME KIND OF BOMB. I'M GOING TO GUESS FIRE-BASED, THANKS TO OUR FRIEND HERE.
STEVE, IT'S ACTIVE. HE MUST'VE HIT THE TIMER WHEN HE SLAMMED INTO IT.
HOW DO WE DEACTIVATE IT?
I WISH I KNEW.
2:00
FRRSSHHHHZZ
OH, WAIT... I DO.
WHAT?
THESE GUYS ARE ROGUE A.I.M., RIGHT? WHEN HAVE YOU EVER RUN INTO AN A.I.M. DEVICE THAT COULD RUN WITHOUT MASSIVE AMOUNTS OF POWER?
PROBABLY PART OF WHY THEY HAD IT DOWN IN THESE OLD TUNNELS. HAD IT HOOKED RIGHT INTO THE GRID.
SO, THIS WAS THE SKULL'S PLAN? TO SET OFF SOME KIND OF INSANE ELECTRICAL FIREBOMB IN THE HEART OF THE CITY...
SOUNDS LIKE HIM, BUT TO WHAT END, OTHER THAN MASS MURDER?

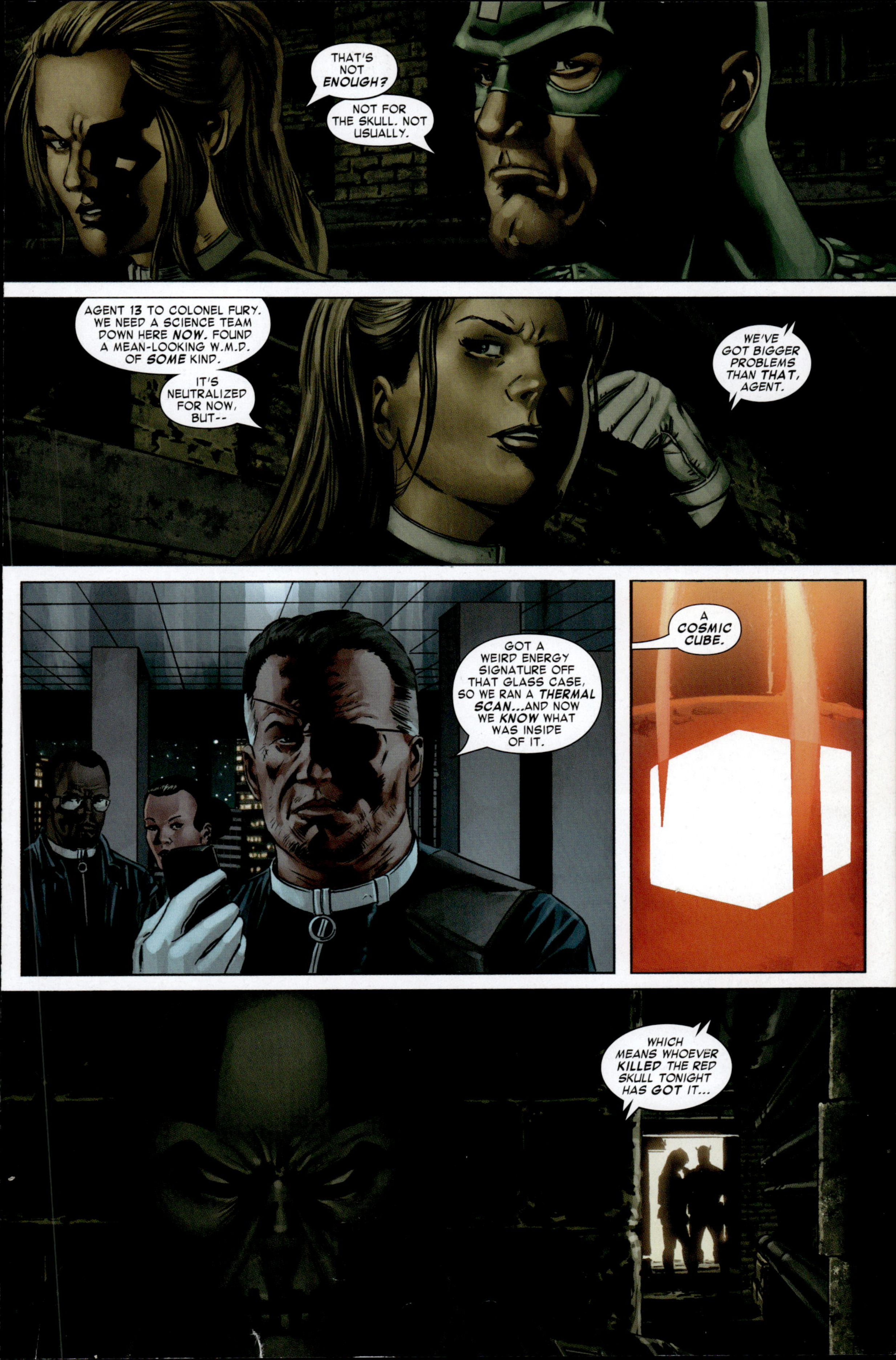
THAT'S NOT ENOUGH?
NOT FOR THE SKULL. NOT USUALLY.
AGENT 13 TO COLONEL FURY. WE NEED A SCIENCE TEAM DOWN HERE NOW. FOUND A MEAN-LOOKING W.M.D. OF SOME KIND.
IT'S NEUTRALIZED FOR NOW, BUT--
WE'VE GOT BIGGER PROBLEMS THAN THAT, AGENT.
GOT A WEIRD ENERGY SIGNATURE OFF THAT GLASS CASE, SO WE RAN A THERMAL SCAN...AND NOW WE KNOW WHAT WAS INSIDE OF IT.
A COSMIC CUBE.
WHICH MEANS WHOEVER KILLED THE RED SKULL TONIGHT HAS GOT IT...

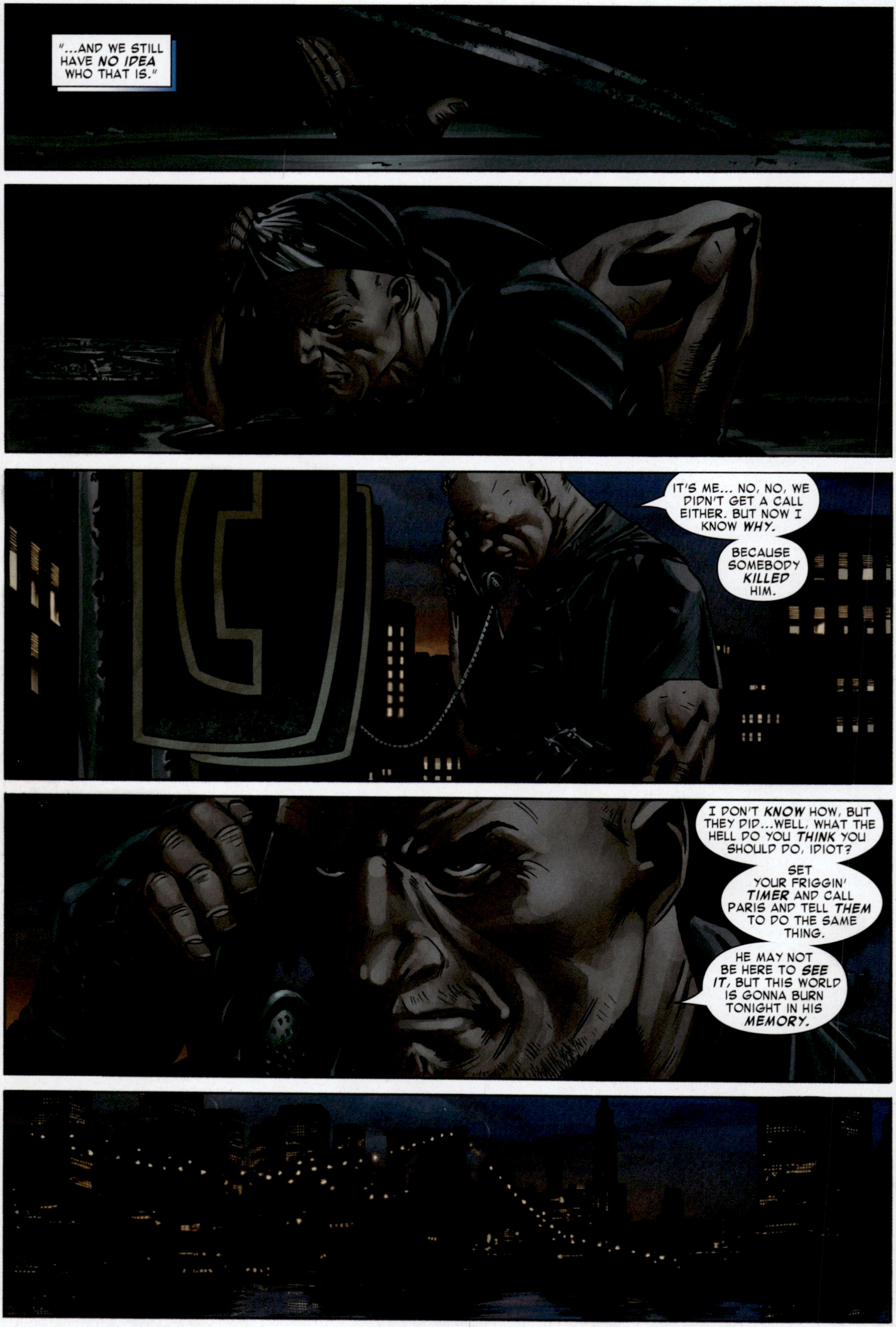
"...AND WE STILL HAVE NO IDEA WHO THAT IS."
IT'S ME... NO, NO, WE DIDN'T GET A CALL EITHER. BUT NOW I KNOW WHY.
BECAUSE SOMEBODY KILLED HIM.
I DON'T KNOW HOW, BUT THEY DID...WELL, WHAT THE HELL DO YOU THINK YOU SHOULD DO, IDIOT?
SET YOUR FRIGGIN' TIMER AND CALL PARIS AND TELL THEM TO DO THE SAME THING.
HE MAY NOT BE HERE TO SEE IT, BUT THIS WORLD IS GONNA BURN TONIGHT IN HIS MEMORY.

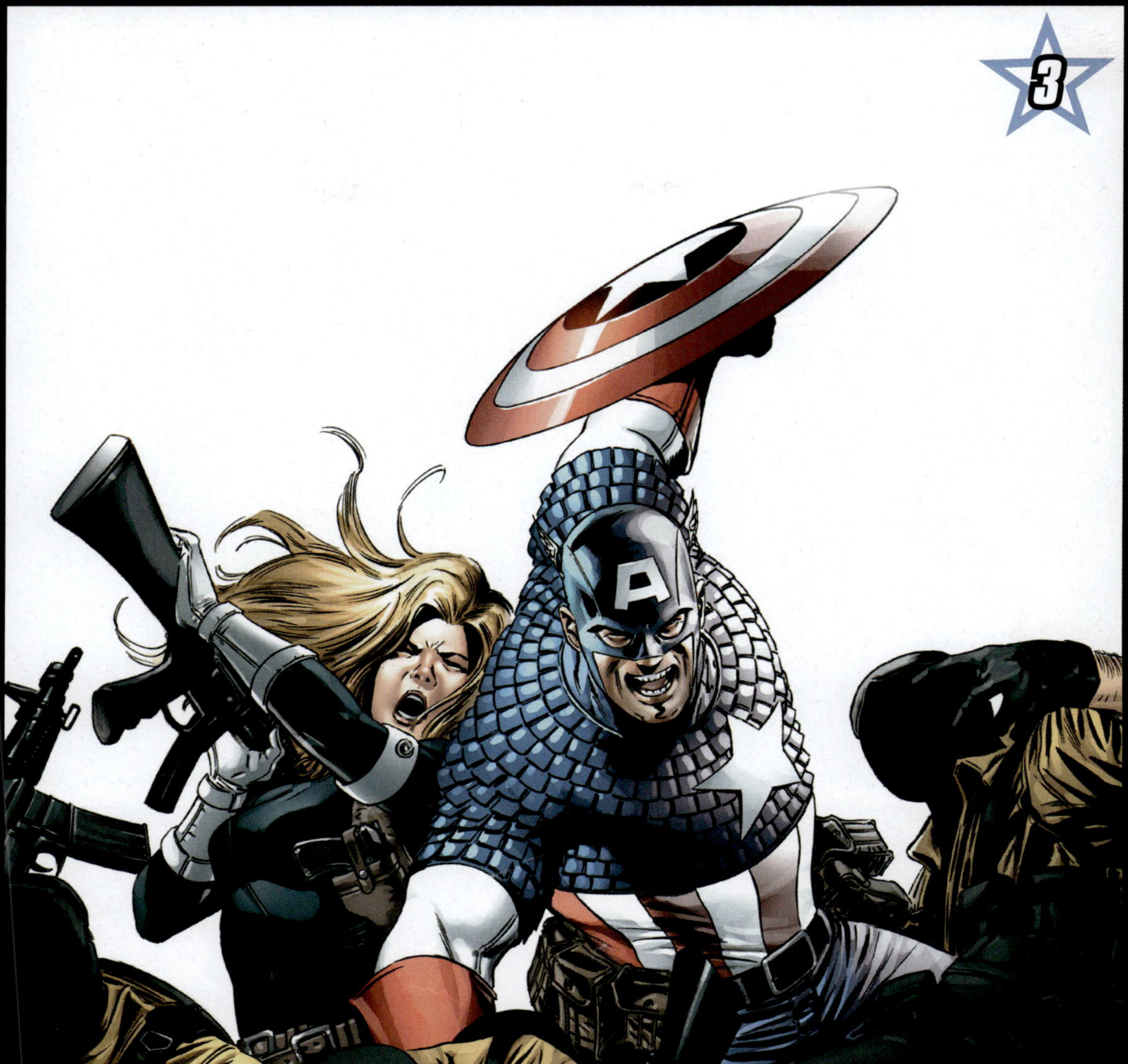
3

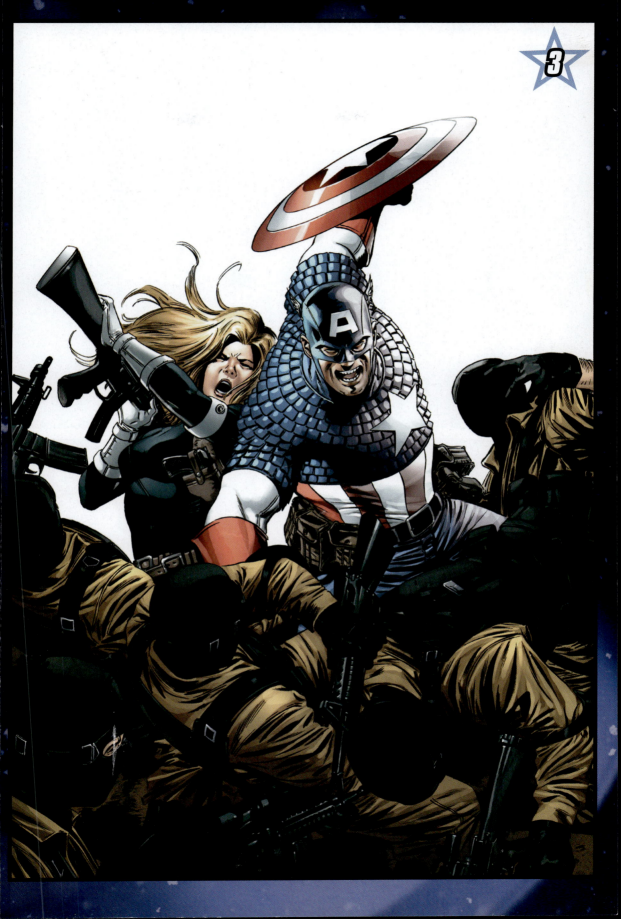

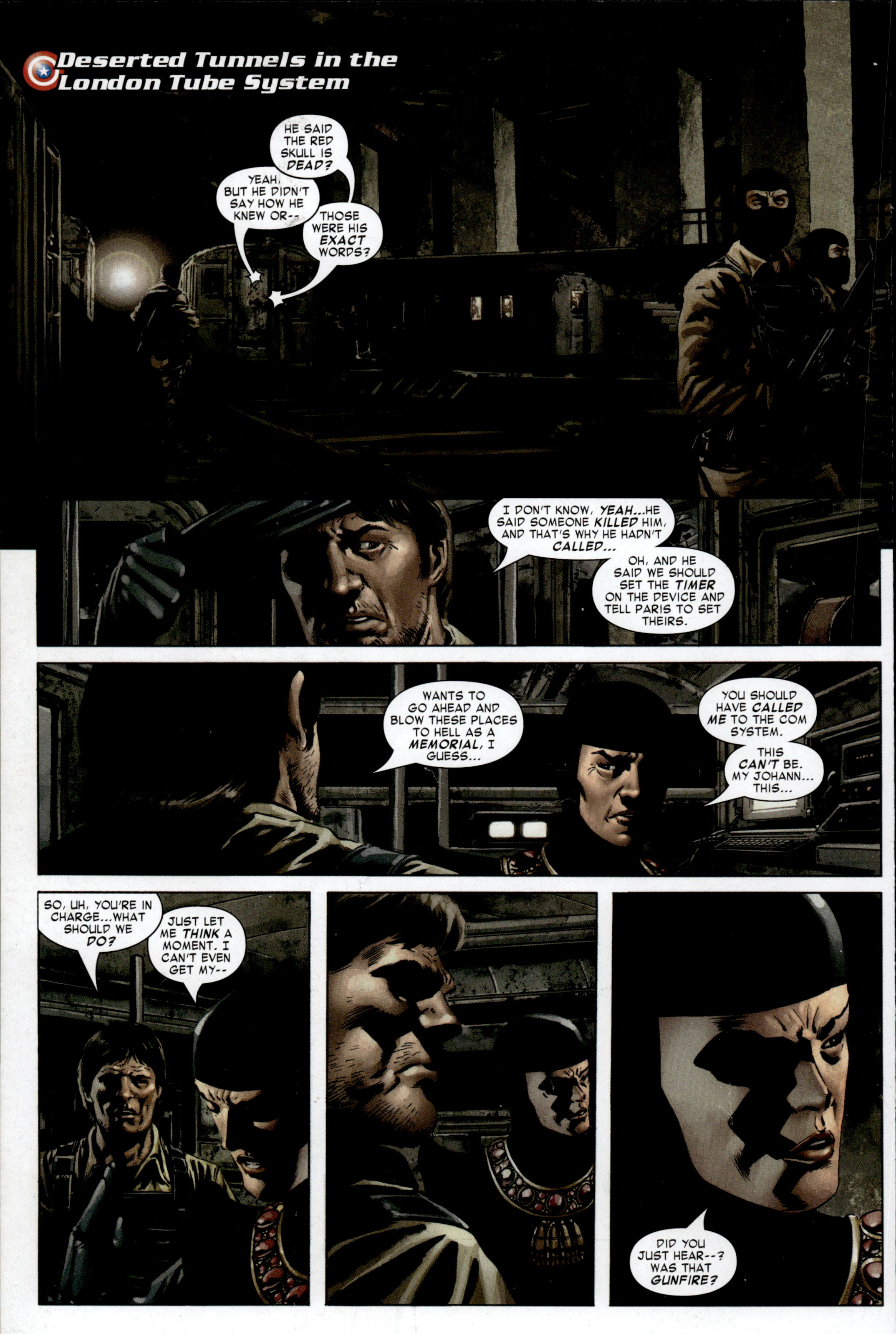
Deserted Tunnels in the London Tube System
HE SAID THE RED SKULL IS DEAD?
YEAH, BUT HE DIDN'T SAY HOW HE KNEW OR--
THOSE WERE HIS EXACT WORDS?
I DON'T KNOW, YEAH...HE SAID SOMEONE KILLED HIM, AND THAT'S WHY HE HADN'T CALLED...
OH, AND HE SAID WE SHOULD SET THE TIMER ON THE DEVICE AND TELL PARIS TO SET THEIRS.
WANTS TO GO AHEAD AND BLOW THESE PLACES TO HELL AS A MEMORIAL, I GUESS...
YOU SHOULD HAVE CALLED ME TO THE COM SYSTEM.
THIS CAN'T BE. MY JOHANN... THIS...
SO, UH, YOU'RE IN CHARGE...WHAT SHOULD WE DO?
JUST LET ME THINK A MOMENT. I CAN'T EVEN GET MY--
DID YOU JUST HEAR--? WAS THAT GUNFIRE?

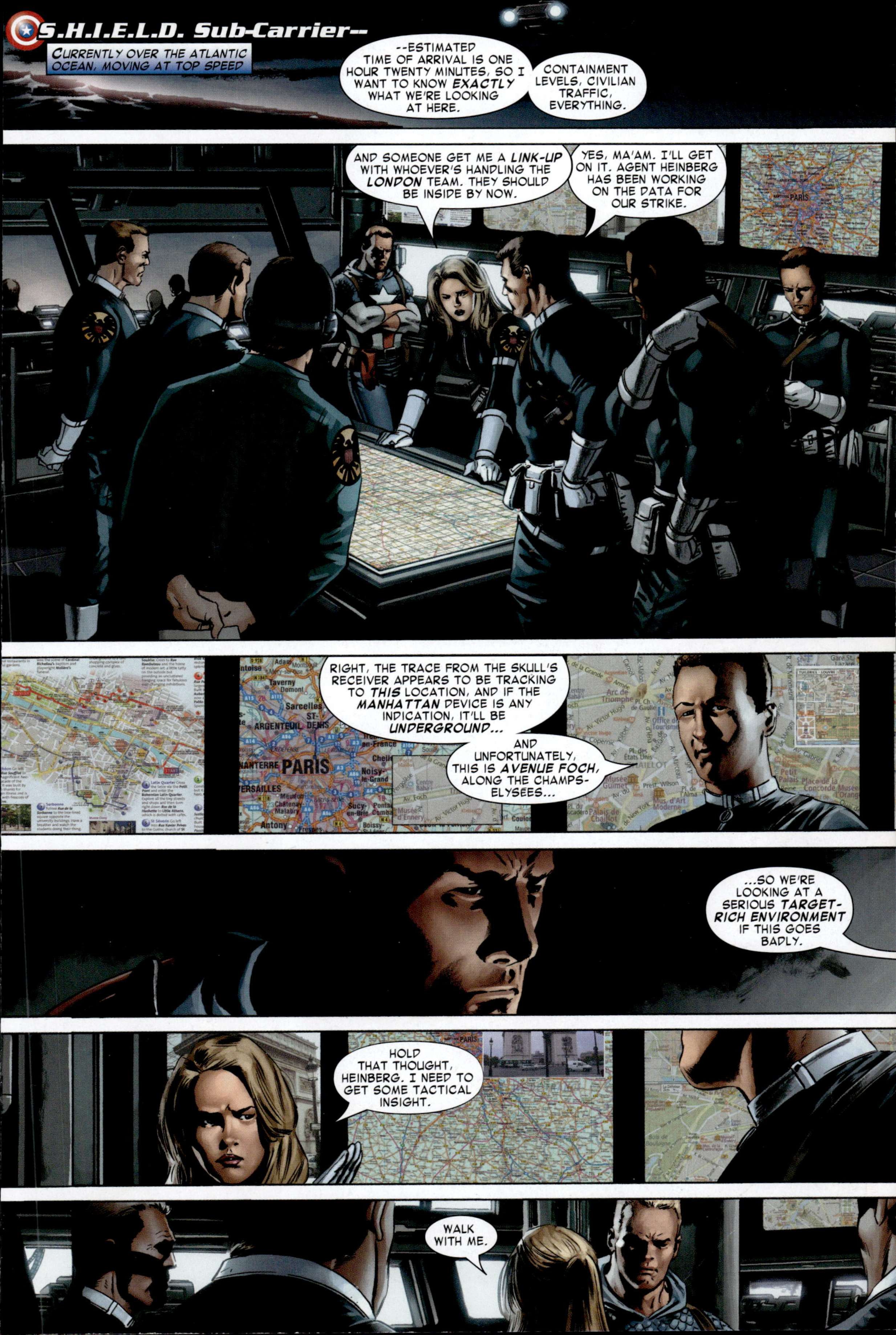

S.H.I.E.L.D. Sub-Carrier--
CURRENTLY OVER THE ATLANTIC OCEAN, MOVING AT TOP SPEED
--ESTIMATED TIME OF ARRIVAL IS ONE HOUR TWENTY MINUTES, SO I WANT TO KNOW EXACTLY WHAT WE'RE LOOKING AT HERE.
CONTAINMENT LEVELS, CIVILIAN TRAFFIC, EVERYTHING.
AND SOMEONE GET ME A LINK-UP WITH WHOEVER'S HANDLING THE LONDON TEAM. THEY SHOULD BE INSIDE BY NOW.
YES, MA'AM. I'LL GET ON IT. AGENT HEINBERG HAS BEEN WORKING ON THE DATA FOR OUR STRIKE.
RIGHT, THE TRACE FROM THE SKULL'S RECEIVER APPEARS TO BE TRACKING TO THIS LOCATION, AND IF THE MANHATTAN DEVICE IS ANY INDICATION, IT'LL BE UNDERGROUND...
AND UNFORTUNATELY, THIS IS AVENUE FOCH, ALONG THE CHAMPS-ELYSEES...
...SO WE'RE LOOKING AT A SERIOUS TARGET-RICH ENVIRONMENT IF THIS GOES BADLY.
HOLD THAT THOUGHT, HEINBERG. I NEED TO GET SOME TACTICAL INSIGHT.
WALK WITH ME.

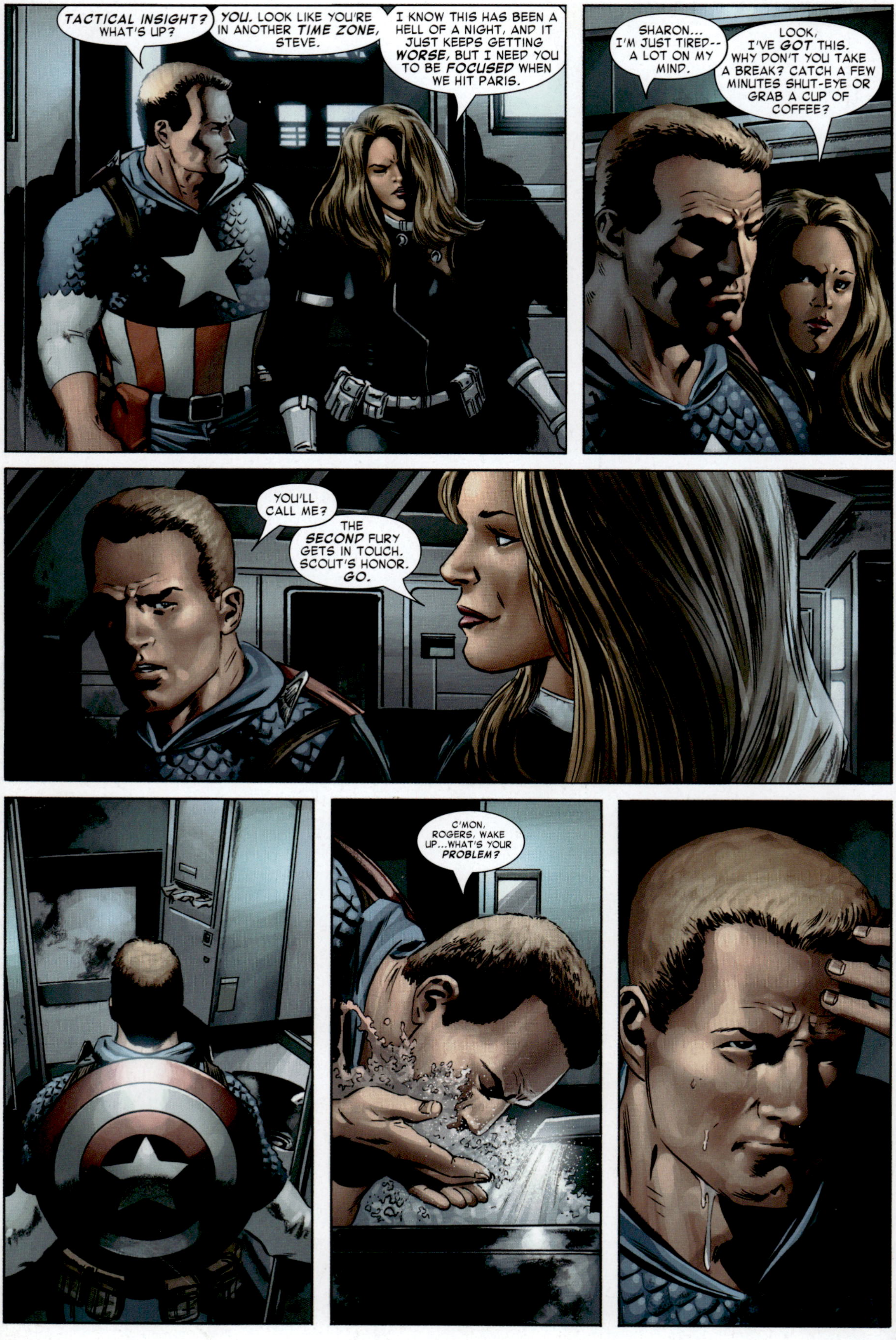
TACTICAL INSIGHT? WHAT'S UP?
YOU. LOOK LIKE YOU'RE IN ANOTHER TIME ZONE, STEVE.
I KNOW THIS HAS BEEN A HELL OF A NIGHT, AND IT JUST KEEPS GETTING WORSE, BUT I NEED YOU TO BE FOCUSED WHEN WE HIT PARIS.
SHARON... I'M JUST TIRED-- A LOT ON MY MIND.
LOOK, I'VE GOT THIS. WHY DON'T YOU TAKE A BREAK? CATCH A FEW MINUTES SHUT-EYE OR GRAB A CUP OF COFFEE?
YOU'LL CALL ME?
THE SECOND FURY GETS IN TOUCH. SCOUT'S HONOR. GO.
C'MON, ROGERS, WAKE UP...WHAT'S YOUR PROBLEM?

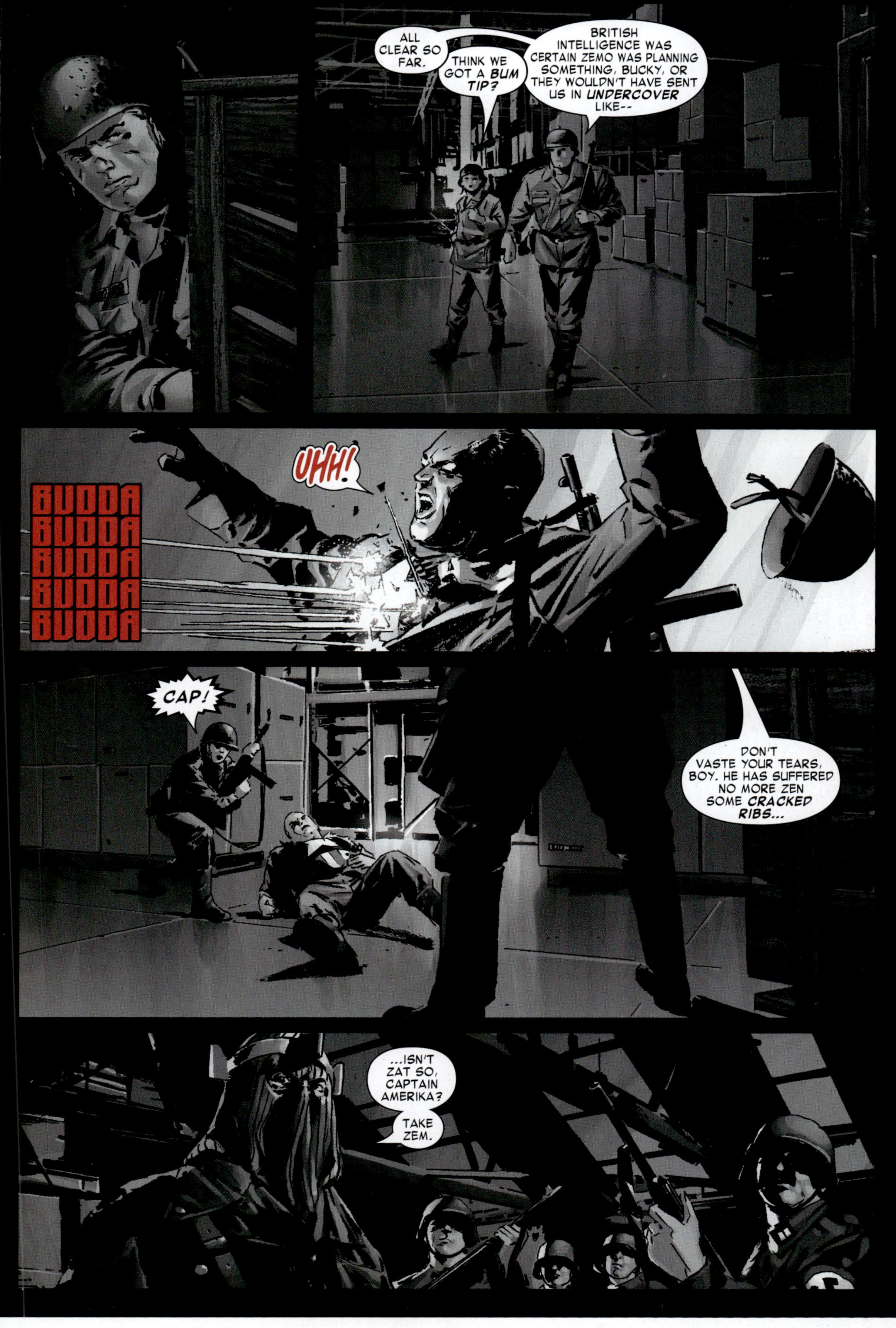
ALL CLEAR SO FAR.
THINK WE GOT A BUM TIP?
BRITISH INTELLIGENCE WAS CERTAIN ZEMO WAS PLANNING SOMETHING, BUCKY, OR THEY WOULDN'T HAVE SENT US IN UNDERCOVER LIKE--
BUDDA BUDDA BUDDA BUDDA BUDDA
UHH!
CAP!
DON'T VASTE YOUR TEARS, BOY. HE HAS SUFFERED NO MORE ZEN SOME CRACKED RIBS...
...ISN'T ZAT SO, CAPTAIN AMERIKA?
TAKE ZEM.

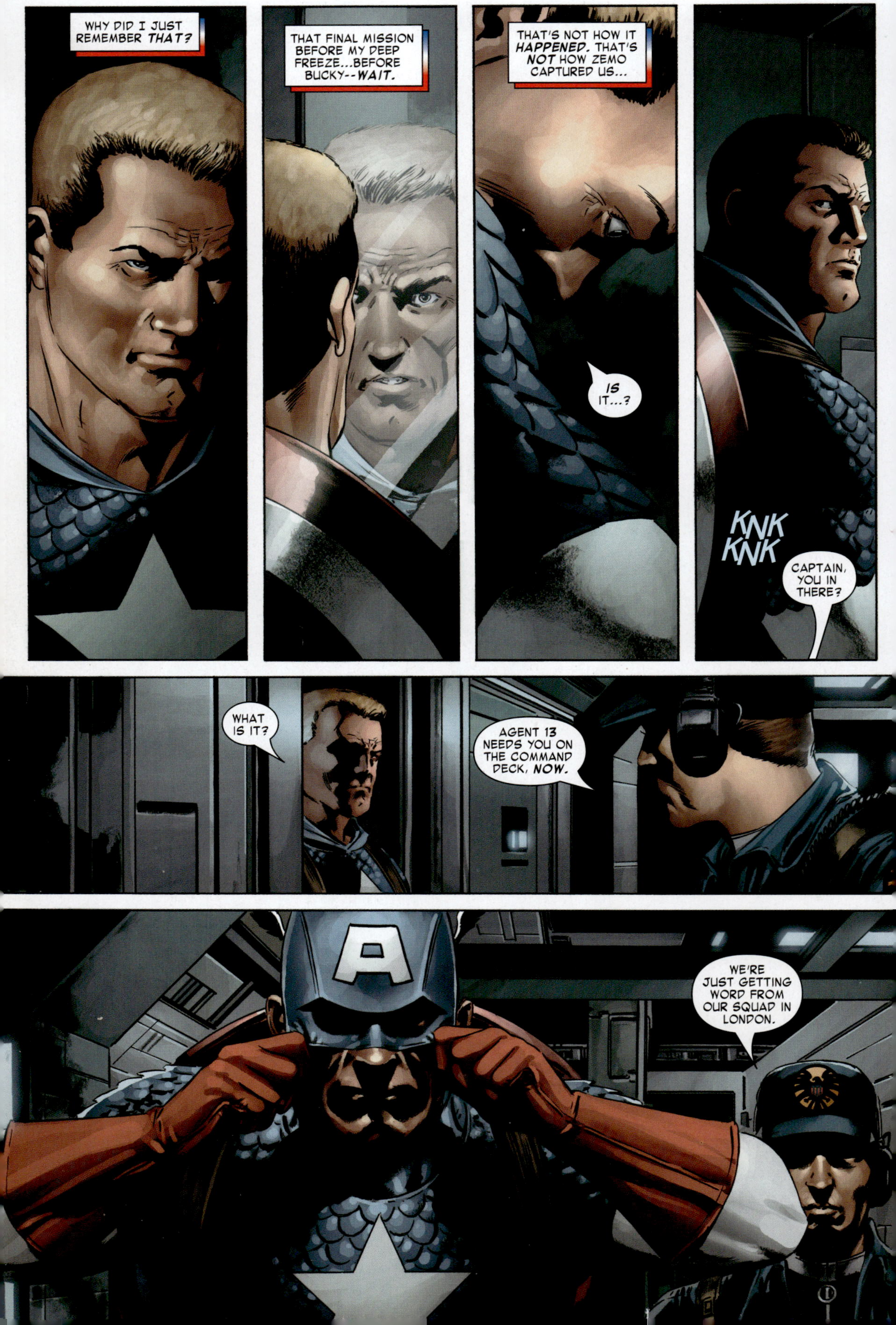
WHY DID I JUST REMEMBER *THAT?*
THAT FINAL MISSION BEFORE MY DEEP FREEZE...BEFORE BUCKY--*WAIT.*
THAT'S NOT HOW IT *HAPPENED.* THAT'S *NOT* HOW ZEMO CAPTURED US...
IS IT...?
KNK KNK
CAPTAIN, YOU IN THERE?
WHAT IS IT?
AGENT 13 NEEDS YOU ON THE COMMAND DECK, **NOW.**
WE'RE JUST GETTING WORD FROM OUR SQUAD IN LONDON.

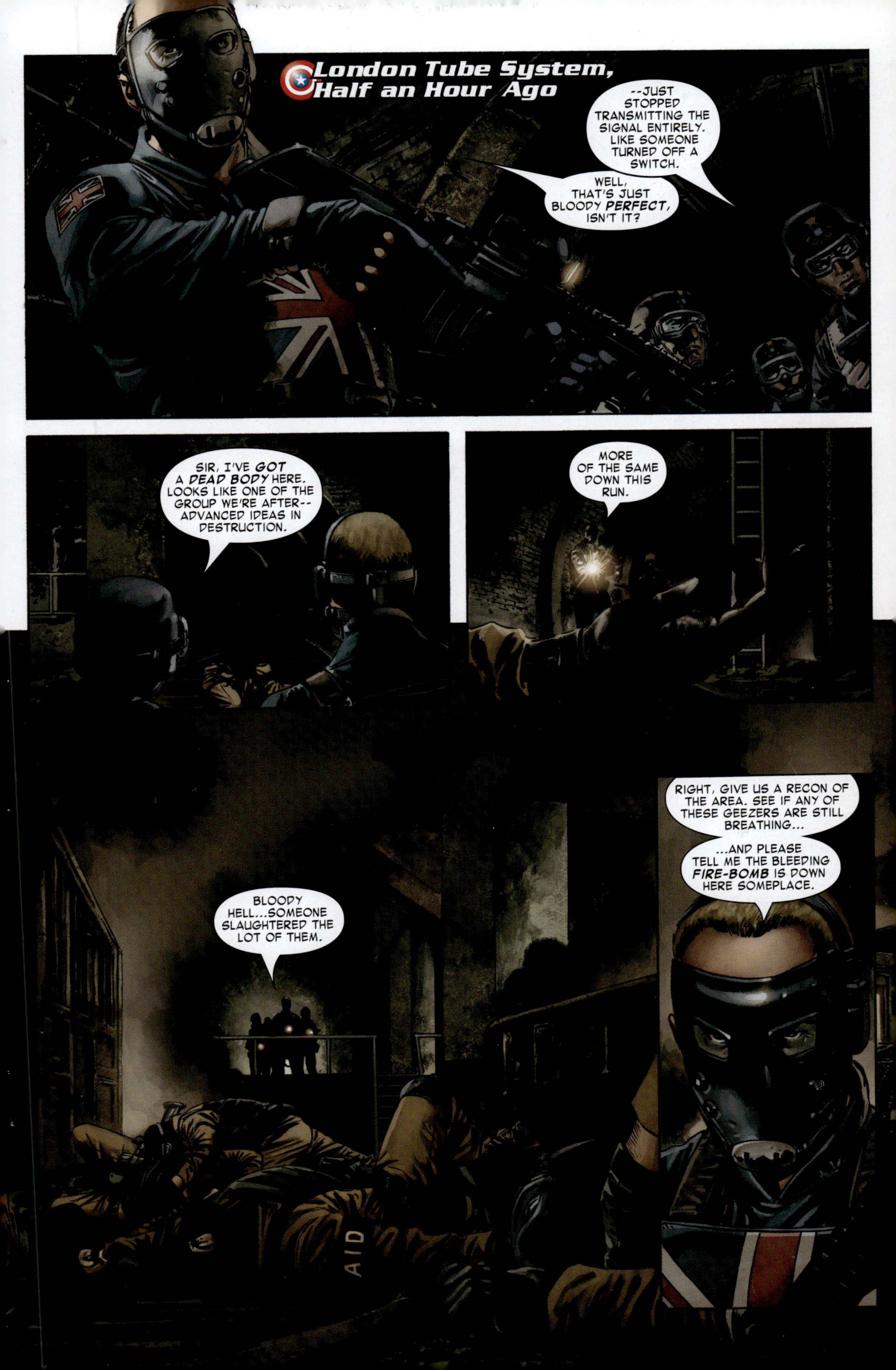
London Tube System, Half an Hour Ago
--JUST STOPPED TRANSMITTING THE SIGNAL ENTIRELY. LIKE SOMEONE TURNED OFF A SWITCH.
WELL, THAT'S JUST BLOODY PERFECT, ISN'T IT?
SIR, I'VE GOT A DEAD BODY HERE. LOOKS LIKE ONE OF THE GROUP WE'RE AFTER--ADVANCED IDEAS IN DESTRUCTION.
MORE OF THE SAME DOWN THIS RUN.
RIGHT, GIVE US A RECON OF THE AREA. SEE IF ANY OF THESE GEEZERS ARE STILL BREATHING...
...AND PLEASE TELL ME THE BLEEDING FIRE-BOMB IS DOWN HERE SOMEPLACE.
BLOODY HELL...SOMEONE SLAUGHTERED THE LOT OF THEM.
AID

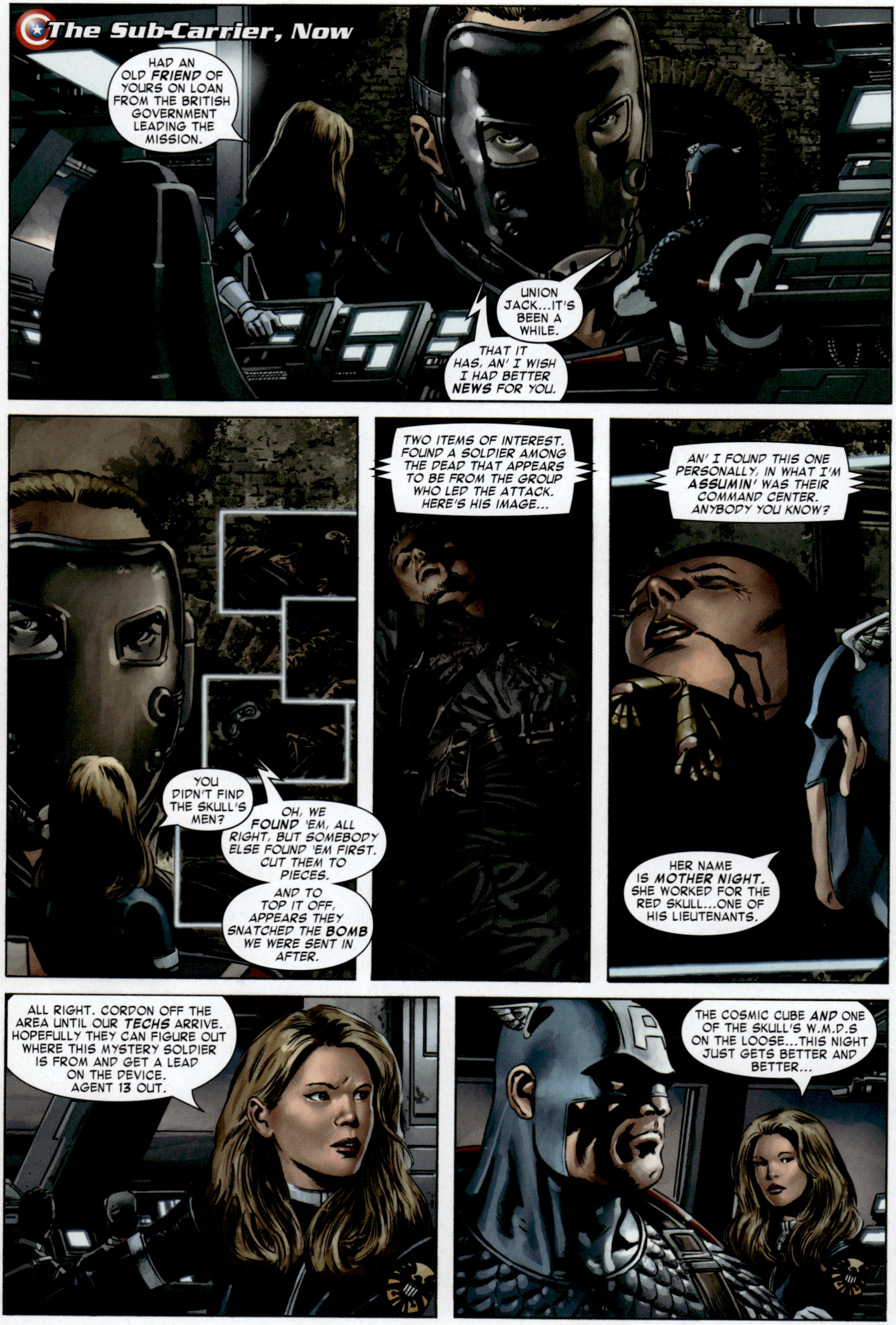
The Sub-Carrier, Now
HAD AN OLD FRIEND OF YOURS ON LOAN FROM THE BRITISH GOVERNMENT LEADING THE MISSION.
UNION JACK...IT'S BEEN A WHILE.
THAT IT HAS, AN' I WISH I HAD BETTER NEWS FOR YOU.
YOU DIDN'T FIND THE SKULL'S MEN?
OH, WE FOUND 'EM, ALL RIGHT, BUT SOMEBODY ELSE FOUND 'EM FIRST. CUT THEM TO PIECES.
AND TO TOP IT OFF, APPEARS THEY SNATCHED THE BOMB WE WERE SENT IN AFTER.
TWO ITEMS OF INTEREST. FOUND A SOLDIER AMONG THE DEAD THAT APPEARS TO BE FROM THE GROUP WHO LED THE ATTACK. HERE'S HIS IMAGE...
AN' I FOUND THIS ONE PERSONALLY, IN WHAT I'M ASSUMIN' WAS THEIR COMMAND CENTER. ANYBODY YOU KNOW?
HER NAME IS MOTHER NIGHT. SHE WORKED FOR THE RED SKULL...ONE OF HIS LIEUTENANTS.
ALL RIGHT. CORDON OFF THE AREA UNTIL OUR TECHS ARRIVE. HOPEFULLY THEY CAN FIGURE OUT WHERE THIS MYSTERY SOLDIER IS FROM AND GET A LEAD ON THE DEVICE. AGENT 13 OUT.
THE COSMIC CUBE AND ONE OF THE SKULL'S W.M.D.S ON THE LOOSE...THIS NIGHT JUST GETS BETTER AND BETTER...

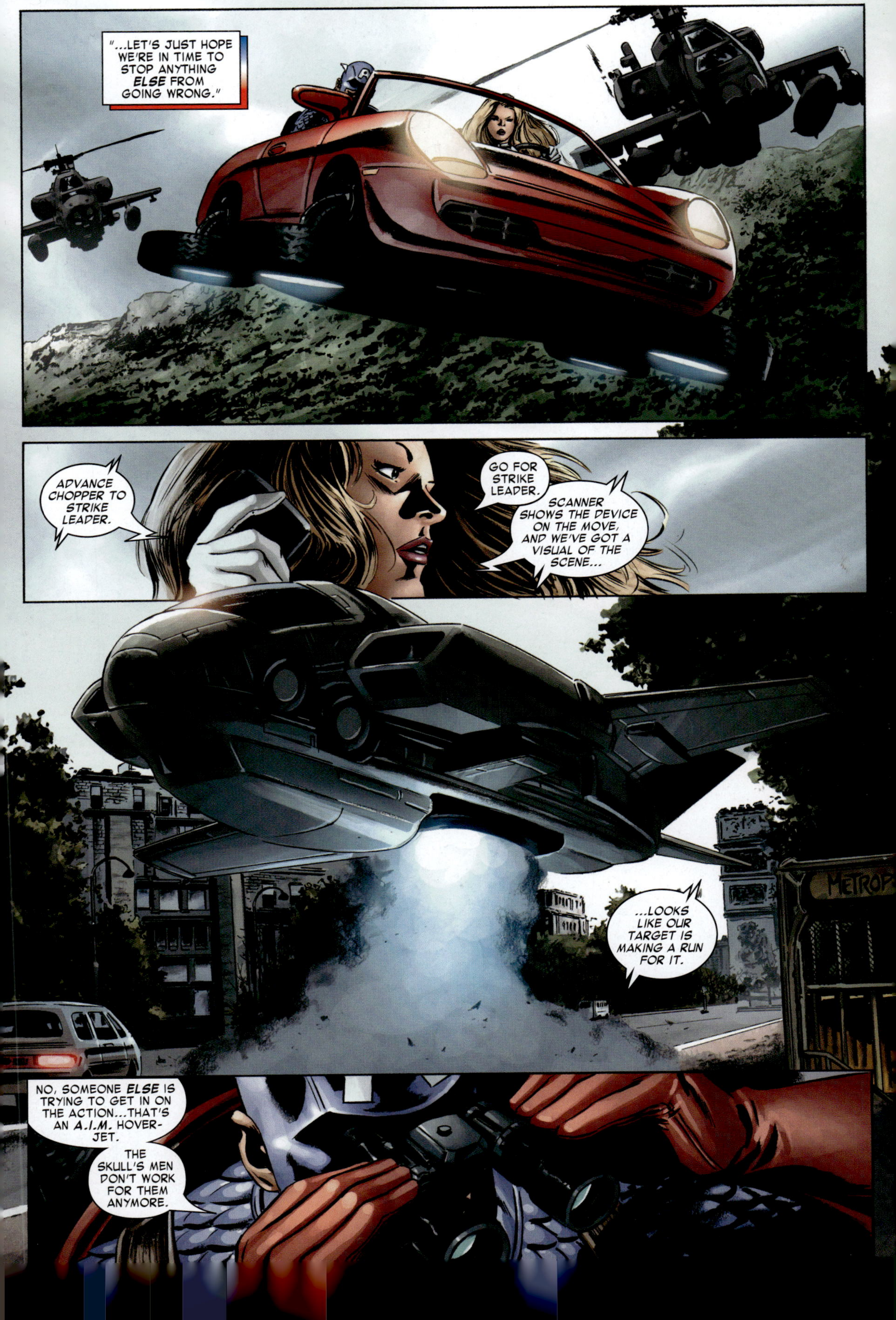
"...LET'S JUST HOPE WE'RE IN TIME TO STOP ANYTHING ELSE FROM GOING WRONG."
ADVANCE CHOPPER TO STRIKE LEADER.
GO FOR STRIKE LEADER.
SCANNER SHOWS THE DEVICE ON THE MOVE, AND WE'VE GOT A VISUAL OF THE SCENE...
...LOOKS LIKE OUR TARGET IS MAKING A RUN FOR IT.
METROP
NO, SOMEONE ELSE IS TRYING TO GET IN ON THE ACTION...THAT'S AN A.I.M. HOVER-JET.
THE SKULL'S MEN DON'T WORK FOR THEM ANYMORE.

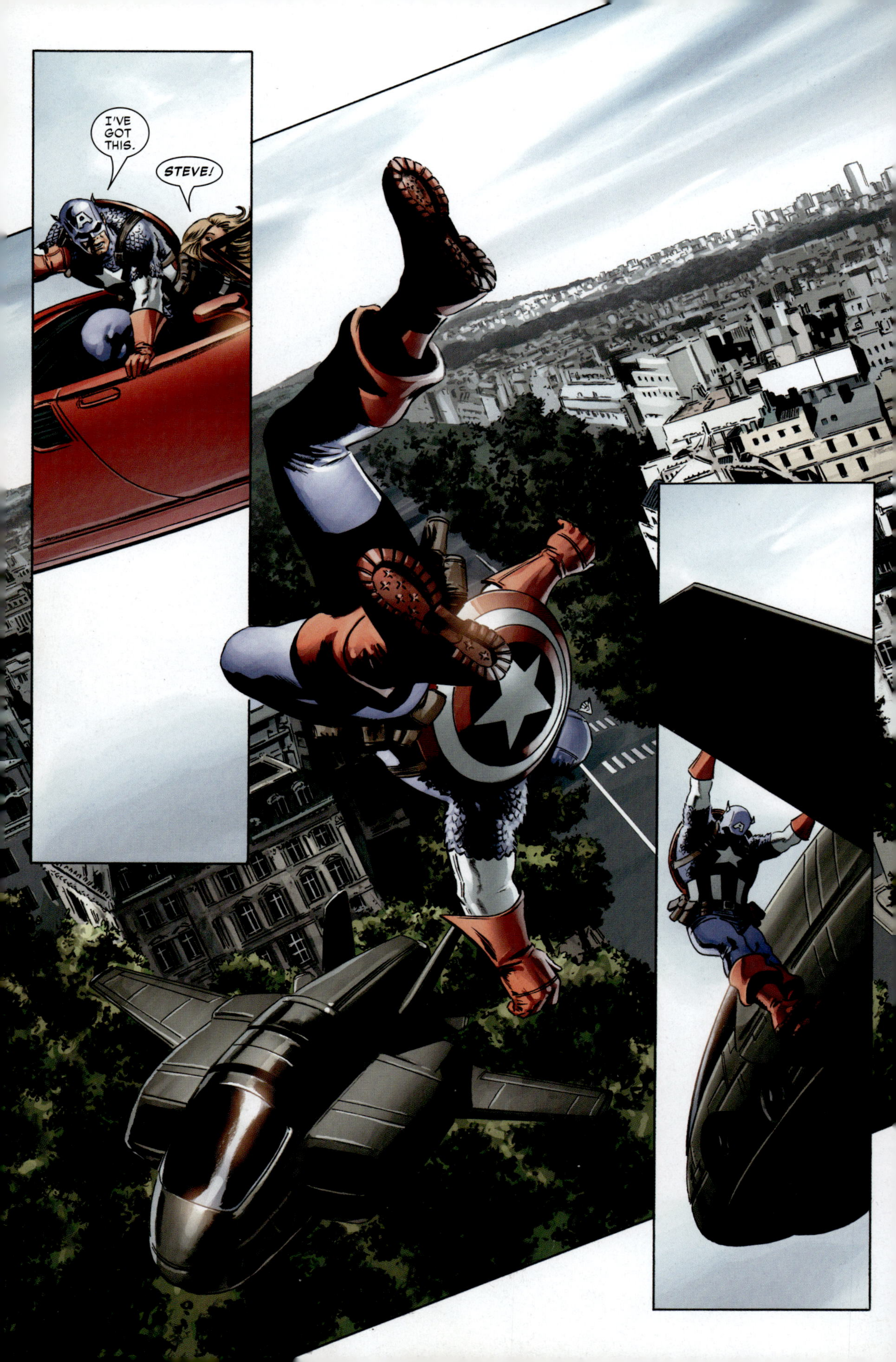
I'VE GOT THIS.
STEVE!

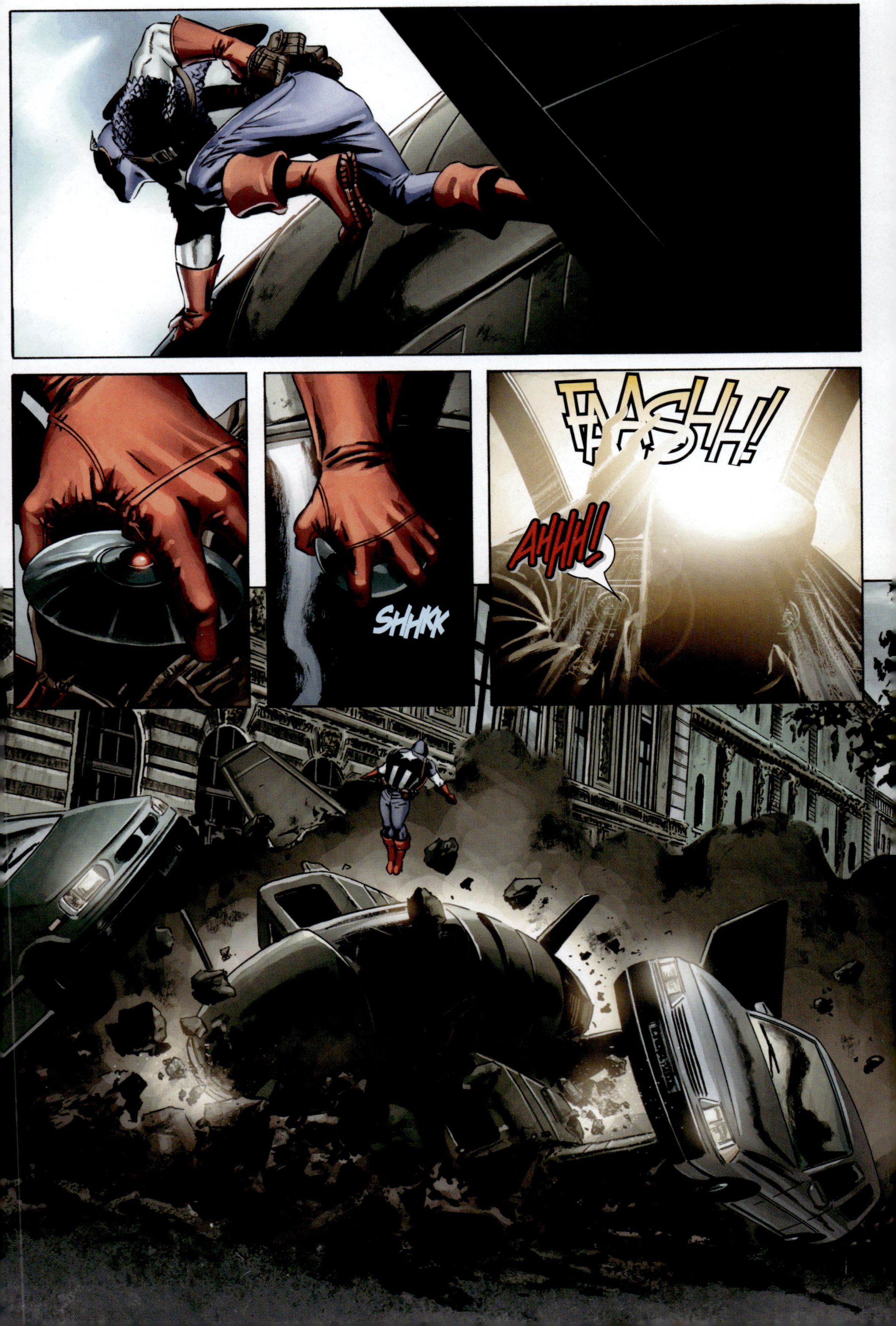
SHHKK
FWASHH!
AHHH!

OPEN FIRE! KILL HIM!

KRAKKRAKKRAKBLAMKRAKKRAKKRAKBLAM

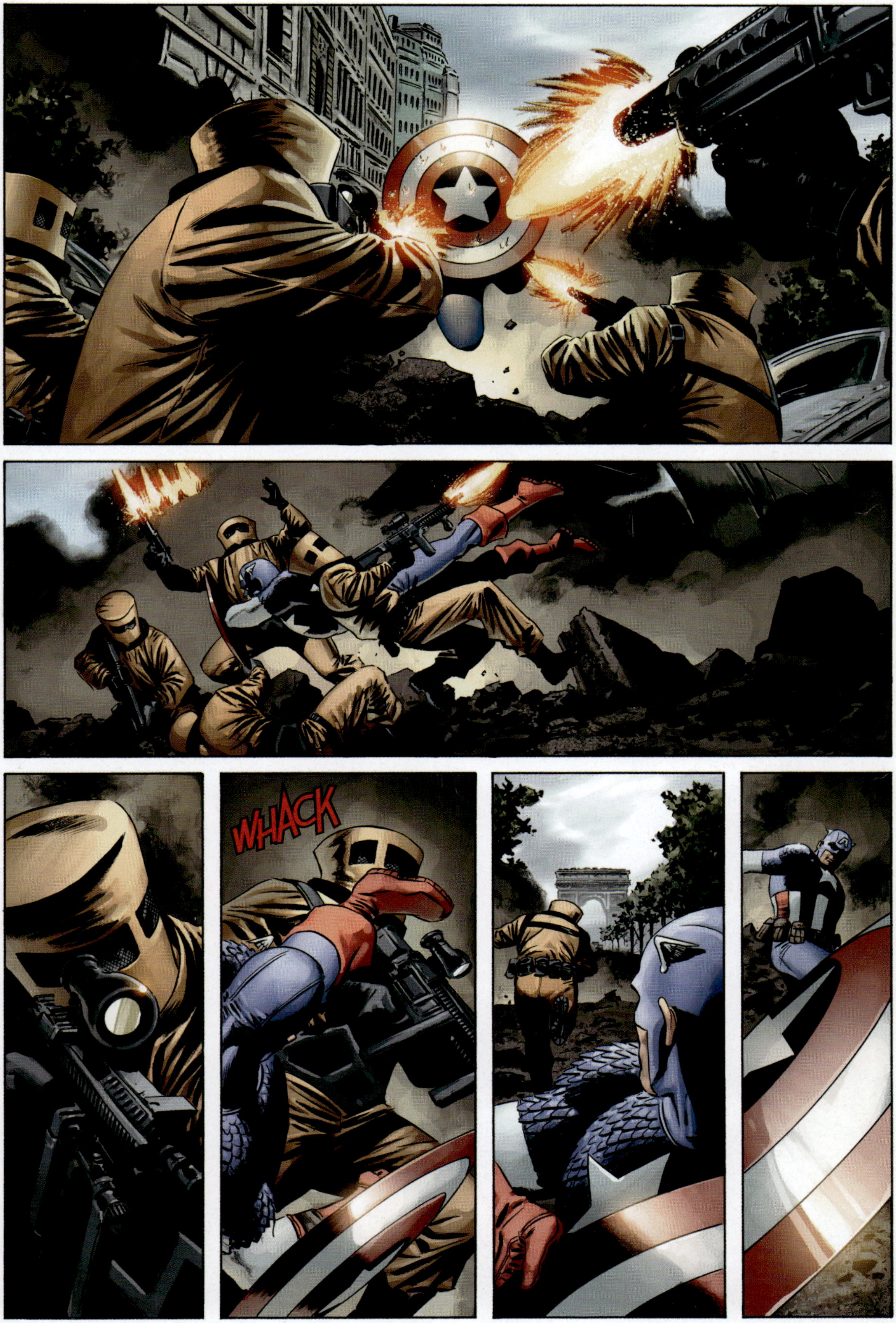
WHACK

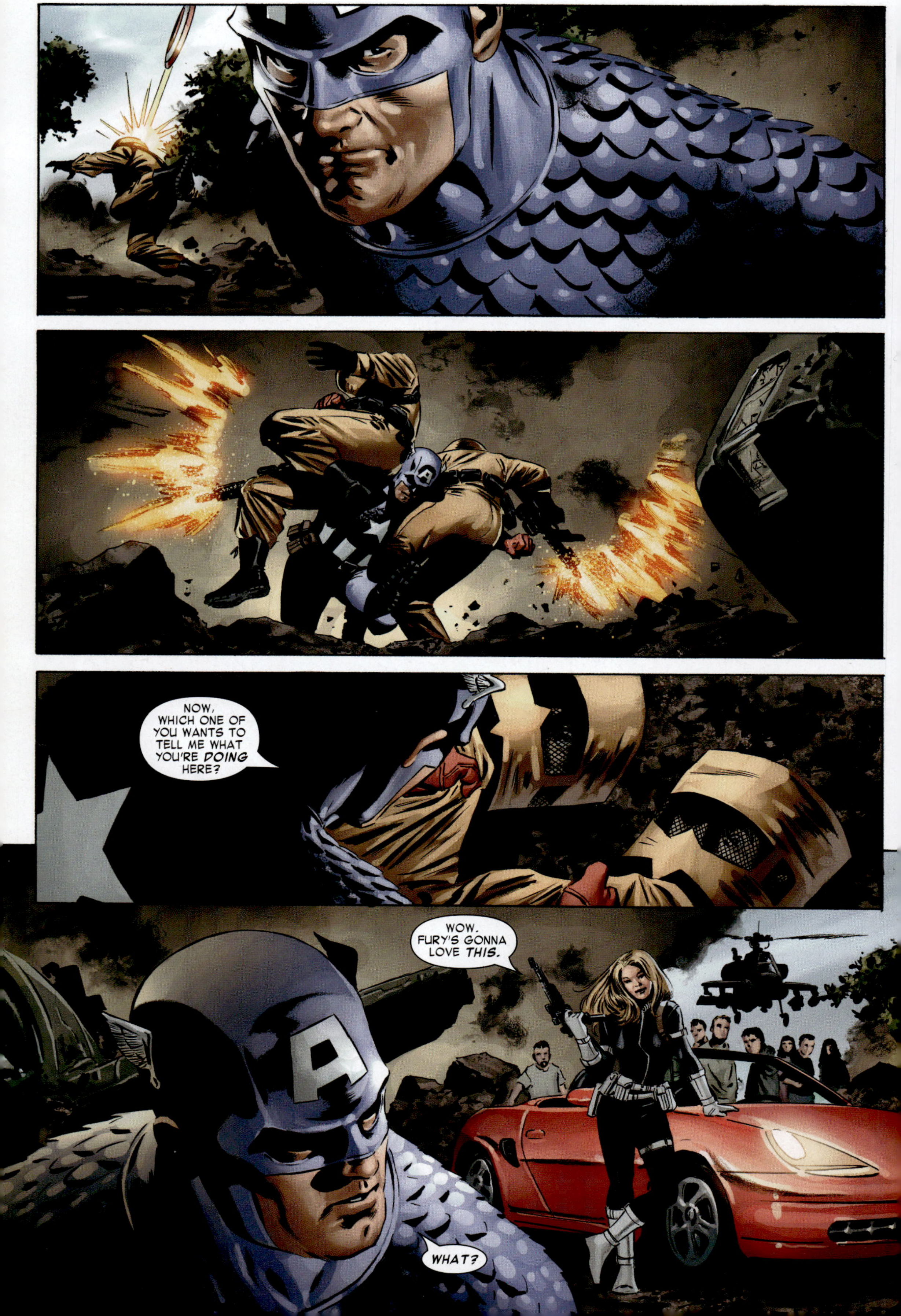
NOW, WHICH ONE OF YOU WANTS TO TELL ME WHAT YOU'RE DOING HERE?
WOW. FURY'S GONNA LOVE THIS.
WHAT?

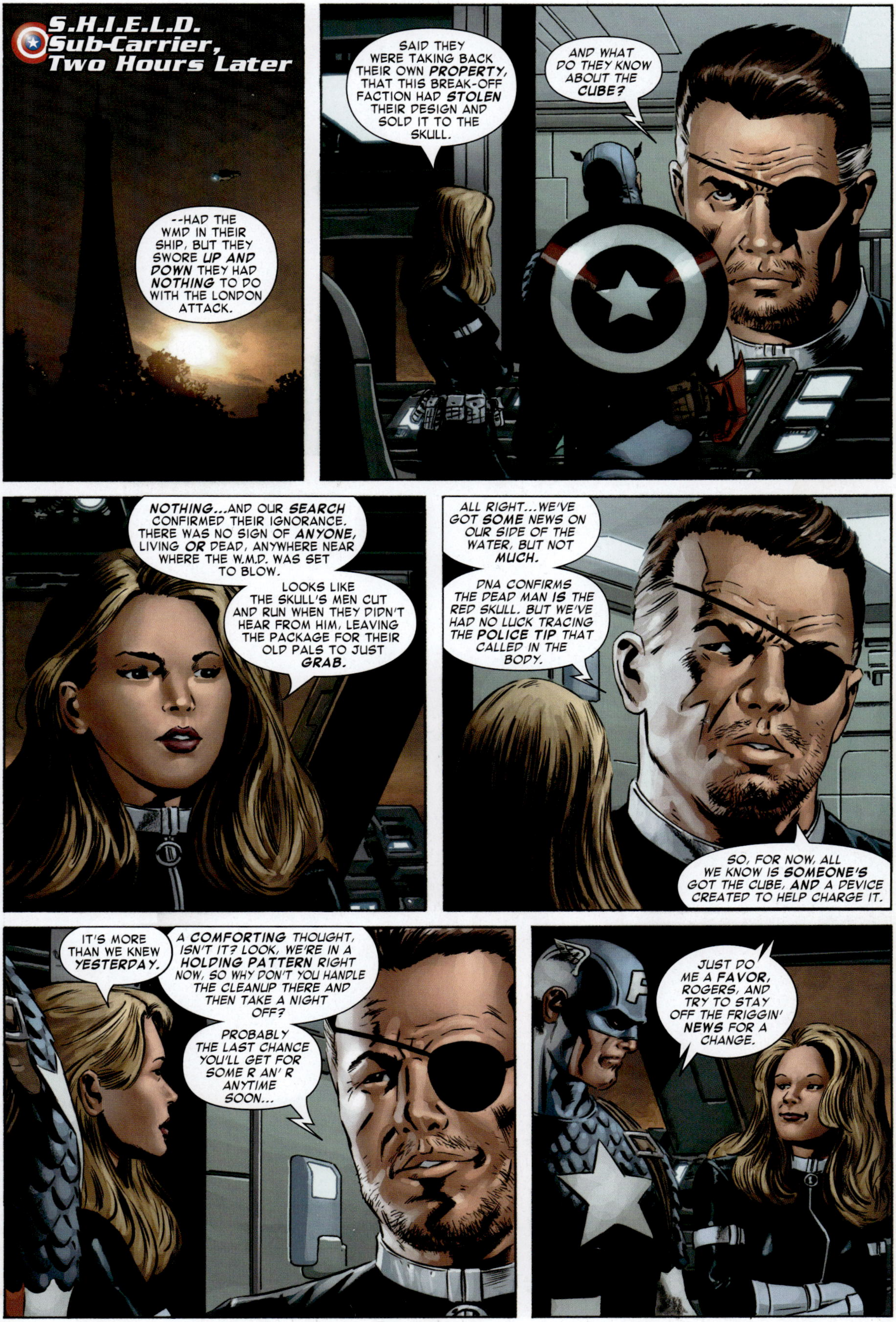
S.H.I.E.L.D. Sub-Carrier, Two Hours Later
--HAD THE WMD IN THEIR SHIP, BUT THEY SWORE UP AND DOWN THEY HAD NOTHING TO DO WITH THE LONDON ATTACK.
SAID THEY WERE TAKING BACK THEIR OWN PROPERTY, THAT THIS BREAK-OFF FACTION HAD STOLEN THEIR DESIGN AND SOLD IT TO THE SKULL.
AND WHAT DO THEY KNOW ABOUT THE CUBE?
NOTHING...AND OUR SEARCH CONFIRMED THEIR IGNORANCE. THERE WAS NO SIGN OF ANYONE, LIVING OR DEAD, ANYWHERE NEAR WHERE THE W.M.D. WAS SET TO BLOW.
LOOKS LIKE THE SKULL'S MEN CUT AND RUN WHEN THEY DIDN'T HEAR FROM HIM, LEAVING THE PACKAGE FOR THEIR OLD PALS TO JUST GRAB.
ALL RIGHT...WE'VE GOT SOME NEWS ON OUR SIDE OF THE WATER, BUT NOT MUCH.
DNA CONFIRMS THE DEAD MAN IS THE RED SKULL. BUT WE'VE HAD NO LUCK TRACING THE POLICE TIP THAT CALLED IN THE BODY.
SO, FOR NOW, ALL WE KNOW IS SOMEONE'S GOT THE CUBE, AND A DEVICE CREATED TO HELP CHARGE IT.
IT'S MORE THAN WE KNEW YESTERDAY.
A COMFORTING THOUGHT, ISN'T IT? LOOK, WE'RE IN A HOLDING PATTERN RIGHT NOW, SO WHY DON'T YOU HANDLE THE CLEANUP THERE AND THEN TAKE A NIGHT OFF?
PROBABLY THE LAST CHANCE YOU'LL GET FOR SOME R AN' R ANYTIME SOON...
JUST DO ME A FAVOR, ROGERS, AND TRY TO STAY OFF THE FRIGGIN' NEWS FOR A CHANGE.

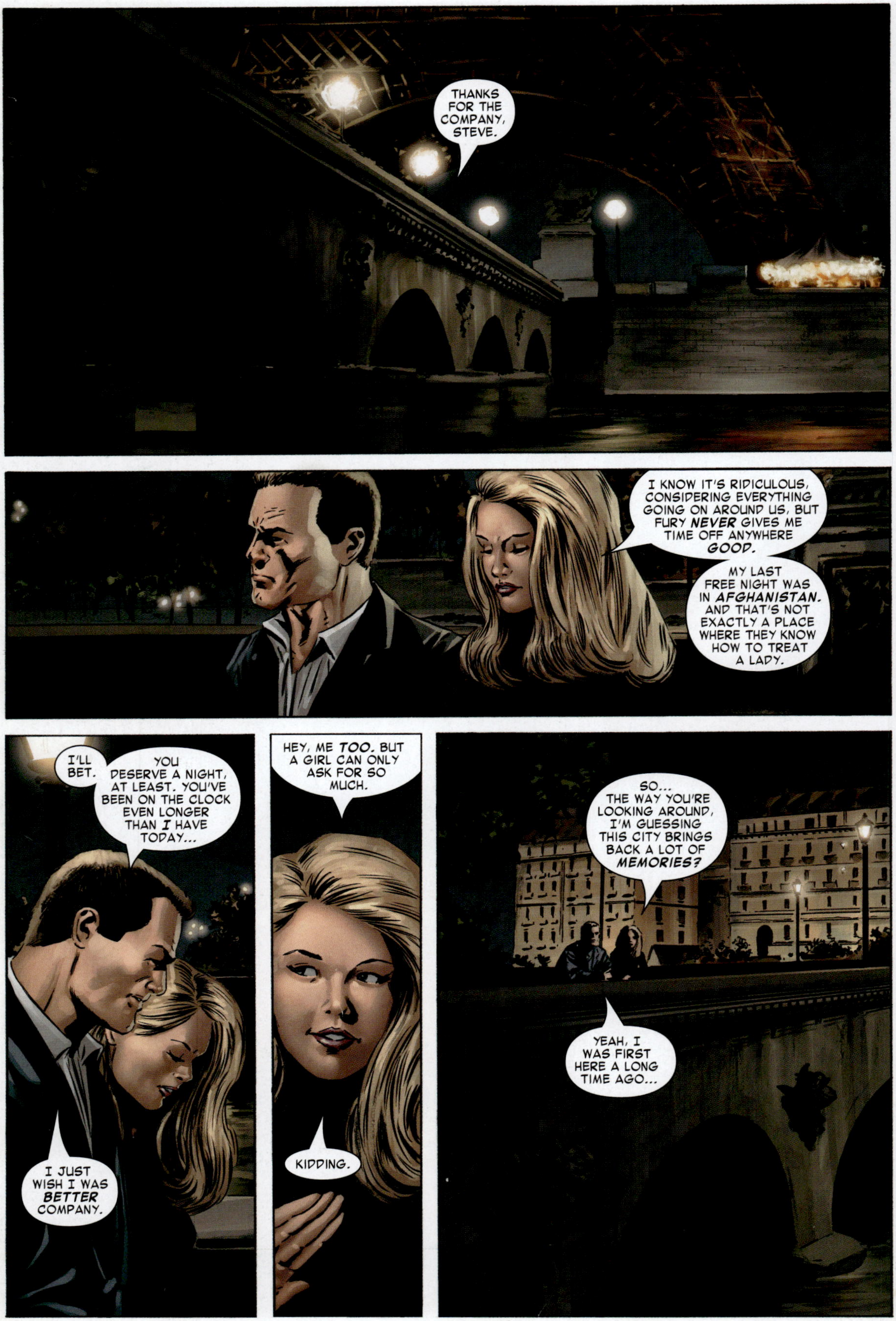
THANKS FOR THE COMPANY, STEVE.
I KNOW IT'S RIDICULOUS, CONSIDERING EVERYTHING GOING ON AROUND US, BUT FURY NEVER GIVES ME TIME OFF ANYWHERE GOOD.
MY LAST FREE NIGHT WAS IN AFGHANISTAN. AND THAT'S NOT EXACTLY A PLACE WHERE THEY KNOW HOW TO TREAT A LADY.
I'LL BET.
YOU DESERVE A NIGHT, AT LEAST. YOU'VE BEEN ON THE CLOCK EVEN LONGER THAN I HAVE TODAY...
I JUST WISH I WAS BETTER COMPANY.
HEY, ME TOO. BUT A GIRL CAN ONLY ASK FOR SO MUCH.
KIDDING.
SO... THE WAY YOU'RE LOOKING AROUND, I'M GUESSING THIS CITY BRINGS BACK A LOT OF MEMORIES?
YEAH, I WAS FIRST HERE A LONG TIME AGO...

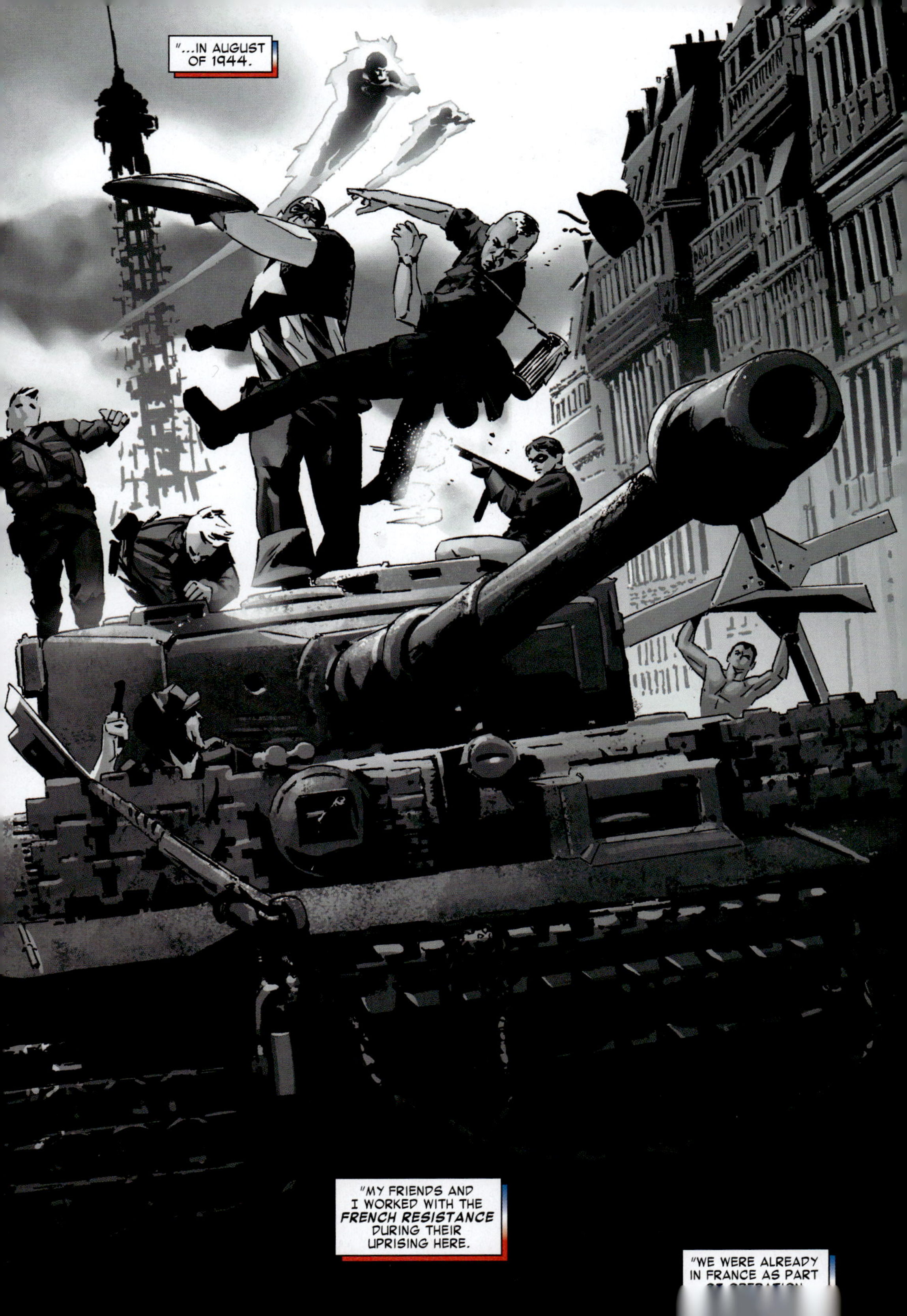
"...IN AUGUST OF 1944.
"MY FRIENDS AND I WORKED WITH THE *FRENCH RESISTANCE* DURING THEIR UPRISING HERE.
"WE WERE ALREADY IN FRANCE AS PART

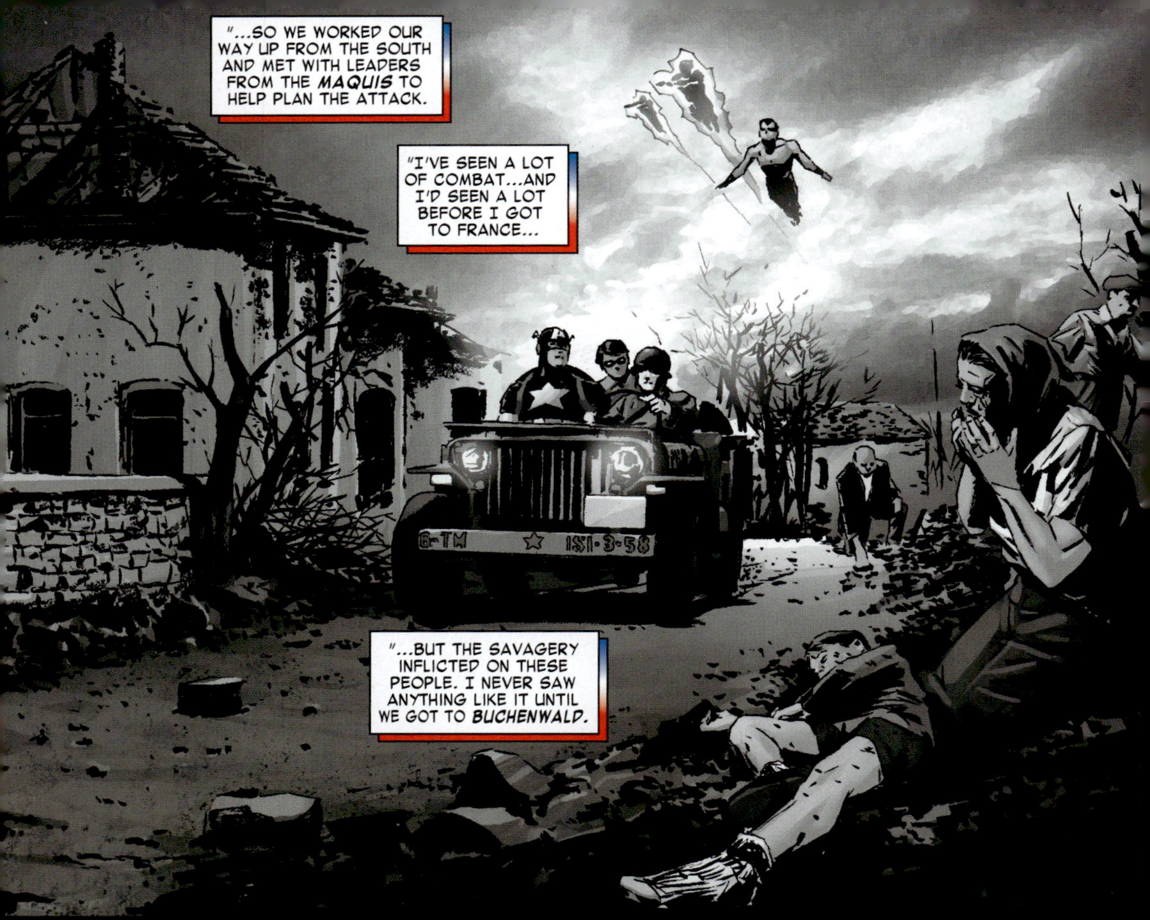
"...SO WE WORKED OUR WAY UP FROM THE SOUTH AND MET WITH LEADERS FROM THE *MAQUIS* TO HELP PLAN THE ATTACK.
"I'VE SEEN A LOT OF COMBAT...AND I'D SEEN A LOT BEFORE I GOT TO FRANCE...
"...BUT THE SAVAGERY INFLICTED ON THESE PEOPLE. I NEVER SAW ANYTHING LIKE IT UNTIL WE GOT TO *BUCHENWALD.*
6-TM
1S1-3-58

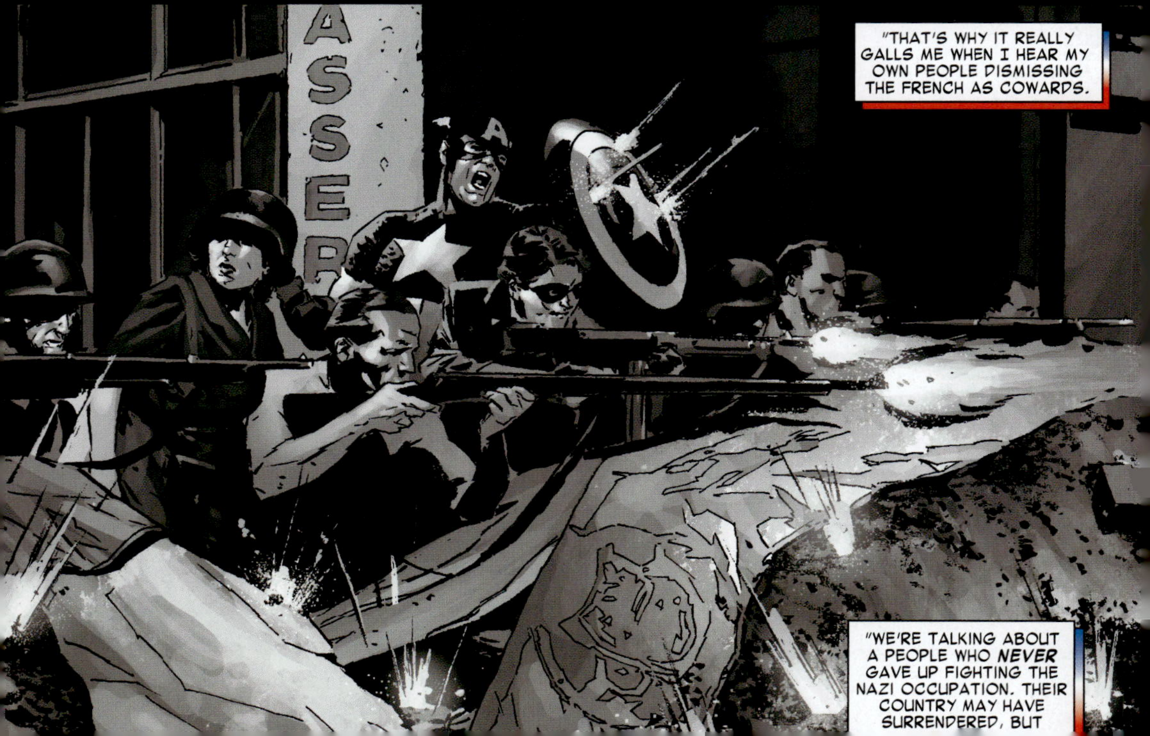
"THAT'S WHY IT REALLY GALLS ME WHEN I HEAR MY OWN PEOPLE DISMISSING THE FRENCH AS COWARDS.
"WE'RE TALKING ABOUT A PEOPLE WHO *NEVER* GAVE UP FIGHTING THE NAZI OCCUPATION. THEIR COUNTRY MAY HAVE SURRENDERED, BUT

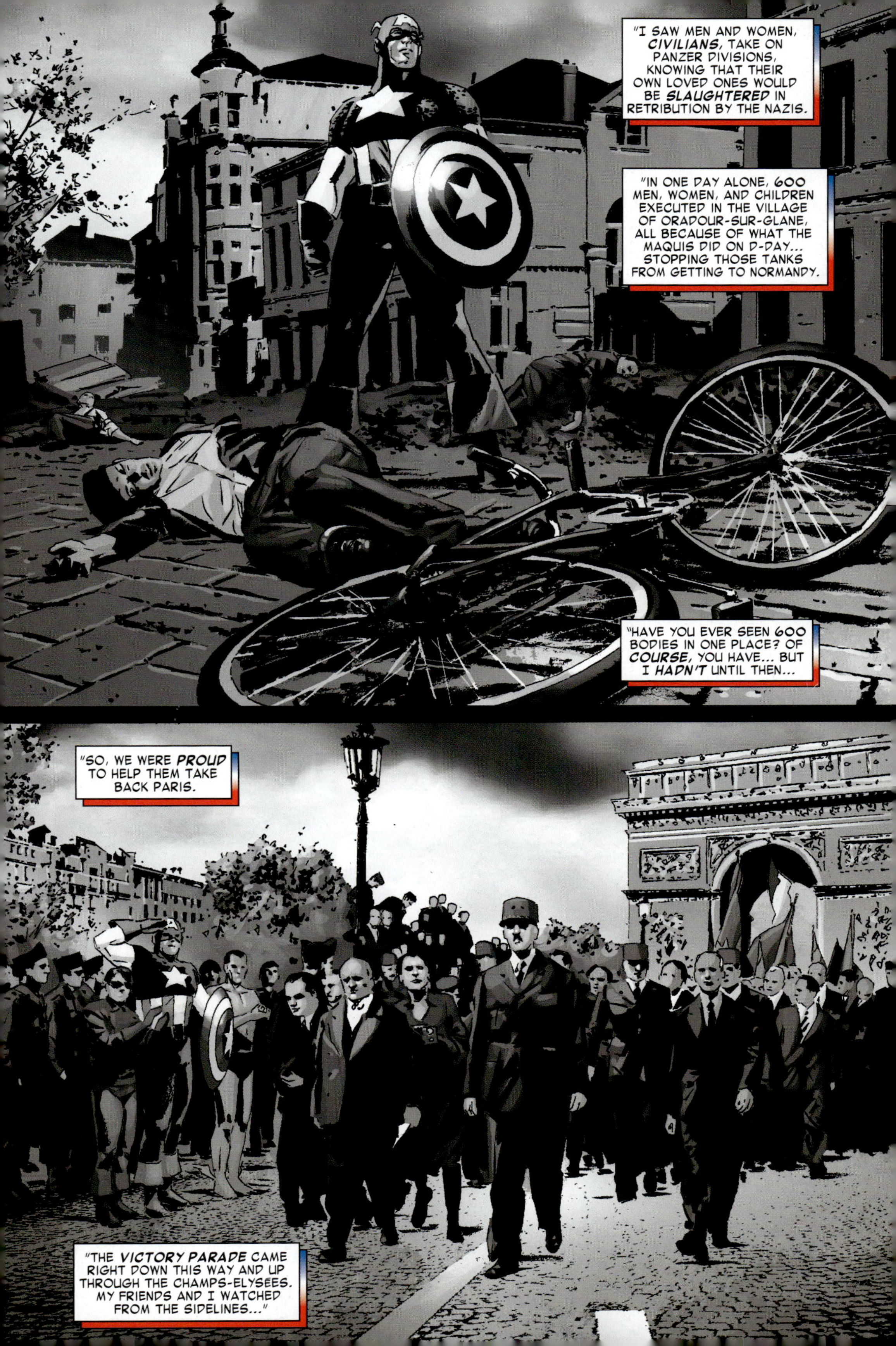
"I SAW MEN AND WOMEN, CIVILIANS, TAKE ON PANZER DIVISIONS, KNOWING THAT THEIR OWN LOVED ONES WOULD BE SLAUGHTERED IN RETRIBUTION BY THE NAZIS.
"IN ONE DAY ALONE, 600 MEN, WOMEN, AND CHILDREN EXECUTED IN THE VILLAGE OF ORADOUR-SUR-GLANE, ALL BECAUSE OF WHAT THE MAQUIS DID ON D-DAY... STOPPING THOSE TANKS FROM GETTING TO NORMANDY.
"HAVE YOU EVER SEEN 600 BODIES IN ONE PLACE? OF COURSE, YOU HAVE... BUT I HADN'T UNTIL THEN...
"SO, WE WERE PROUD TO HELP THEM TAKE BACK PARIS.
"THE VICTORY PARADE CAME RIGHT DOWN THIS WAY AND UP THROUGH THE CHAMPS-ELYSEES. MY FRIENDS AND I WATCHED FROM THE SIDELINES..."

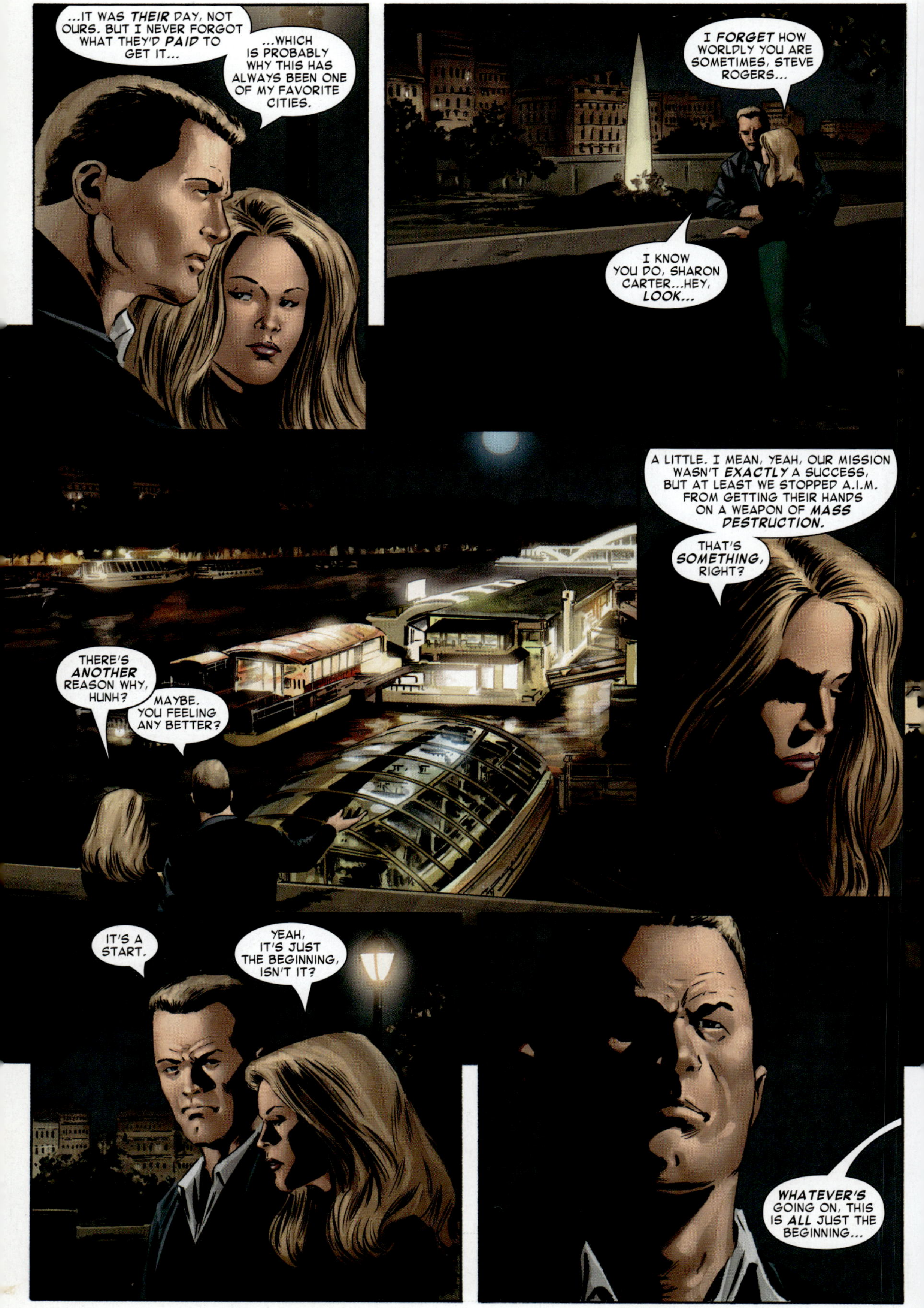
...IT WAS THEIR DAY, NOT OURS. BUT I NEVER FORGOT WHAT THEY'D PAID TO GET IT...
...WHICH IS PROBABLY WHY THIS HAS ALWAYS BEEN ONE OF MY FAVORITE CITIES.
I FORGET HOW WORLDLY YOU ARE SOMETIMES, STEVE ROGERS...
I KNOW YOU DO, SHARON CARTER...HEY, LOOK...
THERE'S ANOTHER REASON WHY, HUNH?
MAYBE. YOU FEELING ANY BETTER?
A LITTLE. I MEAN, YEAH, OUR MISSION WASN'T EXACTLY A SUCCESS, BUT AT LEAST WE STOPPED A.I.M. FROM GETTING THEIR HANDS ON A WEAPON OF MASS DESTRUCTION.
THAT'S SOMETHING, RIGHT?
IT'S A START.
YEAH, IT'S JUST THE BEGINNING, ISN'T IT?
WHATEVER'S GOING ON, THIS IS ALL JUST THE BEGINNING...

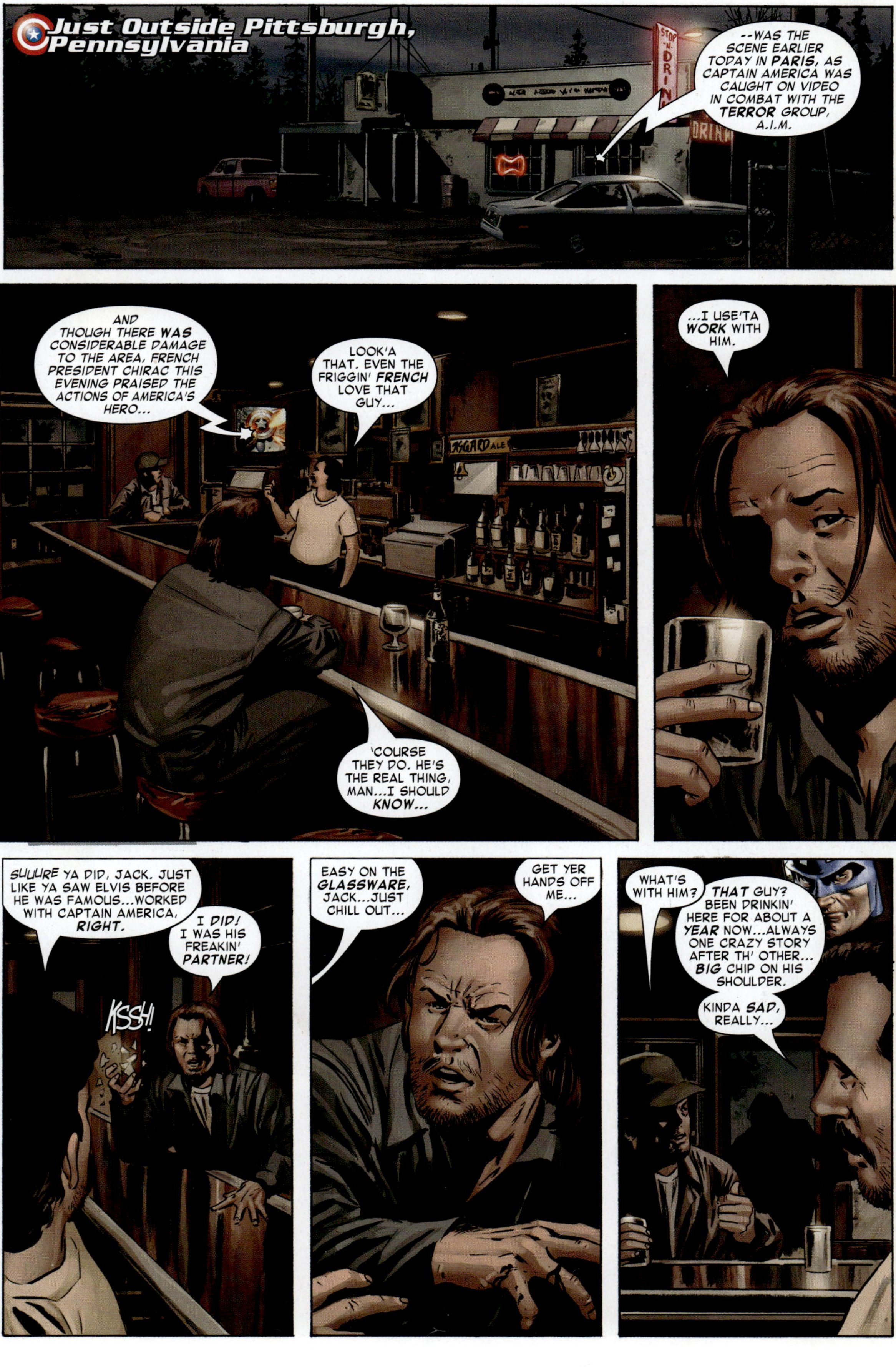
Just Outside Pittsburgh, Pennsylvania
--WAS THE SCENE EARLIER TODAY IN PARIS, AS CAPTAIN AMERICA WAS CAUGHT ON VIDEO IN COMBAT WITH THE TERROR GROUP, A.I.M.
AND THOUGH THERE WAS CONSIDERABLE DAMAGE TO THE AREA, FRENCH PRESIDENT CHIRAC THIS EVENING PRAISED THE ACTIONS OF AMERICA'S HERO...
LOOK'A THAT. EVEN THE FRIGGIN' FRENCH LOVE THAT GUY...
'COURSE THEY DO. HE'S THE REAL THING, MAN...I SHOULD KNOW...
...I USE'TA WORK WITH HIM.
SUUURE YA DID, JACK. JUST LIKE YA SAW ELVIS BEFORE HE WAS FAMOUS...WORKED WITH CAPTAIN AMERICA, RIGHT.
I DID! I WAS HIS FREAKIN' PARTNER!
KSSH!
EASY ON THE GLASSWARE, JACK...JUST CHILL OUT...
GET YER HANDS OFF ME...
WHAT'S WITH HIM?
THAT GUY? BEEN DRINKIN' HERE FOR ABOUT A YEAR NOW...ALWAYS ONE CRAZY STORY AFTER TH' OTHER... BIG CHIP ON HIS SHOULDER.
KINDA SAD, REALLY...

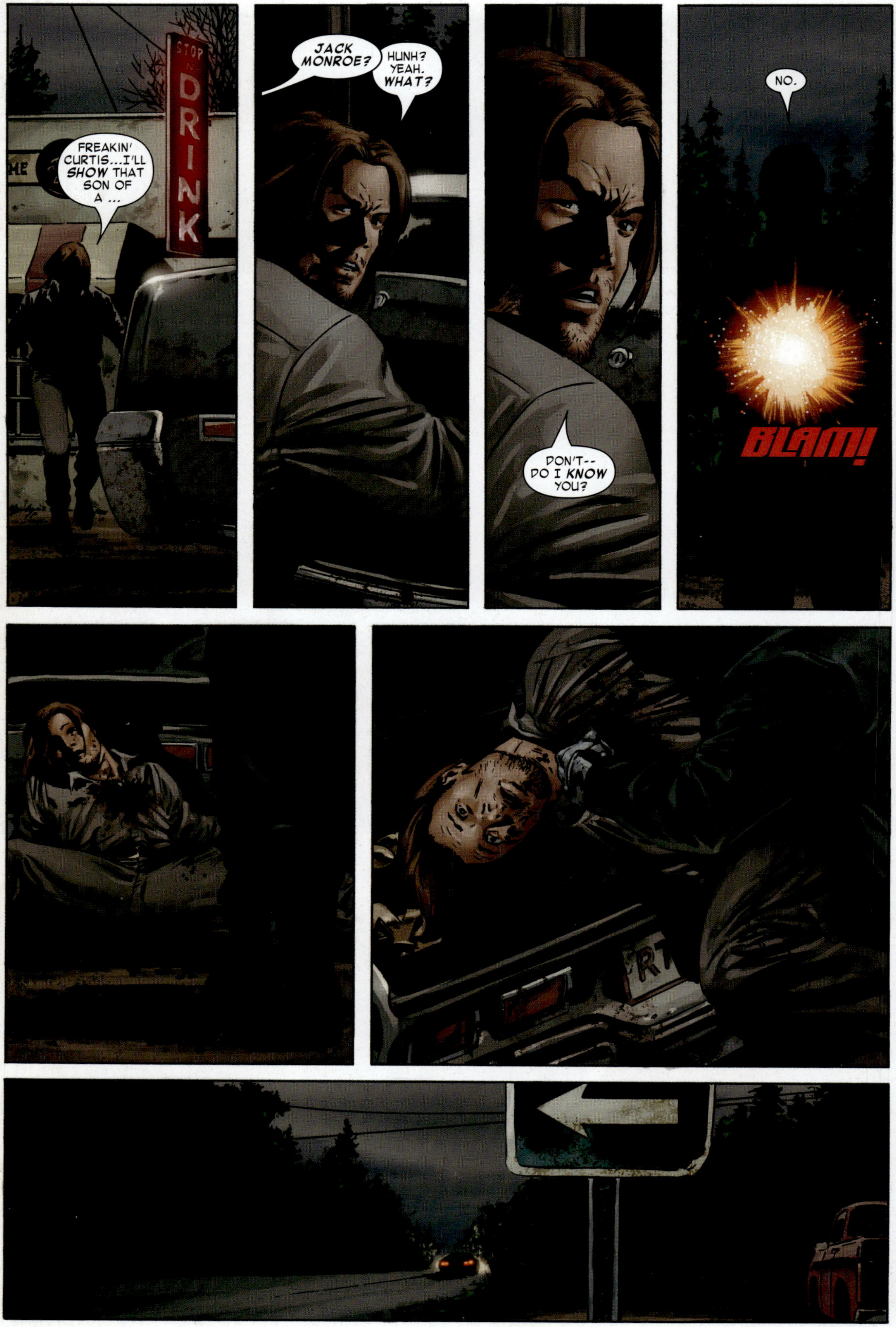

FREAKIN' CURTIS...I'LL SHOW THAT SON OF A ...
JACK MONROE?
HUNH? YEAH. WHAT?
DON'T-- DO I KNOW YOU?
NO.
BLAM!

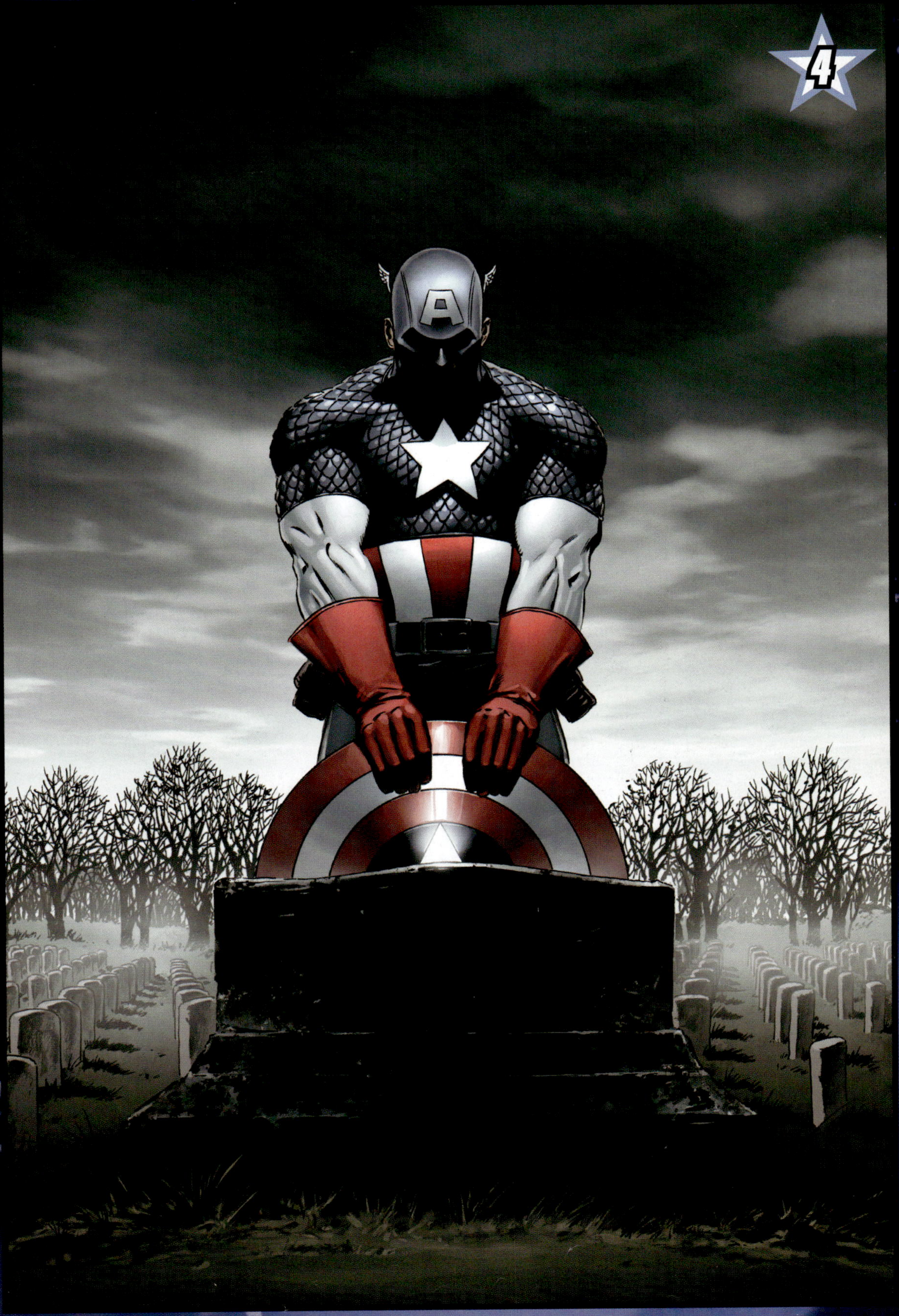
4

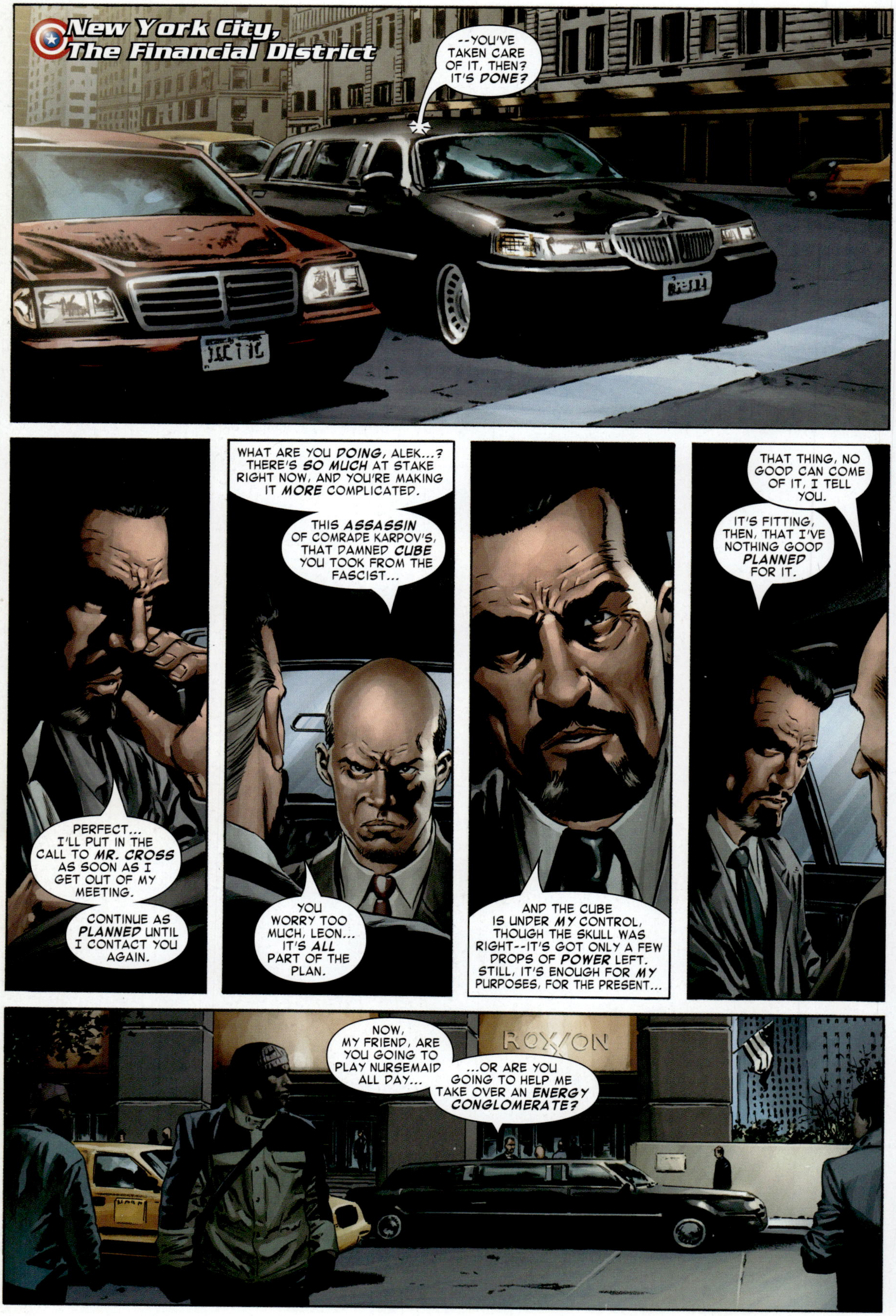
New York City, The Financial District
--YOU'VE TAKEN CARE OF IT, THEN? IT'S DONE?
PERFECT... I'LL PUT IN THE CALL TO MR. CROSS AS SOON AS I GET OUT OF MY MEETING.
CONTINUE AS PLANNED UNTIL I CONTACT YOU AGAIN.
WHAT ARE YOU DOING, ALEK...? THERE'S SO MUCH AT STAKE RIGHT NOW, AND YOU'RE MAKING IT MORE COMPLICATED.
THIS ASSASSIN OF COMRADE KARPOV'S, THAT DAMNED CUBE YOU TOOK FROM THE FASCIST...
YOU WORRY TOO MUCH, LEON... IT'S ALL PART OF THE PLAN.
AND THE CUBE IS UNDER MY CONTROL, THOUGH THE SKULL WAS RIGHT--IT'S GOT ONLY A FEW DROPS OF POWER LEFT. STILL, IT'S ENOUGH FOR MY PURPOSES, FOR THE PRESENT...
THAT THING, NO GOOD CAN COME OF IT, I TELL YOU.
IT'S FITTING, THEN, THAT I'VE NOTHING GOOD PLANNED FOR IT.
NOW, MY FRIEND, ARE YOU GOING TO PLAY NURSEMAID ALL DAY...
...OR ARE YOU GOING TO HELP ME TAKE OVER AN ENERGY CONGLOMERATE?
ROXXON

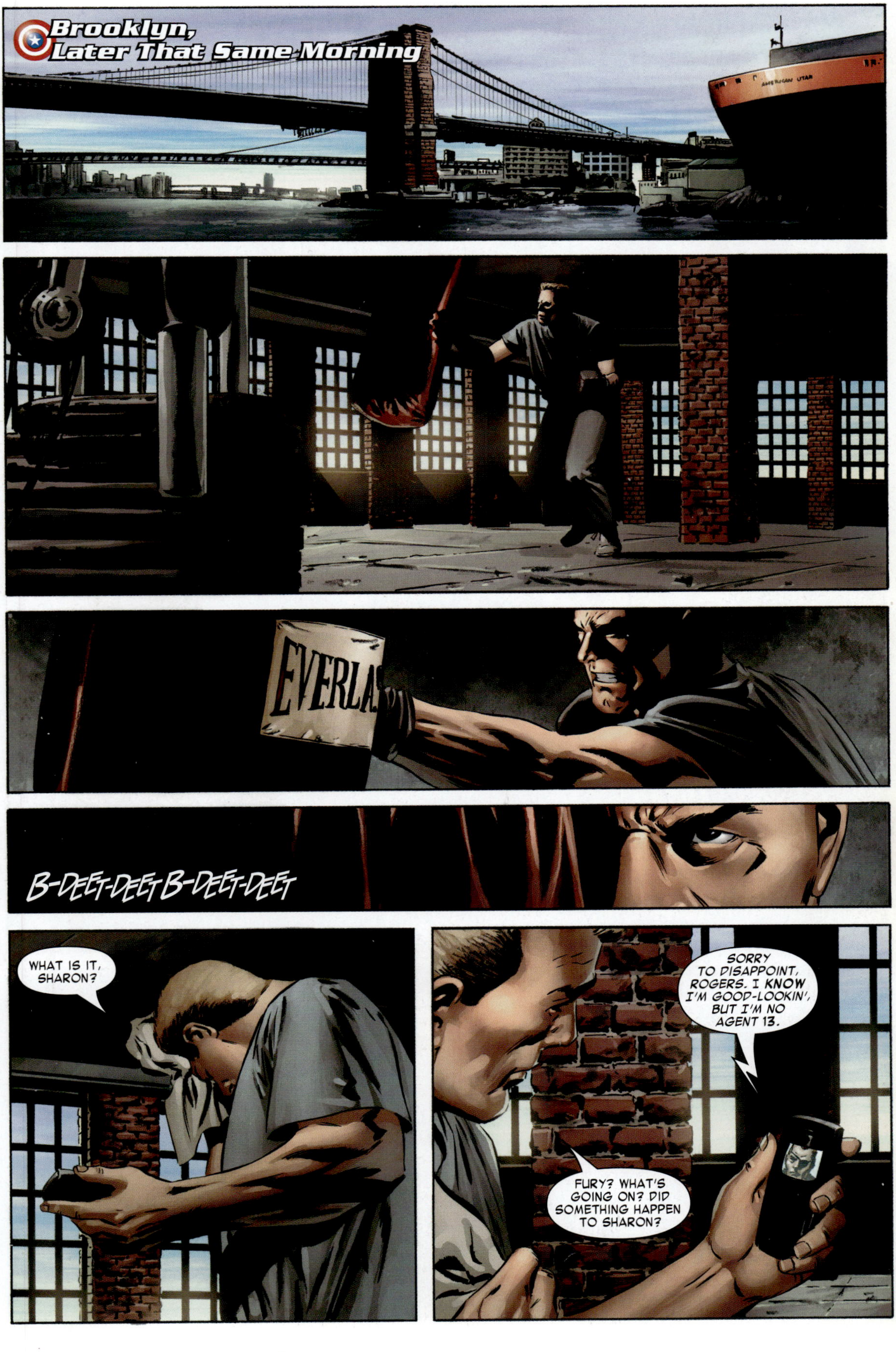
Brooklyn, Later That Same Morning
EVERLAS
B-DEET-DEET B-DEET-DEET
WHAT IS IT, SHARON?
SORRY TO DISAPPOINT, ROGERS. I KNOW I'M GOOD-LOOKIN', BUT I'M NO AGENT 13.
FURY? WHAT'S GOING ON? DID SOMETHING HAPPEN TO SHARON?

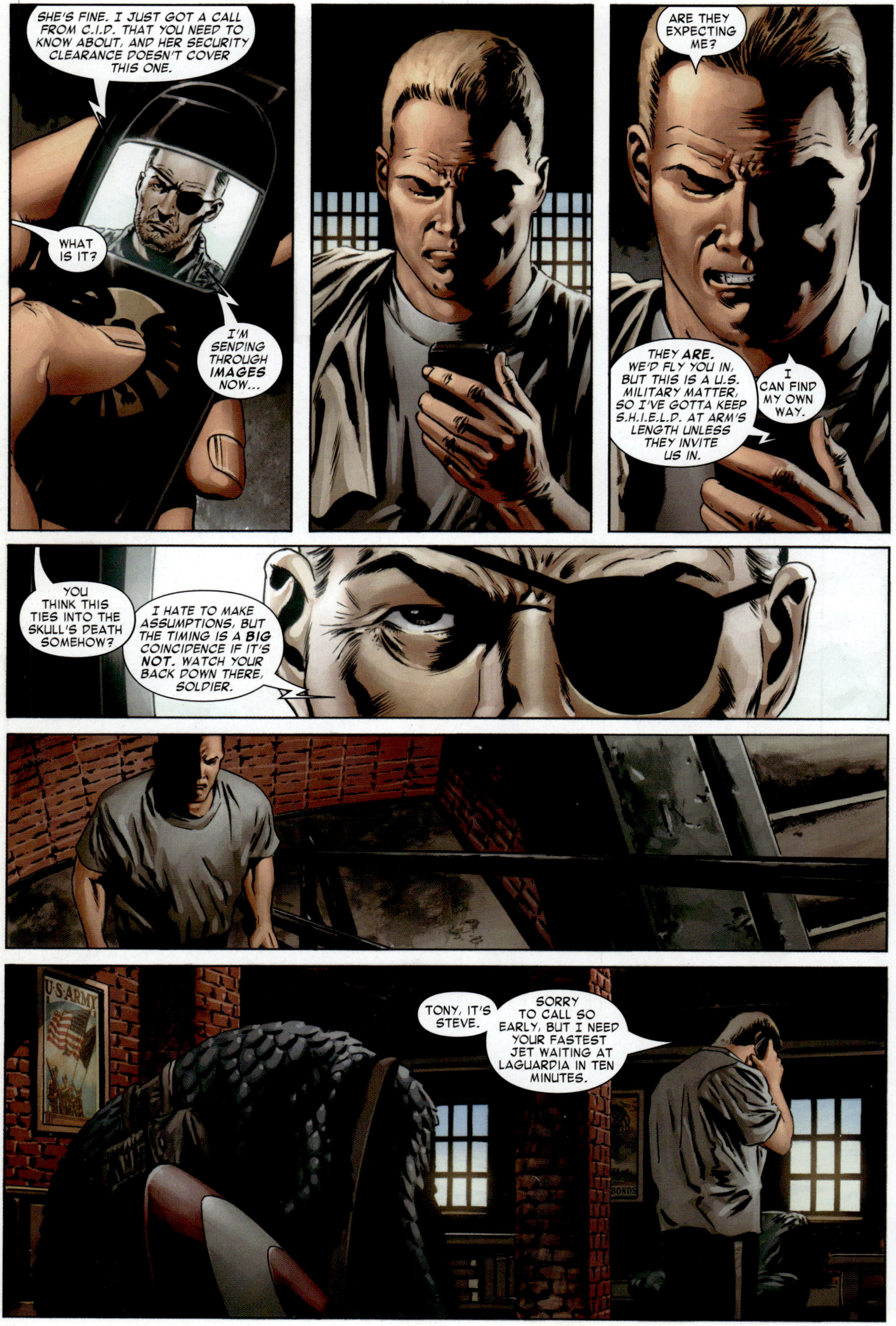
SHE'S FINE. I JUST GOT A CALL FROM C.I.D. THAT YOU NEED TO KNOW ABOUT, AND HER SECURITY CLEARANCE DOESN'T COVER THIS ONE.
WHAT IS IT?
I'M SENDING THROUGH IMAGES NOW...
ARE THEY EXPECTING ME?
THEY ARE. WE'D FLY YOU IN, BUT THIS IS A U.S. MILITARY MATTER, SO I'VE GOTTA KEEP S.H.I.E.L.D. AT ARM'S LENGTH UNLESS THEY INVITE US IN.
I CAN FIND MY OWN WAY.
YOU THINK THIS TIES INTO THE SKULL'S DEATH SOMEHOW?
I HATE TO MAKE ASSUMPTIONS, BUT THE TIMING IS A BIG COINCIDENCE IF IT'S NOT. WATCH YOUR BACK DOWN THERE, SOLDIER.
U.S. ARMY
TONY, IT'S STEVE.
SORRY TO CALL SO EARLY, BUT I NEED YOUR FASTEST JET WAITING AT LAGUARDIA IN TEN MINUTES.
BONDS

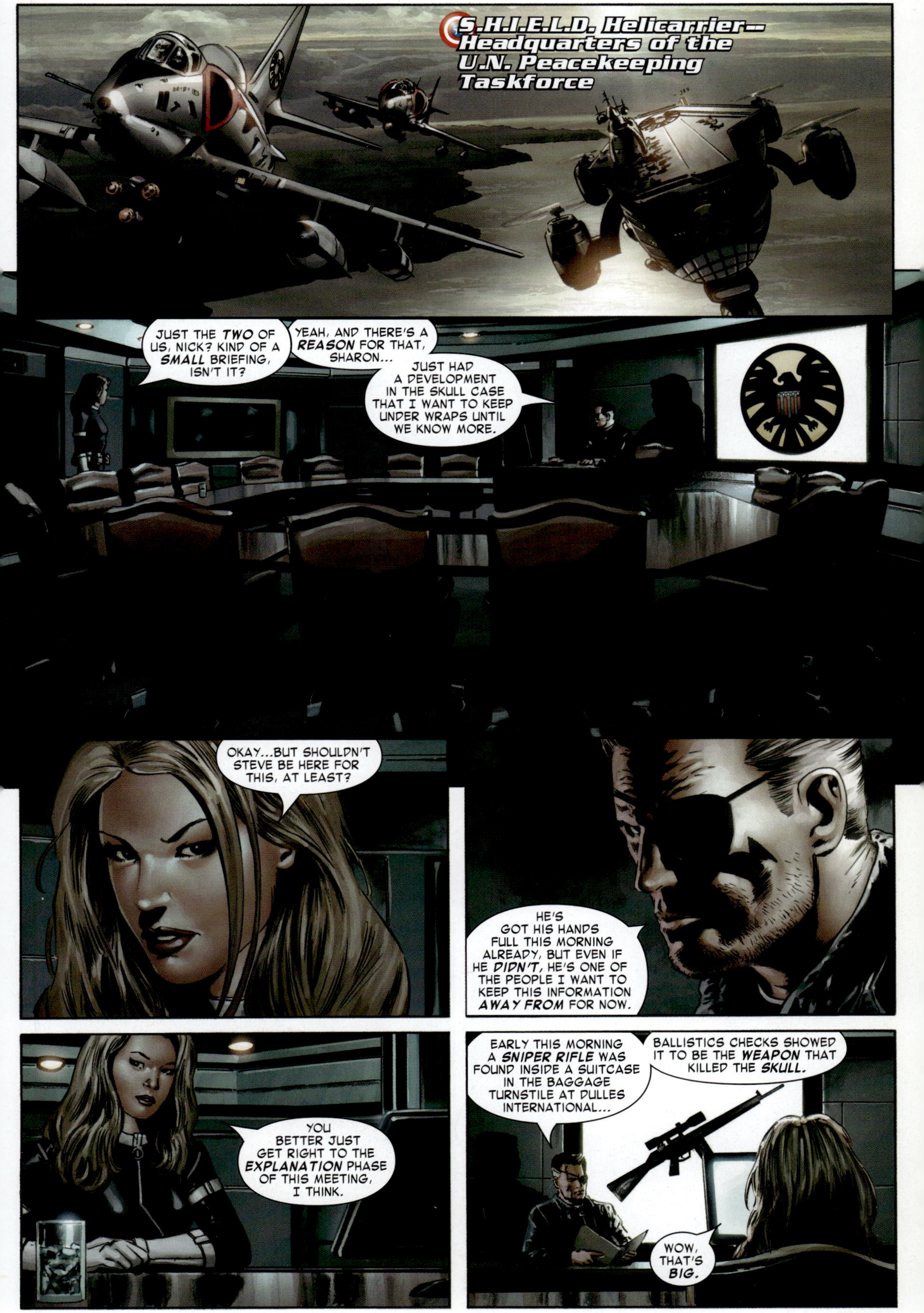
S.H.I.E.L.D. Helicarrier--Headquarters of the U.N. Peacekeeping Taskforce
JUST THE TWO OF US, NICK? KIND OF A SMALL BRIEFING, ISN'T IT?
YEAH, AND THERE'S A REASON FOR THAT, SHARON...
JUST HAD A DEVELOPMENT IN THE SKULL CASE THAT I WANT TO KEEP UNDER WRAPS UNTIL WE KNOW MORE.
OKAY...BUT SHOULDN'T STEVE BE HERE FOR THIS, AT LEAST?
HE'S GOT HIS HANDS FULL THIS MORNING ALREADY, BUT EVEN IF HE DIDN'T, HE'S ONE OF THE PEOPLE I WANT TO KEEP THIS INFORMATION AWAY FROM FOR NOW.
YOU BETTER JUST GET RIGHT TO THE EXPLANATION PHASE OF THIS MEETING, I THINK.
EARLY THIS MORNING A SNIPER RIFLE WAS FOUND INSIDE A SUITCASE IN THE BAGGAGE TURNSTILE AT DULLES INTERNATIONAL...
BALLISTICS CHECKS SHOWED IT TO BE THE WEAPON THAT KILLED THE SKULL.
WOW, THAT'S BIG.

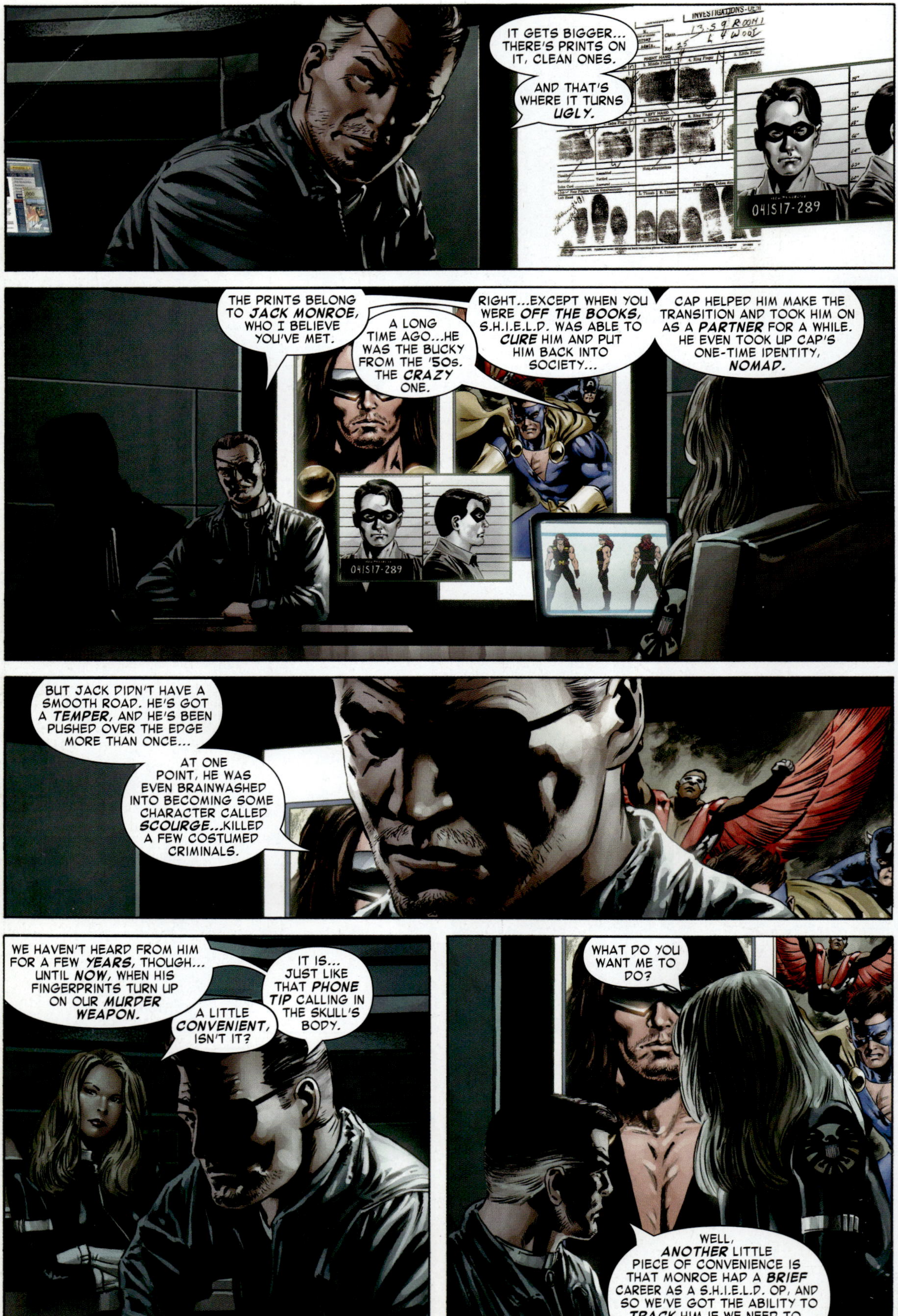
IT GETS BIGGER... THERE'S PRINTS ON IT, CLEAN ONES.
AND THAT'S WHERE IT TURNS UGLY.
041S17-289
THE PRINTS BELONG TO JACK MONROE, WHO I BELIEVE YOU'VE MET.
A LONG TIME AGO...HE WAS THE BUCKY FROM THE '50s. THE CRAZY ONE.
RIGHT...EXCEPT WHEN YOU WERE OFF THE BOOKS, S.H.I.E.L.D. WAS ABLE TO CURE HIM AND PUT HIM BACK INTO SOCIETY...
CAP HELPED HIM MAKE THE TRANSITION AND TOOK HIM ON AS A PARTNER FOR A WHILE. HE EVEN TOOK UP CAP'S ONE-TIME IDENTITY, NOMAD.
041S17-289
BUT JACK DIDN'T HAVE A SMOOTH ROAD. HE'S GOT A TEMPER, AND HE'S BEEN PUSHED OVER THE EDGE MORE THAN ONCE...
AT ONE POINT, HE WAS EVEN BRAINWASHED INTO BECOMING SOME CHARACTER CALLED SCOURGE...KILLED A FEW COSTUMED CRIMINALS.
WE HAVEN'T HEARD FROM HIM FOR A FEW YEARS, THOUGH... UNTIL NOW, WHEN HIS FINGERPRINTS TURN UP ON OUR MURDER WEAPON.
A LITTLE CONVENIENT, ISN'T IT?
IT IS... JUST LIKE THAT PHONE TIP CALLING IN THE SKULL'S BODY.
WHAT DO YOU WANT ME TO DO?
WELL, ANOTHER LITTLE PIECE OF CONVENIENCE IS THAT MONROE HAD A BRIEF CAREER AS A S.H.I.E.L.D. OP, AND SO WE'VE GOT THE ABILITY TO TRACK HIM IF WE NEED TO...

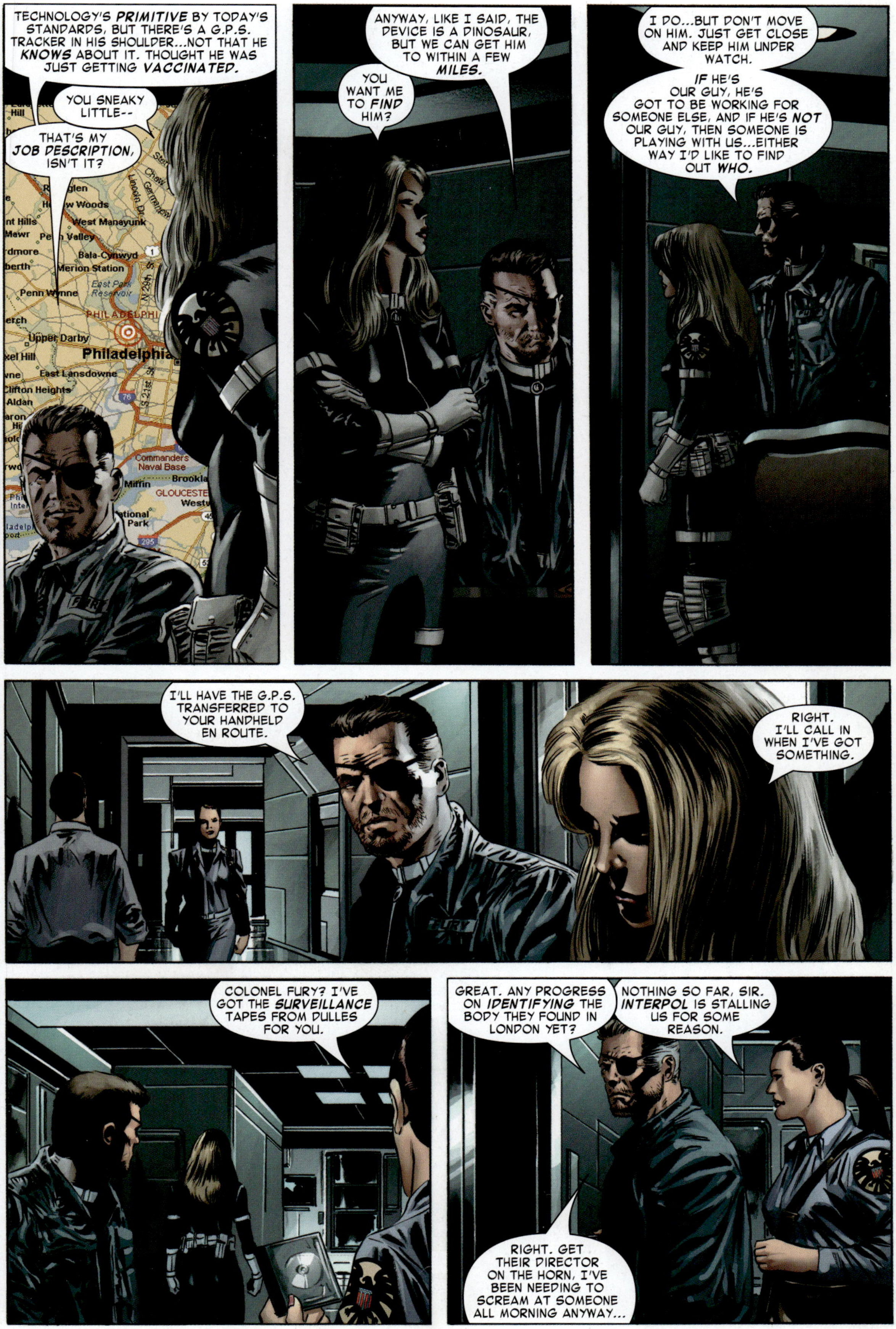

TECHNOLOGY'S PRIMITIVE BY TODAY'S STANDARDS, BUT THERE'S A G.P.S. TRACKER IN HIS SHOULDER...NOT THAT HE KNOWS ABOUT IT. THOUGHT HE WAS JUST GETTING VACCINATED.
YOU SNEAKY LITTLE--
THAT'S MY JOB DESCRIPTION, ISN'T IT?
West Manayunk
Merion Station
Penn Wynne
Upper Darby
Philadelphia
East Lansdowne
Clifton Heights
Commanders Naval Base
YOU WANT ME TO FIND HIM?
ANYWAY, LIKE I SAID, THE DEVICE IS A DINOSAUR, BUT WE CAN GET HIM TO WITHIN A FEW MILES.
I DO...BUT DON'T MOVE ON HIM. JUST GET CLOSE AND KEEP HIM UNDER WATCH.
IF HE'S OUR GUY, HE'S GOT TO BE WORKING FOR SOMEONE ELSE, AND IF HE'S NOT OUR GUY, THEN SOMEONE IS PLAYING WITH US...EITHER WAY I'D LIKE TO FIND OUT WHO.
I'LL HAVE THE G.P.S. TRANSFERRED TO YOUR HANDHELD EN ROUTE.
RIGHT. I'LL CALL IN WHEN I'VE GOT SOMETHING.
COLONEL FURY? I'VE GOT THE SURVEILLANCE TAPES FROM DULLES FOR YOU.
GREAT. ANY PROGRESS ON IDENTIFYING THE BODY THEY FOUND IN LONDON YET?
NOTHING SO FAR, SIR. INTERPOL IS STALLING US FOR SOME REASON.
RIGHT. GET THEIR DIRECTOR ON THE HORN, I'VE BEEN NEEDING TO SCREAM AT SOMEONE ALL MORNING ANYWAY...

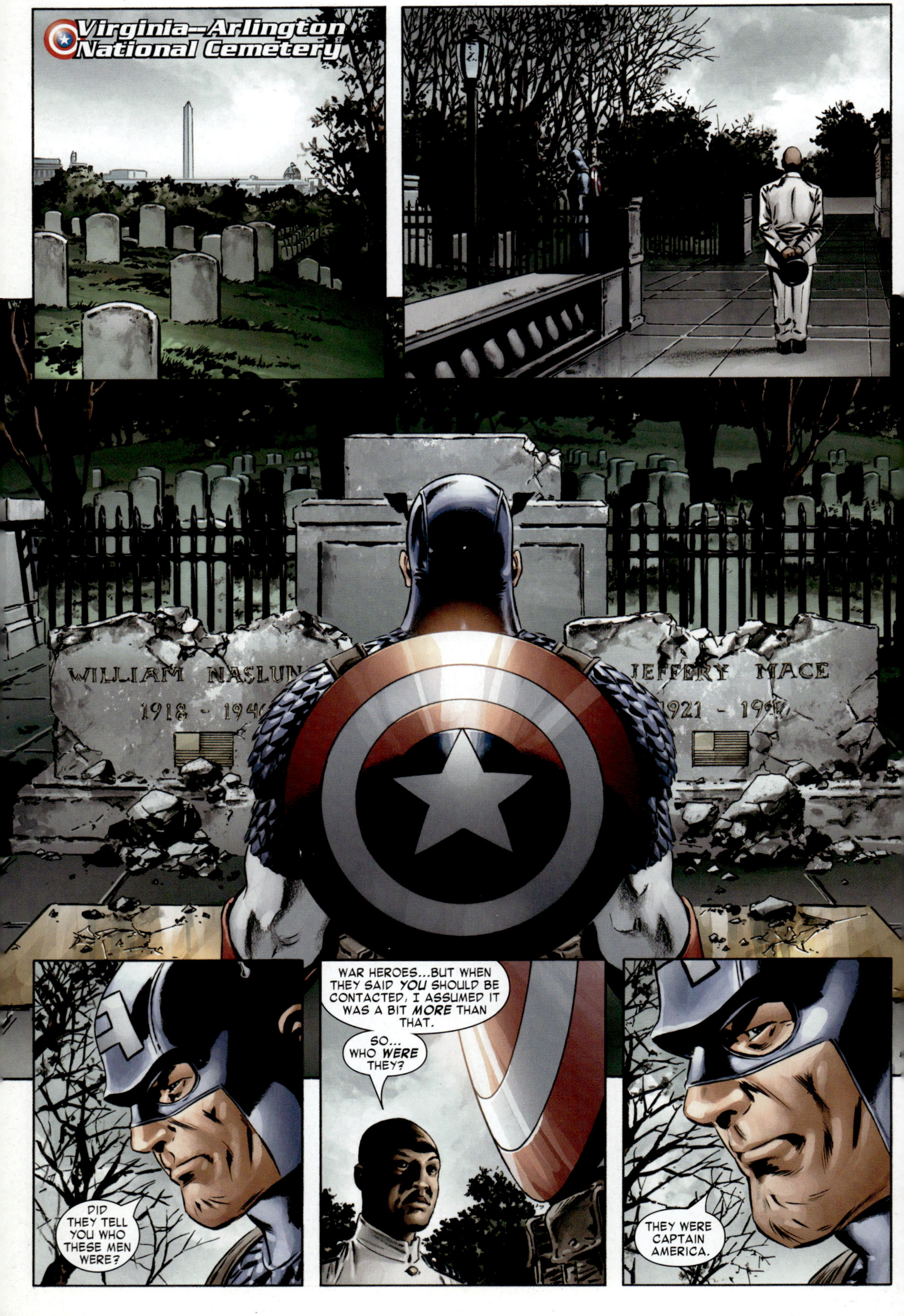
Virginia--Arlington National Cemetery
WILLIAM NASLUN
1918 - 194
JEFFERY MACE
1921 - 19
DID THEY TELL YOU WHO THESE MEN WERE?
WAR HEROES...BUT WHEN THEY SAID YOU SHOULD BE CONTACTED, I ASSUMED IT WAS A BIT MORE THAN THAT.
SO... WHO WERE THEY?
THEY WERE CAPTAIN AMERICA.

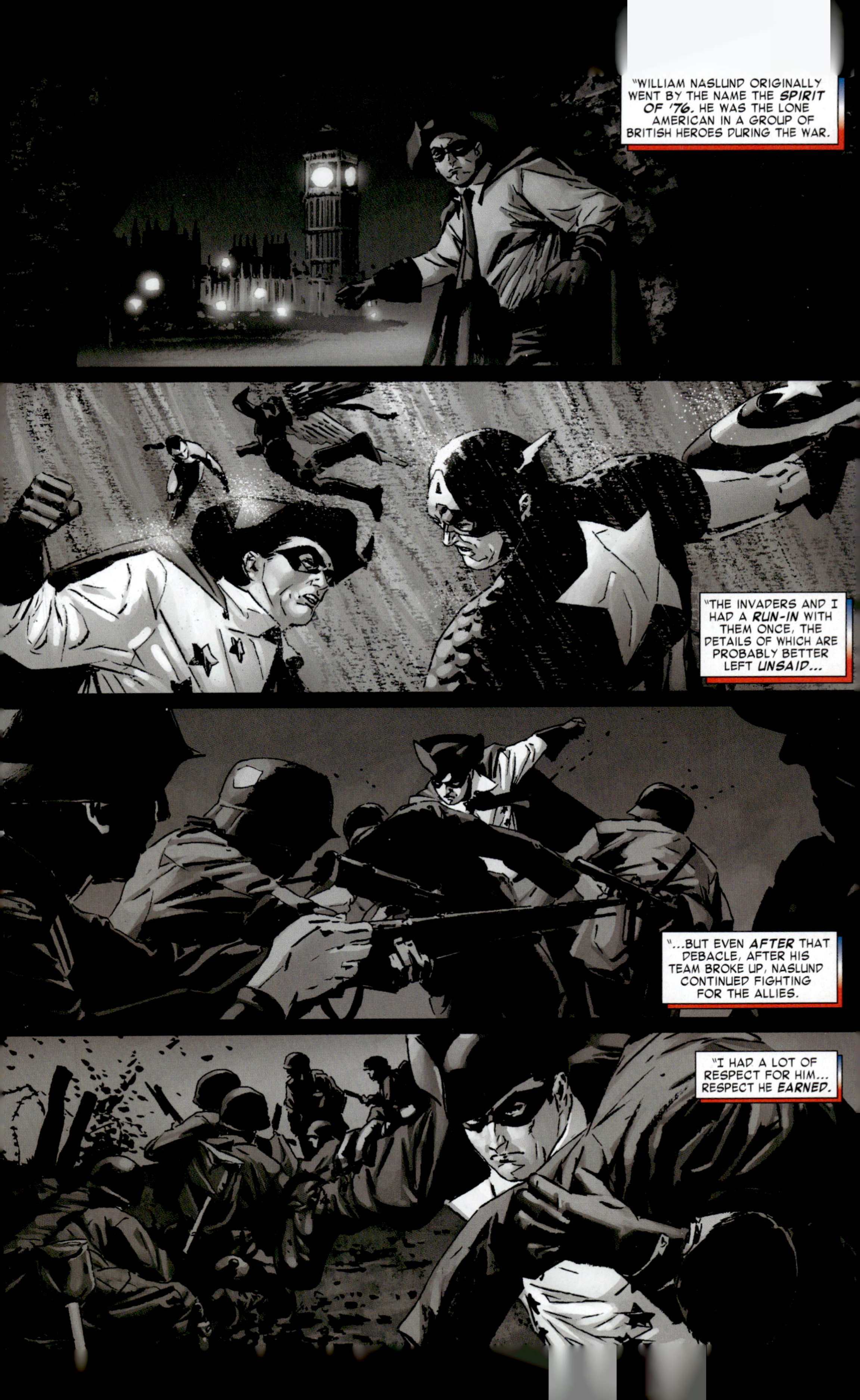
"WILLIAM NASLUND ORIGINALLY WENT BY THE NAME THE SPIRIT OF '76. HE WAS THE LONE AMERICAN IN A GROUP OF BRITISH HEROES DURING THE WAR.
"THE INVADERS AND I HAD A RUN-IN WITH THEM ONCE, THE DETAILS OF WHICH ARE PROBABLY BETTER LEFT UNSAID...
"...BUT EVEN AFTER THAT DEBACLE, AFTER HIS TEAM BROKE UP, NASLUND CONTINUED FIGHTING FOR THE ALLIES.
"I HAD A LOT OF RESPECT FOR HIM... RESPECT HE EARNED.

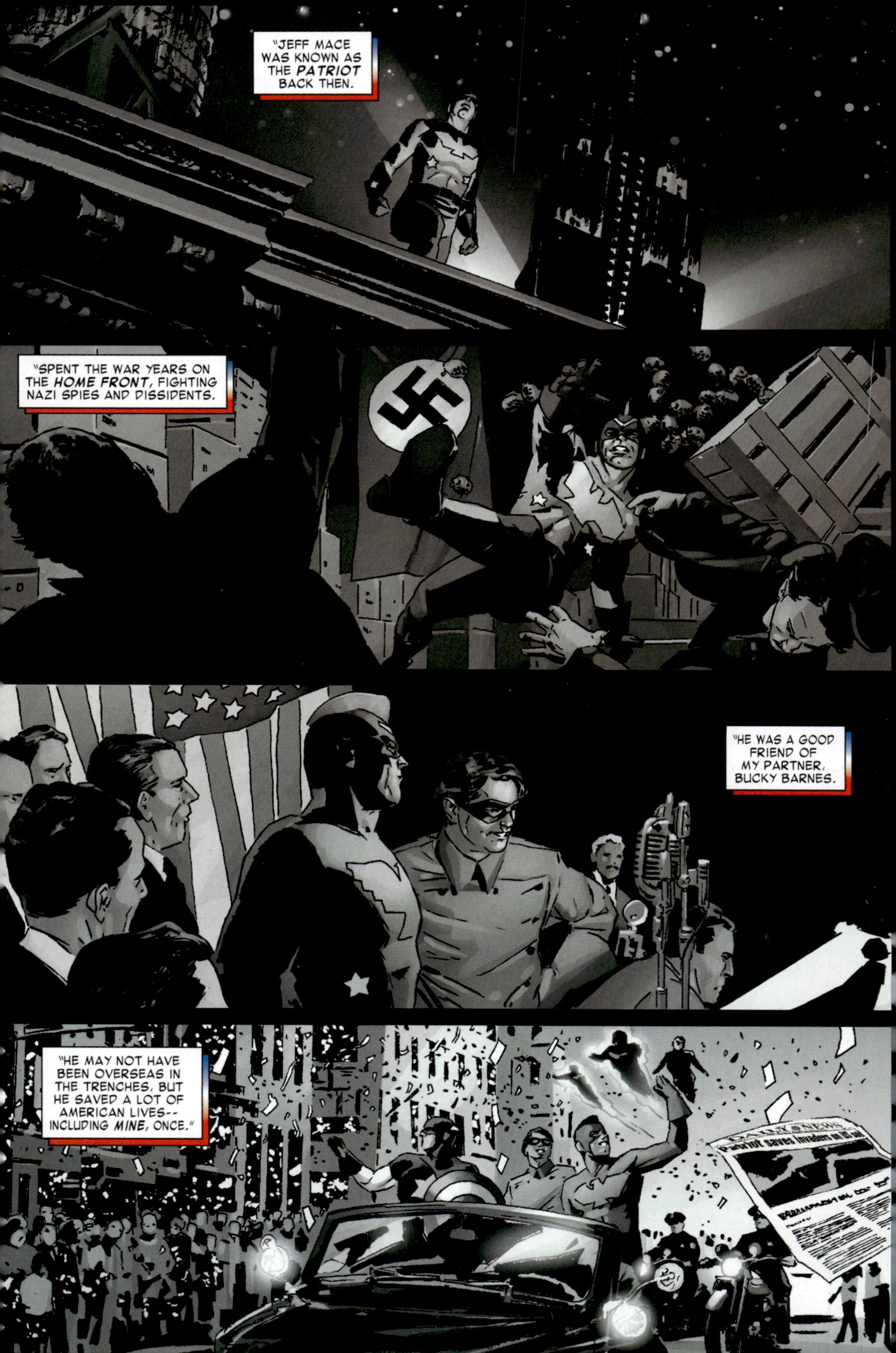
"JEFF MACE WAS KNOWN AS THE *PATRIOT* BACK THEN.
"SPENT THE WAR YEARS ON THE *HOME FRONT*, FIGHTING NAZI SPIES AND DISSIDENTS.
"HE WAS A GOOD FRIEND OF MY PARTNER, BUCKY BARNES.
"HE MAY NOT HAVE BEEN OVERSEAS IN THE TRENCHES, BUT HE SAVED A LOT OF AMERICAN LIVES-- INCLUDING *MINE*, ONCE."
DAILY NEWS
Patriot saves Invaders

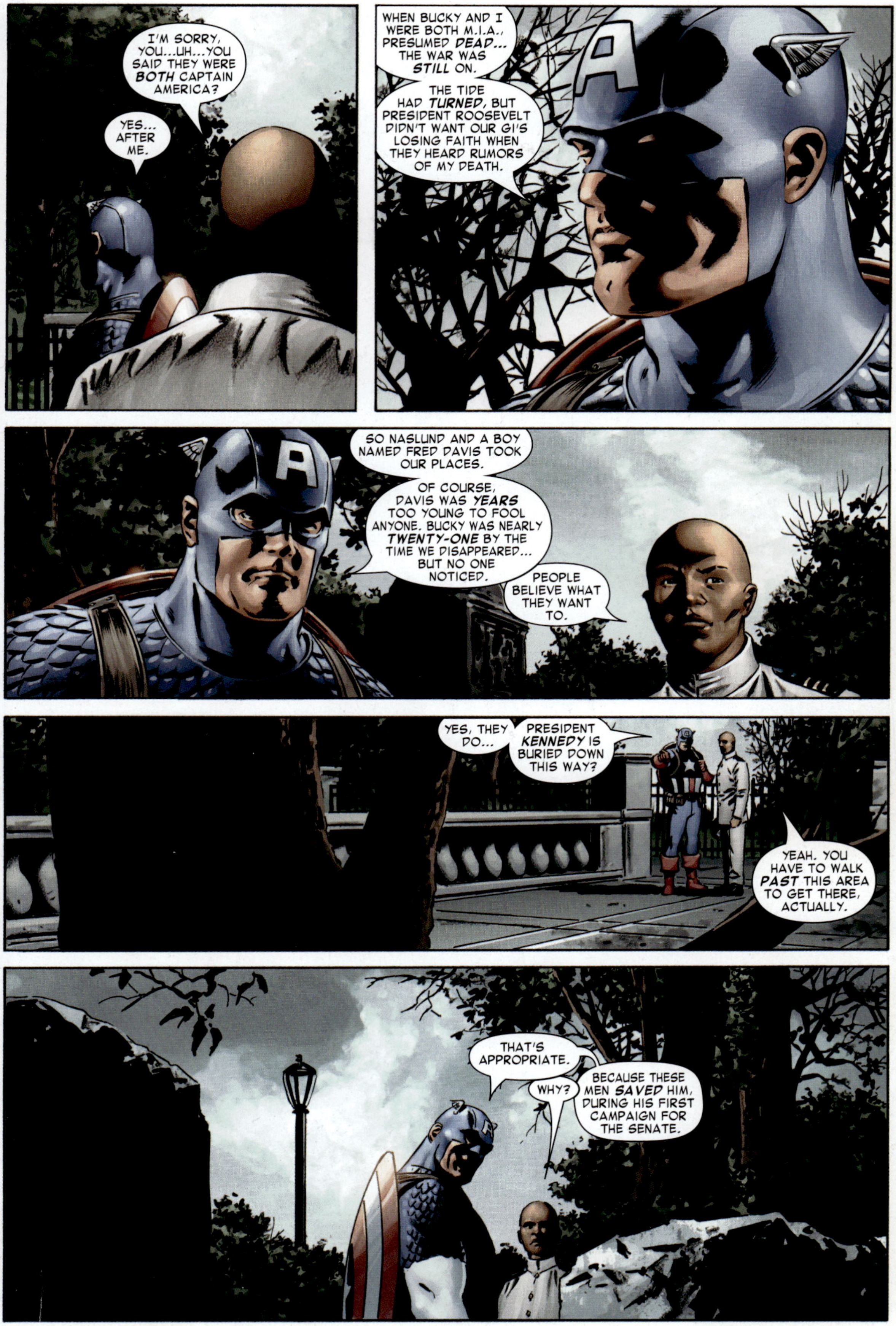
I'M SORRY, YOU...UH...YOU SAID THEY WERE BOTH CAPTAIN AMERICA?
YES... AFTER ME.
WHEN BUCKY AND I WERE BOTH M.I.A., PRESUMED DEAD... THE WAR WAS STILL ON.
THE TIDE HAD TURNED, BUT PRESIDENT ROOSEVELT DIDN'T WANT OUR GI'S LOSING FAITH WHEN THEY HEARD RUMORS OF MY DEATH.
SO NASLUND AND A BOY NAMED FRED DAVIS TOOK OUR PLACES.
OF COURSE, DAVIS WAS YEARS TOO YOUNG TO FOOL ANYONE. BUCKY WAS NEARLY TWENTY-ONE BY THE TIME WE DISAPPEARED... BUT NO ONE NOTICED.
PEOPLE BELIEVE WHAT THEY WANT TO.
YES, THEY DO...
PRESIDENT KENNEDY IS BURIED DOWN THIS WAY?
YEAH. YOU HAVE TO WALK PAST THIS AREA TO GET THERE, ACTUALLY.
THAT'S APPROPRIATE.
WHY?
BECAUSE THESE MEN SAVED HIM, DURING HIS FIRST CAMPAIGN FOR THE SENATE.

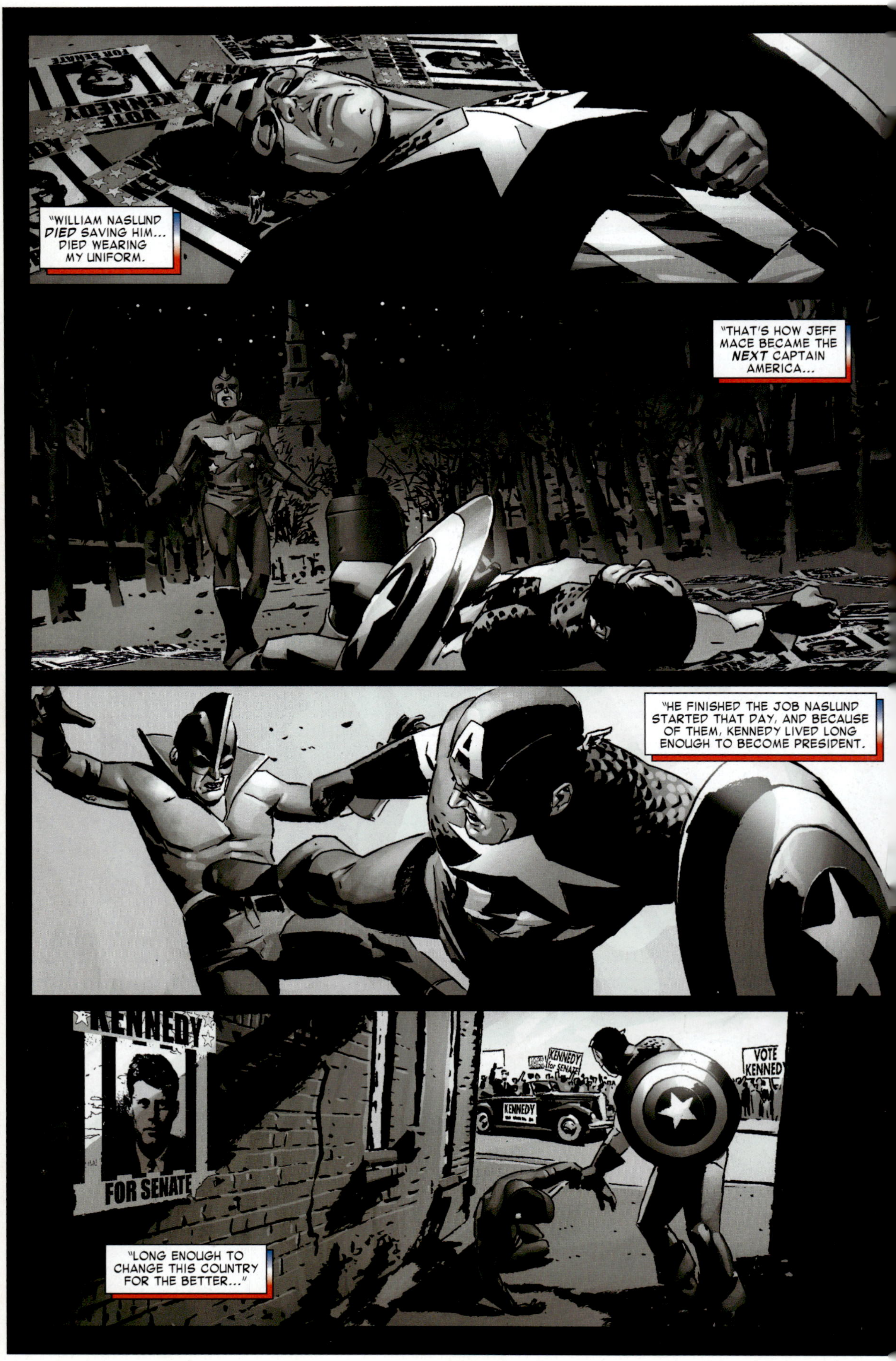

"WILLIAM NASLUND DIED SAVING HIM... DIED WEARING MY UNIFORM.
"THAT'S HOW JEFF MACE BECAME THE NEXT CAPTAIN AMERICA...
"HE FINISHED THE JOB NASLUND STARTED THAT DAY, AND BECAUSE OF THEM, KENNEDY LIVED LONG ENOUGH TO BECOME PRESIDENT.
KENNEDY
FOR SENATE
KENNEDY for SENATE
KENNEDY
VOTE KENNED
"LONG ENOUGH TO CHANGE THIS COUNTRY FOR THE BETTER..."

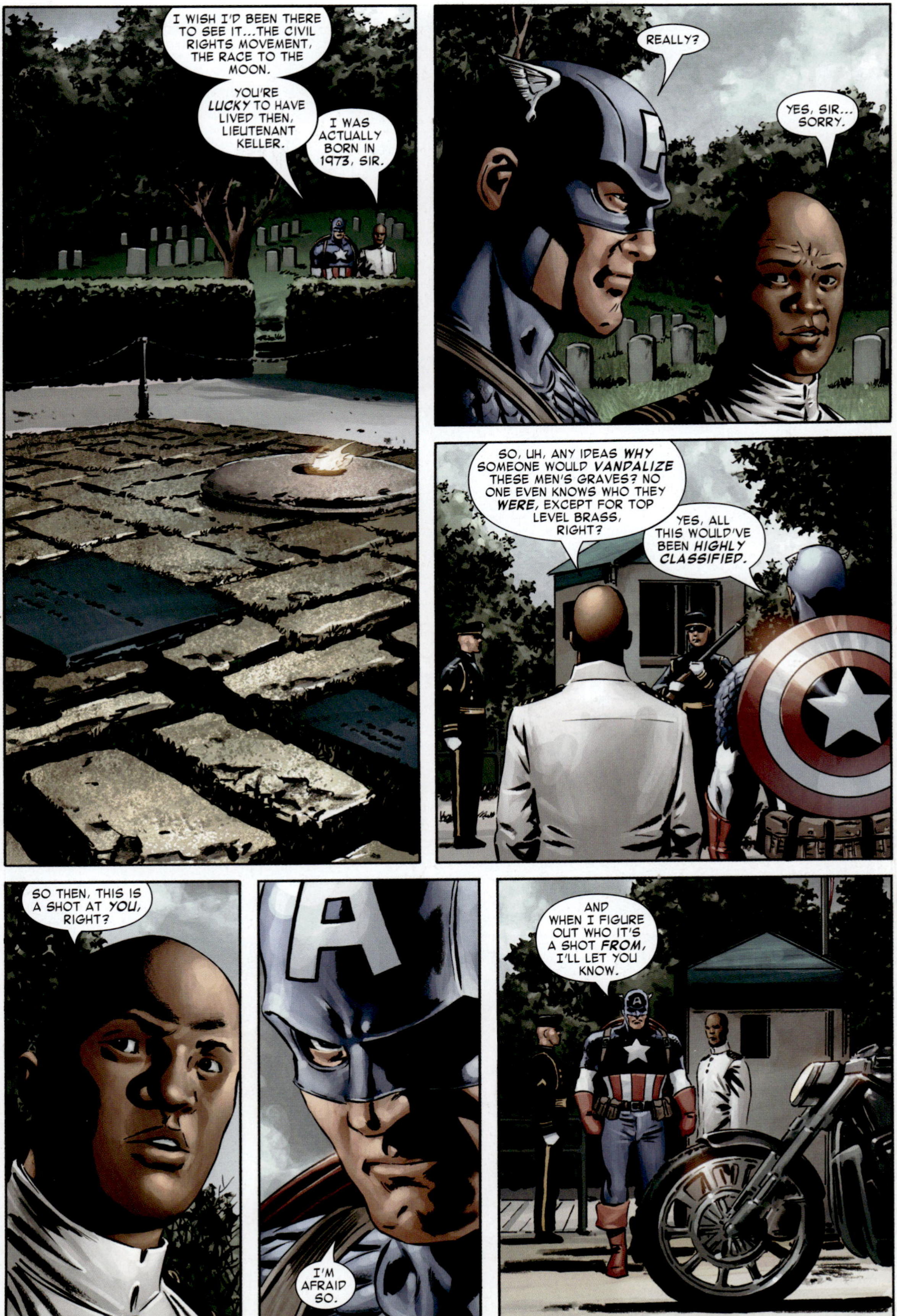
I WISH I'D BEEN THERE TO SEE IT...THE CIVIL RIGHTS MOVEMENT, THE RACE TO THE MOON.
YOU'RE LUCKY TO HAVE LIVED THEN, LIEUTENANT KELLER.
I WAS ACTUALLY BORN IN 1973, SIR.
REALLY?
YES, SIR... SORRY.
SO, UH, ANY IDEAS WHY SOMEONE WOULD VANDALIZE THESE MEN'S GRAVES? NO ONE EVEN KNOWS WHO THEY WERE, EXCEPT FOR TOP LEVEL BRASS, RIGHT?
YES, ALL THIS WOULD'VE BEEN HIGHLY CLASSIFIED.
SO THEN, THIS IS A SHOT AT YOU, RIGHT?
I'M AFRAID SO.
AND WHEN I FIGURE OUT WHO IT'S A SHOT FROM, I'LL LET YOU KNOW.

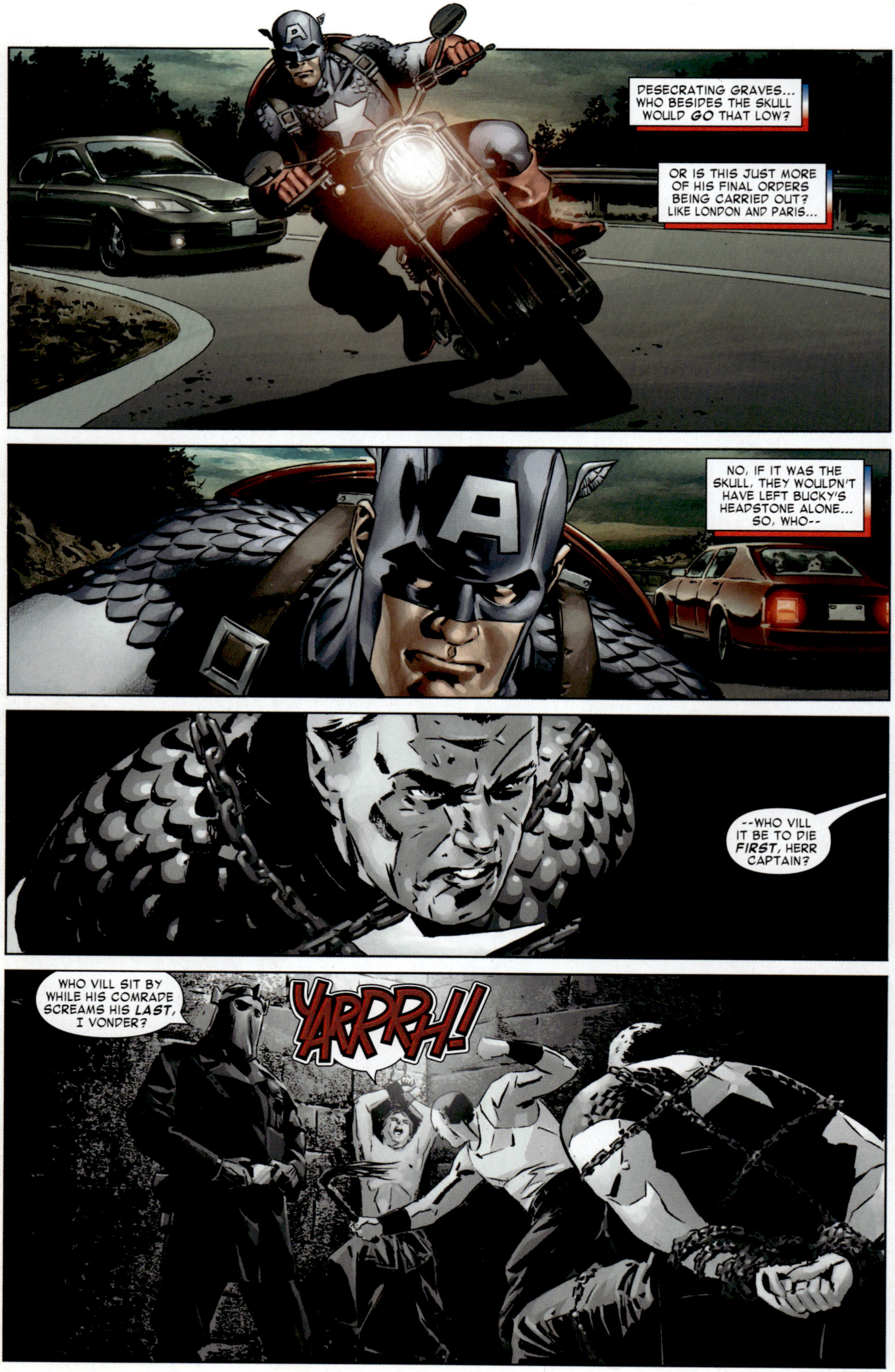
DESECRATING GRAVES... WHO BESIDES THE SKULL WOULD GO THAT LOW?
OR IS THIS JUST MORE OF HIS FINAL ORDERS BEING CARRIED OUT? LIKE LONDON AND PARIS...
NO, IF IT WAS THE SKULL, THEY WOULDN'T HAVE LEFT BUCKY'S HEADSTONE ALONE... SO, WHO--
--WHO VILL IT BE TO DIE FIRST, HERR CAPTAIN?
WHO VILL SIT BY WHILE HIS COMRADE SCREAMS HIS LAST, I VONDER?
YARRRH!

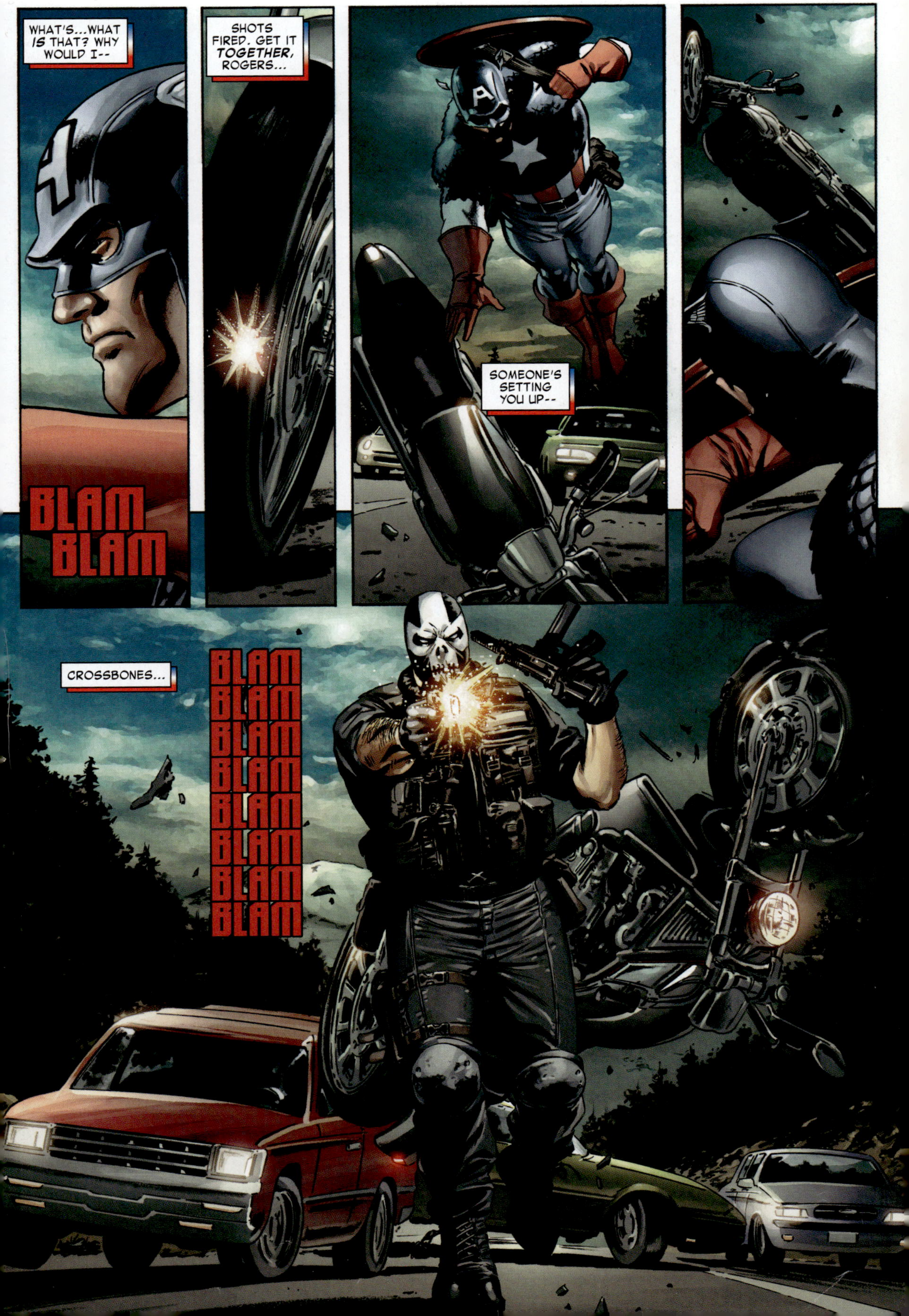
WHAT'S...WHAT *IS* THAT? WHY WOULD I--
BLAM
BLAM
SHOTS FIRED. GET IT *TOGETHER*, ROGERS...
SOMEONE'S SETTING YOU UP--
CROSSBONES...
BLAM
BLAM
BLAM
BLAM
BLAM
BLAM
BLAM
BLAM

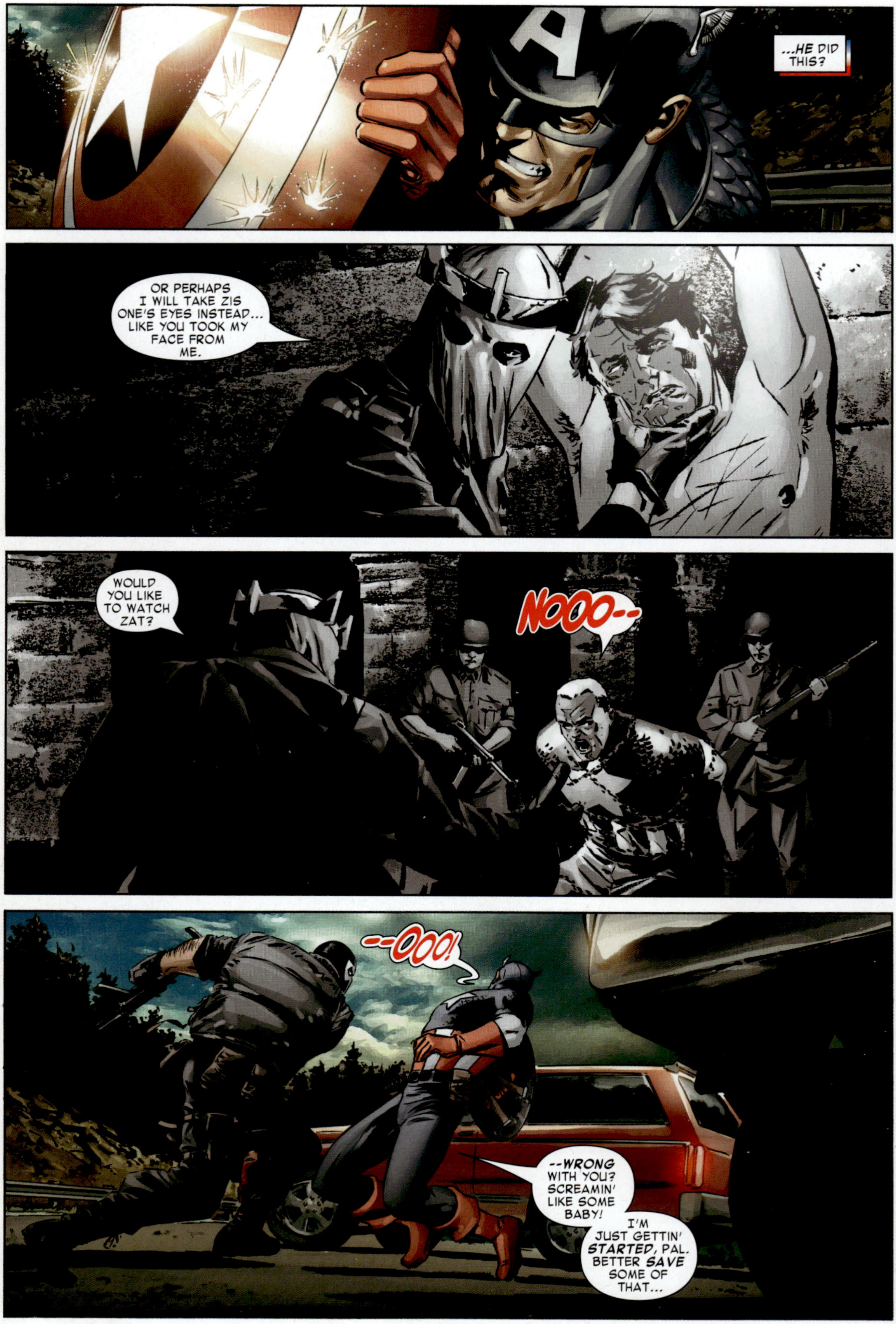
...HE DID THIS?
OR PERHAPS I WILL TAKE ZIS ONE'S EYES INSTEAD... LIKE YOU TOOK MY FACE FROM ME.
WOULD YOU LIKE TO WATCH ZAT?
NOOO--
--OOO!
--WRONG WITH YOU? SCREAMIN' LIKE SOME BABY!
I'M JUST GETTIN' STARTED, PAL. BETTER SAVE SOME OF THAT...

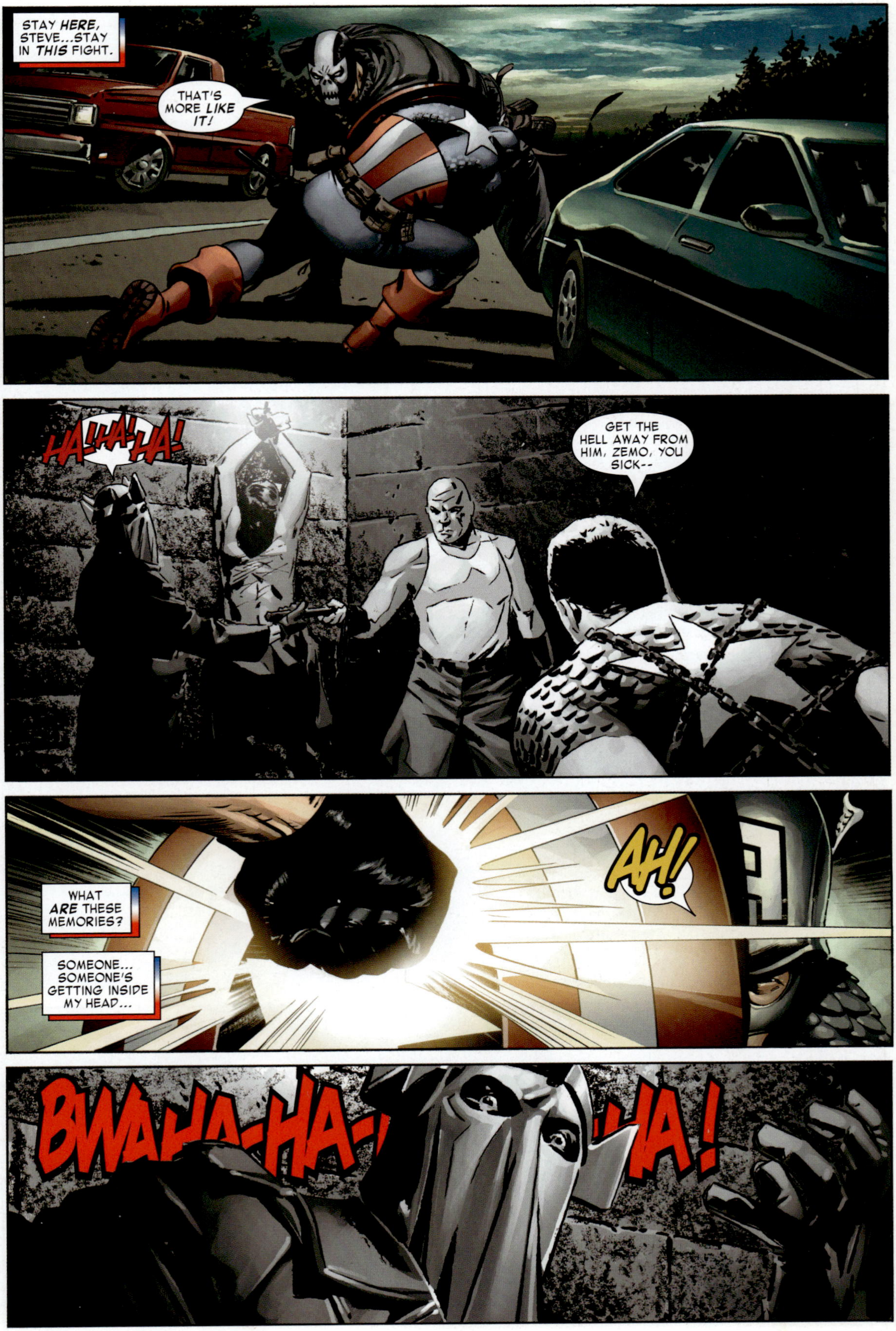
STAY HERE, STEVE...STAY IN THIS FIGHT.
THAT'S MORE LIKE IT!
HA! HA! HA!
GET THE HELL AWAY FROM HIM, ZEMO, YOU SICK--
WHAT ARE THESE MEMORIES?
AH!
SOMEONE... SOMEONE'S GETTING INSIDE MY HEAD...
BWAHA-HA-HA!

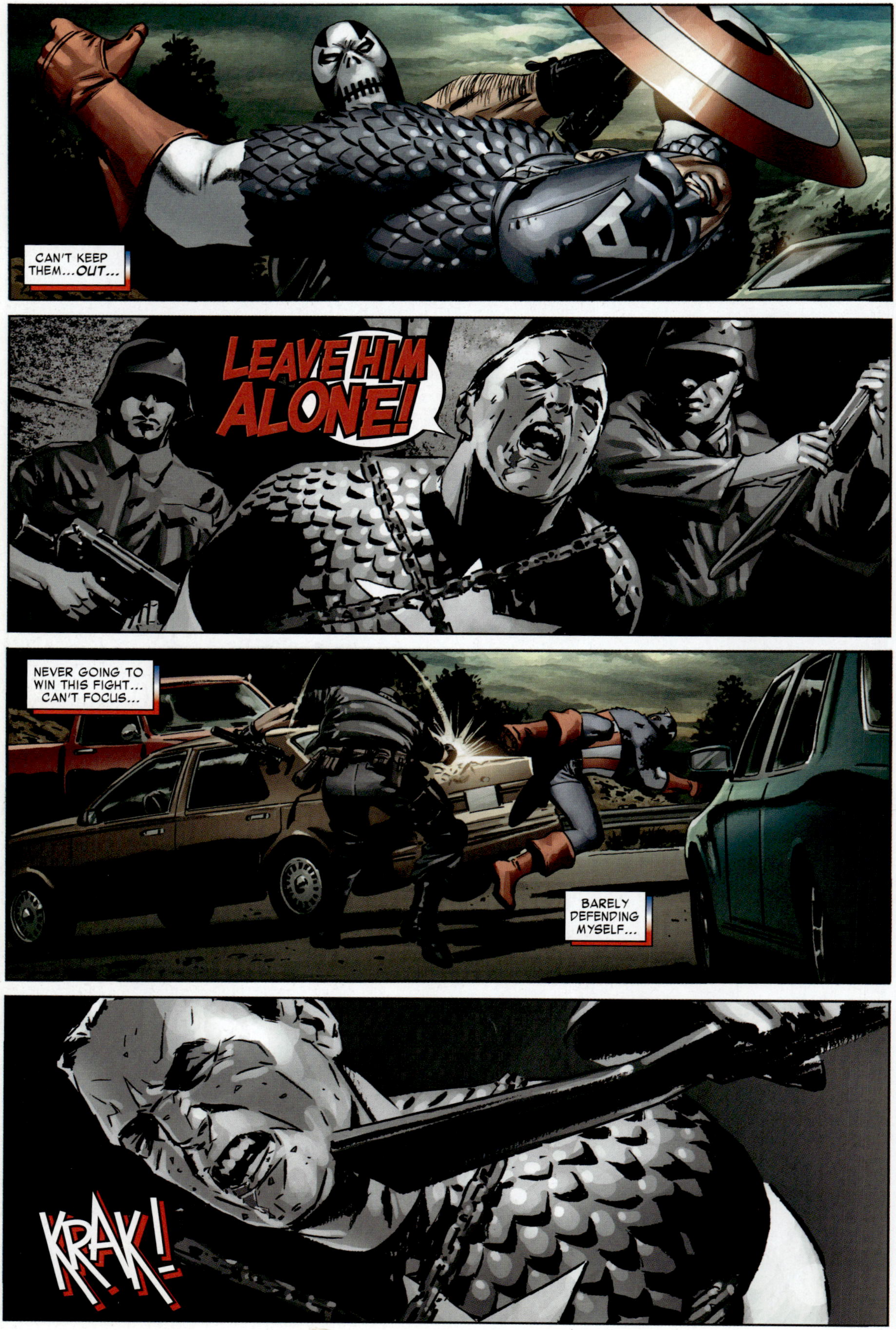
CAN'T KEEP THEM...OUT...
LEAVE HIM ALONE!
NEVER GOING TO WIN THIS FIGHT... CAN'T FOCUS...
BARELY DEFENDING MYSELF...
KRAK!

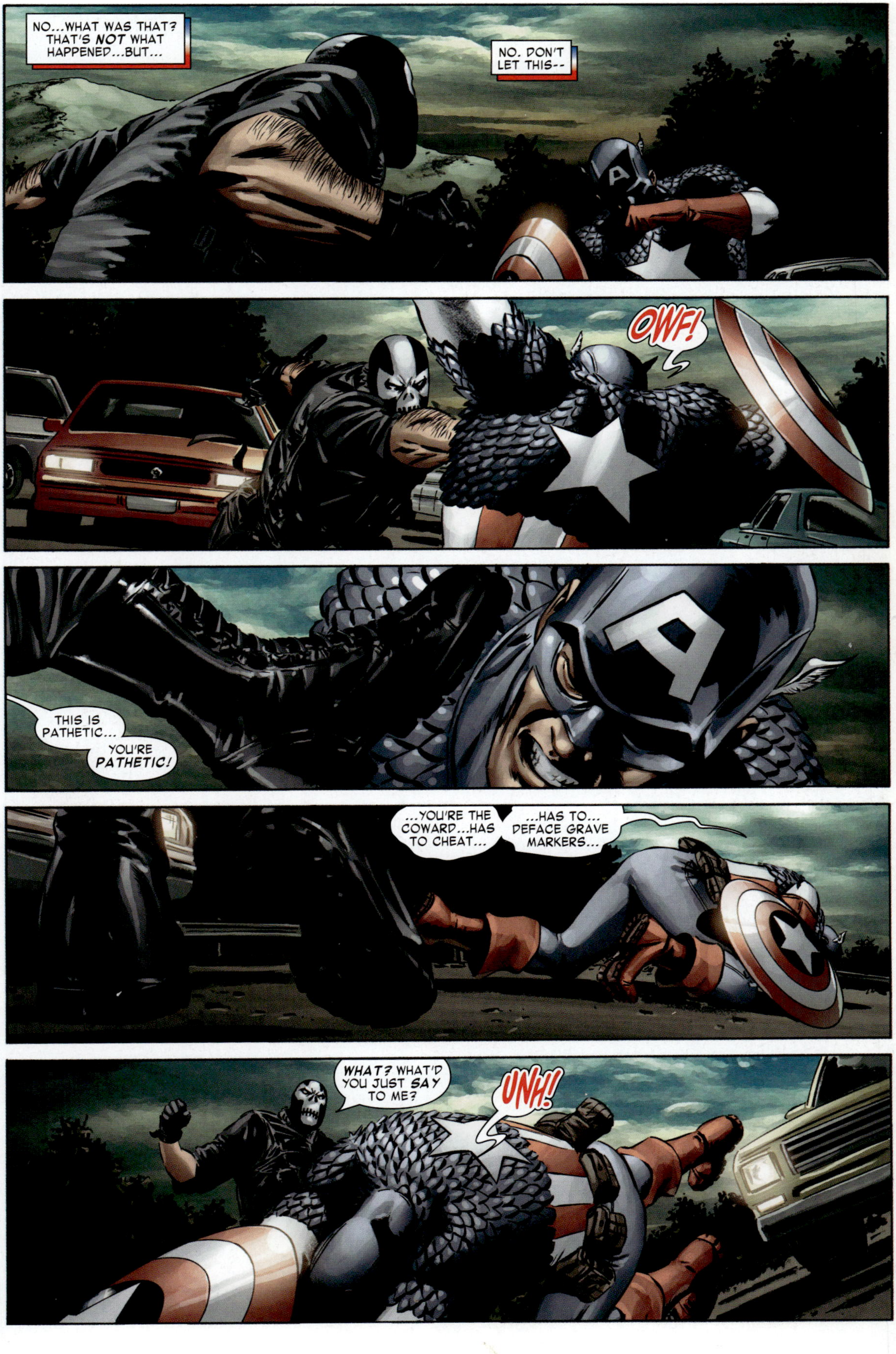
NO...WHAT WAS THAT? THAT'S NOT WHAT HAPPENED...BUT...
NO. DON'T LET THIS--
OWF!
THIS IS PATHETIC...
YOU'RE PATHETIC!
...YOU'RE THE COWARD...HAS TO CHEAT...
...HAS TO... DEFACE GRAVE MARKERS...
WHAT? WHAT'D YOU JUST SAY TO ME?
UNH!

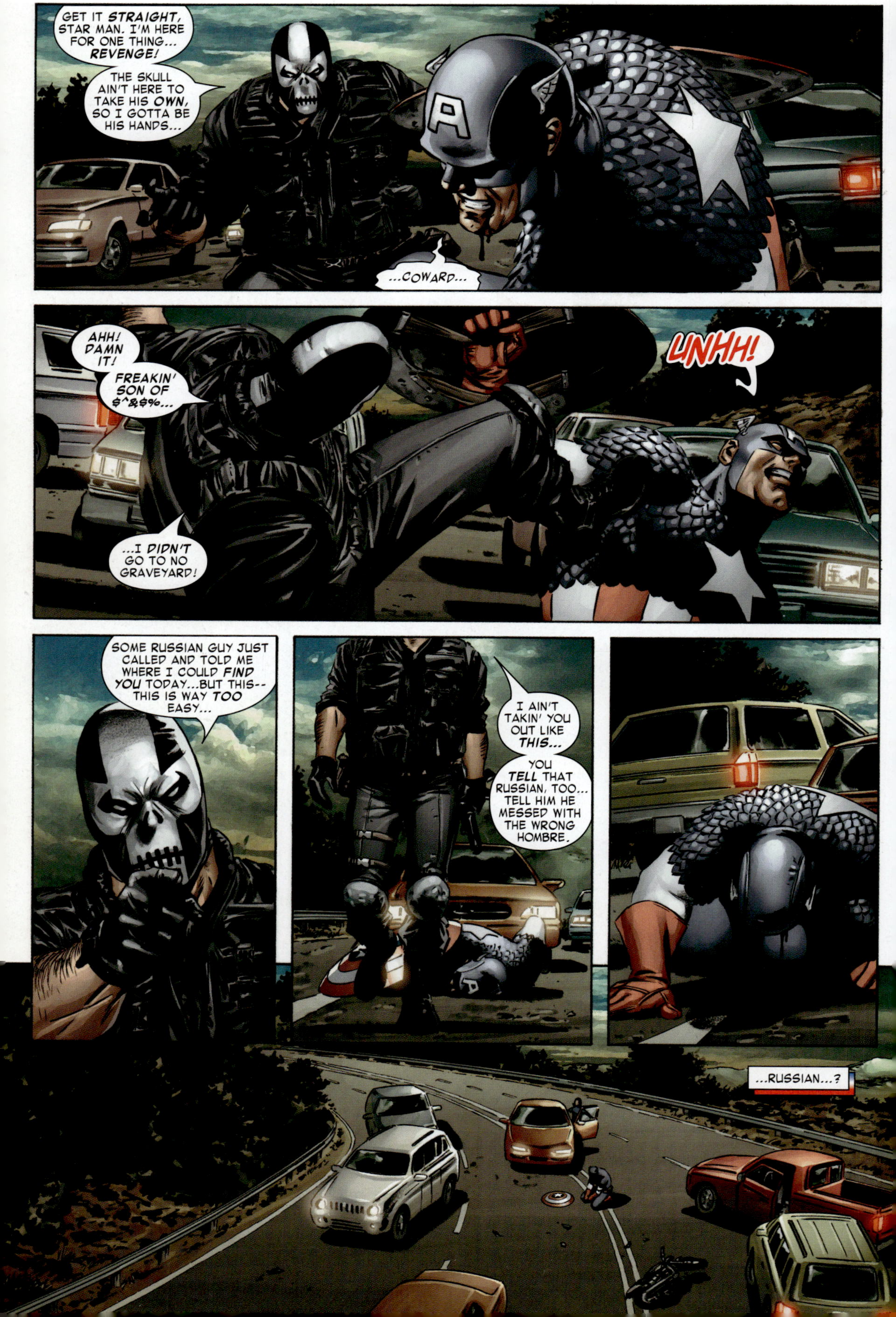
GET IT STRAIGHT, STAR MAN. I'M HERE FOR ONE THING... REVENGE!
THE SKULL AIN'T HERE TO TAKE HIS OWN, SO I GOTTA BE HIS HANDS...
...COWARD...
AHH! DAMN IT!
FREAKIN' SON OF $^&$%...
UNHH!
...I DIDN'T GO TO NO GRAVEYARD!
SOME RUSSIAN GUY JUST CALLED AND TOLD ME WHERE I COULD FIND YOU TODAY...BUT THIS-- THIS IS WAY TOO EASY...
I AIN'T TAKIN' YOU OUT LIKE THIS...
YOU TELL THAT RUSSIAN, TOO... TELL HIM HE MESSED WITH THE WRONG HOMBRE.
...RUSSIAN...?

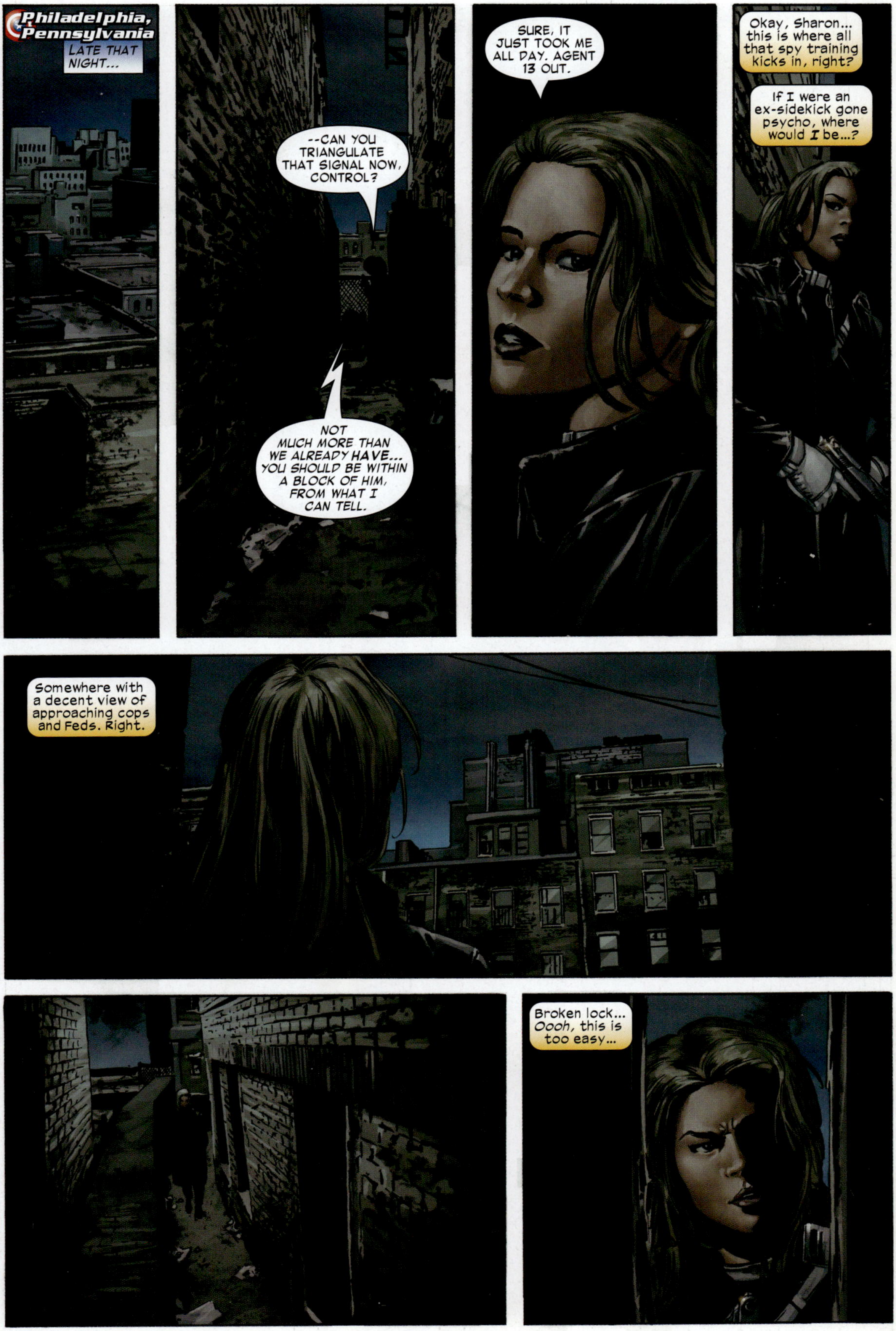
Philadelphia, Pennsylvania
LATE THAT NIGHT...
--CAN YOU TRIANGULATE THAT SIGNAL NOW, CONTROL?
NOT MUCH MORE THAN WE ALREADY HAVE... YOU SHOULD BE WITHIN A BLOCK OF HIM, FROM WHAT I CAN TELL.
SURE, IT JUST TOOK ME ALL DAY. AGENT 13 OUT.
Okay, Sharon... this is where all that spy training kicks in, right?
If I were an ex-sidekick gone psycho, where would I be...?
Somewhere with a decent view of approaching cops and Feds. Right.
Broken lock... Oooh, this is too easy...

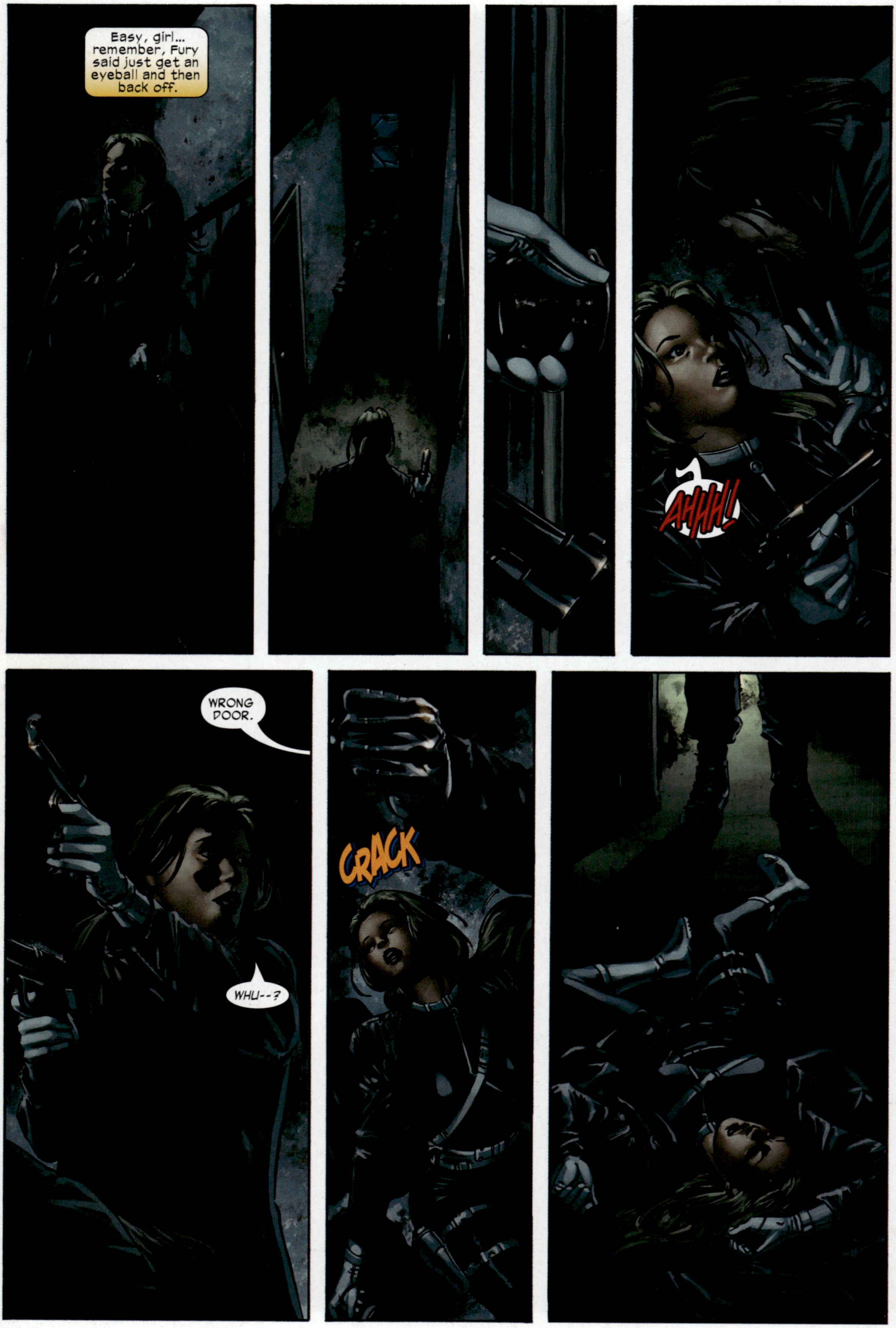
Easy, girl... remember, Fury said just get an eyeball and then back off.
AHHH!
WRONG DOOR.
WHU--?
CRACK

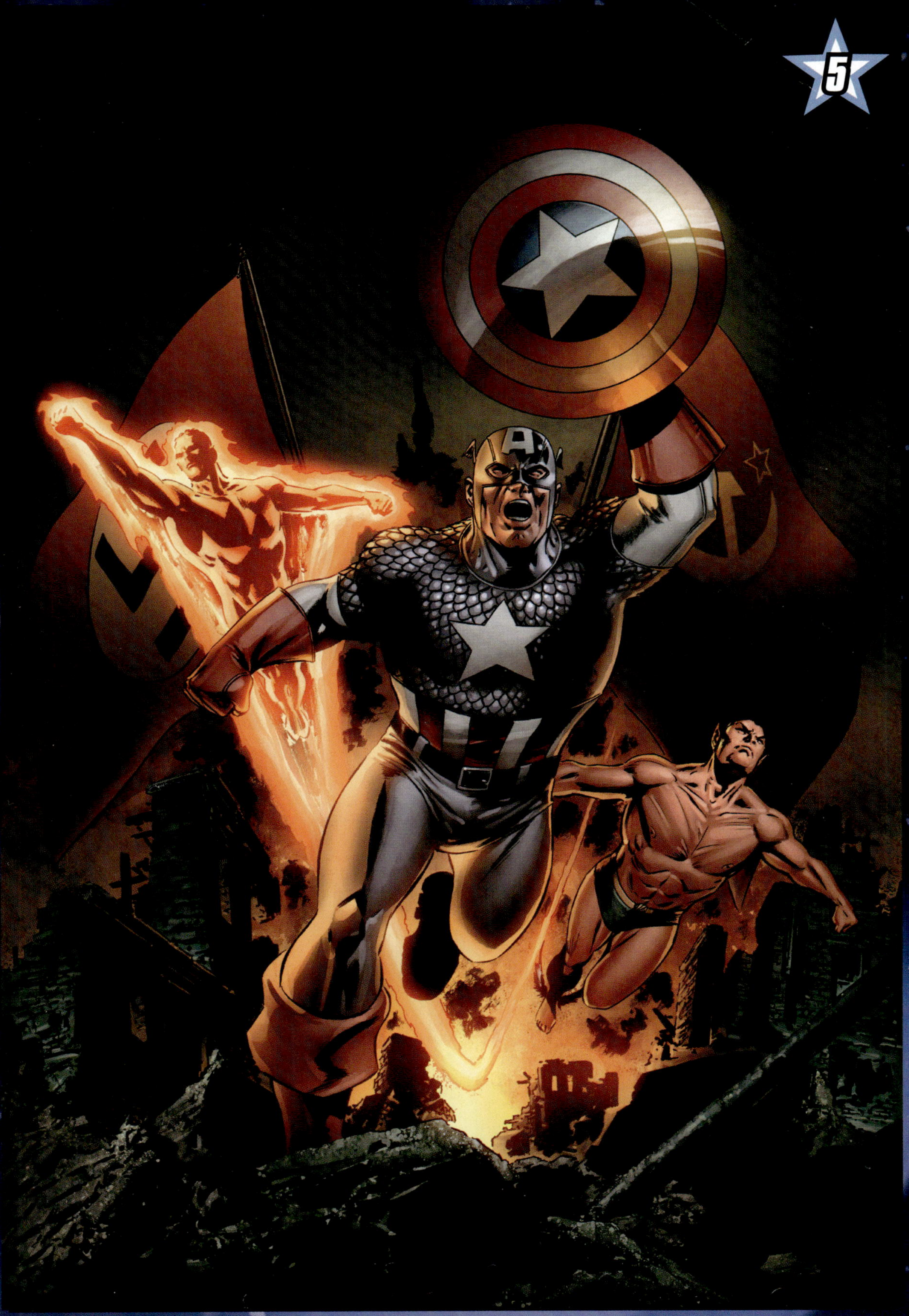
5

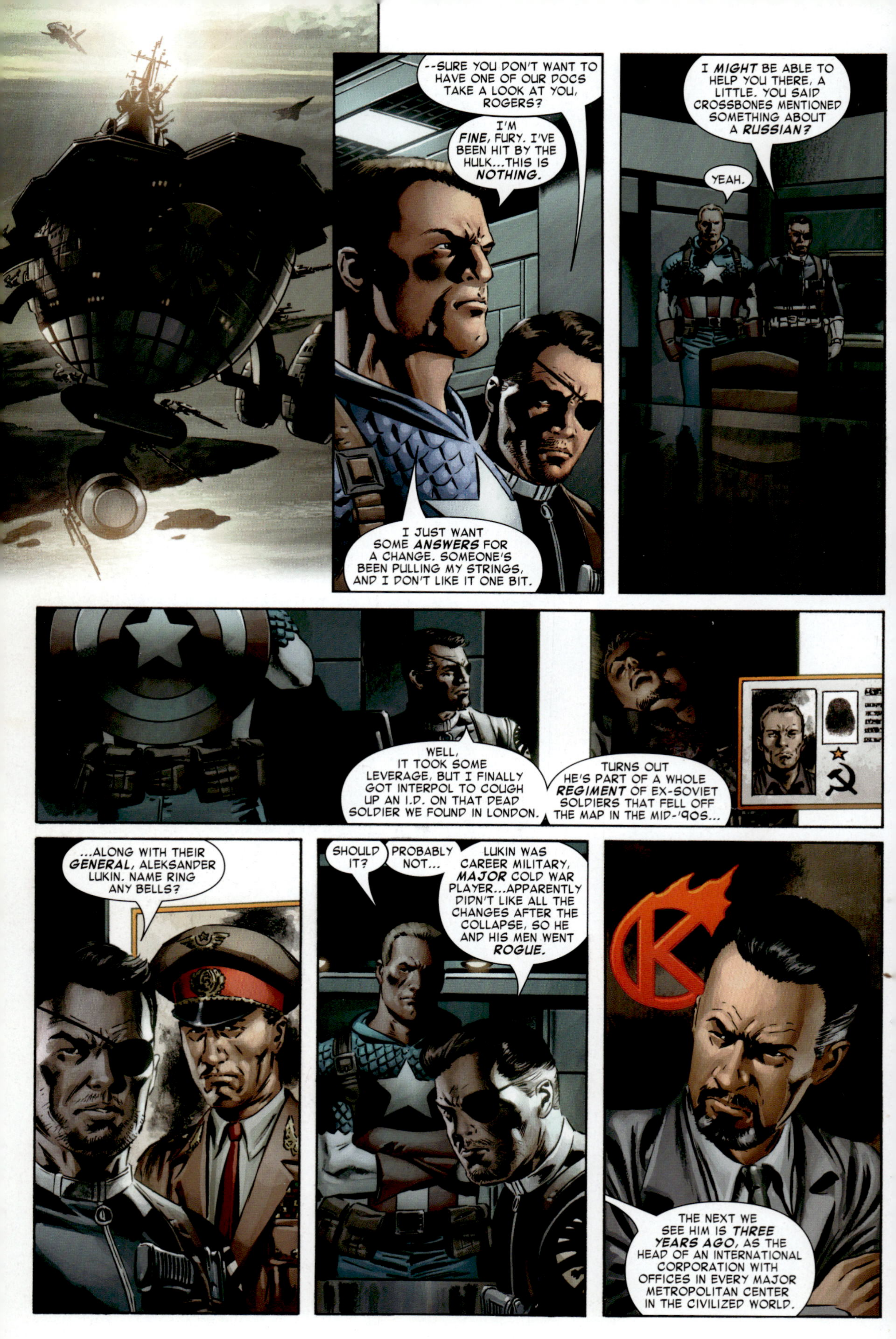
--SURE YOU DON'T WANT TO HAVE ONE OF OUR DOCS TAKE A LOOK AT YOU, ROGERS?
I'M FINE, FURY. I'VE BEEN HIT BY THE HULK...THIS IS NOTHING.
I JUST WANT SOME ANSWERS FOR A CHANGE. SOMEONE'S BEEN PULLING MY STRINGS, AND I DON'T LIKE IT ONE BIT.
I MIGHT BE ABLE TO HELP YOU THERE, A LITTLE. YOU SAID CROSSBONES MENTIONED SOMETHING ABOUT A RUSSIAN?
YEAH.
WELL, IT TOOK SOME LEVERAGE, BUT I FINALLY GOT INTERPOL TO COUGH UP AN I.D. ON THAT DEAD SOLDIER WE FOUND IN LONDON.
TURNS OUT HE'S PART OF A WHOLE REGIMENT OF EX-SOVIET SOLDIERS THAT FELL OFF THE MAP IN THE MID-'90S...
...ALONG WITH THEIR GENERAL, ALEKSANDER LUKIN. NAME RING ANY BELLS?
SHOULD IT?
PROBABLY NOT...
LUKIN WAS CAREER MILITARY, MAJOR COLD WAR PLAYER...APPARENTLY DIDN'T LIKE ALL THE CHANGES AFTER THE COLLAPSE, SO HE AND HIS MEN WENT ROGUE.
THE NEXT WE SEE HIM IS THREE YEARS AGO, AS THE HEAD OF AN INTERNATIONAL CORPORATION WITH OFFICES IN EVERY MAJOR METROPOLITAN CENTER IN THE CIVILIZED WORLD.

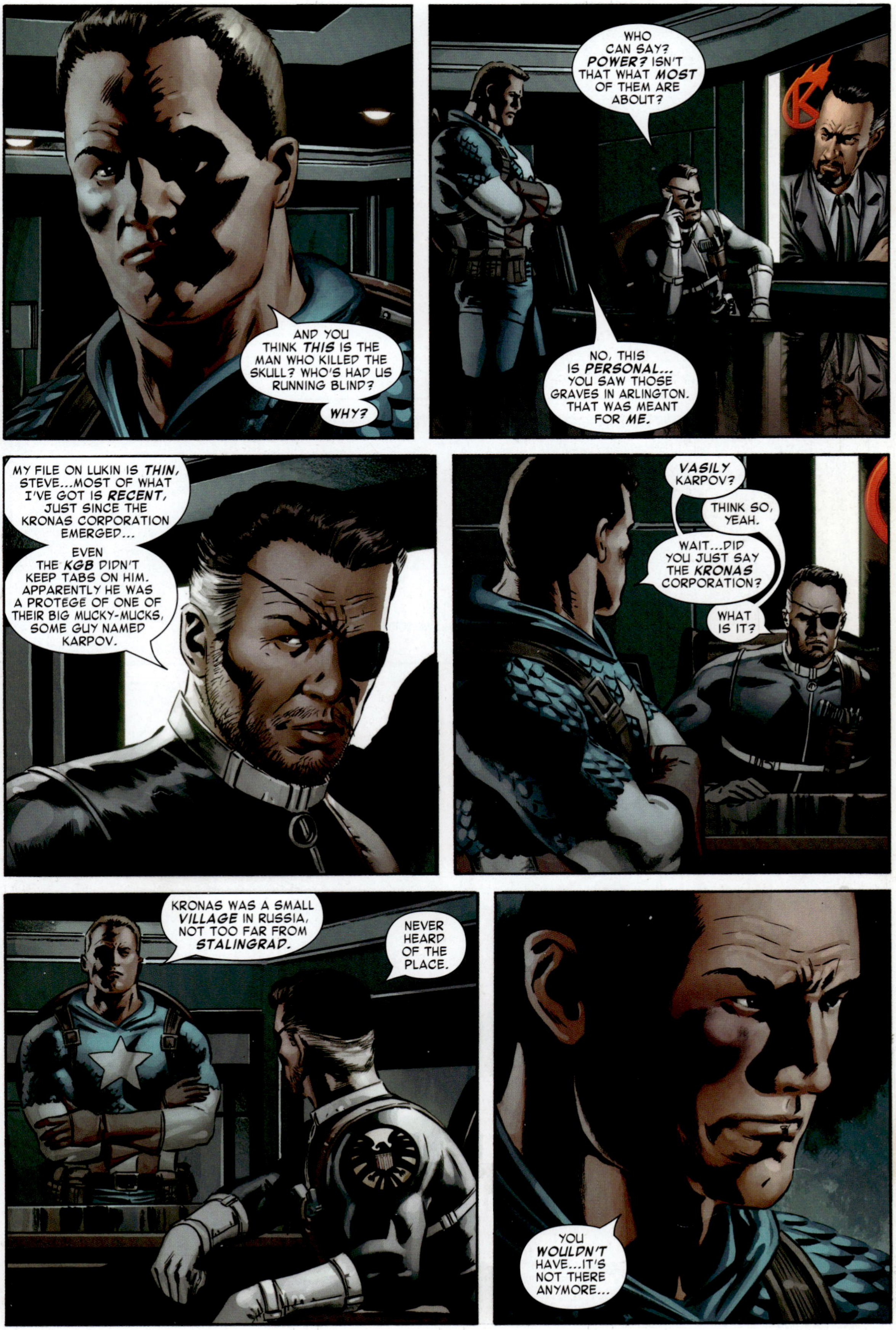
AND YOU THINK THIS IS THE MAN WHO KILLED THE SKULL? WHO'S HAD US RUNNING BLIND?
WHY?
WHO CAN SAY? POWER? ISN'T THAT WHAT MOST OF THEM ARE ABOUT?
NO, THIS IS PERSONAL... YOU SAW THOSE GRAVES IN ARLINGTON. THAT WAS MEANT FOR ME.
MY FILE ON LUKIN IS THIN, STEVE...MOST OF WHAT I'VE GOT IS RECENT, JUST SINCE THE KRONAS CORPORATION EMERGED...
EVEN THE KGB DIDN'T KEEP TABS ON HIM. APPARENTLY HE WAS A PROTEGE OF ONE OF THEIR BIG MUCKY-MUCKS, SOME GUY NAMED KARPOV.
VASILY KARPOV?
THINK SO, YEAH.
WAIT...DID YOU JUST SAY THE KRONAS CORPORATION?
WHAT IS IT?
KRONAS WAS A SMALL VILLAGE IN RUSSIA, NOT TOO FAR FROM STALINGRAD.
NEVER HEARD OF THE PLACE.
YOU WOULDN'T HAVE...IT'S NOT THERE ANYMORE...

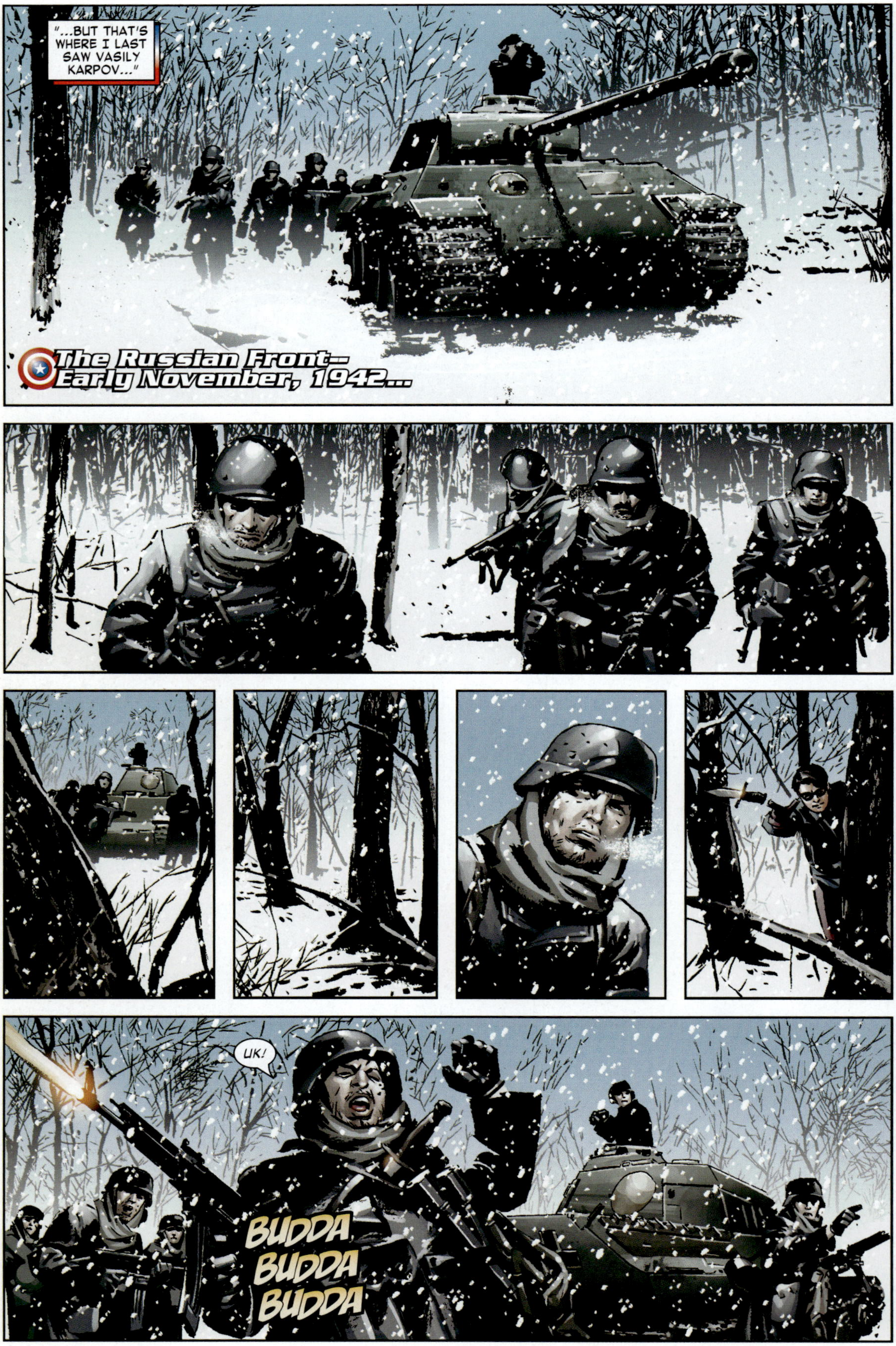
"...BUT THAT'S WHERE I LAST SAW VASILY KARPOV..."
The Russian Front--
Early November, 1942...
UK!
BUDDA
BUDDA
BUDDA

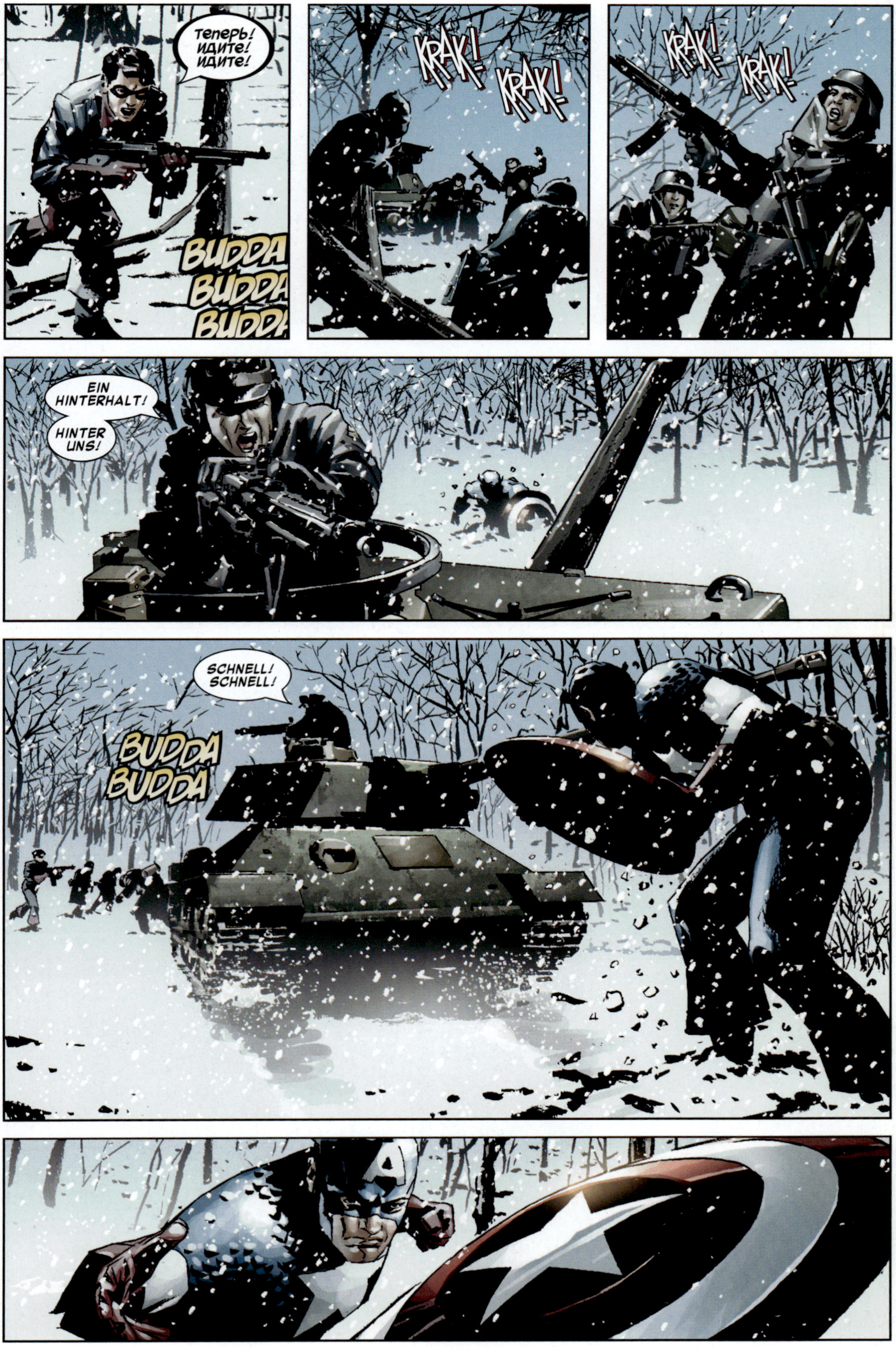
ТЕПЕРЬ! ИДИТЕ! ИДИТЕ!
BUDDA BUDDA BUDDA
KRAK! KRAK!
KRAK! KRAK!
EIN HINTERHALT!
HINTER UNS!
SCHNELL! SCHNELL!
BUDDA BUDDA

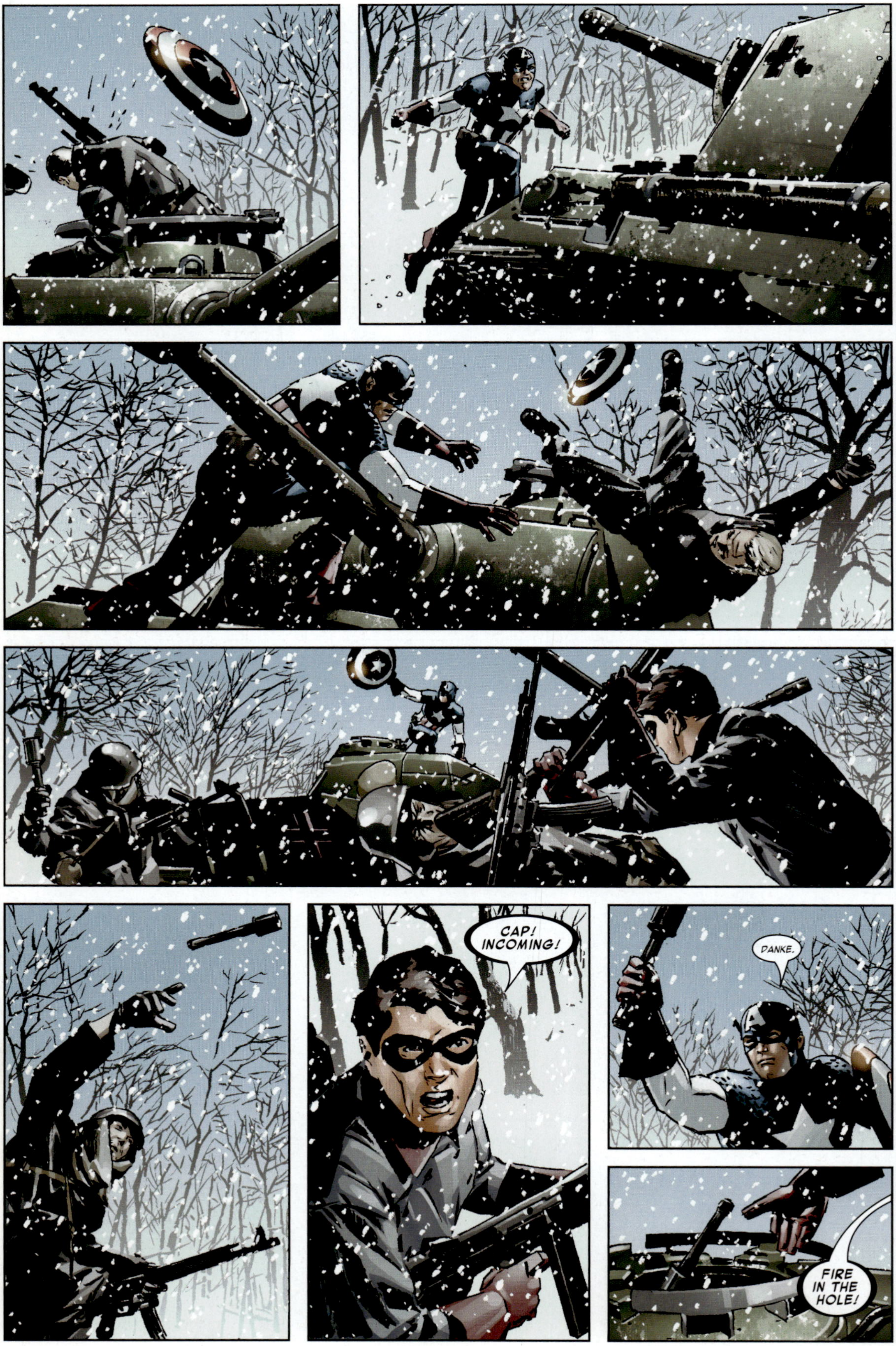
CAP! INCOMING!
DANKE.
FIRE IN THE HOLE!

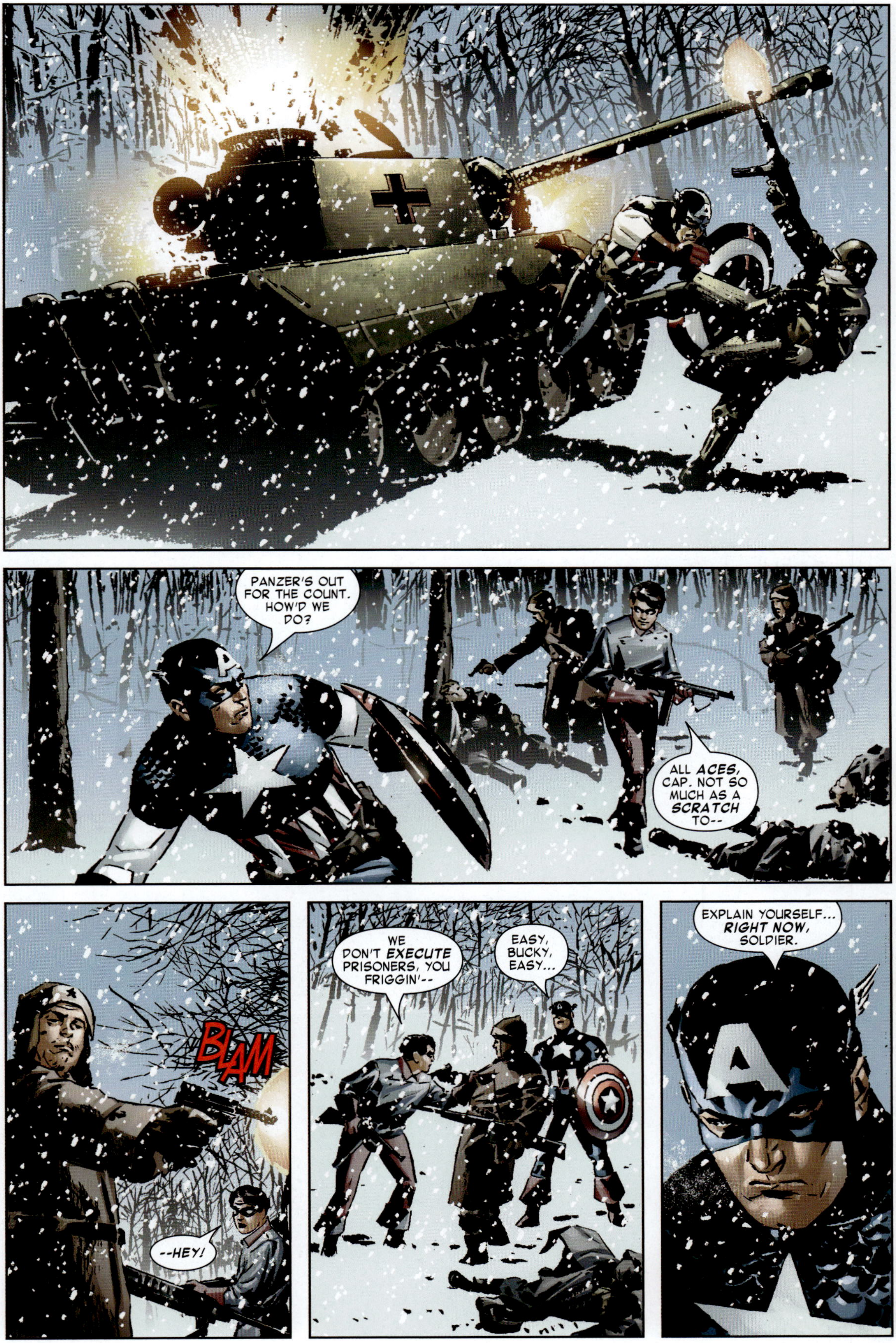
PANZER'S OUT FOR THE COUNT. HOW'D WE DO?
ALL ACES, CAP. NOT SO MUCH AS A SCRATCH TO--
BLAM
--HEY!
WE DON'T EXECUTE PRISONERS, YOU FRIGGIN'--
EASY, BUCKY, EASY...
EXPLAIN YOURSELF... RIGHT NOW, SOLDIER.

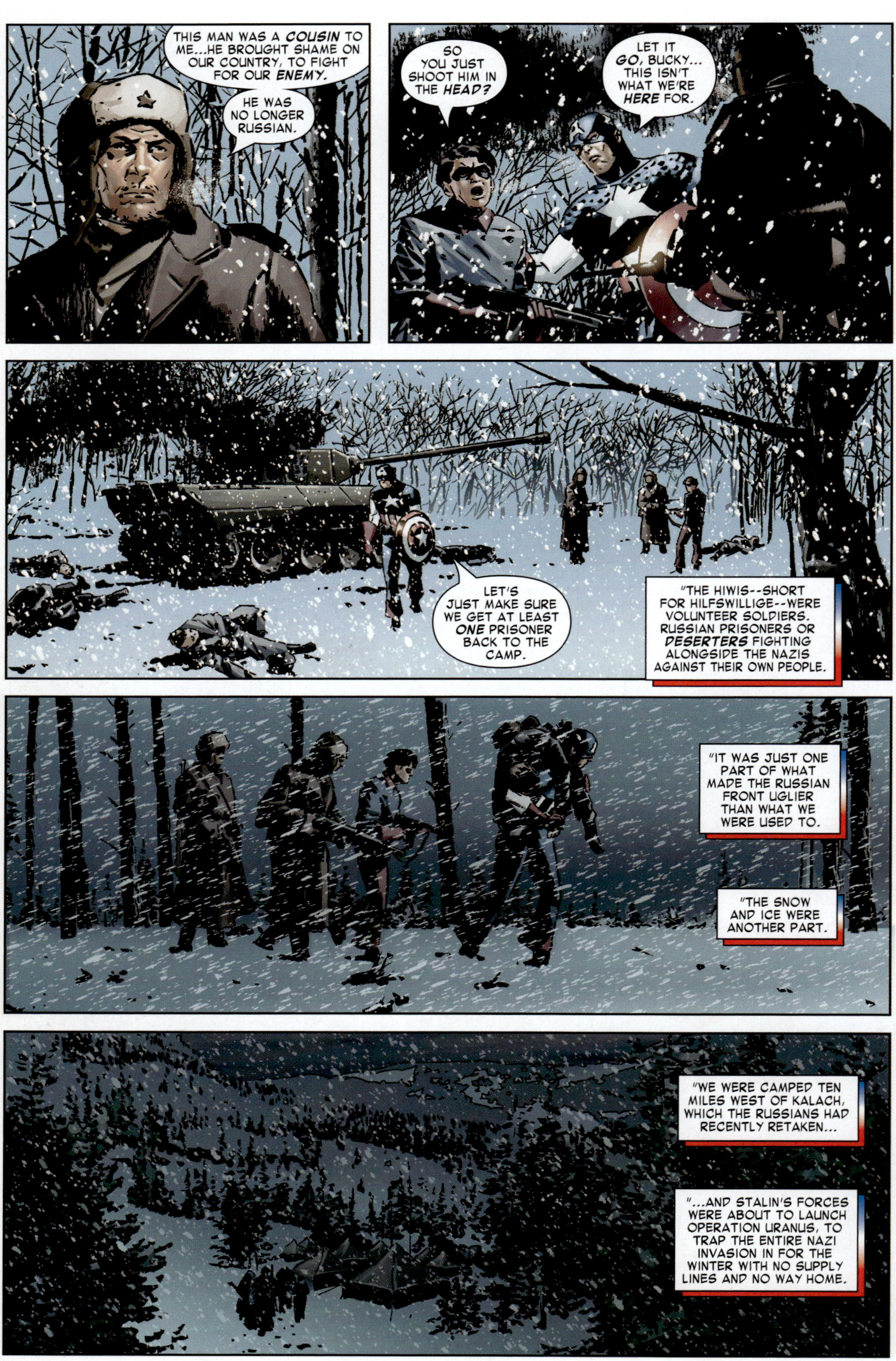

THIS MAN WAS A COUSIN TO ME...HE BROUGHT SHAME ON OUR COUNTRY, TO FIGHT FOR OUR ENEMY.
HE WAS NO LONGER RUSSIAN.
SO YOU JUST SHOOT HIM IN THE HEAD?
LET IT GO, BUCKY... THIS ISN'T WHAT WE'RE HERE FOR.
LET'S JUST MAKE SURE WE GET AT LEAST ONE PRISONER BACK TO THE CAMP.
"THE HIWIS--SHORT FOR HILFSWILLIGE--WERE VOLUNTEER SOLDIERS. RUSSIAN PRISONERS OR DESERTERS FIGHTING ALONGSIDE THE NAZIS AGAINST THEIR OWN PEOPLE.
"IT WAS JUST ONE PART OF WHAT MADE THE RUSSIAN FRONT UGLIER THAN WHAT WE WERE USED TO.
"THE SNOW AND ICE WERE ANOTHER PART.
"WE WERE CAMPED TEN MILES WEST OF KALACH, WHICH THE RUSSIANS HAD RECENTLY RETAKEN...
"...AND STALIN'S FORCES WERE ABOUT TO LAUNCH OPERATION URANUS, TO TRAP THE ENTIRE NAZI INVASION IN FOR THE WINTER WITH NO SUPPLY LINES AND NO WAY HOME.

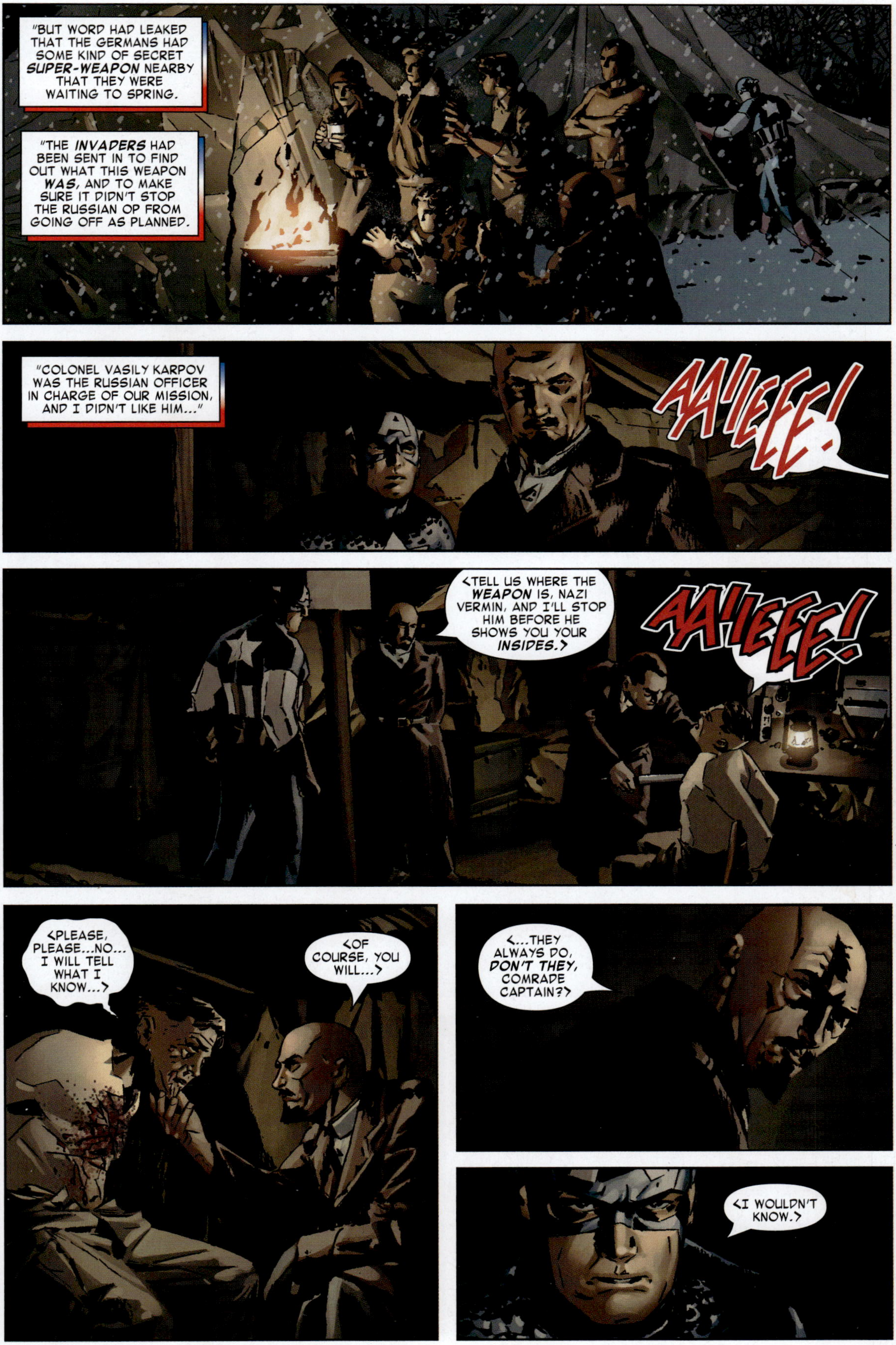
"BUT WORD HAD LEAKED THAT THE GERMANS HAD SOME KIND OF SECRET SUPER-WEAPON NEARBY THAT THEY WERE WAITING TO SPRING.
"THE INVADERS HAD BEEN SENT IN TO FIND OUT WHAT THIS WEAPON WAS, AND TO MAKE SURE IT DIDN'T STOP THE RUSSIAN OP FROM GOING OFF AS PLANNED.
"COLONEL VASILY KARPOV WAS THE RUSSIAN OFFICER IN CHARGE OF OUR MISSION, AND I DIDN'T LIKE HIM..."
AAIIEEE!
<TELL US WHERE THE WEAPON IS, NAZI VERMIN, AND I'LL STOP HIM BEFORE HE SHOWS YOU YOUR INSIDES.>
AAIIEEE!
<PLEASE, PLEASE...NO... I WILL TELL WHAT I KNOW...>
<OF COURSE, YOU WILL...>
<...THEY ALWAYS DO, DON'T THEY, COMRADE CAPTAIN?>
<I WOULDN'T KNOW.>

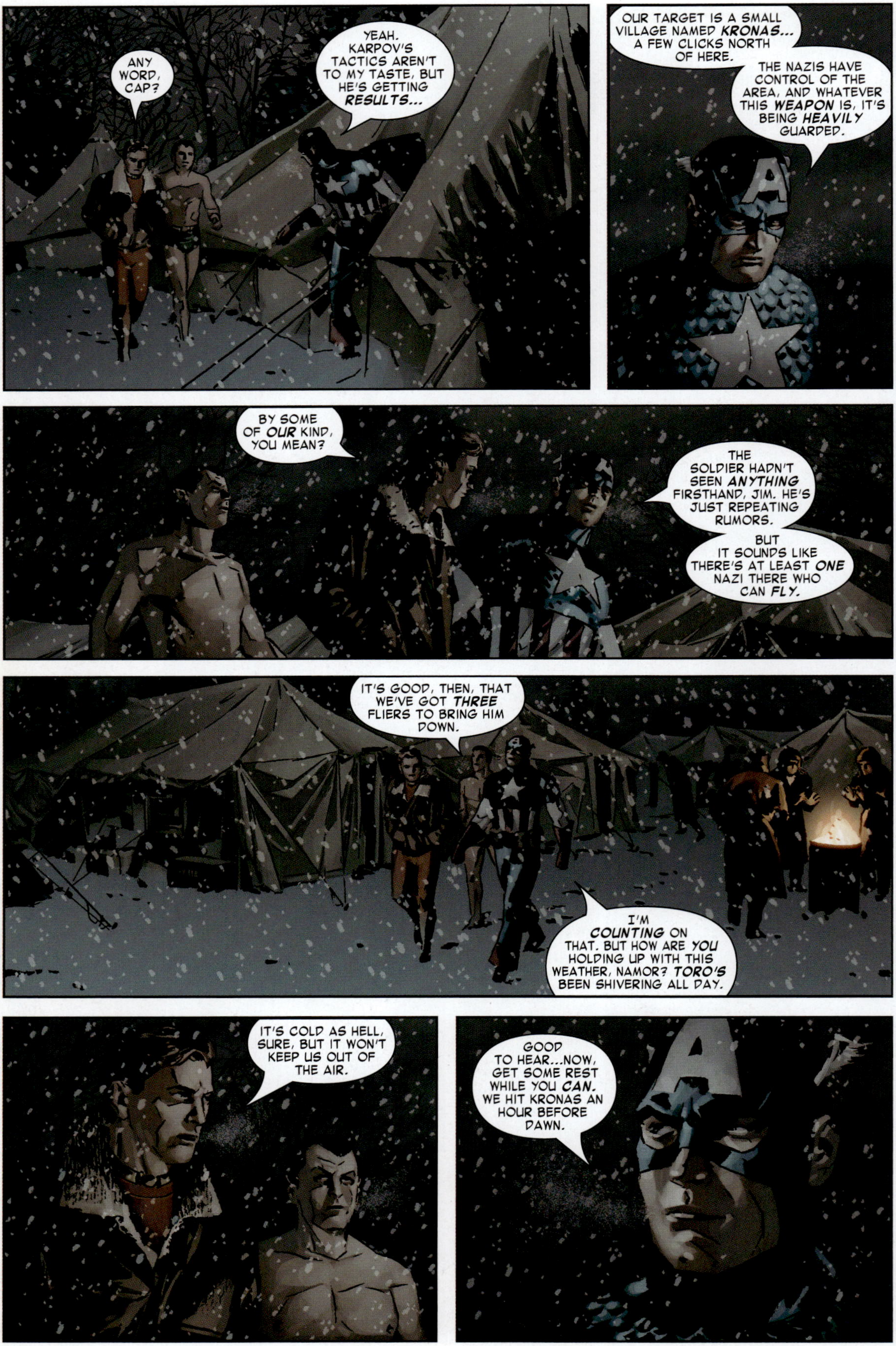
ANY WORD, CAP?
YEAH. KARPOV'S TACTICS AREN'T TO MY TASTE, BUT HE'S GETTING RESULTS...
OUR TARGET IS A SMALL VILLAGE NAMED KRONAS... A FEW CLICKS NORTH OF HERE.
THE NAZIS HAVE CONTROL OF THE AREA, AND WHATEVER THIS WEAPON IS, IT'S BEING HEAVILY GUARDED.
BY SOME OF OUR KIND, YOU MEAN?
THE SOLDIER HADN'T SEEN ANYTHING FIRSTHAND, JIM. HE'S JUST REPEATING RUMORS.
BUT IT SOUNDS LIKE THERE'S AT LEAST ONE NAZI THERE WHO CAN FLY.
IT'S GOOD, THEN, THAT WE'VE GOT THREE FLIERS TO BRING HIM DOWN.
I'M COUNTING ON THAT. BUT HOW ARE YOU HOLDING UP WITH THIS WEATHER, NAMOR? TORO'S BEEN SHIVERING ALL DAY.
IT'S COLD AS HELL, SURE, BUT IT WON'T KEEP US OUT OF THE AIR.
GOOD TO HEAR...NOW, GET SOME REST WHILE YOU CAN. WE HIT KRONAS AN HOUR BEFORE DAWN.

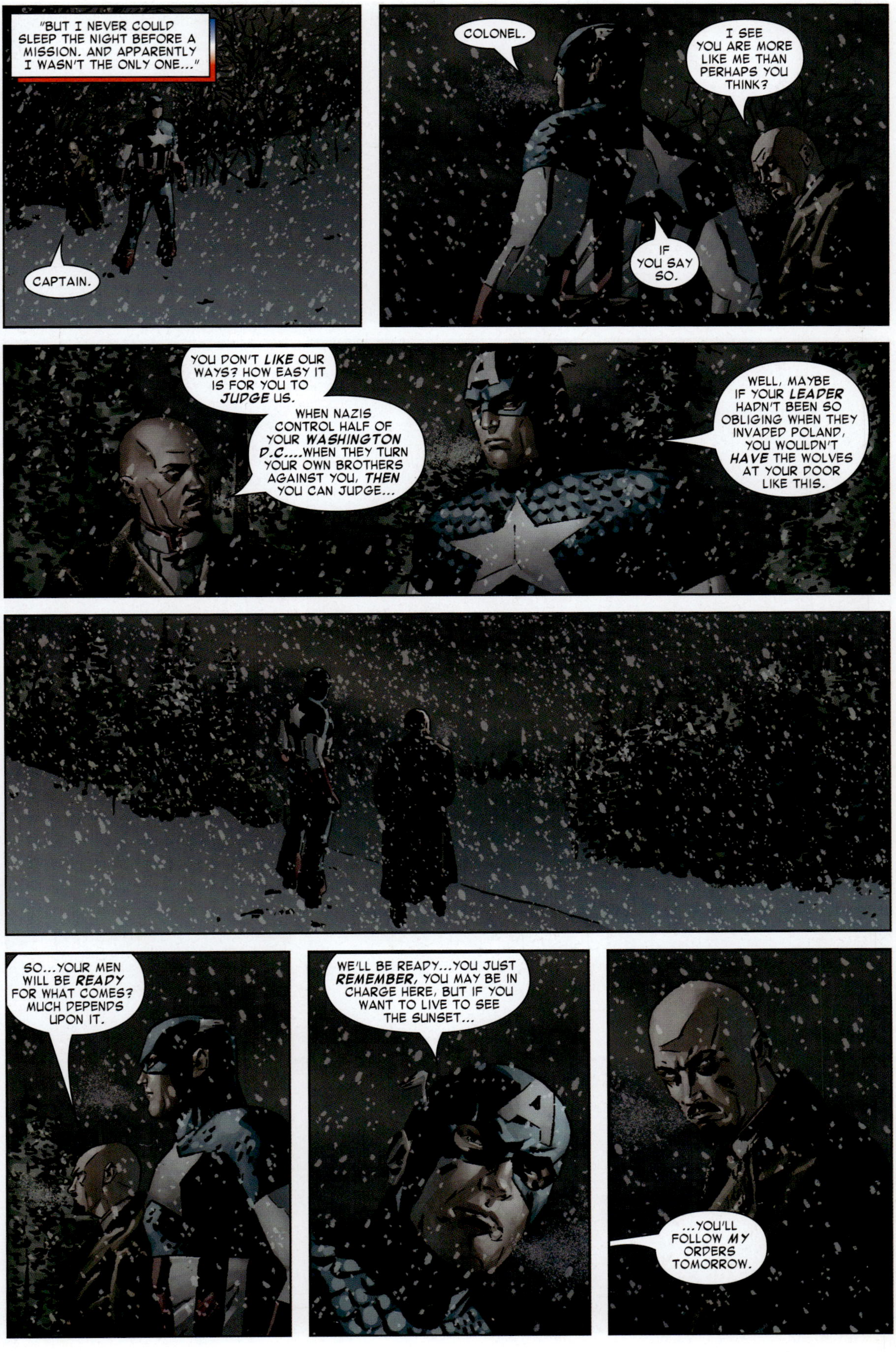
"BUT I NEVER COULD SLEEP THE NIGHT BEFORE A MISSION. AND APPARENTLY I WASN'T THE ONLY ONE..."
CAPTAIN.
COLONEL.
I SEE YOU ARE MORE LIKE ME THAN PERHAPS YOU THINK?
IF YOU SAY SO.
YOU DON'T LIKE OUR WAYS? HOW EASY IT IS FOR YOU TO JUDGE US.
WHEN NAZIS CONTROL HALF OF YOUR WASHINGTON D.C.... WHEN THEY TURN YOUR OWN BROTHERS AGAINST YOU, THEN YOU CAN JUDGE...
WELL, MAYBE IF YOUR LEADER HADN'T BEEN SO OBLIGING WHEN THEY INVADED POLAND, YOU WOULDN'T HAVE THE WOLVES AT YOUR DOOR LIKE THIS.
SO...YOUR MEN WILL BE READY FOR WHAT COMES? MUCH DEPENDS UPON IT.
WE'LL BE READY...YOU JUST REMEMBER, YOU MAY BE IN CHARGE HERE, BUT IF YOU WANT TO LIVE TO SEE THE SUNSET...
...YOU'LL FOLLOW MY ORDERS TOMORROW.

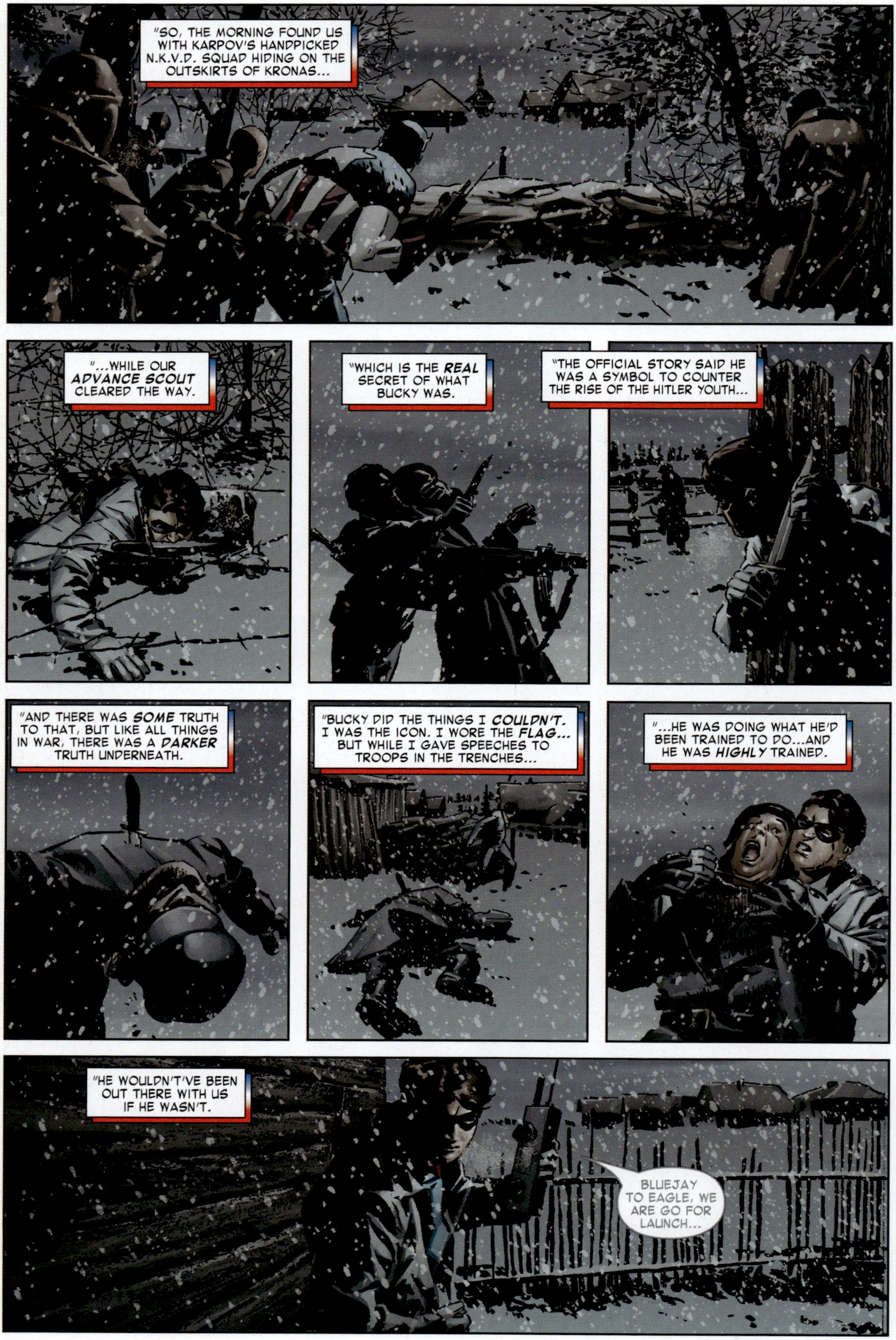
"SO, THE MORNING FOUND US WITH KARPOV'S HANDPICKED N.K.V.D. SQUAD HIDING ON THE OUTSKIRTS OF KRONAS...
"...WHILE OUR ADVANCE SCOUT CLEARED THE WAY.
"WHICH IS THE REAL SECRET OF WHAT BUCKY WAS.
"THE OFFICIAL STORY SAID HE WAS A SYMBOL TO COUNTER THE RISE OF THE HITLER YOUTH...
"AND THERE WAS SOME TRUTH TO THAT, BUT LIKE ALL THINGS IN WAR, THERE WAS A DARKER TRUTH UNDERNEATH.
"BUCKY DID THE THINGS I COULDN'T. I WAS THE ICON. I WORE THE FLAG... BUT WHILE I GAVE SPEECHES TO TROOPS IN THE TRENCHES...
"...HE WAS DOING WHAT HE'D BEEN TRAINED TO DO...AND HE WAS HIGHLY TRAINED.
"HE WOULDN'T'VE BEEN OUT THERE WITH US IF HE WASN'T.
BLUEJAY TO EAGLE, WE ARE GO FOR LAUNCH...

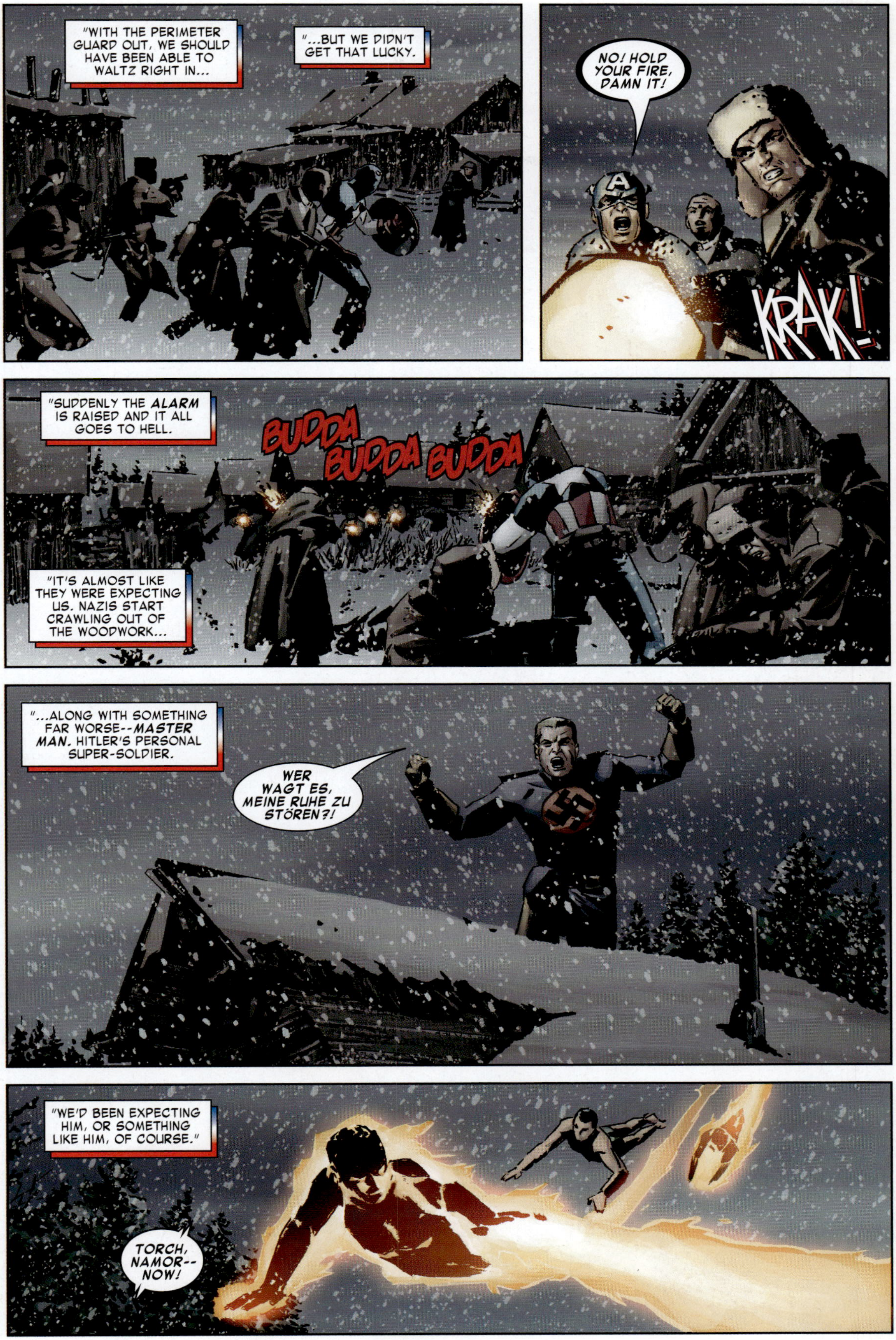
"WITH THE PERIMETER GUARD OUT, WE SHOULD HAVE BEEN ABLE TO WALTZ RIGHT IN...
"...BUT WE DIDN'T GET THAT LUCKY.
NO! HOLD YOUR FIRE, DAMN IT!
KRAK!
"SUDDENLY THE ALARM IS RAISED AND IT ALL GOES TO HELL.
BUDDA BUDDA BUDDA
"IT'S ALMOST LIKE THEY WERE EXPECTING US. NAZIS START CRAWLING OUT OF THE WOODWORK...
"...ALONG WITH SOMETHING FAR WORSE--MASTER MAN. HITLER'S PERSONAL SUPER-SOLDIER.
WER WAGT ES, MEINE RUHE ZU STÖREN?!
"WE'D BEEN EXPECTING HIM, OR SOMETHING LIKE HIM, OF COURSE."
TORCH, NAMOR-- NOW!

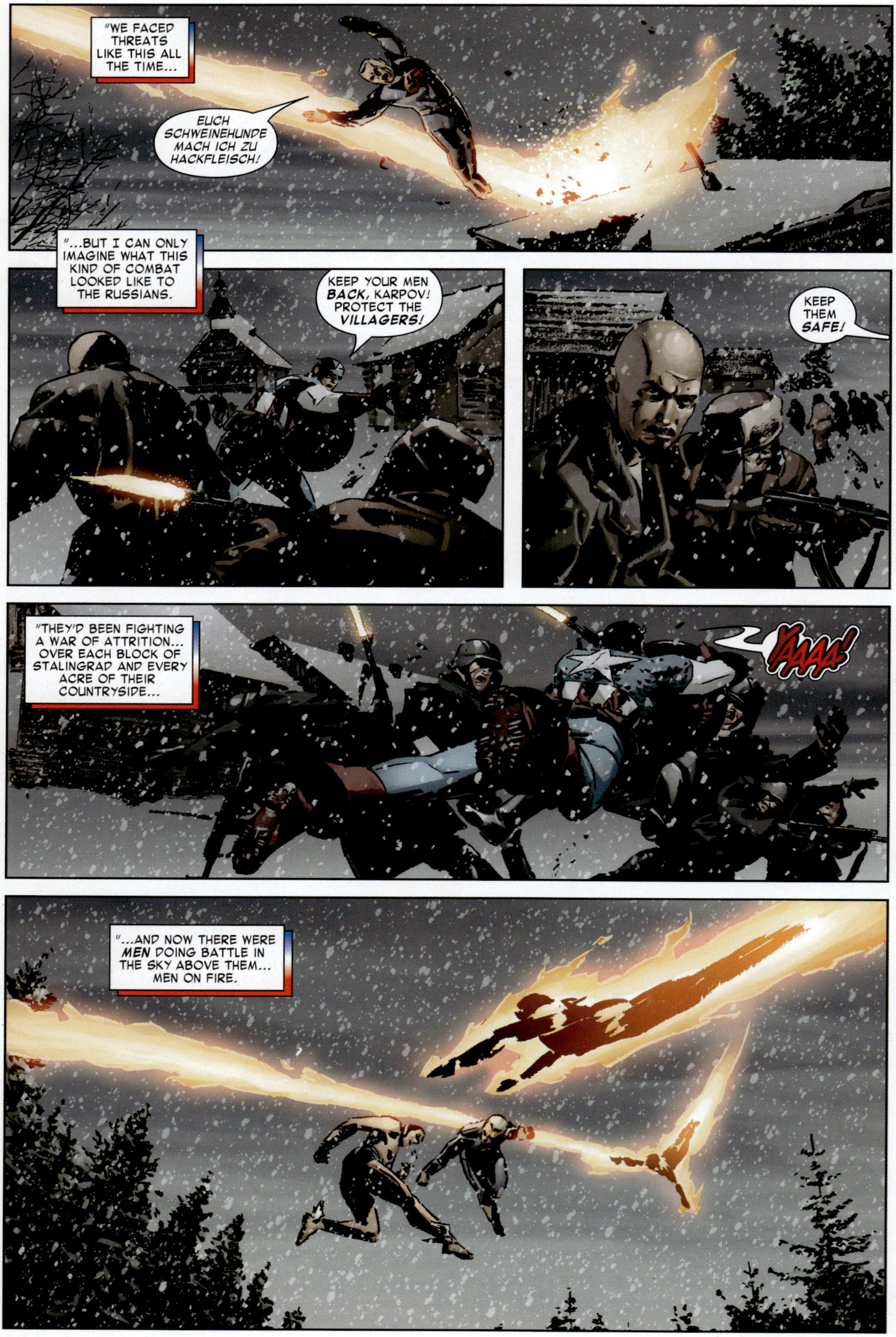
"WE FACED THREATS LIKE THIS ALL THE TIME...
EUCH SCHWEINEHUNDE MACH ICH ZU HACKFLEISCH!
"...BUT I CAN ONLY IMAGINE WHAT THIS KIND OF COMBAT LOOKED LIKE TO THE RUSSIANS.
KEEP YOUR MEN BACK, KARPOV! PROTECT THE VILLAGERS!
KEEP THEM SAFE!
"THEY'D BEEN FIGHTING A WAR OF ATTRITION... OVER EACH BLOCK OF STALINGRAD AND EVERY ACRE OF THEIR COUNTRYSIDE...
YAAAA!
"...AND NOW THERE WERE MEN DOING BATTLE IN THE SKY ABOVE THEM... MEN ON FIRE.

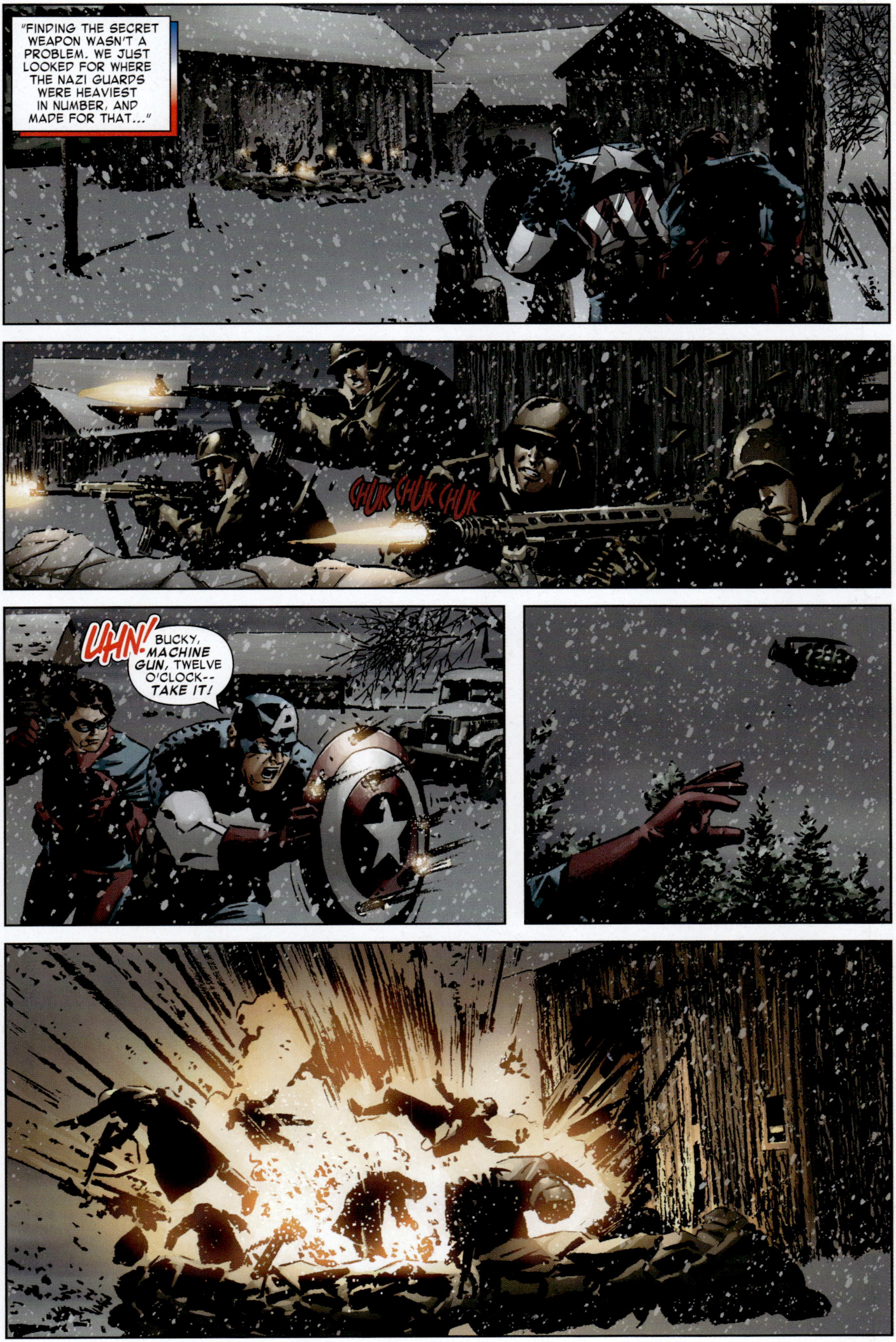
"FINDING THE SECRET WEAPON WASN'T A PROBLEM. WE JUST LOOKED FOR WHERE THE NAZI GUARDS WERE HEAVIEST IN NUMBER, AND MADE FOR THAT..."
CHUK CHUK CHUK
UHN!
BUCKY, MACHINE GUN, TWELVE O'CLOCK-- TAKE IT!

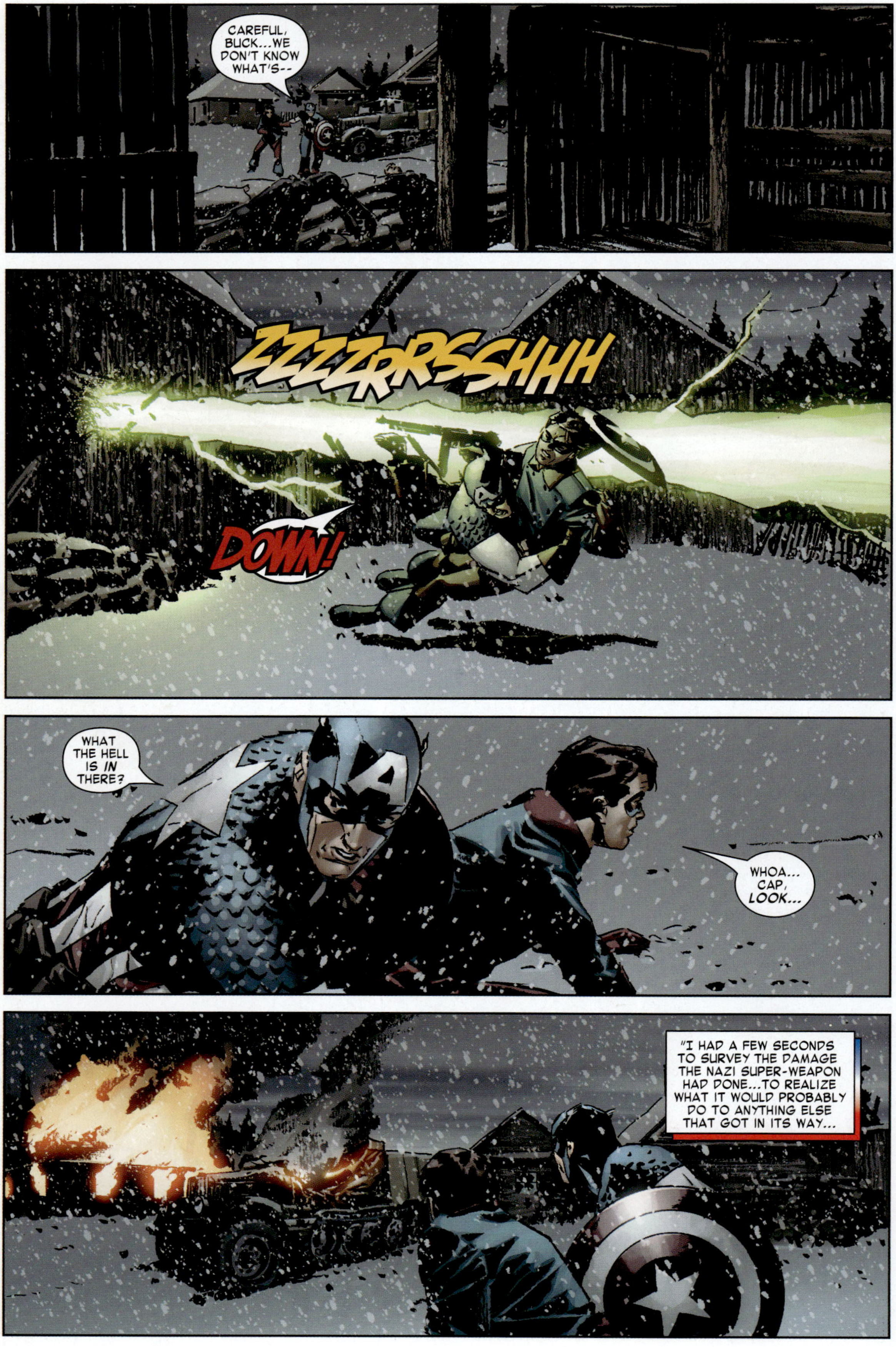
CAREFUL, BUCK...WE DON'T KNOW WHAT'S--
ZZZZRRSSHHH
DOWN!
WHAT THE HELL IS *IN* THERE?
WHOA... CAP, *LOOK*...
"I HAD A FEW SECONDS TO SURVEY THE DAMAGE THE NAZI SUPER-WEAPON HAD DONE...TO REALIZE WHAT IT WOULD PROBABLY DO TO ANYTHING ELSE THAT GOT IN ITS WAY...

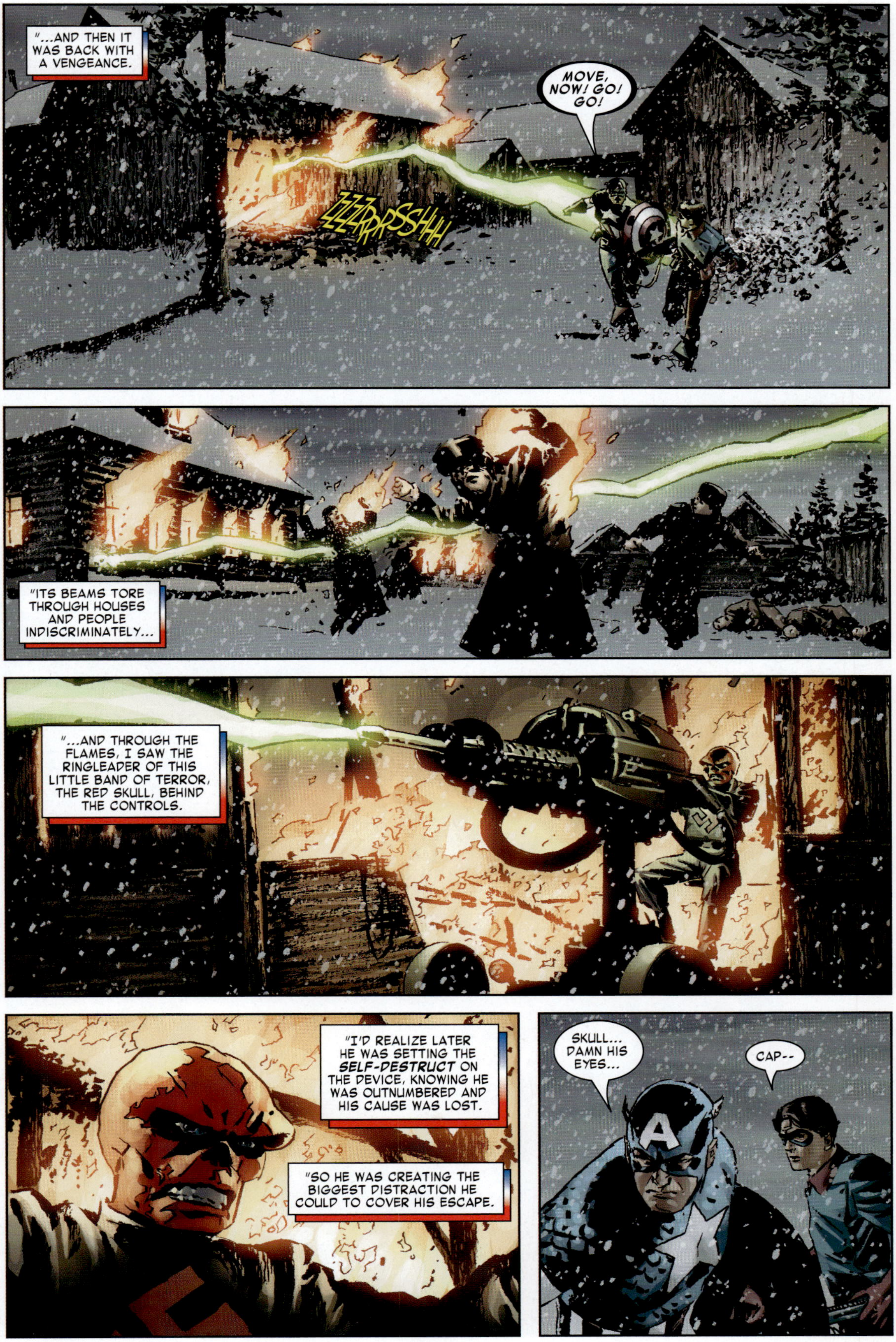
"...AND THEN IT WAS BACK WITH A VENGEANCE.
MOVE, NOW! GO! GO!
ZZZZRRRSSHHH
"ITS BEAMS TORE THROUGH HOUSES AND PEOPLE INDISCRIMINATELY...
"...AND THROUGH THE FLAMES, I SAW THE RINGLEADER OF THIS LITTLE BAND OF TERROR, THE RED SKULL, BEHIND THE CONTROLS.
"I'D REALIZE LATER HE WAS SETTING THE ***SELF-DESTRUCT*** ON THE DEVICE, KNOWING HE WAS OUTNUMBERED AND HIS CAUSE WAS LOST.
"SO HE WAS CREATING THE BIGGEST DISTRACTION HE COULD TO COVER HIS ESCAPE.
SKULL... DAMN HIS EYES...
CAP--

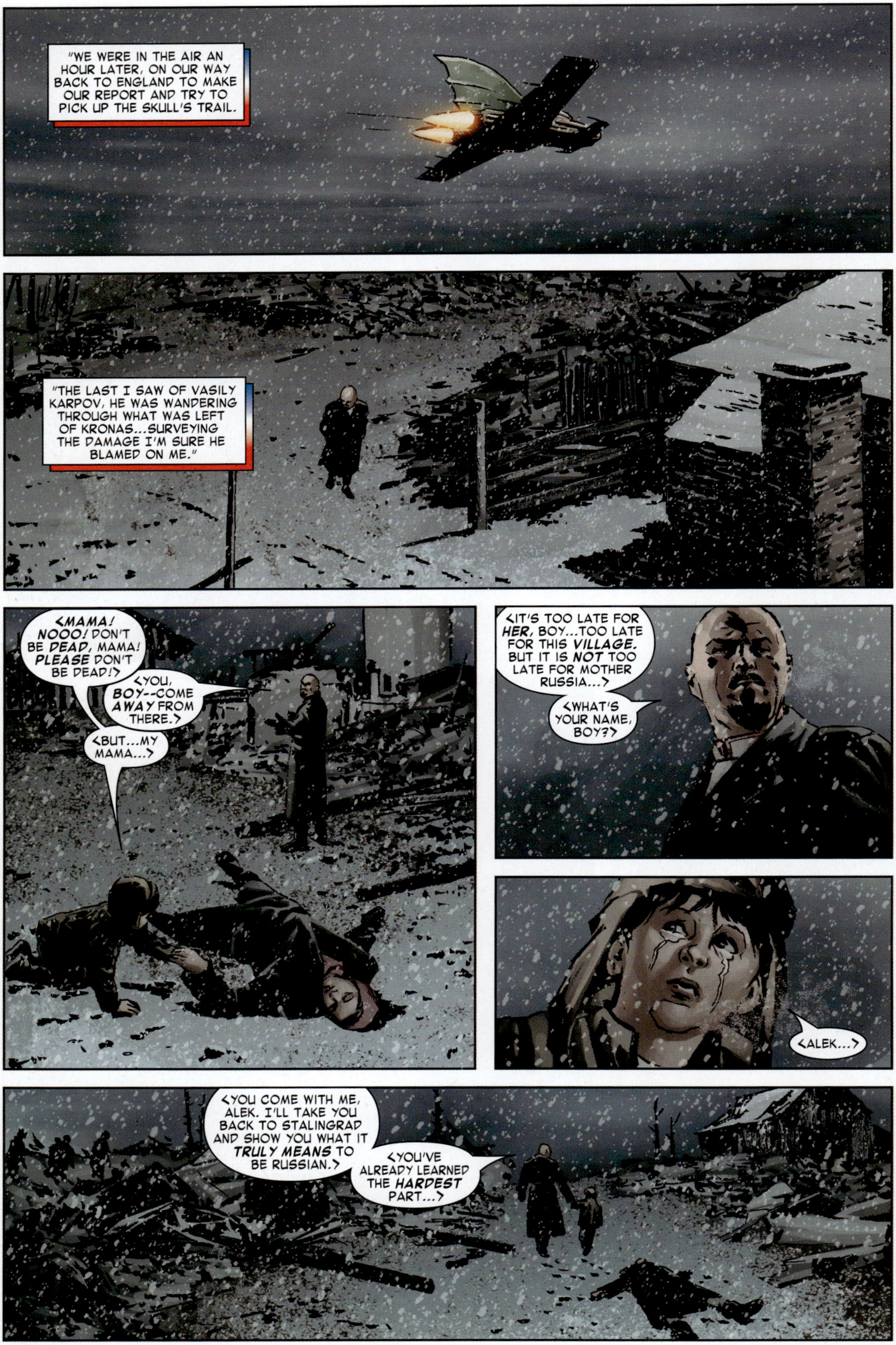
"WE WERE IN THE AIR AN HOUR LATER, ON OUR WAY BACK TO ENGLAND TO MAKE OUR REPORT AND TRY TO PICK UP THE SKULL'S TRAIL.
"THE LAST I SAW OF VASILY KARPOV, HE WAS WANDERING THROUGH WHAT WAS LEFT OF KRONAS...SURVEYING THE DAMAGE I'M SURE HE BLAMED ON ME."
<MAMA! NOOO! DON'T BE DEAD, MAMA! PLEASE DON'T BE DEAD!>
<YOU, BOY--COME AWAY FROM THERE.>
<BUT...MY MAMA...>
<IT'S TOO LATE FOR HER, BOY...TOO LATE FOR THIS VILLAGE. BUT IT IS NOT TOO LATE FOR MOTHER RUSSIA...>
<WHAT'S YOUR NAME, BOY?>
<ALEK...>
<YOU COME WITH ME, ALEK. I'LL TAKE YOU BACK TO STALINGRAD AND SHOW YOU WHAT IT TRULY MEANS TO BE RUSSIAN.>
<YOU'VE ALREADY LEARNED THE HARDEST PART...>

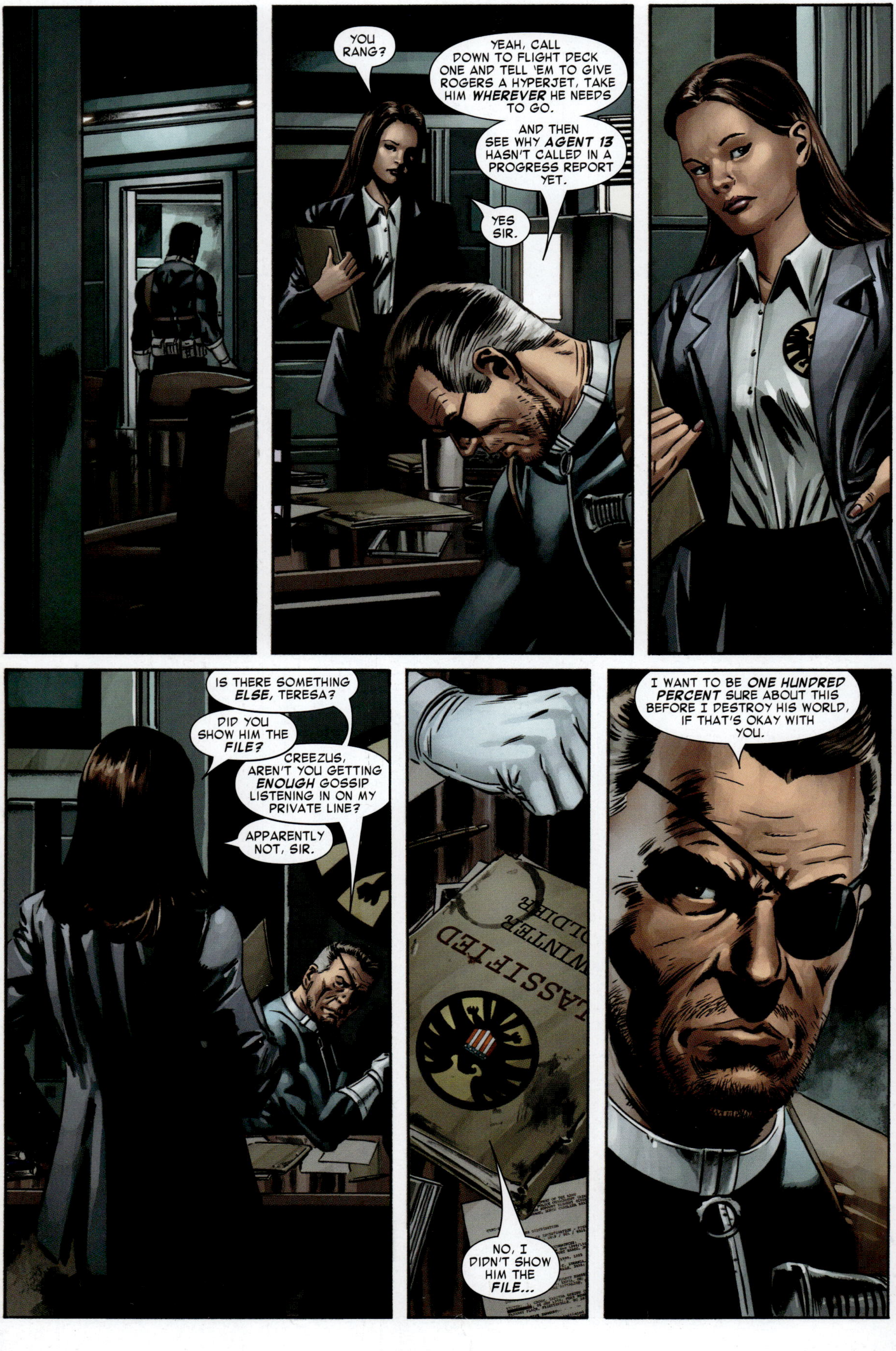
YOU RANG?
YEAH, CALL DOWN TO FLIGHT DECK ONE AND TELL 'EM TO GIVE ROGERS A HYPERJET, TAKE HIM WHEREVER HE NEEDS TO GO.
AND THEN SEE WHY AGENT 13 HASN'T CALLED IN A PROGRESS REPORT YET.
YES SIR.
IS THERE SOMETHING ELSE, TERESA?
DID YOU SHOW HIM THE FILE?
CREEZUS, AREN'T YOU GETTING ENOUGH GOSSIP LISTENING IN ON MY PRIVATE LINE?
APPARENTLY NOT, SIR.
CLASSIFIED
WINTER SOLDIER
NO, I DIDN'T SHOW HIM THE FILE...
I WANT TO BE ONE HUNDRED PERCENT SURE ABOUT THIS BEFORE I DESTROY HIS WORLD, IF THAT'S OKAY WITH YOU.

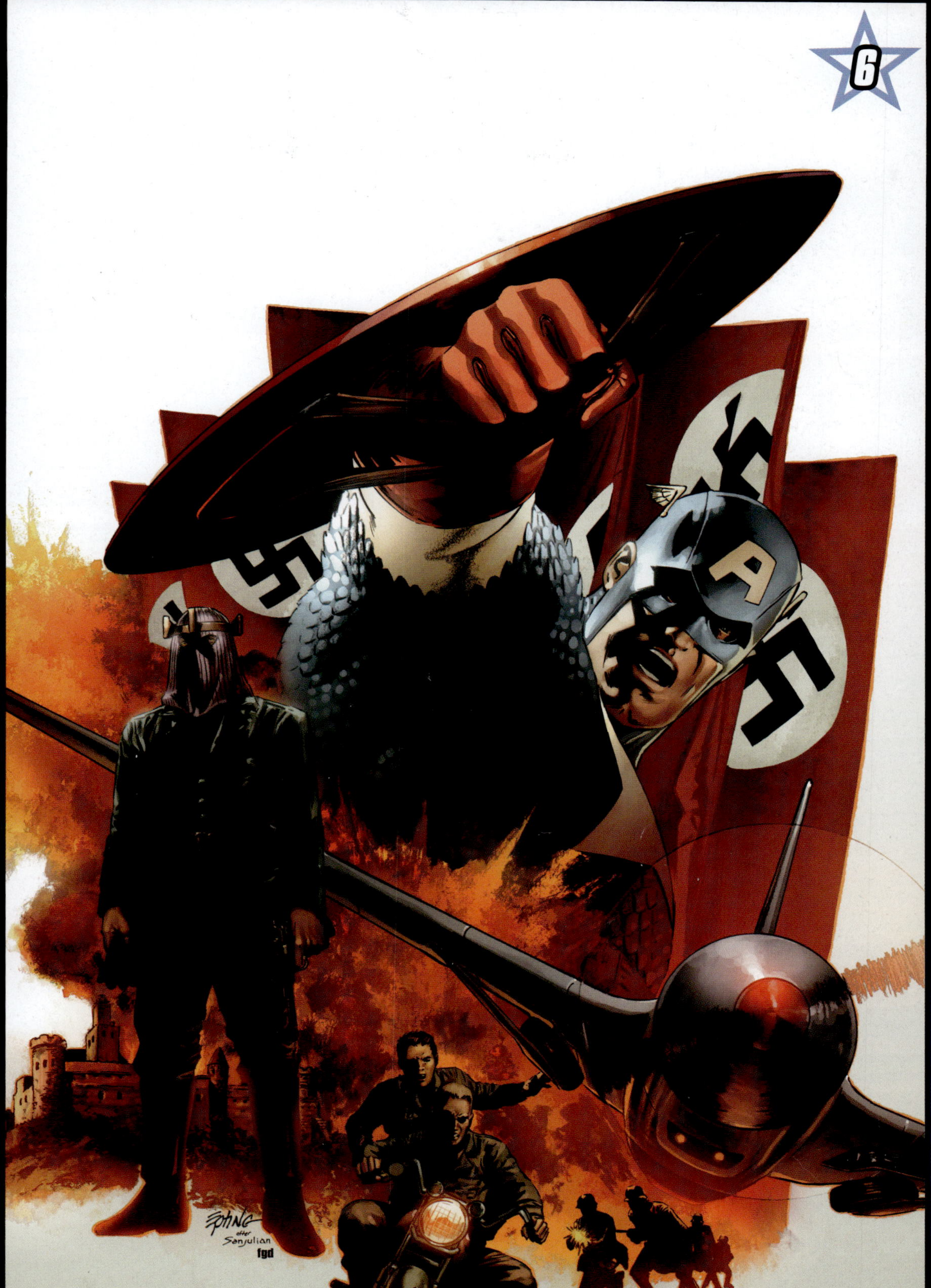
6
Epting
after
Sanjulian
fgd

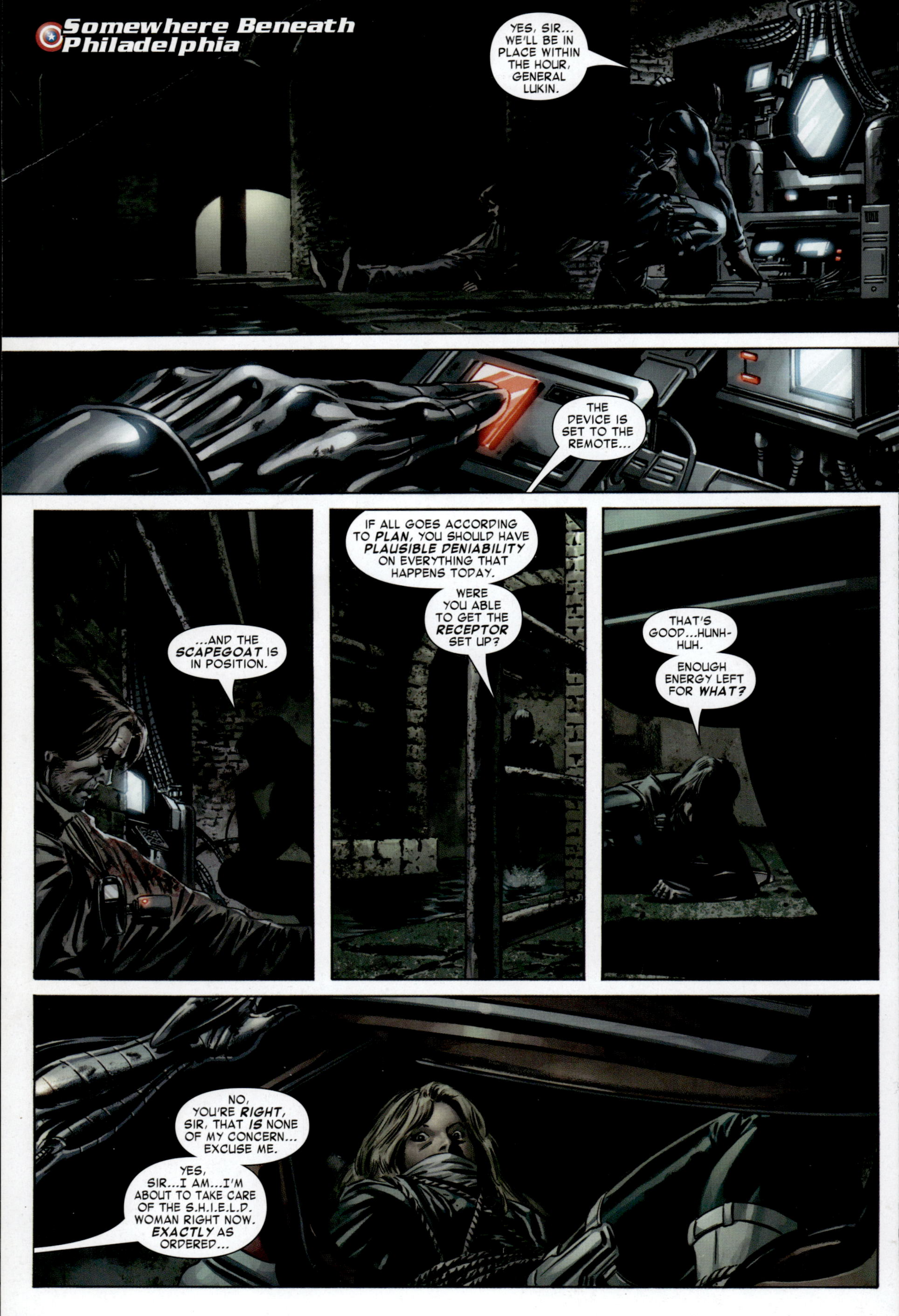
Somewhere Beneath Philadelphia
YES, SIR... WE'LL BE IN PLACE WITHIN THE HOUR, GENERAL LUKIN.
THE DEVICE IS SET TO THE REMOTE...
...AND THE SCAPEGOAT IS IN POSITION.
IF ALL GOES ACCORDING TO PLAN, YOU SHOULD HAVE PLAUSIBLE DENIABILITY ON EVERYTHING THAT HAPPENS TODAY.
WERE YOU ABLE TO GET THE RECEPTOR SET UP?
THAT'S GOOD...HUNH-HUH.
ENOUGH ENERGY LEFT FOR WHAT?
NO, YOU'RE RIGHT, SIR, THAT IS NONE OF MY CONCERN... EXCUSE ME.
YES, SIR...I AM...I'M ABOUT TO TAKE CARE OF THE S.H.I.E.L.D. WOMAN RIGHT NOW. EXACTLY AS ORDERED...

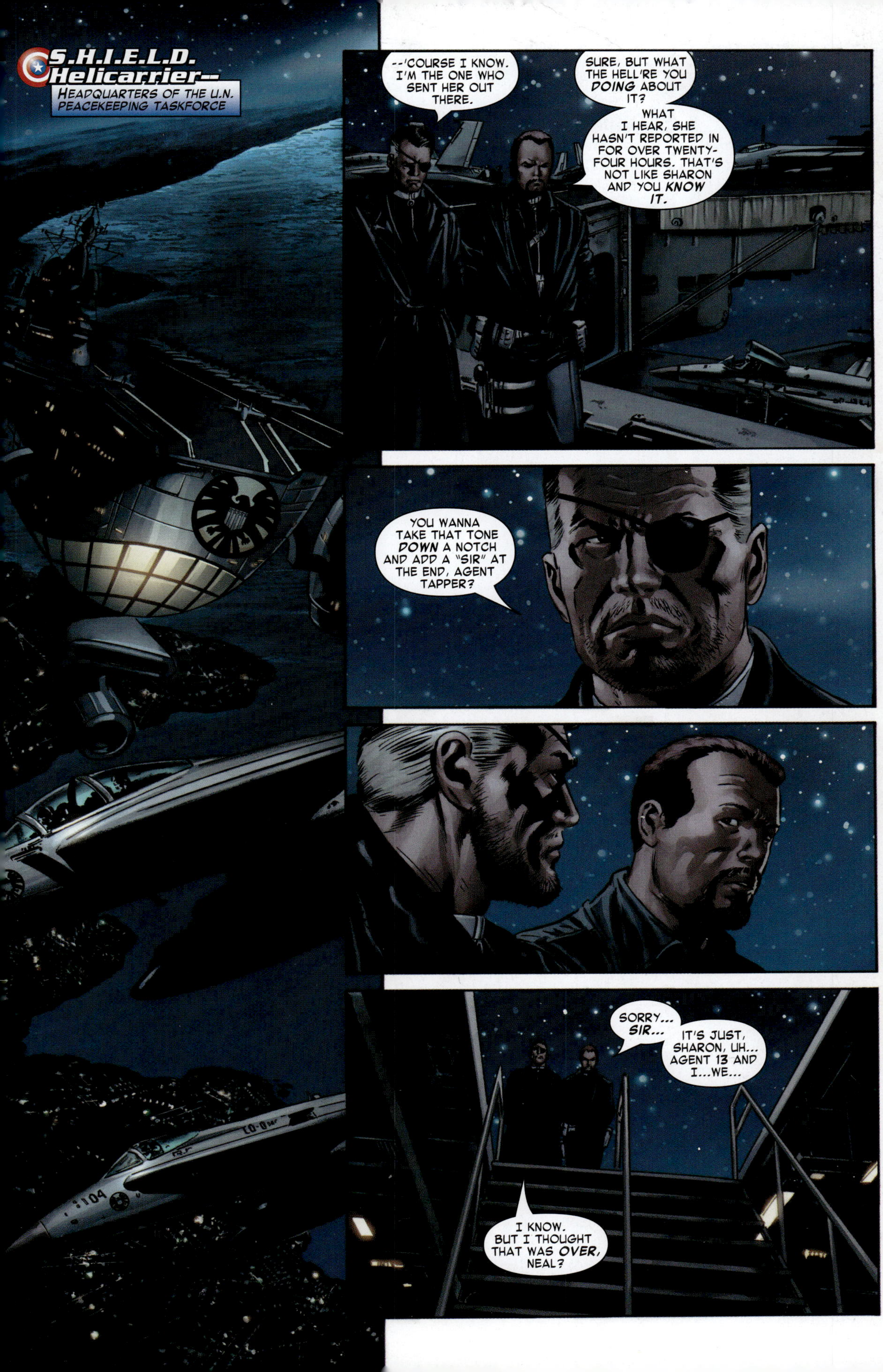
S.H.I.E.L.D. Helicarrier--
HEADQUARTERS OF THE U.N. PEACEKEEPING TASKFORCE
--'COURSE I KNOW. I'M THE ONE WHO SENT HER OUT THERE.
SURE, BUT WHAT THE HELL'RE YOU DOING ABOUT IT?
WHAT I HEAR, SHE HASN'T REPORTED IN FOR OVER TWENTY-FOUR HOURS. THAT'S NOT LIKE SHARON AND YOU KNOW IT.
YOU WANNA TAKE THAT TONE DOWN A NOTCH AND ADD A "SIR" AT THE END, AGENT TAPPER?
SORRY... SIR...
IT'S JUST, SHARON, UH... AGENT 13 AND I...WE...
I KNOW. BUT I THOUGHT THAT WAS OVER, NEAL?

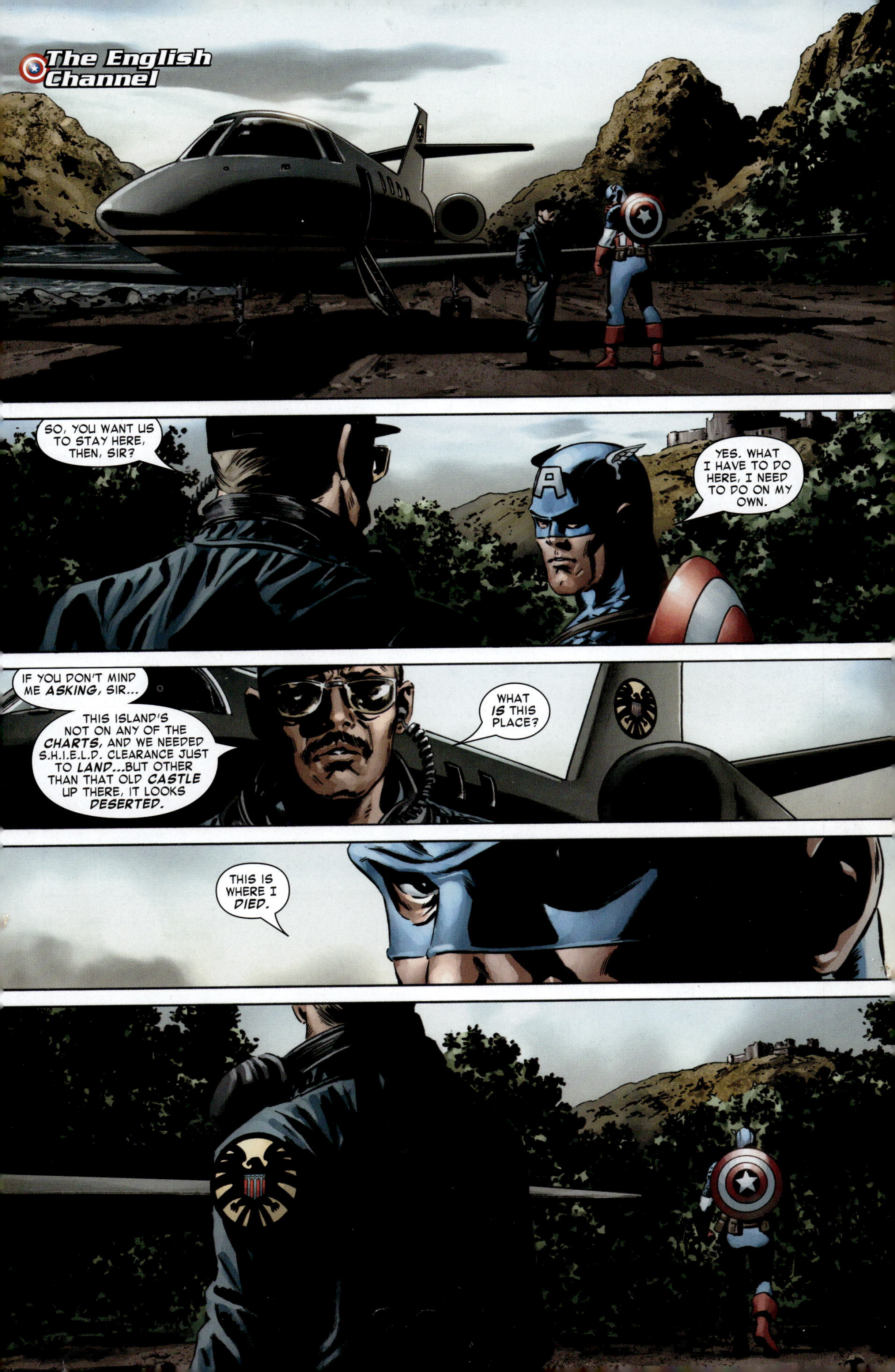
The English Channel
SO, YOU WANT US TO STAY HERE, THEN, SIR?
YES. WHAT I HAVE TO DO HERE, I NEED TO DO ON MY OWN.
IF YOU DON'T MIND ME ASKING, SIR...
THIS ISLAND'S NOT ON ANY OF THE CHARTS, AND WE NEEDED S.H.I.E.L.D. CLEARANCE JUST TO LAND...BUT OTHER THAN THAT OLD CASTLE UP THERE, IT LOOKS DESERTED.
WHAT IS THIS PLACE?
THIS IS WHERE I DIED.

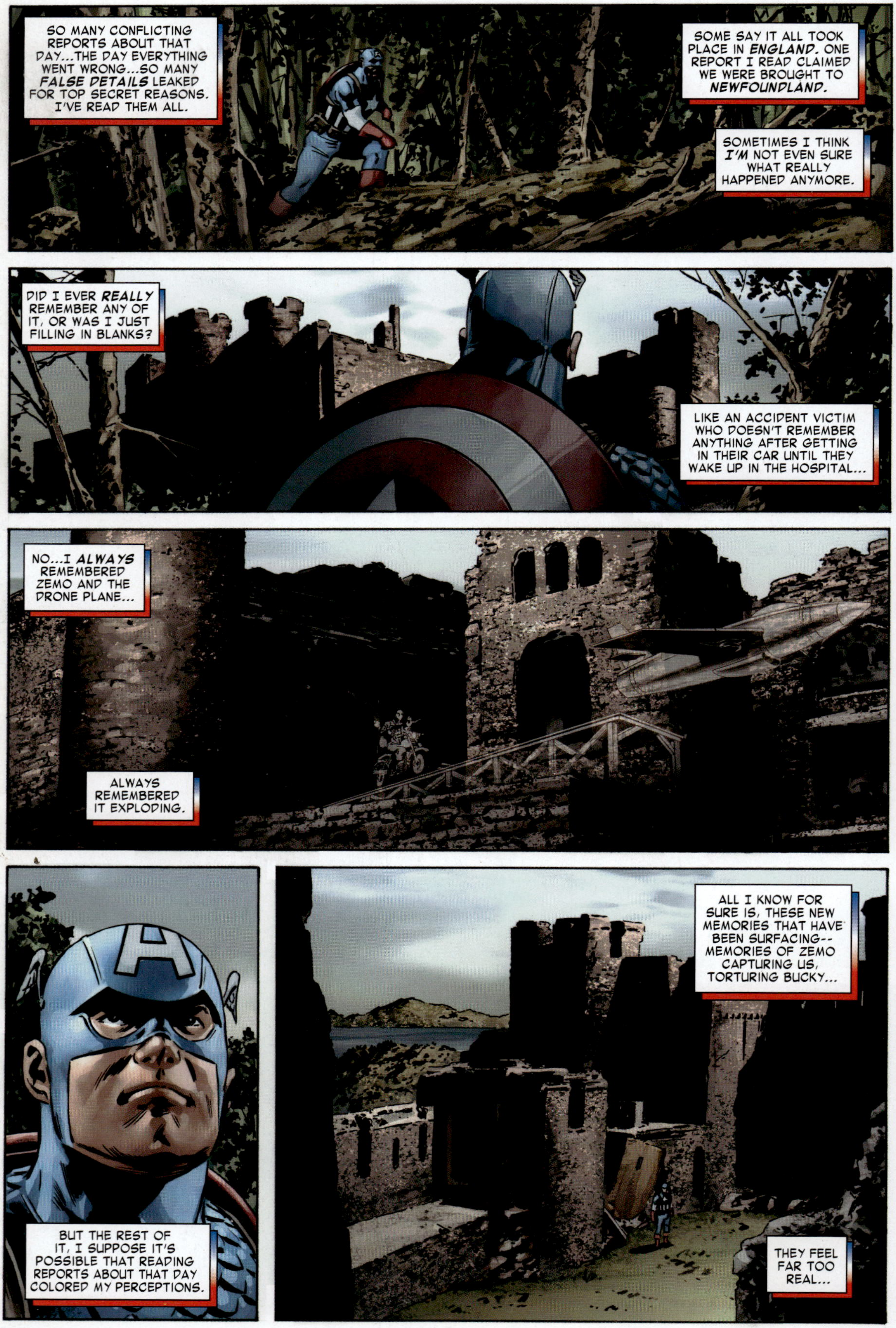
SO MANY CONFLICTING REPORTS ABOUT THAT DAY...THE DAY EVERYTHING WENT WRONG...SO MANY **FALSE DETAILS** LEAKED FOR TOP SECRET REASONS. I'VE READ THEM ALL.
SOME SAY IT ALL TOOK PLACE IN **ENGLAND.** ONE REPORT I READ CLAIMED WE WERE BROUGHT TO **NEWFOUNDLAND.**
SOMETIMES I THINK **I'M** NOT EVEN SURE WHAT REALLY HAPPENED ANYMORE.
DID I EVER **REALLY** REMEMBER ANY OF IT, OR WAS I JUST FILLING IN BLANKS?
LIKE AN ACCIDENT VICTIM WHO DOESN'T REMEMBER ANYTHING AFTER GETTING IN THEIR CAR UNTIL THEY WAKE UP IN THE HOSPITAL...
NO...I **ALWAYS** REMEMBERED ZEMO AND THE DRONE PLANE...
ALWAYS REMEMBERED IT EXPLODING.
BUT THE REST OF IT, I SUPPOSE IT'S POSSIBLE THAT READING REPORTS ABOUT THAT DAY COLORED MY PERCEPTIONS.
ALL I KNOW FOR SURE IS, THESE NEW MEMORIES THAT HAVE BEEN SURFACING-- MEMORIES OF ZEMO CAPTURING US, TORTURING BUCKY...
THEY FEEL FAR TOO REAL...

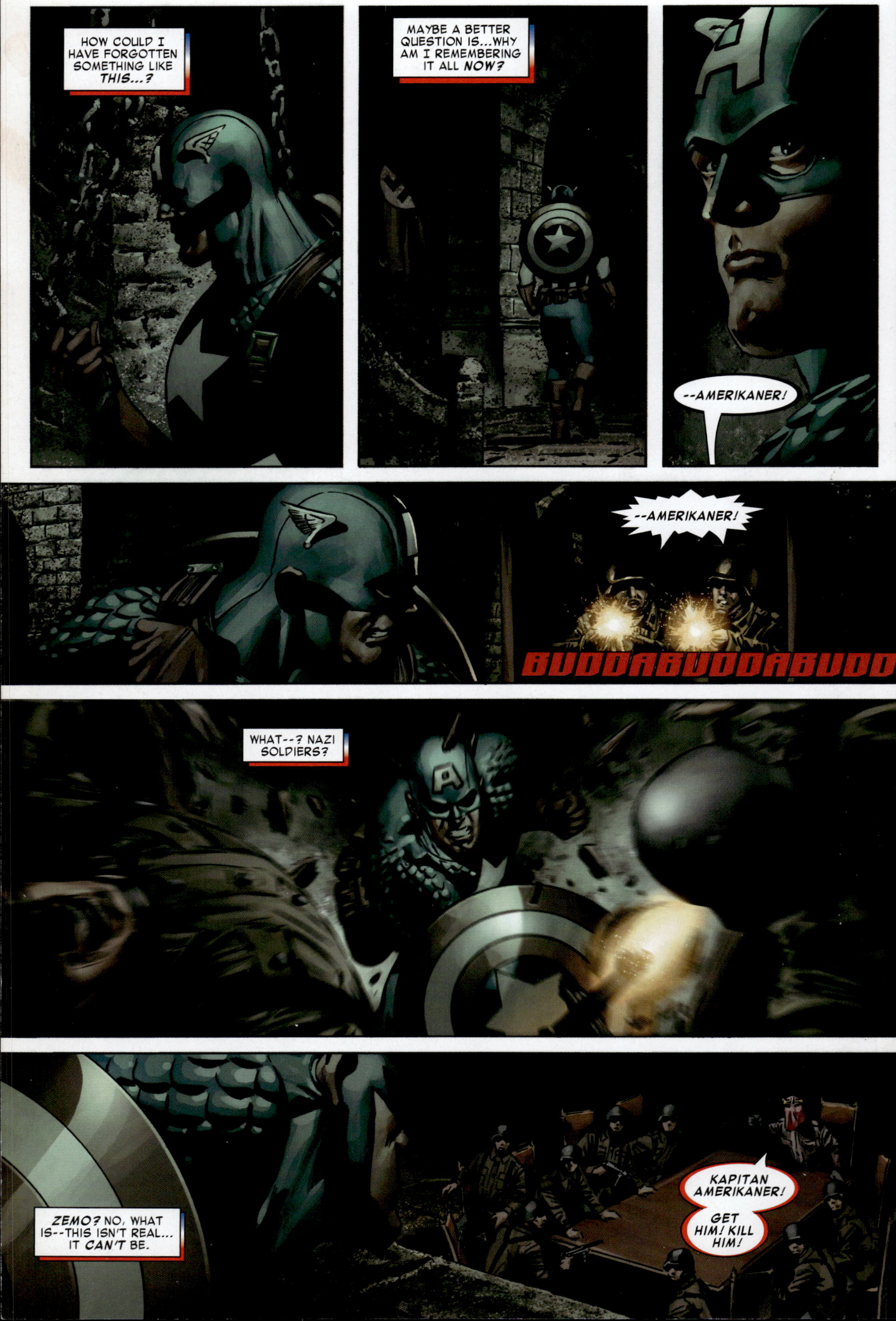
HOW COULD I HAVE FORGOTTEN SOMETHING LIKE THIS...?
MAYBE A BETTER QUESTION IS...WHY AM I REMEMBERING IT ALL NOW?
--AMERIKANER!
--AMERIKANER!
BUDDABUDDABUDD
WHAT--? NAZI SOLDIERS?
KAPITAN AMERIKANER!
GET HIM! KILL HIM!
ZEMO? NO, WHAT IS--THIS ISN'T REAL... IT CAN'T BE.

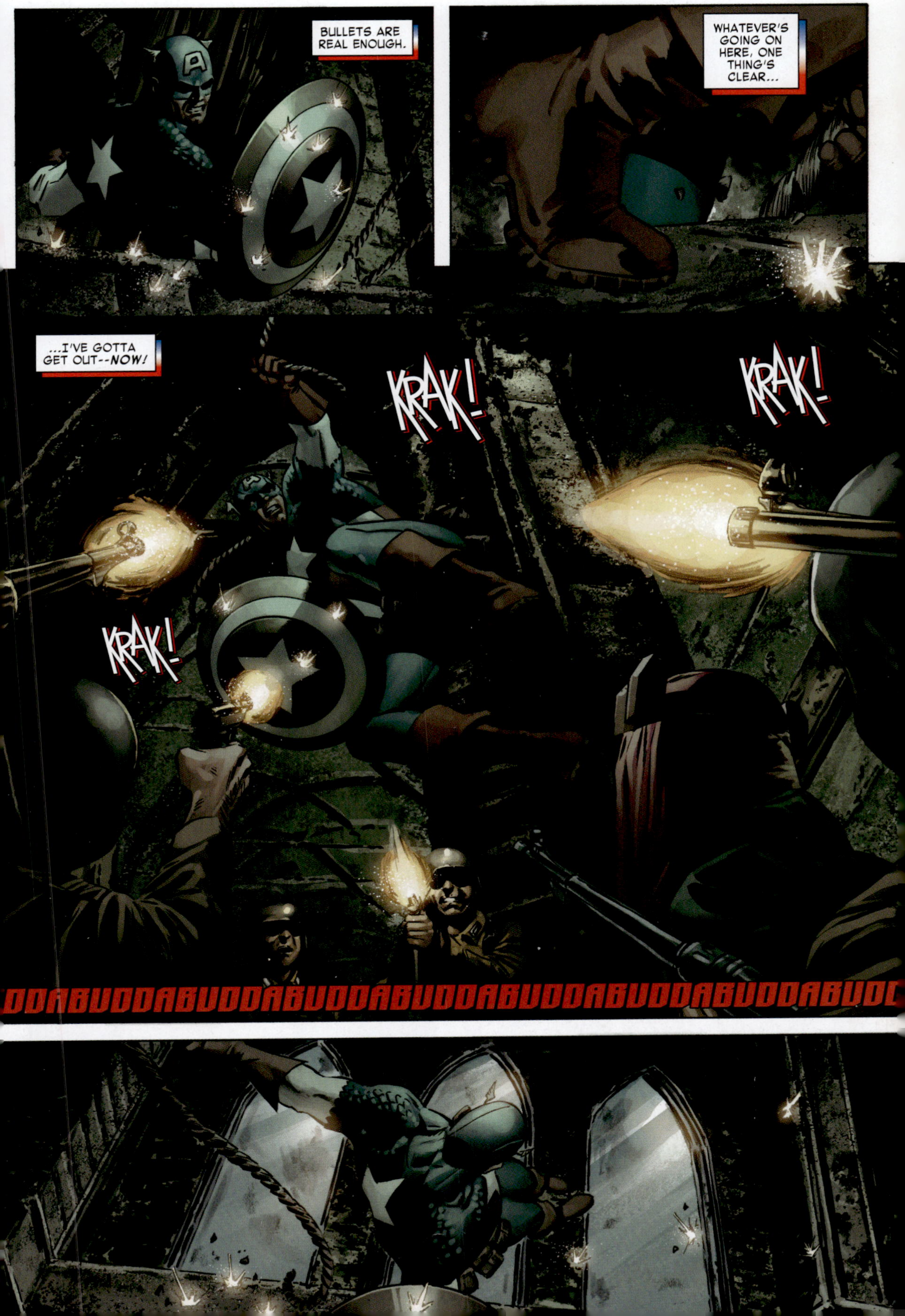
BULLETS ARE REAL ENOUGH.
WHATEVER'S GOING ON HERE, ONE THING'S CLEAR...
...I'VE GOTTA GET OUT--NOW!
KRAK!
KRAK!
KRAK!
DDABUDDABUDDABUDDABUDDABUDDABUDDABUDDABUDDABUD

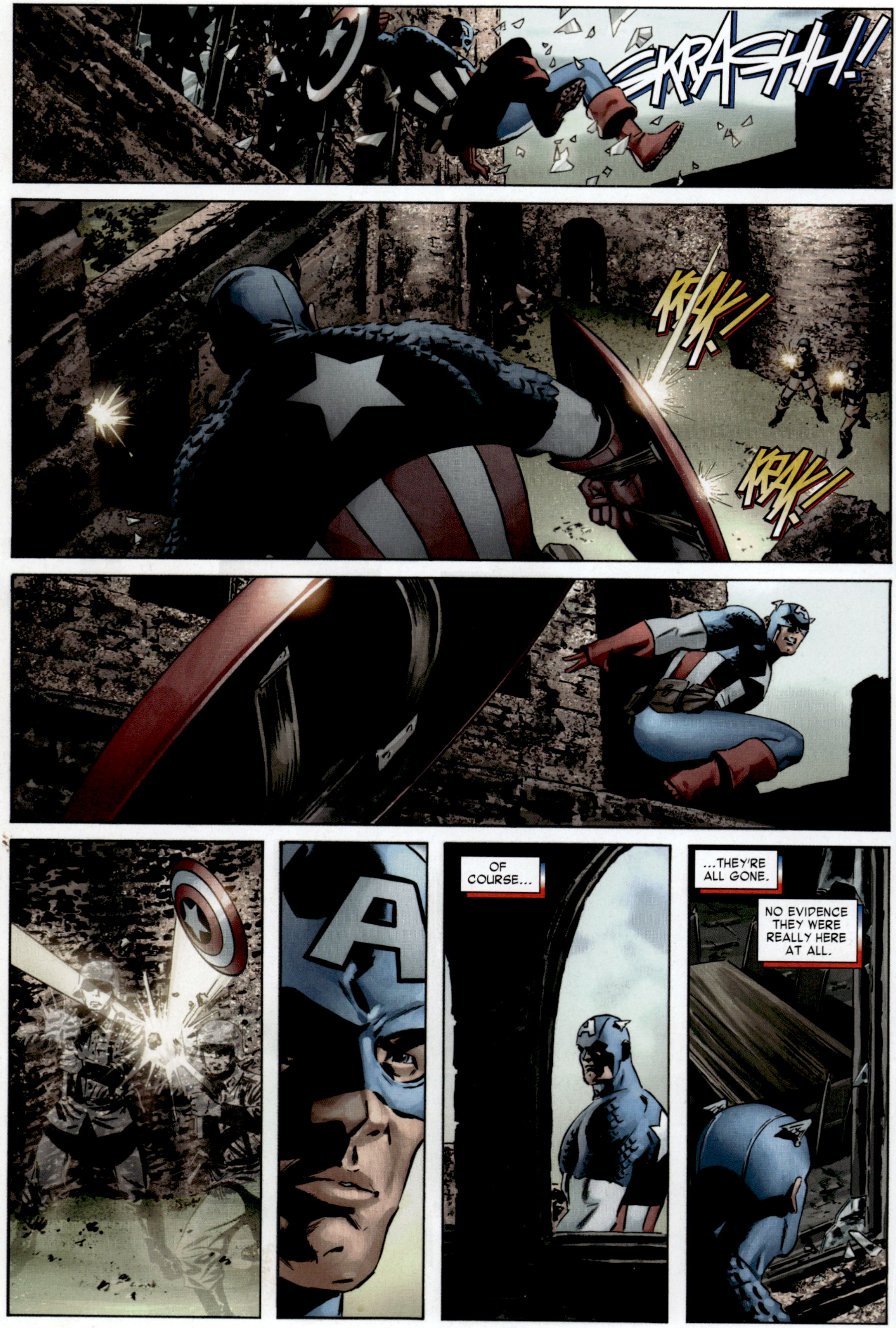
SKRASHH!!
KRAK!
KRAK!
OF COURSE...
...THEY'RE ALL GONE.
NO EVIDENCE THEY WERE REALLY HERE AT ALL.

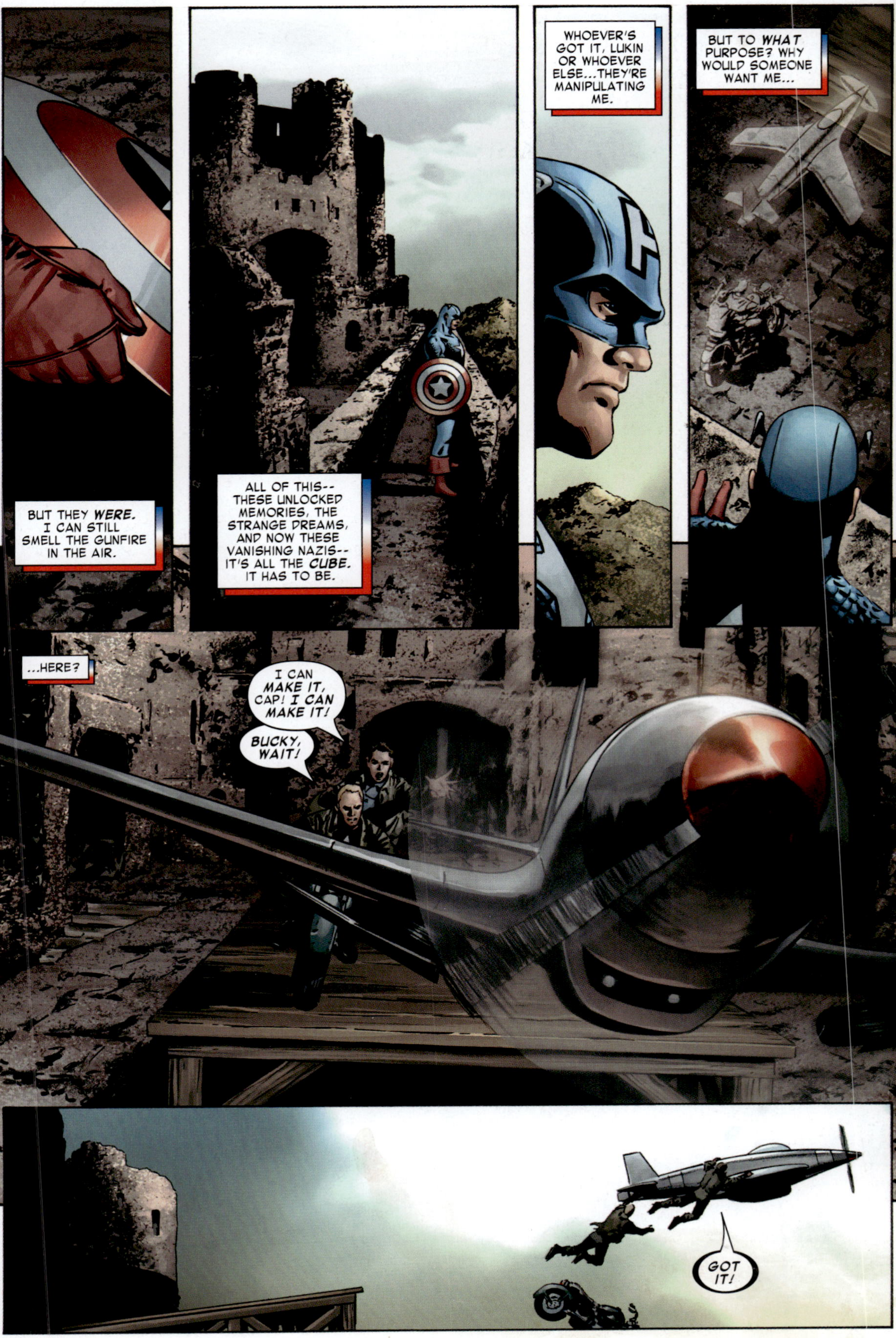
BUT THEY WERE. I CAN STILL SMELL THE GUNFIRE IN THE AIR.
ALL OF THIS-- THESE UNLOCKED MEMORIES, THE STRANGE DREAMS, AND NOW THESE VANISHING NAZIS-- IT'S ALL THE CUBE. IT HAS TO BE.
WHOEVER'S GOT IT, LUKIN OR WHOEVER ELSE...THEY'RE MANIPULATING ME.
BUT TO WHAT PURPOSE? WHY WOULD SOMEONE WANT ME...
...HERE?
I CAN MAKE IT, CAP! I CAN MAKE IT!
BUCKY, WAIT!
GOT IT!

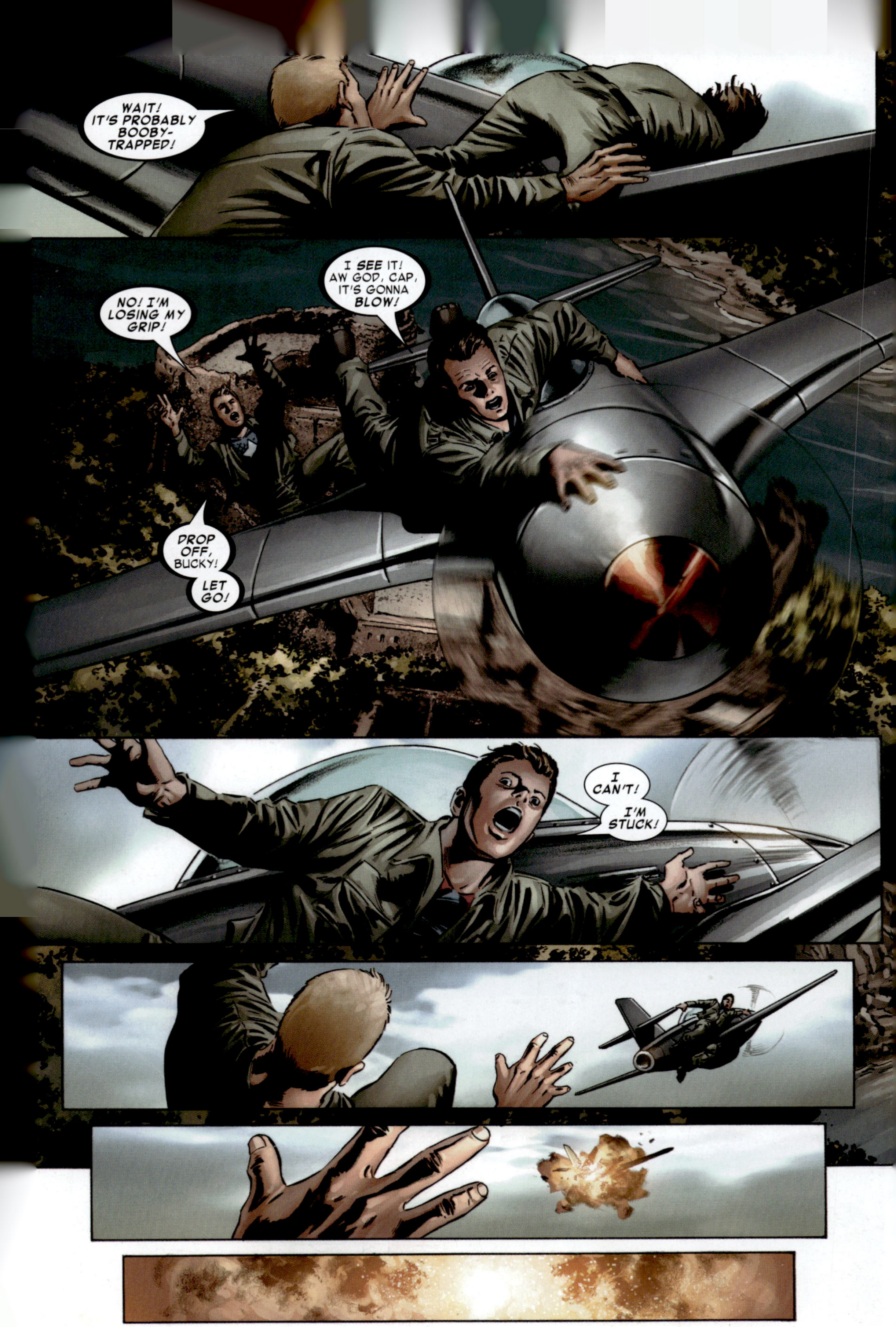
WAIT! IT'S PROBABLY BOOBY-TRAPPED!
NO! I'M LOSING MY GRIP!
I SEE IT! AW GOD, CAP, IT'S GONNA BLOW!
DROP OFF, BUCKY!
LET GO!
I CAN'T!
I'M STUCK!

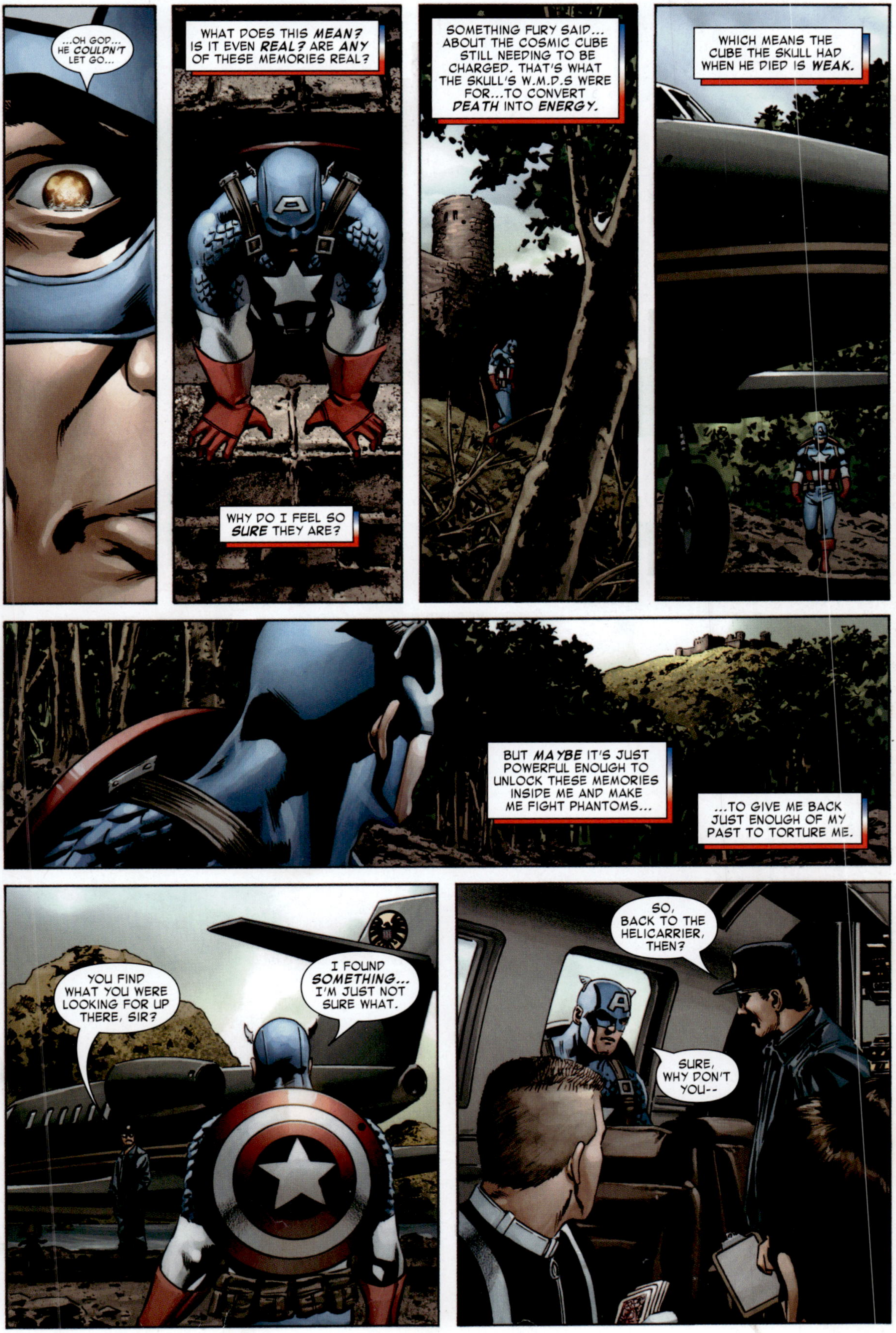
...OH GOD... HE COULDN'T LET GO...
WHAT DOES THIS MEAN? IS IT EVEN REAL? ARE ANY OF THESE MEMORIES REAL?
WHY DO I FEEL SO SURE THEY ARE?
SOMETHING FURY SAID... ABOUT THE COSMIC CUBE STILL NEEDING TO BE CHARGED. THAT'S WHAT THE SKULL'S W.M.D.S WERE FOR...TO CONVERT DEATH INTO ENERGY.
WHICH MEANS THE CUBE THE SKULL HAD WHEN HE DIED IS WEAK.
BUT MAYBE IT'S JUST POWERFUL ENOUGH TO UNLOCK THESE MEMORIES INSIDE ME AND MAKE ME FIGHT PHANTOMS...
...TO GIVE ME BACK JUST ENOUGH OF MY PAST TO TORTURE ME.
YOU FIND WHAT YOU WERE LOOKING FOR UP THERE, SIR?
I FOUND SOMETHING... I'M JUST NOT SURE WHAT.
SO, BACK TO THE HELICARRIER, THEN?
SURE, WHY DON'T YOU--

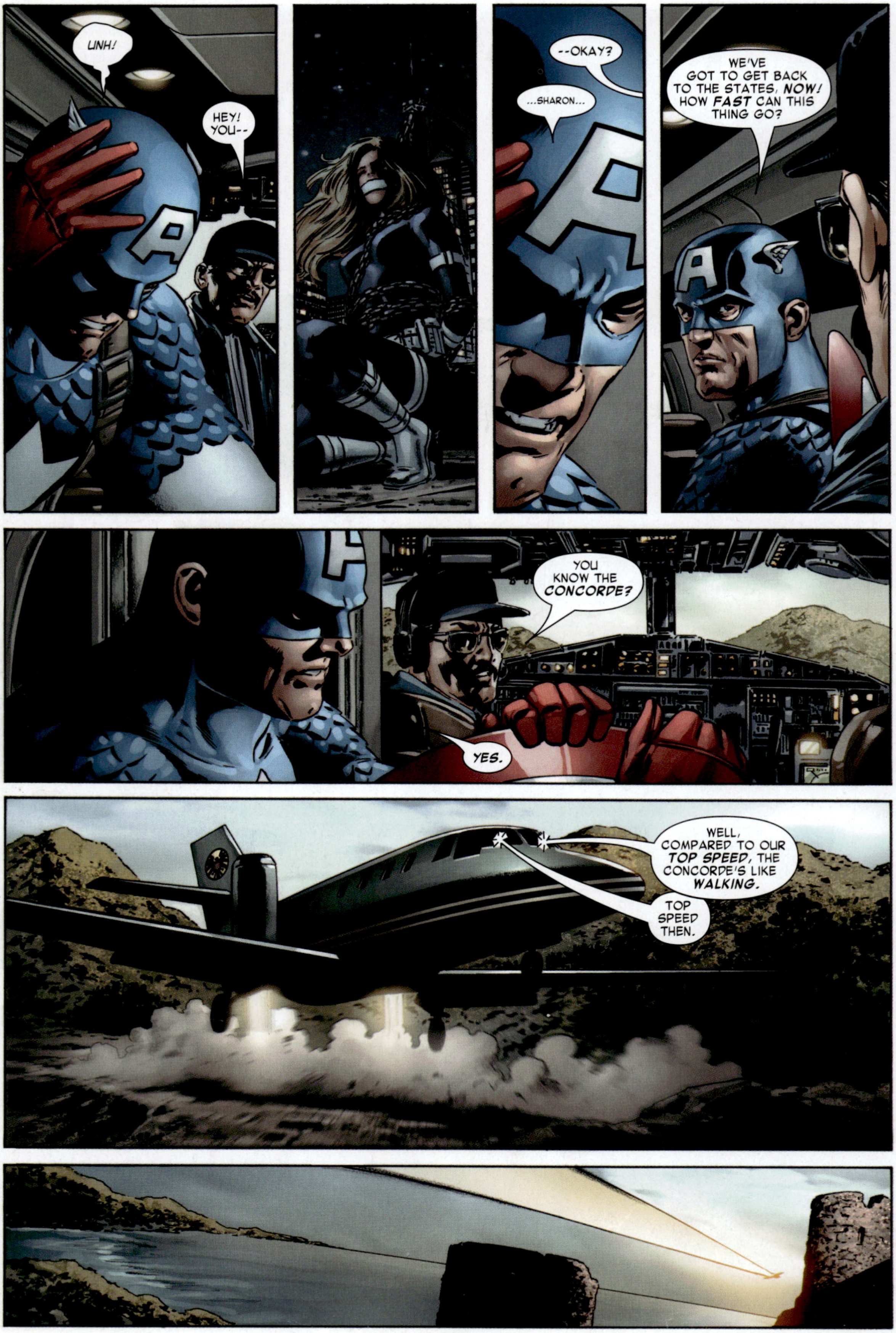
UNH!
HEY! YOU--
...SHARON...
--OKAY?
WE'VE GOT TO GET BACK TO THE STATES, NOW! HOW FAST CAN THIS THING GO?
YOU KNOW THE CONCORDE?
YES.
WELL, COMPARED TO OUR TOP SPEED, THE CONCORDE'S LIKE WALKING.
TOP SPEED THEN.

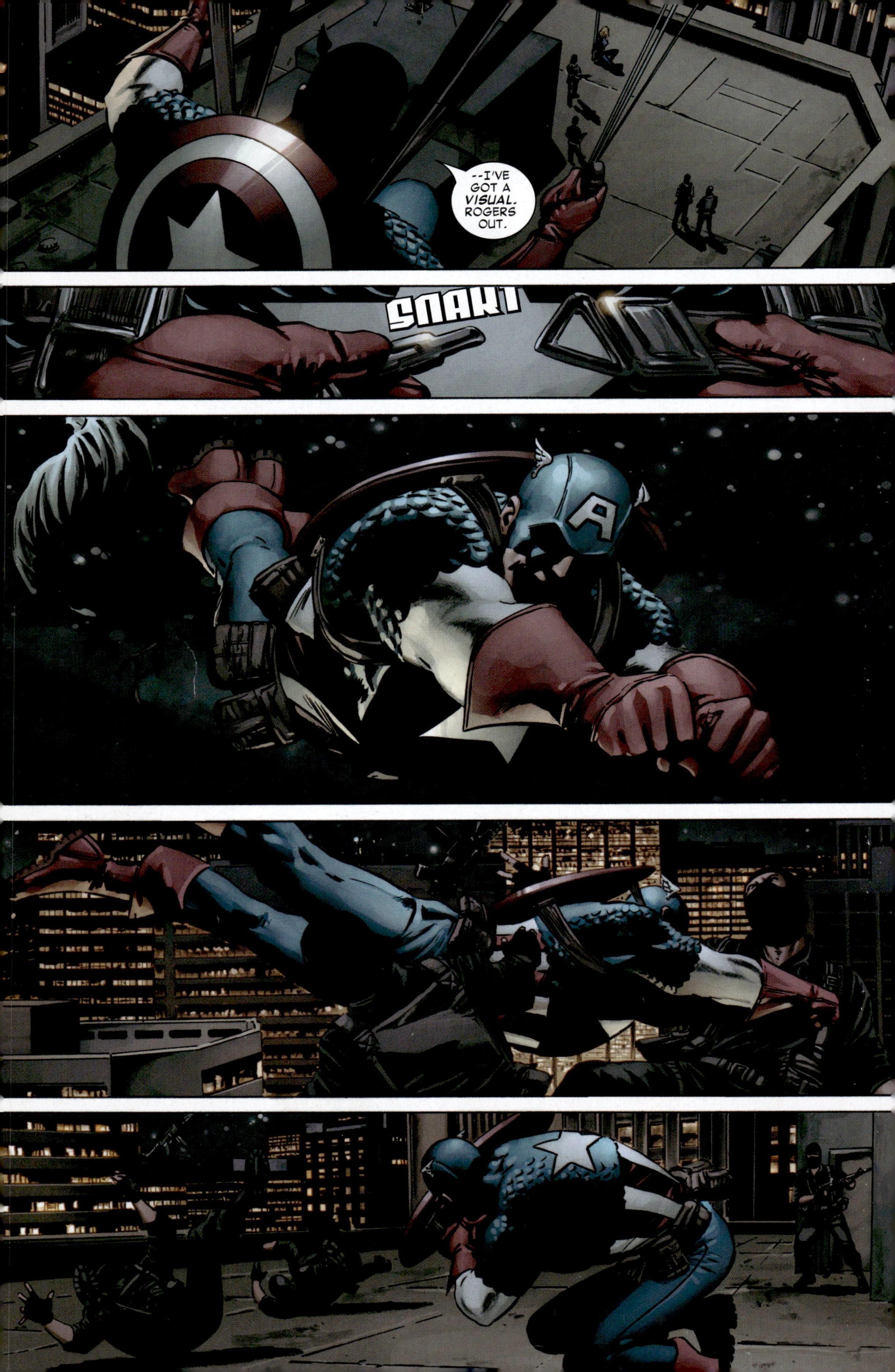
--I'VE GOT A VISUAL. ROGERS OUT.
SNAKT

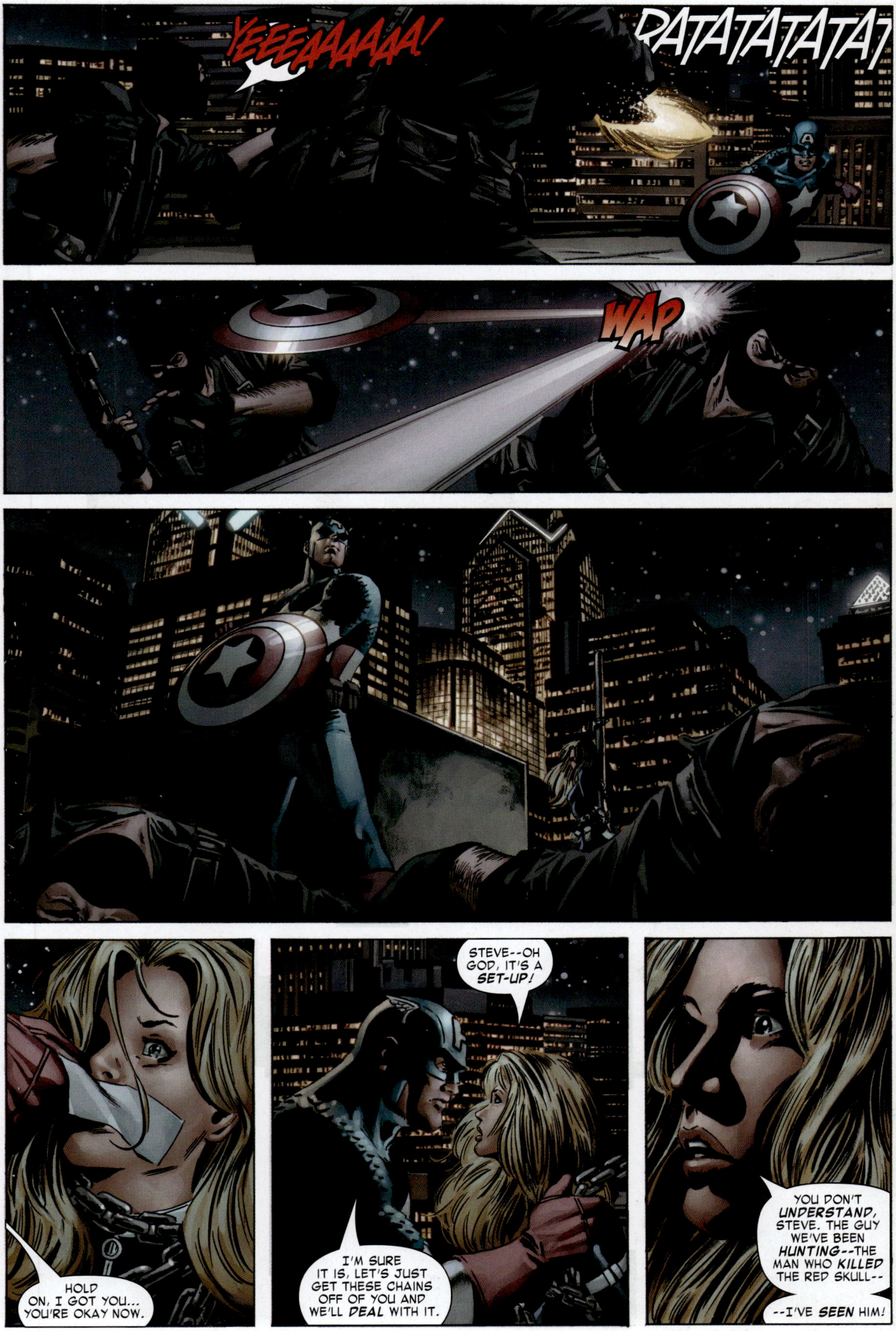
YEEEAAAAAA!
RATATATATAT
WAP
HOLD ON, I GOT YOU... YOU'RE OKAY NOW.
STEVE--OH GOD, IT'S A SET-UP!
I'M SURE IT IS, LET'S JUST GET THESE CHAINS OFF OF YOU AND WE'LL DEAL WITH IT.
YOU DON'T UNDERSTAND, STEVE. THE GUY WE'VE BEEN HUNTING--THE MAN WHO KILLED THE RED SKULL--
--I'VE SEEN HIM!

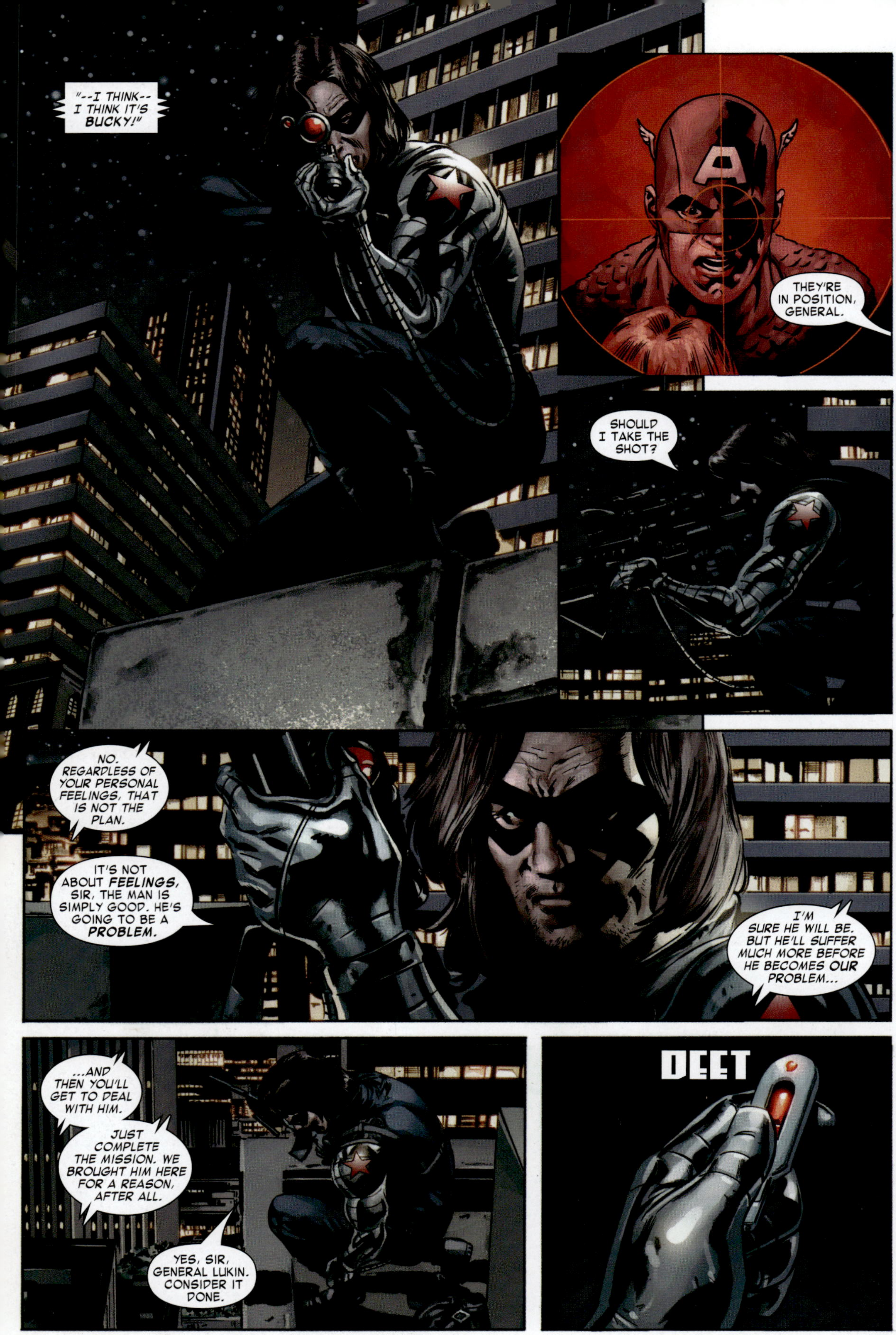
"--I THINK--
I THINK IT'S
BUCKY!"
THEY'RE IN POSITION, GENERAL.
SHOULD I TAKE THE SHOT?
NO. REGARDLESS OF YOUR PERSONAL FEELINGS, THAT IS NOT THE PLAN.
IT'S NOT ABOUT FEELINGS, SIR, THE MAN IS SIMPLY GOOD. HE'S GOING TO BE A PROBLEM.
I'M SURE HE WILL BE. BUT HE'LL SUFFER MUCH MORE BEFORE HE BECOMES OUR PROBLEM...
...AND THEN YOU'LL GET TO DEAL WITH HIM.
JUST COMPLETE THE MISSION. WE BROUGHT HIM HERE FOR A REASON, AFTER ALL.
YES, SIR, GENERAL LUKIN. CONSIDER IT DONE.
DEET

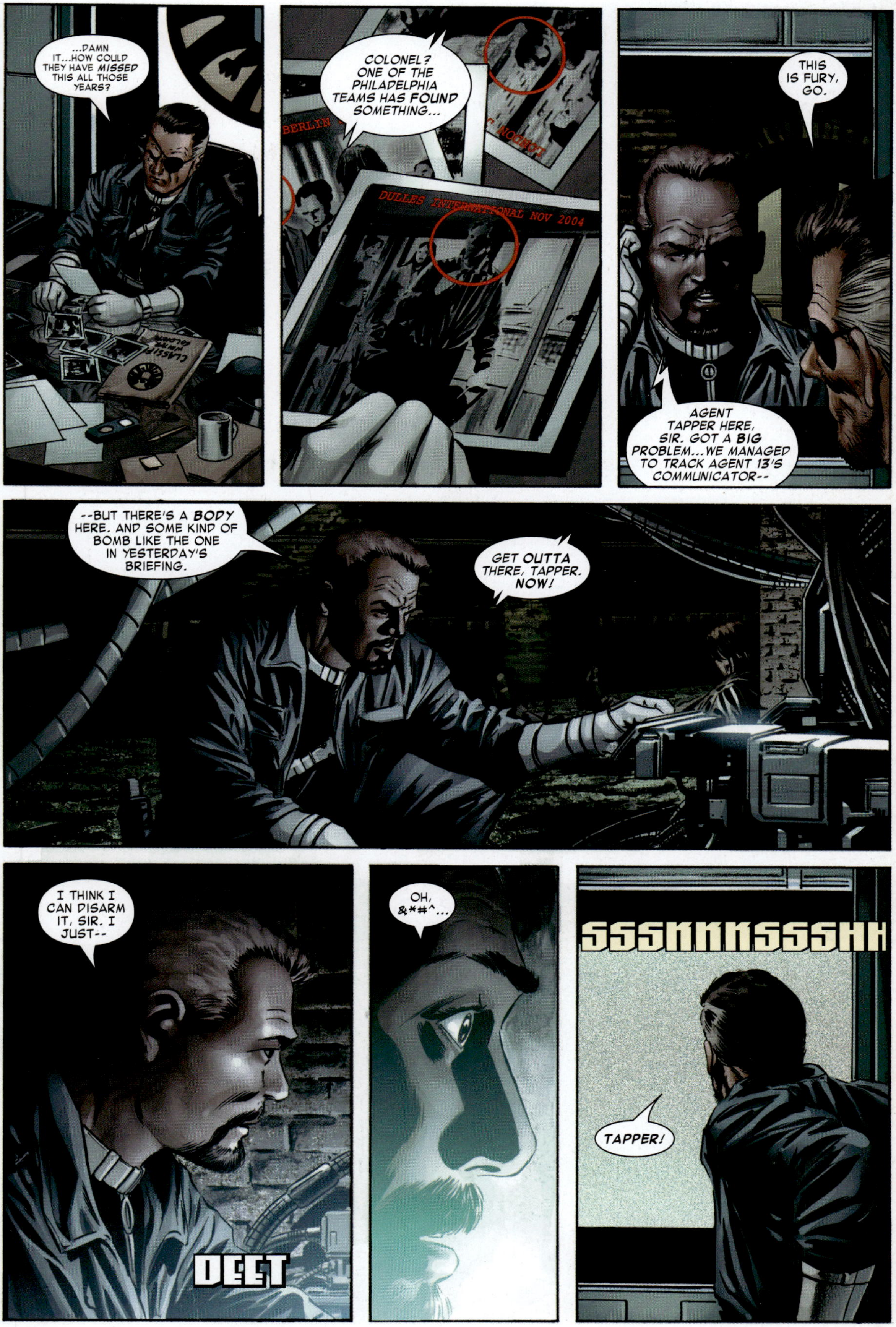
...DAMN IT...HOW COULD THEY HAVE MISSED THIS ALL THOSE YEARS?
COLONEL? ONE OF THE PHILADELPHIA TEAMS HAS FOUND SOMETHING...
BERLIN
DULLES INTERNATIONAL NOV 2004
THIS IS FURY, GO.
AGENT TAPPER HERE, SIR. GOT A BIG PROBLEM...WE MANAGED TO TRACK AGENT 13'S COMMUNICATOR--
--BUT THERE'S A BODY HERE. AND SOME KIND OF BOMB LIKE THE ONE IN YESTERDAY'S BRIEFING.
GET OUTTA THERE, TAPPER. NOW!
I THINK I CAN DISARM IT, SIR. I JUST--
DEET
OH, &*#^...
SSSKKKSSSHH
TAPPER!

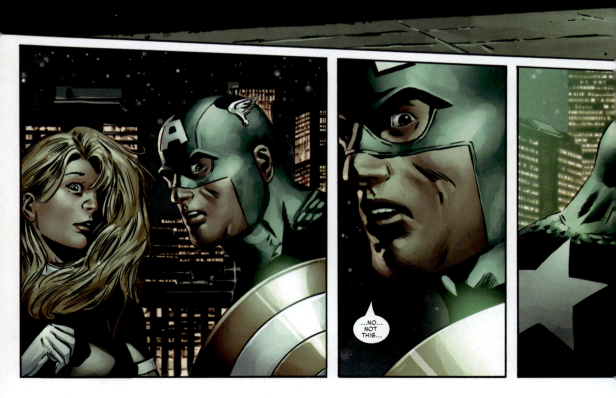

...NO...
NOT
THIS...

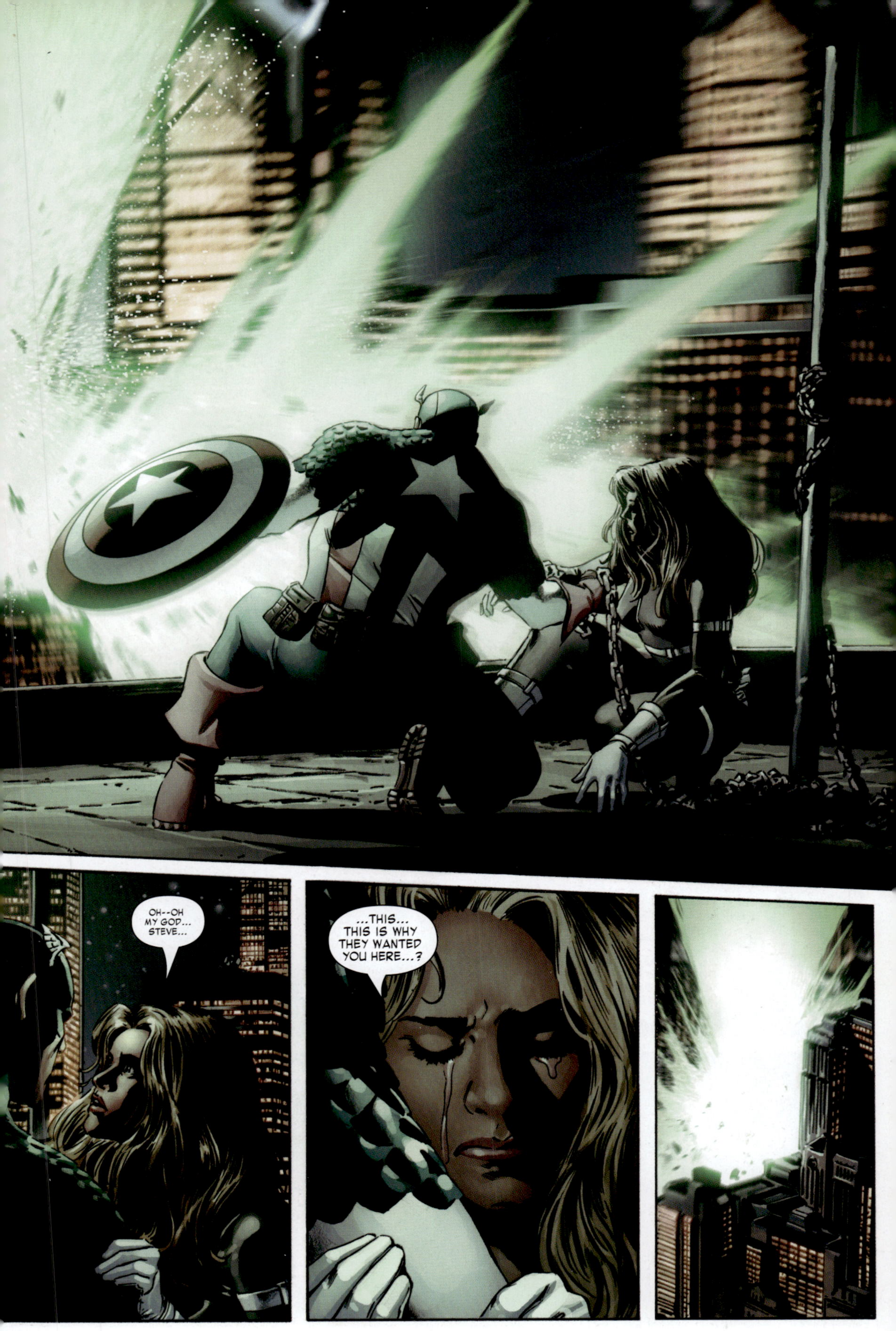
OH--OH MY GOD... STEVE...
...THIS... THIS IS WHY THEY WANTED YOU HERE...?

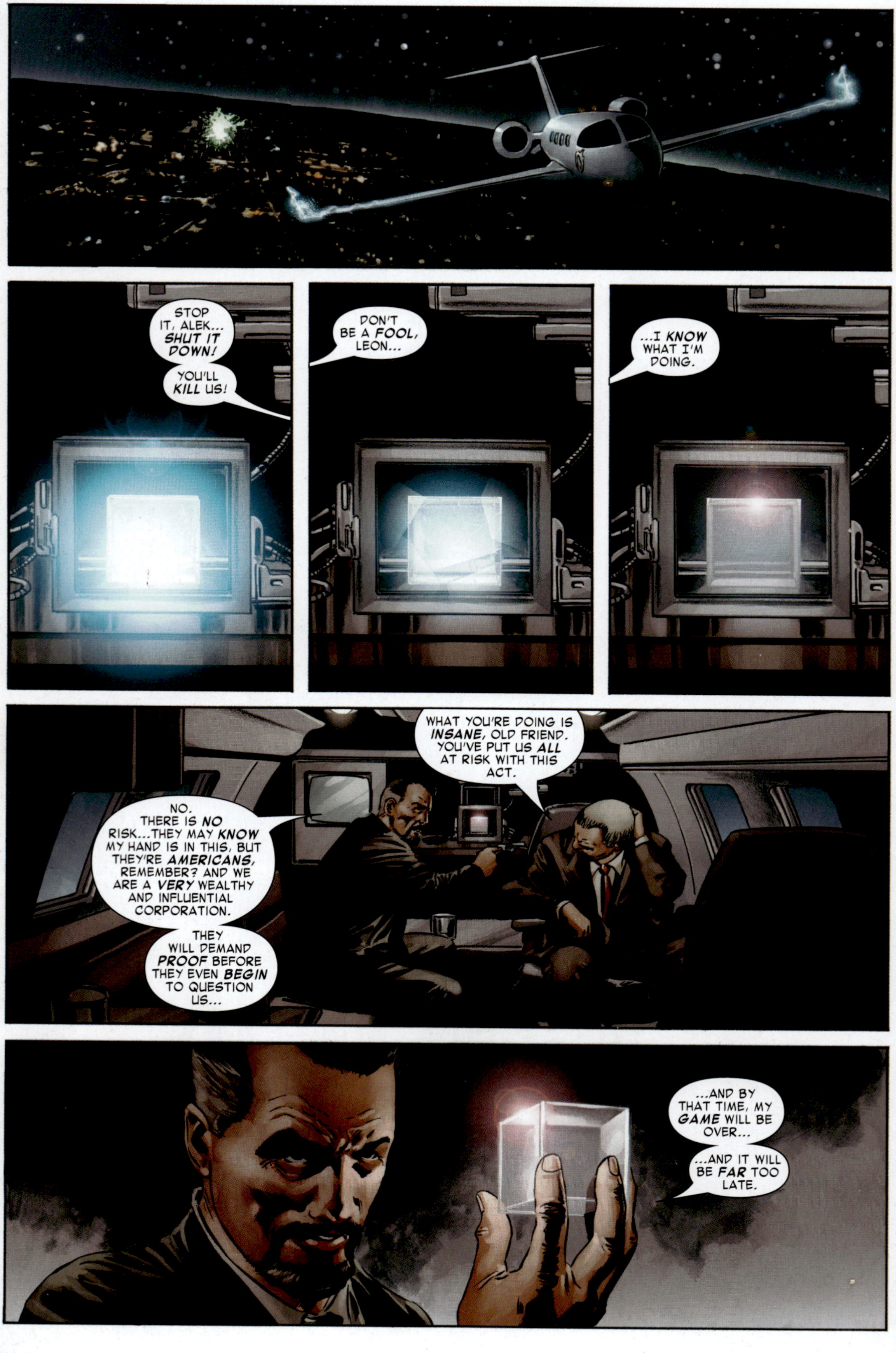
STOP IT, ALEK... SHUT IT DOWN!
YOU'LL KILL US!
DON'T BE A FOOL, LEON...
...I KNOW WHAT I'M DOING.
WHAT YOU'RE DOING IS INSANE, OLD FRIEND. YOU'VE PUT US ALL AT RISK WITH THIS ACT.
NO. THERE IS NO RISK...THEY MAY KNOW MY HAND IS IN THIS, BUT THEY'RE AMERICANS, REMEMBER? AND WE ARE A VERY WEALTHY AND INFLUENTIAL CORPORATION.
THEY WILL DEMAND PROOF BEFORE THEY EVEN BEGIN TO QUESTION US...
...AND BY THAT TIME, MY GAME WILL BE OVER...
...AND IT WILL BE FAR TOO LATE.

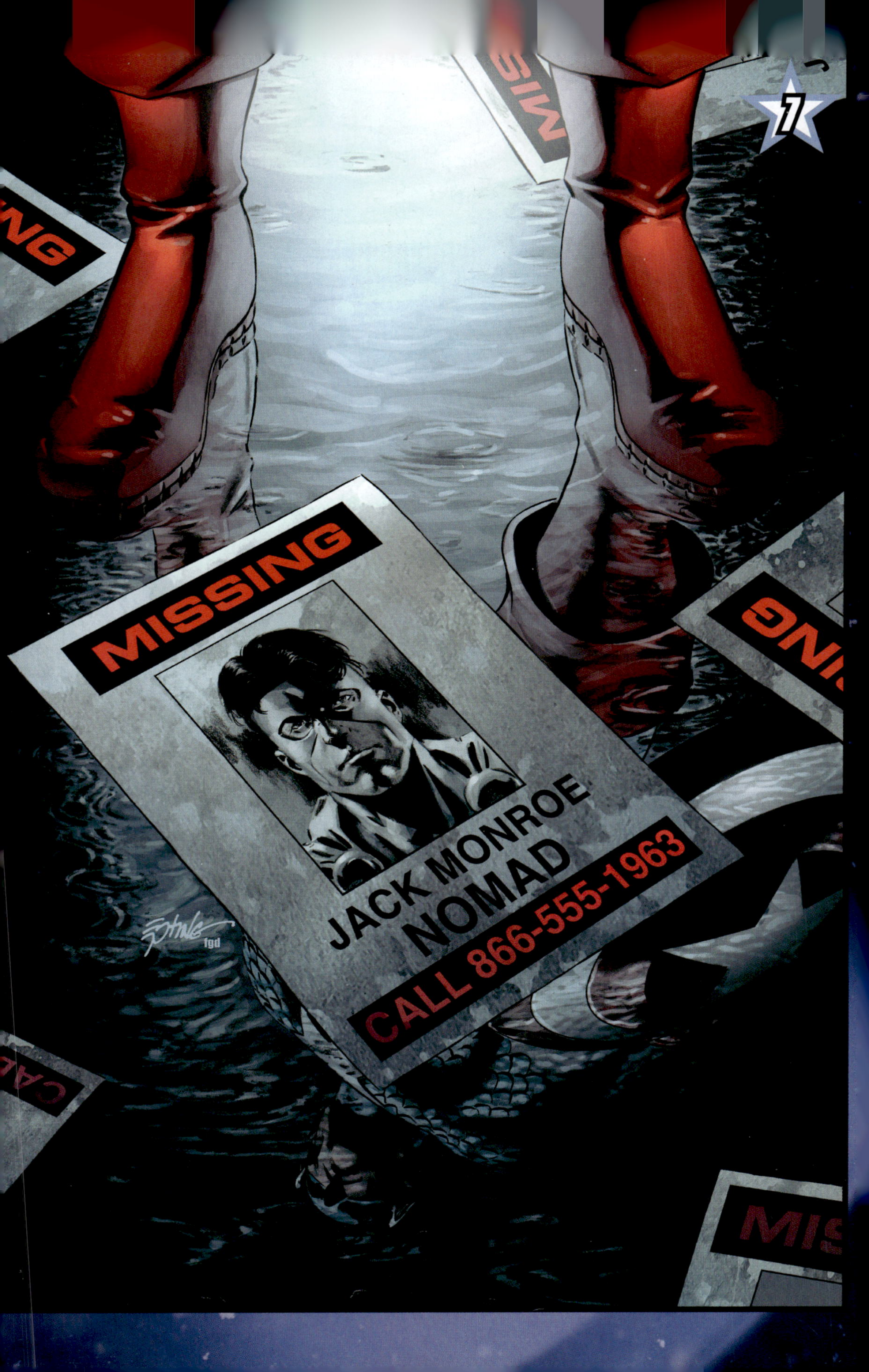
7
MISSING
JACK MONROE
NOMAD
CALL 866-555-1963

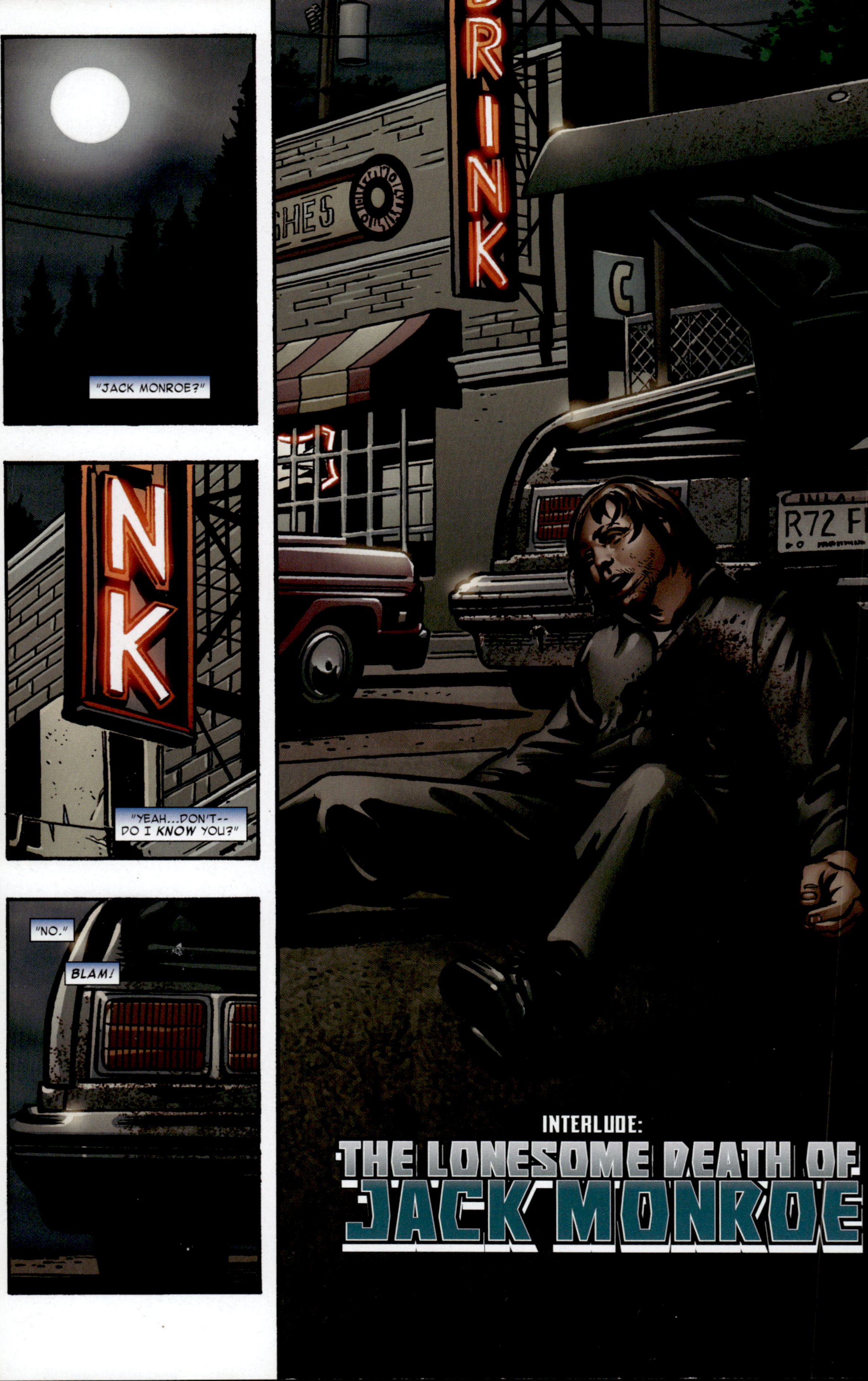
"JACK MONROE?"
"YEAH...DON'T--
DO I KNOW YOU?"
"NO."
BLAM!
DRINK
INTERLUDE:
THE LONESOME DEATH OF
JACK MONROE

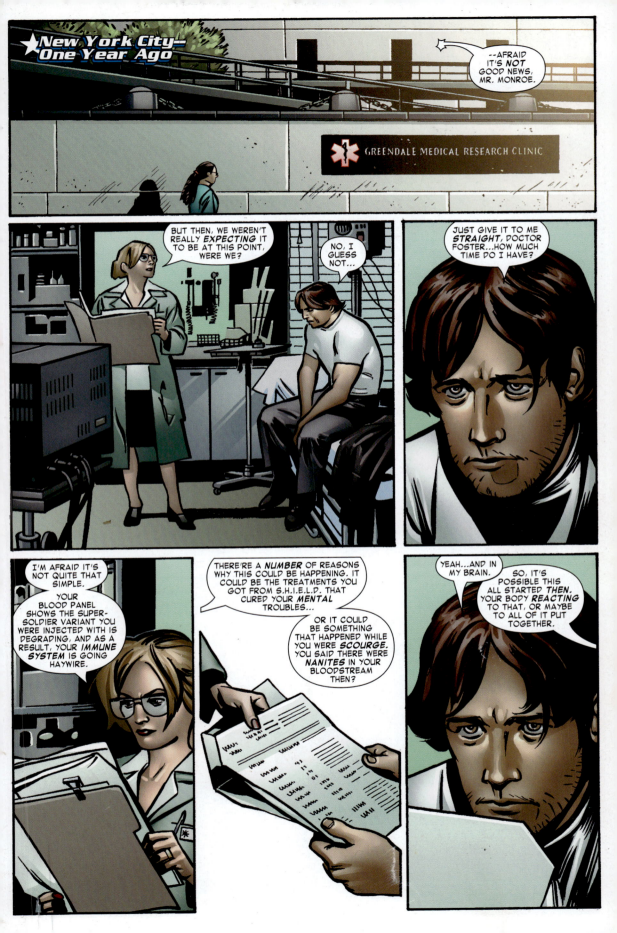

So Dr. Jane Foster, after all the effort it took to find someone with meta-human experience to help me, now tells me I'm going to die. She just isn't sure how soon.

But she tells me it's not going to be pleasant.

First I'm going to continue losing my added strength and stamina as the Super-Soldier Serum fades.

And then I'm going to start to get sick. Really sick. Because my immune system will be almost nonexistent by then.

Oh yeah, and it's highly likely that I'll start to lose my mind as this goes along. Just to make it fun.

Something about the original serum's effects on me. I don't know...I stop listening after a while.

She says I should start saying goodbye to my friends and family, start getting my affairs in order.

Do I even have any affairs left to organize? Do I even have any friends and family?

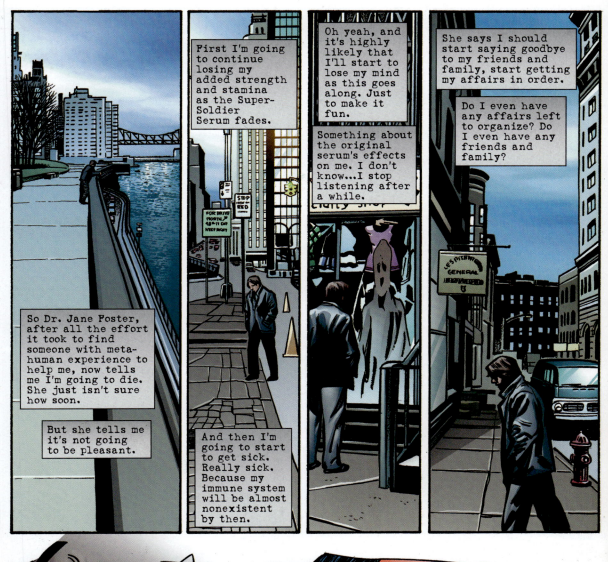

I suppose the only person I really think of as a friend is Cap...but that's such a twisted history...

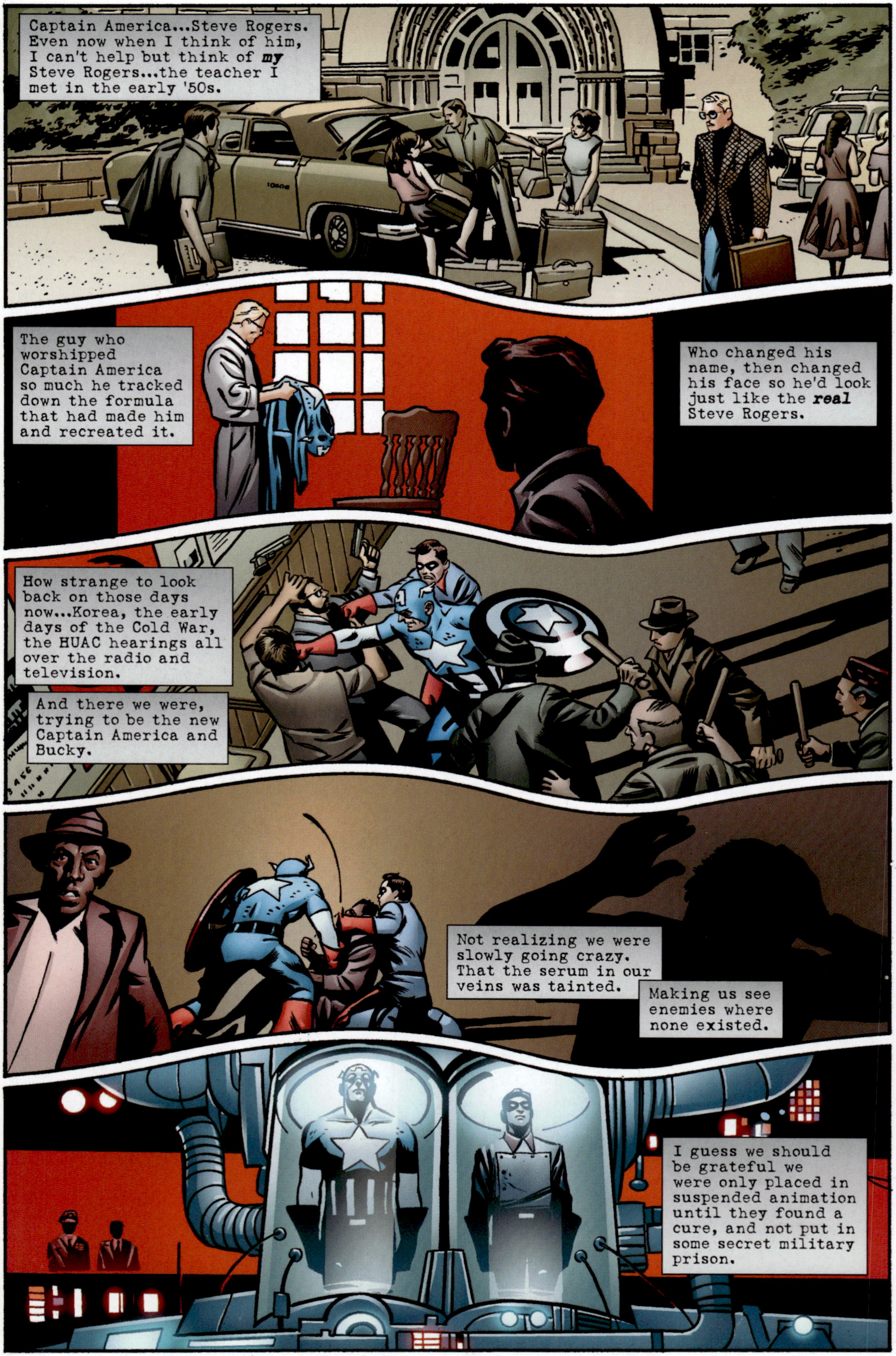
Captain America...Steve Rogers. Even now when I think of him, I can't help but think of *my* Steve Rogers...the teacher I met in the early '50s.
The guy who worshipped Captain America so much he tracked down the formula that had made him and recreated it.
Who changed his name, then changed his face so he'd look just like the *real* Steve Rogers.
How strange to look back on those days now...Korea, the early days of the Cold War, the HUAC hearings all over the radio and television.
And there we were, trying to be the new Captain America and Bucky.
Not realizing we were slowly going crazy. That the serum in our veins was tainted.
Making us see enemies where none existed.
I guess we should be grateful we were only placed in suspended animation until they found a cure, and not put in some secret military prison.

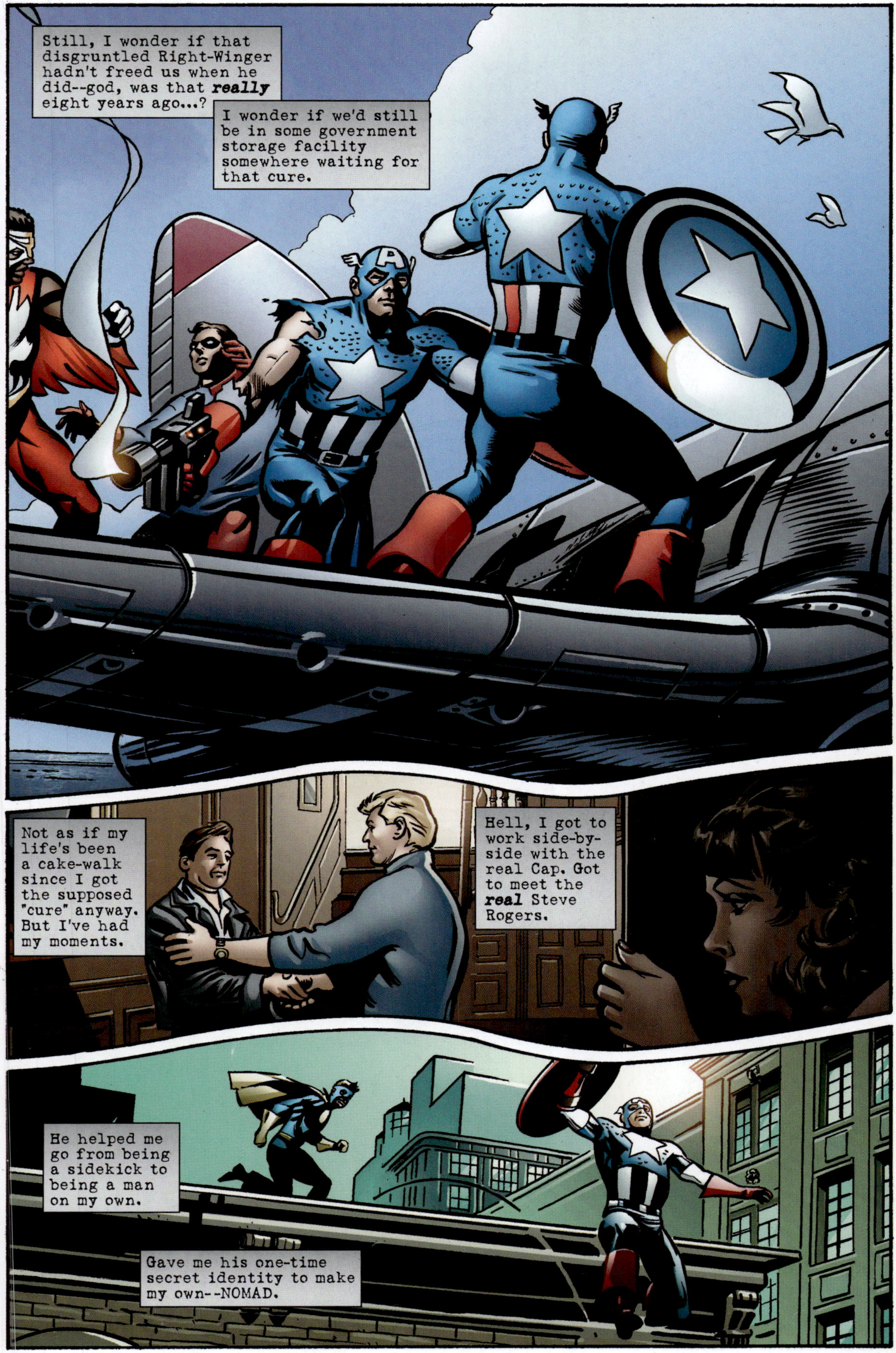
Still, I wonder if that disgruntled Right-Winger hadn't freed us when he did--god, was that **really** eight years ago...?
I wonder if we'd still be in some government storage facility somewhere waiting for that cure.
Not as if my life's been a cake-walk since I got the supposed "cure" anyway. But I've had my moments.
Hell, I got to work side-by-side with the real Cap. Got to meet the **real** Steve Rogers.
He helped me go from being a sidekick to being a man on my own.
Gave me his one-time secret identity to make my own--NOMAD.

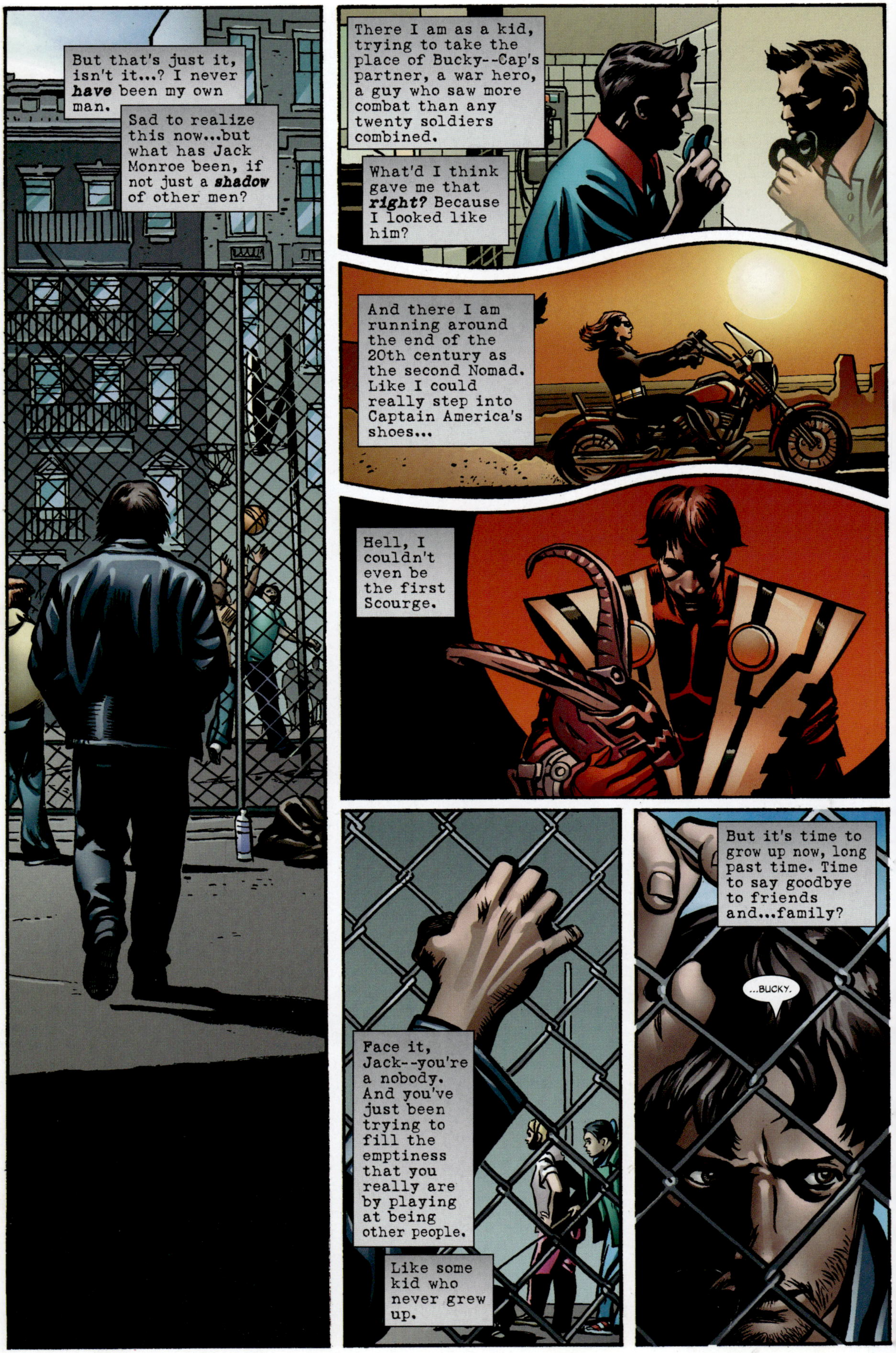
But that's just it, isn't it...? I never **have** been my own man.
Sad to realize this now...but what has Jack Monroe been, if not just a **shadow** of other men?
There I am as a kid, trying to take the place of Bucky--Cap's partner, a war hero, a guy who saw more combat than any twenty soldiers combined.
What'd I think gave me that **right?** Because I looked like him?
And there I am running around the end of the 20th century as the second Nomad. Like I could really step into Captain America's shoes...
Hell, I couldn't even be the first Scourge.
Face it, Jack--you're a nobody. And you've just been trying to fill the emptiness that you really are by playing at being other people.
Like some kid who never grew up.
But it's time to grow up now, long past time. Time to say goodbye to friends and...family?
...BUCKY.

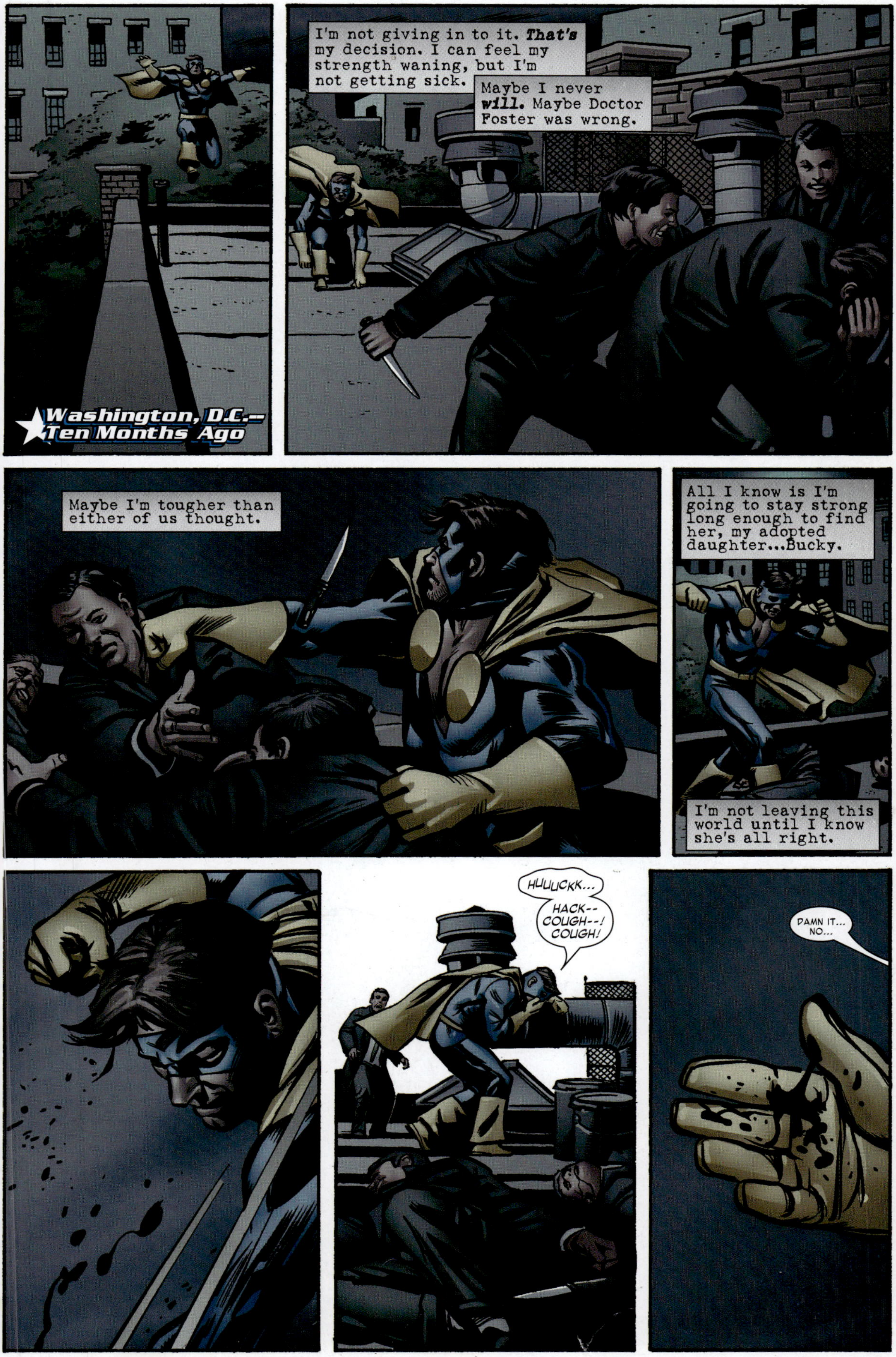
Washington, D.C.-- Ten Months Ago
I'm not giving in to it. That's my decision. I can feel my strength waning, but I'm not getting sick.
Maybe I never will. Maybe Doctor Foster was wrong.
Maybe I'm tougher than either of us thought.
All I know is I'm going to stay strong long enough to find her, my adopted daughter...Bucky.
I'm not leaving this world until I know she's all right.
HUUUCKK...
HACK-- COUGH--! COUGH!
DAMN IT... NO...

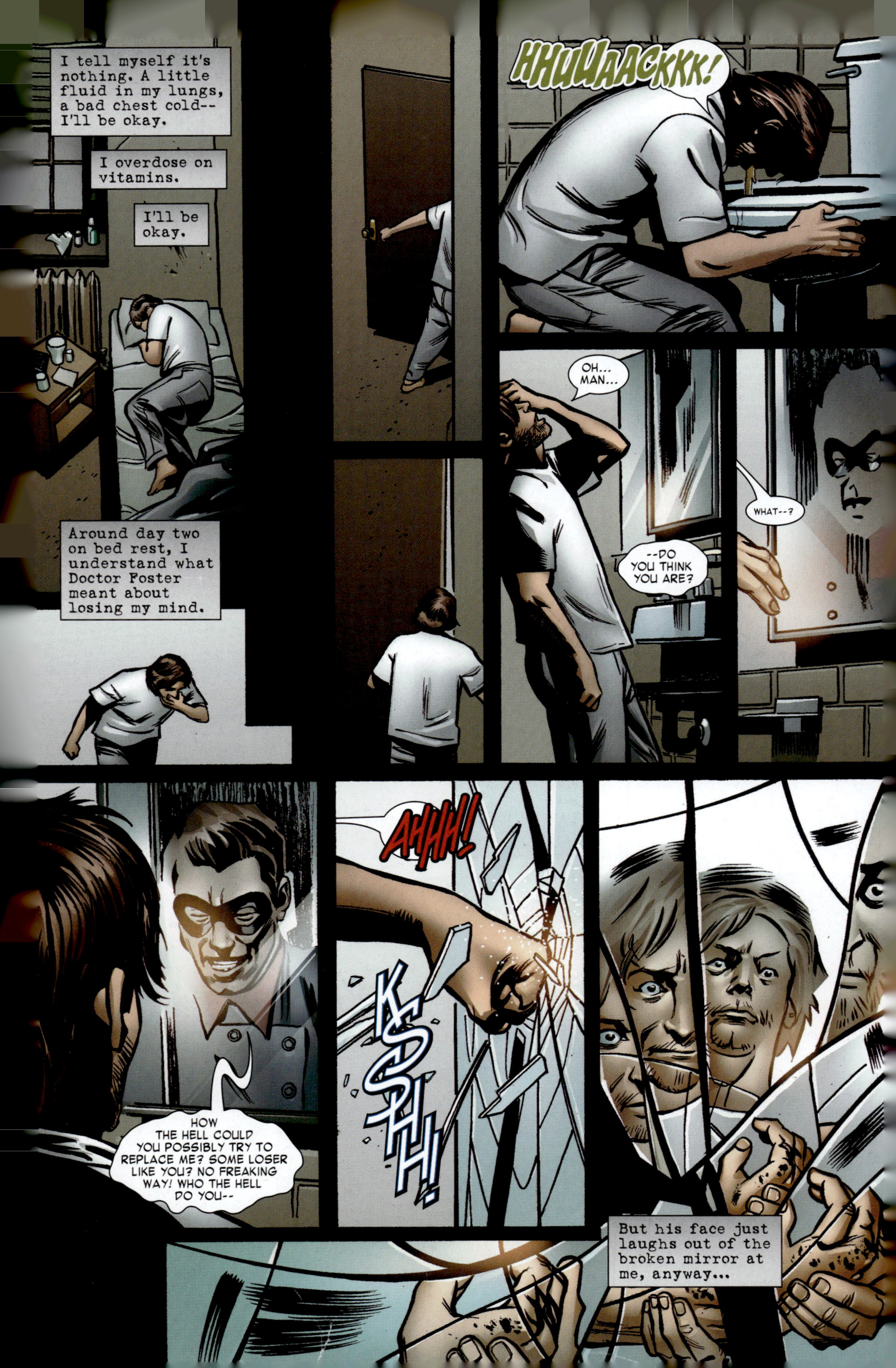

I tell myself it's nothing. A little fluid in my lungs, a bad chest cold--I'll be okay.
I overdose on vitamins.
I'll be okay.
HHUUAACKKK!
Around day two on bed rest, I understand what Doctor Foster meant about losing my mind.
OH... MAN...
WHAT--?
--DO YOU THINK YOU ARE?
HOW THE HELL COULD YOU POSSIBLY TRY TO REPLACE ME? SOME LOSER LIKE YOU? NO FREAKING WAY! WHO THE HELL DO YOU--
AHHH!
KSHH!
But his face just laughs out of the broken mirror at me, anyway...

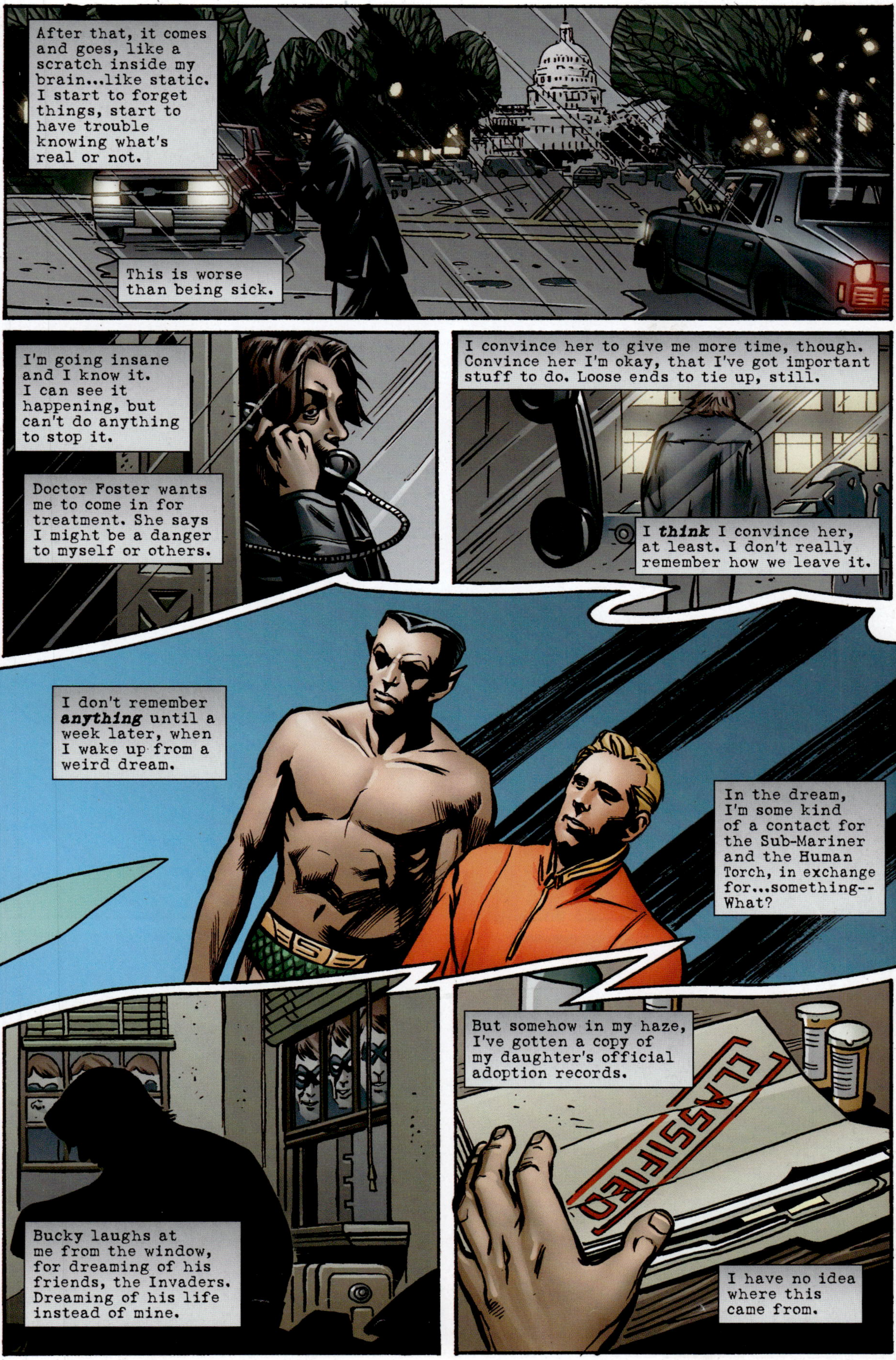
After that, it comes and goes, like a scratch inside my brain...like static. I start to forget things, start to have trouble knowing what's real or not.
This is worse than being sick.
I'm going insane and I know it. I can see it happening, but can't do anything to stop it.
Doctor Foster wants me to come in for treatment. She says I might be a danger to myself or others.
I convince her to give me more time, though. Convince her I'm okay, that I've got important stuff to do. Loose ends to tie up, still.
I *think* I convince her, at least. I don't really remember how we leave it.
I don't remember ***anything*** until a week later, when I wake up from a weird dream.
In the dream, I'm some kind of a contact for the Sub-Mariner and the Human Torch, in exchange for...something-- What?
Bucky laughs at me from the window, for dreaming of his friends, the Invaders. Dreaming of his life instead of mine.
But somehow in my haze, I've gotten a copy of my daughter's official adoption records.
CLASSIFIED
I have no idea where this came from.

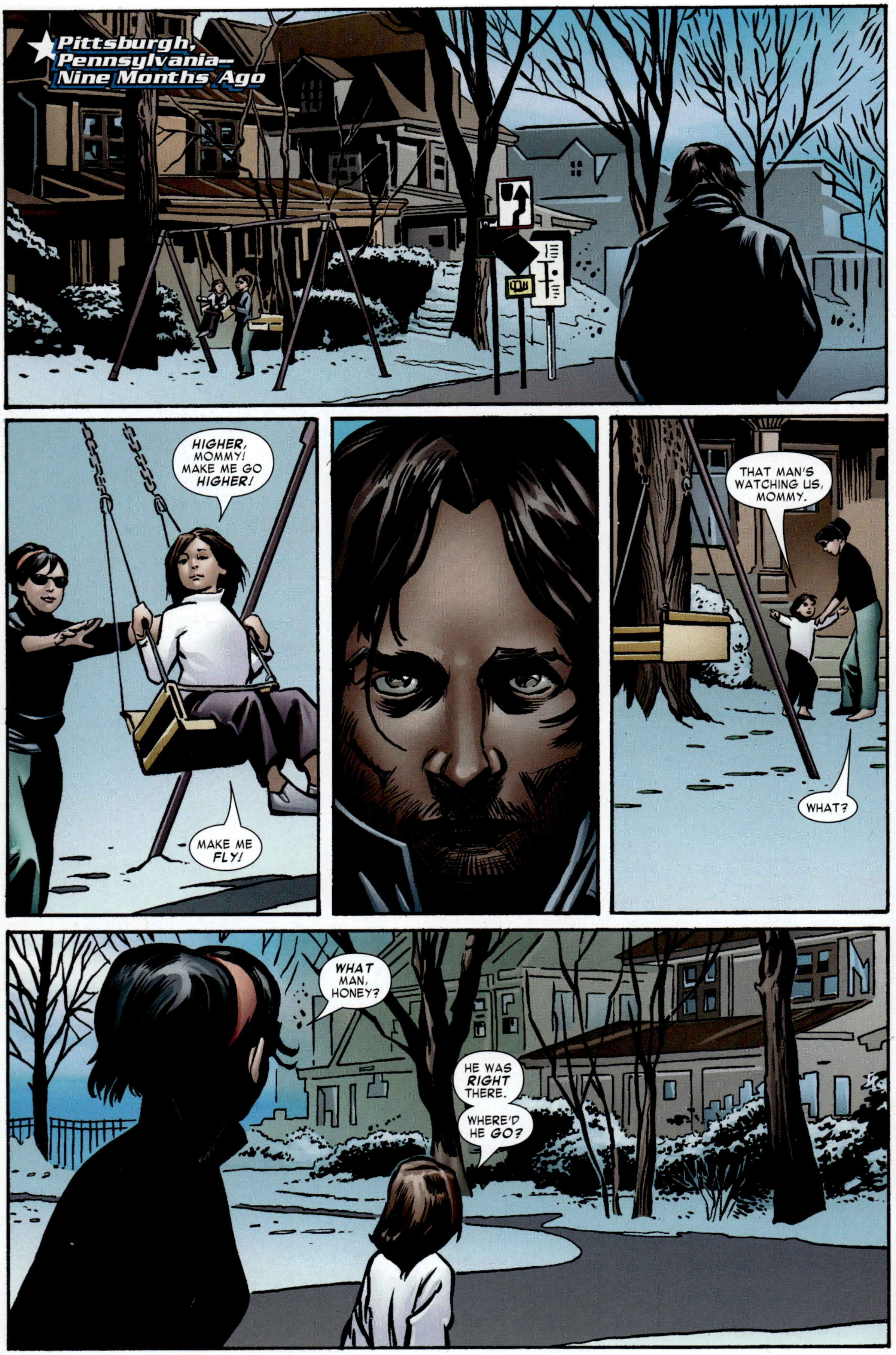
Pittsburgh, Pennsylvania— Nine Months Ago
HIGHER, MOMMY! MAKE ME GO HIGHER!
MAKE ME FLY!
THAT MAN'S WATCHING US, MOMMY.
WHAT?
WHAT MAN, HONEY?
HE WAS RIGHT THERE.
WHERE'D HE GO?

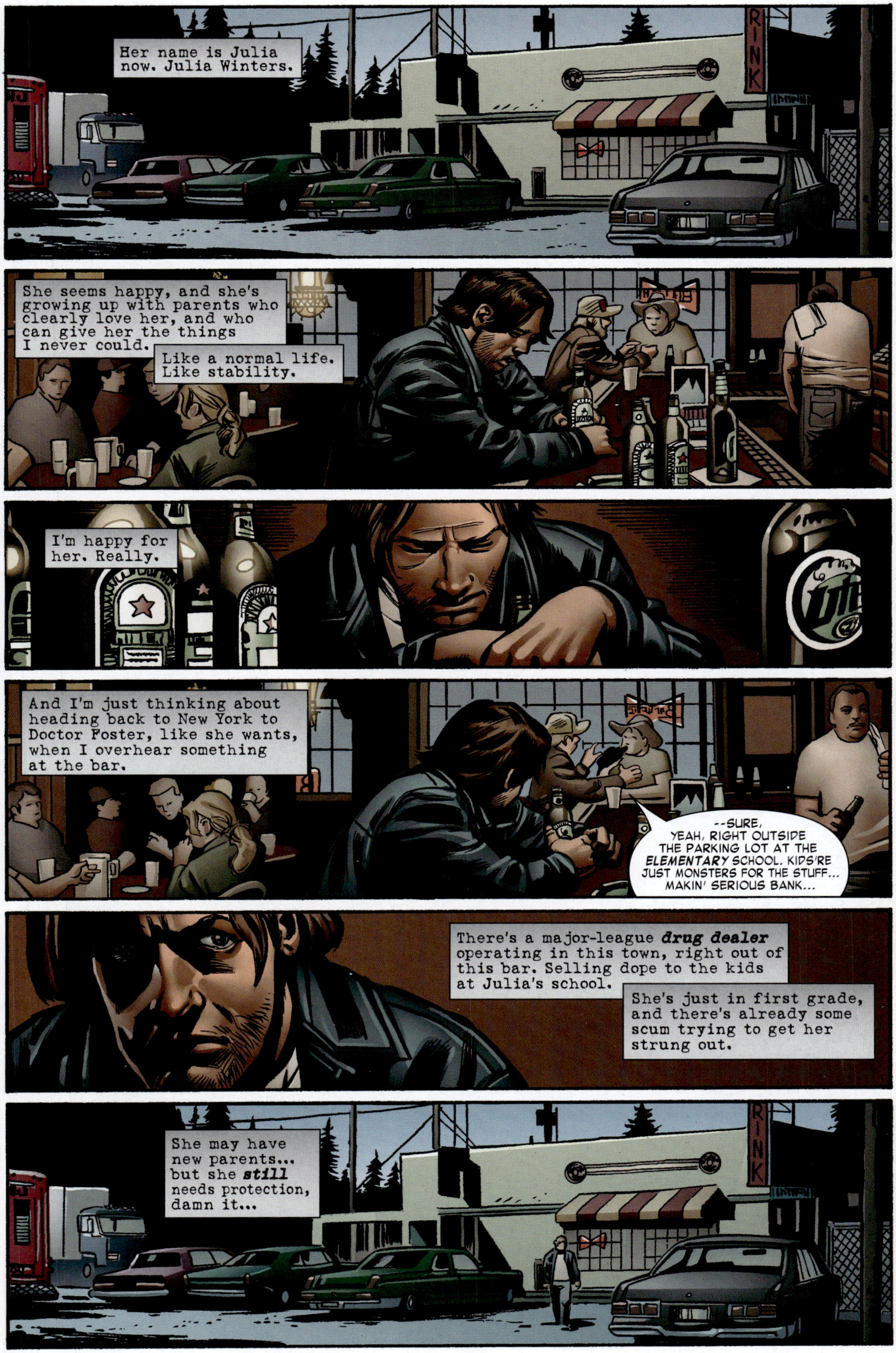

Her name is Julia now. Julia Winters.
She seems happy, and she's growing up with parents who clearly love her, and who can give her the things I never could.
Like a normal life. Like stability.
I'm happy for her. Really.
And I'm just thinking about heading back to New York to Doctor Foster, like she wants, when I overhear something at the bar.
--SURE, YEAH, RIGHT OUTSIDE THE PARKING LOT AT THE ELEMENTARY SCHOOL. KIDS'RE JUST MONSTERS FOR THE STUFF... MAKIN' SERIOUS BANK...
There's a major-league drug dealer operating in this town, right out of this bar. Selling dope to the kids at Julia's school.
She's just in first grade, and there's already some scum trying to get her strung out.
She may have new parents... but she still needs protection, damn it...

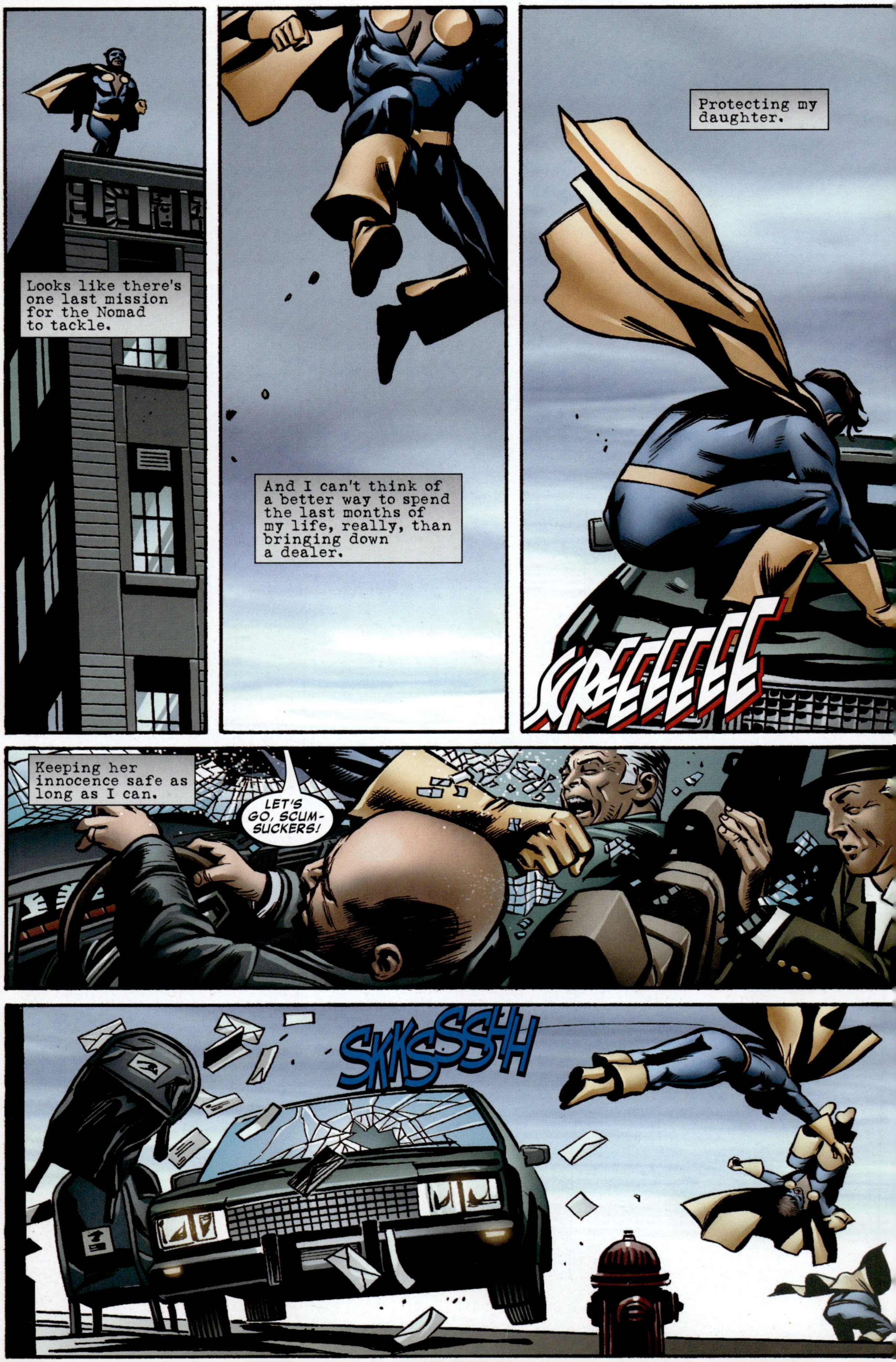
Looks like there's one last mission for the Nomad to tackle.
And I can't think of a better way to spend the last months of my life, really, than bringing down a dealer.
Protecting my daughter.
SCREEEEEEE
Keeping her innocence safe as long as I can.
LET'S GO, SCUM-SUCKERS!
SKKSSSHH

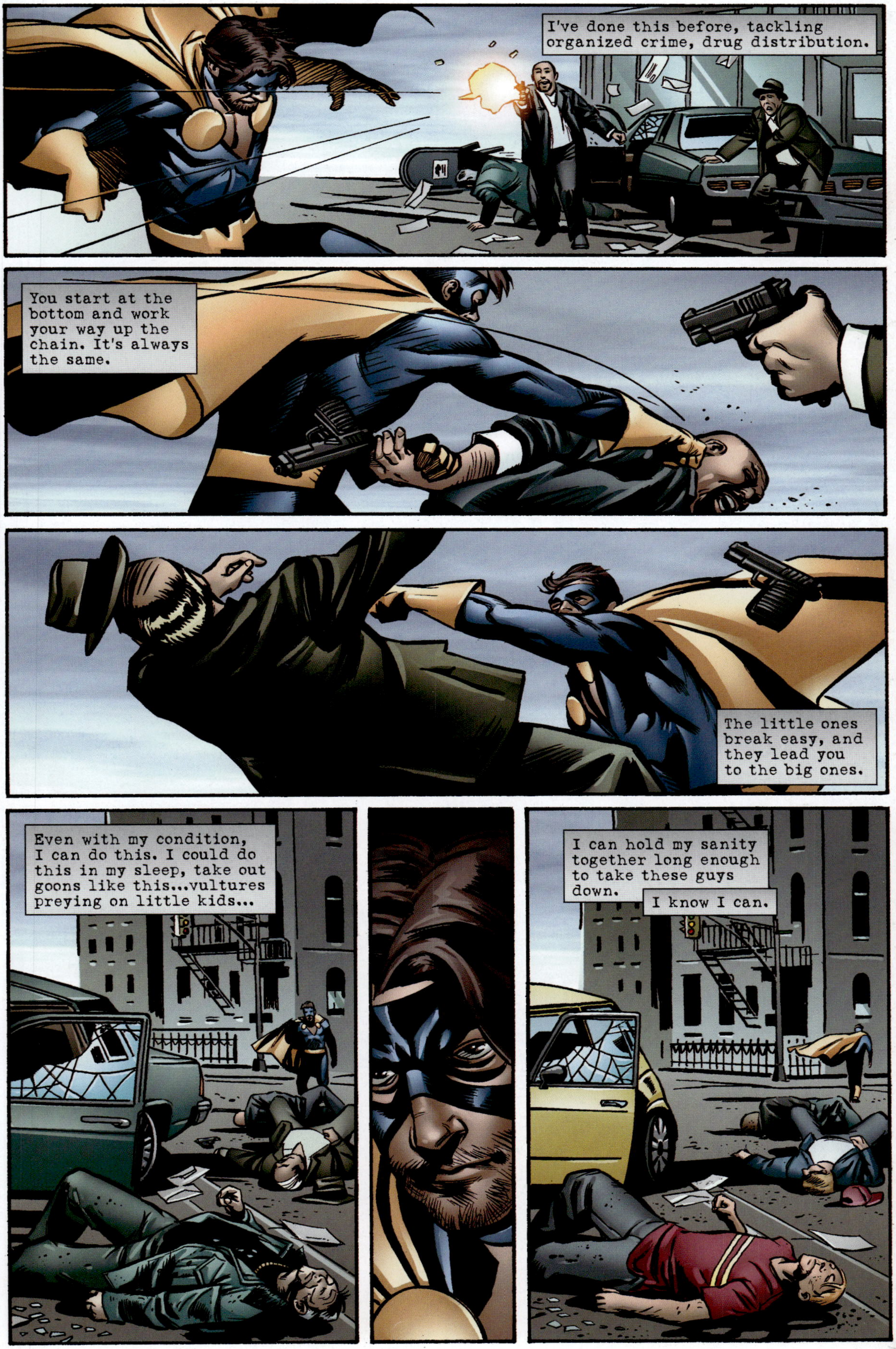
I've done this before, tackling organized crime, drug distribution.
You start at the bottom and work your way up the chain. It's always the same.
The little ones break easy, and they lead you to the big ones.
Even with my condition, I can do this. I could do this in my sleep, take out goons like this...vultures preying on little kids...
I can hold my sanity together long enough to take these guys down.
I know I can.

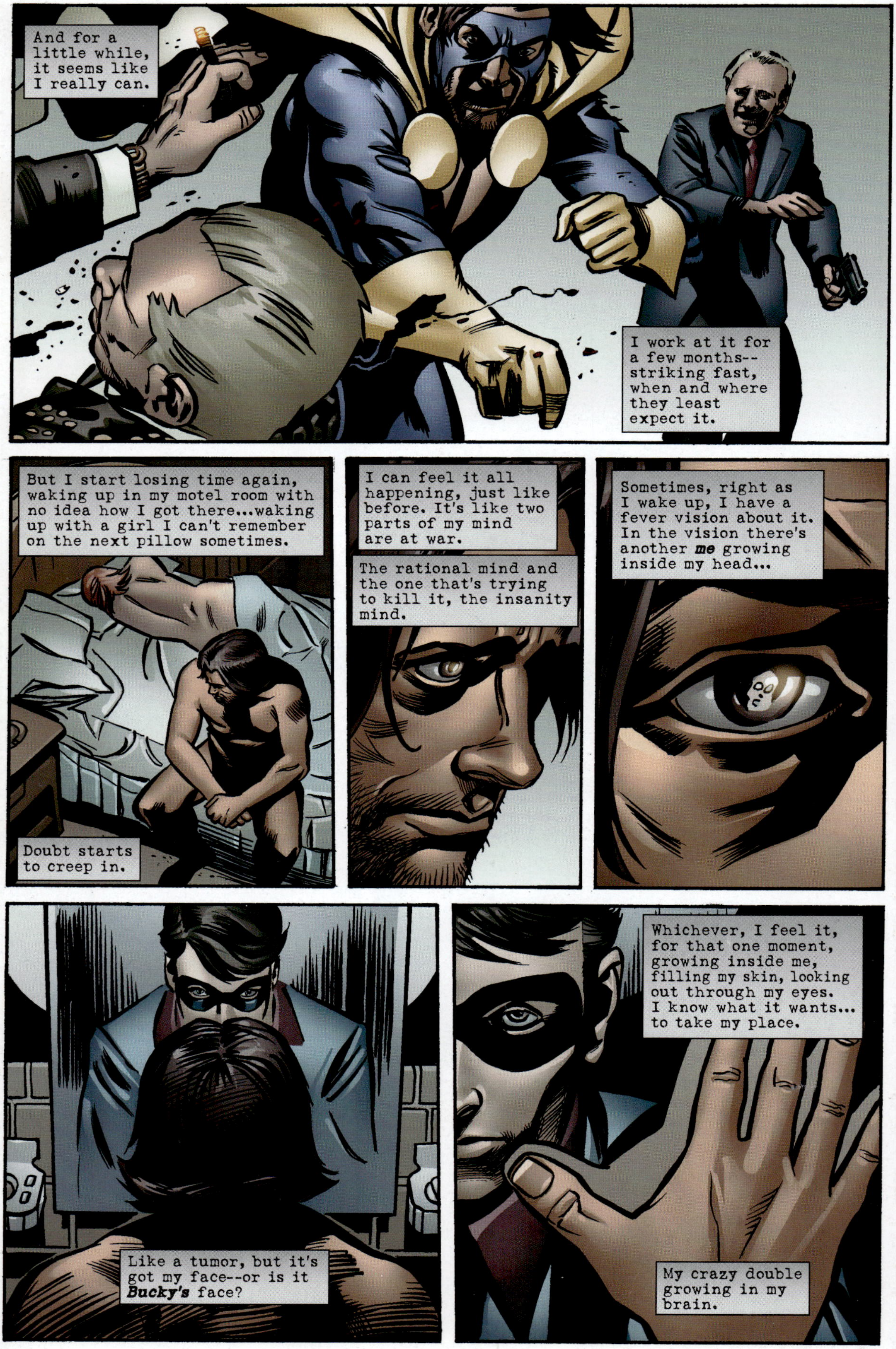
And for a little while, it seems like I really can.
I work at it for a few months--striking fast, when and where they least expect it.
But I start losing time again, waking up in my motel room with no idea how I got there...waking up with a girl I can't remember on the next pillow sometimes.
Doubt starts to creep in.
I can feel it all happening, just like before. It's like two parts of my mind are at war.
The rational mind and the one that's trying to kill it, the insanity mind.
Sometimes, right as I wake up, I have a fever vision about it. In the vision there's another *me* growing inside my head...
Like a tumor, but it's got my face--or is it ***Bucky's*** face?
Whichever, I feel it, for that one moment, growing inside me, filling my skin, looking out through my eyes. I know what it wants... to take my place.
My crazy double growing in my brain.

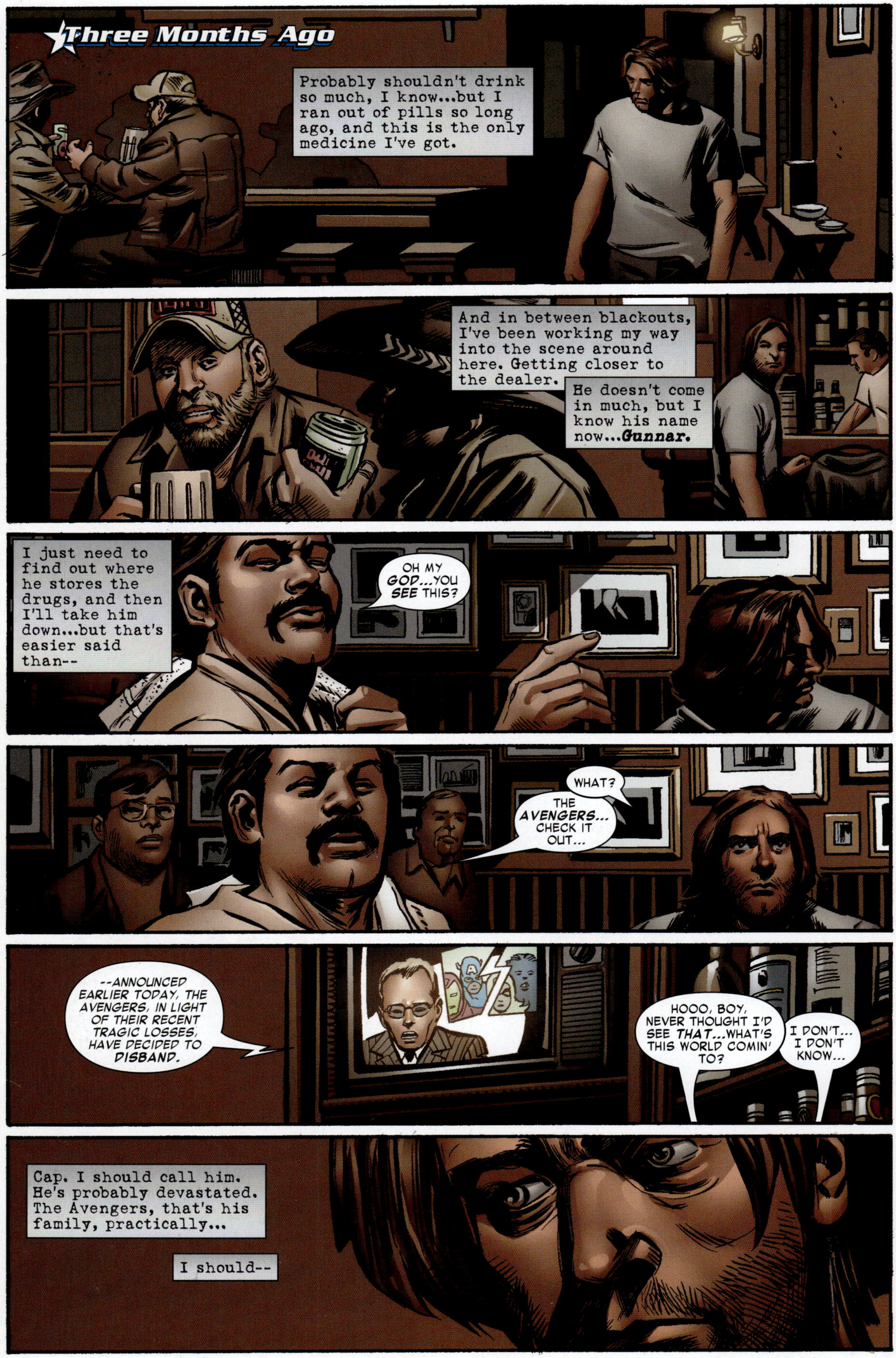
Three Months Ago
Probably shouldn't drink so much, I know...but I ran out of pills so long ago, and this is the only medicine I've got.
And in between blackouts, I've been working my way into the scene around here. Getting closer to the dealer.
He doesn't come in much, but I know his name now...Gunnar.
I just need to find out where he stores the drugs, and then I'll take him down...but that's easier said than--
OH MY GOD...YOU SEE THIS?
WHAT?
THE AVENGERS... CHECK IT OUT...
--ANNOUNCED EARLIER TODAY, THE AVENGERS, IN LIGHT OF THEIR RECENT TRAGIC LOSSES, HAVE DECIDED TO DISBAND.
HOOO, BOY, NEVER THOUGHT I'D SEE THAT...WHAT'S THIS WORLD COMIN' TO?
I DON'T... I DON'T KNOW...
Cap. I should call him. He's probably devastated. The Avengers, that's his family, practically...
I should--

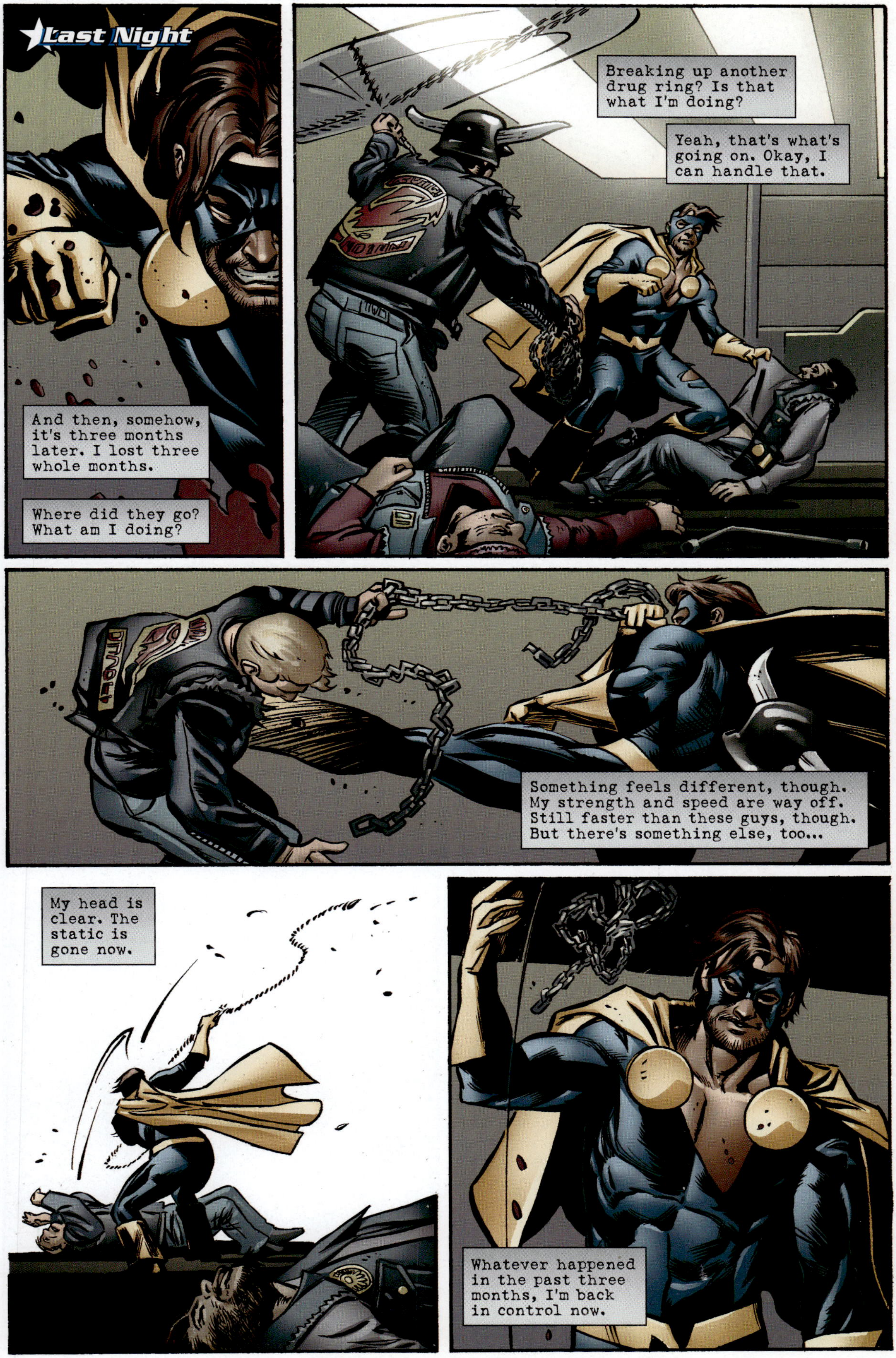
Last Night
And then, somehow, it's three months later. I lost three whole months.
Where did they go? What am I doing?
Breaking up another drug ring? Is that what I'm doing?
Yeah, that's what's going on. Okay, I can handle that.
Something feels different, though. My strength and speed are way off. Still faster than these guys, though. But there's something else, too...
My head is clear. The static is gone now.
Whatever happened in the past three months, I'm back in control now.

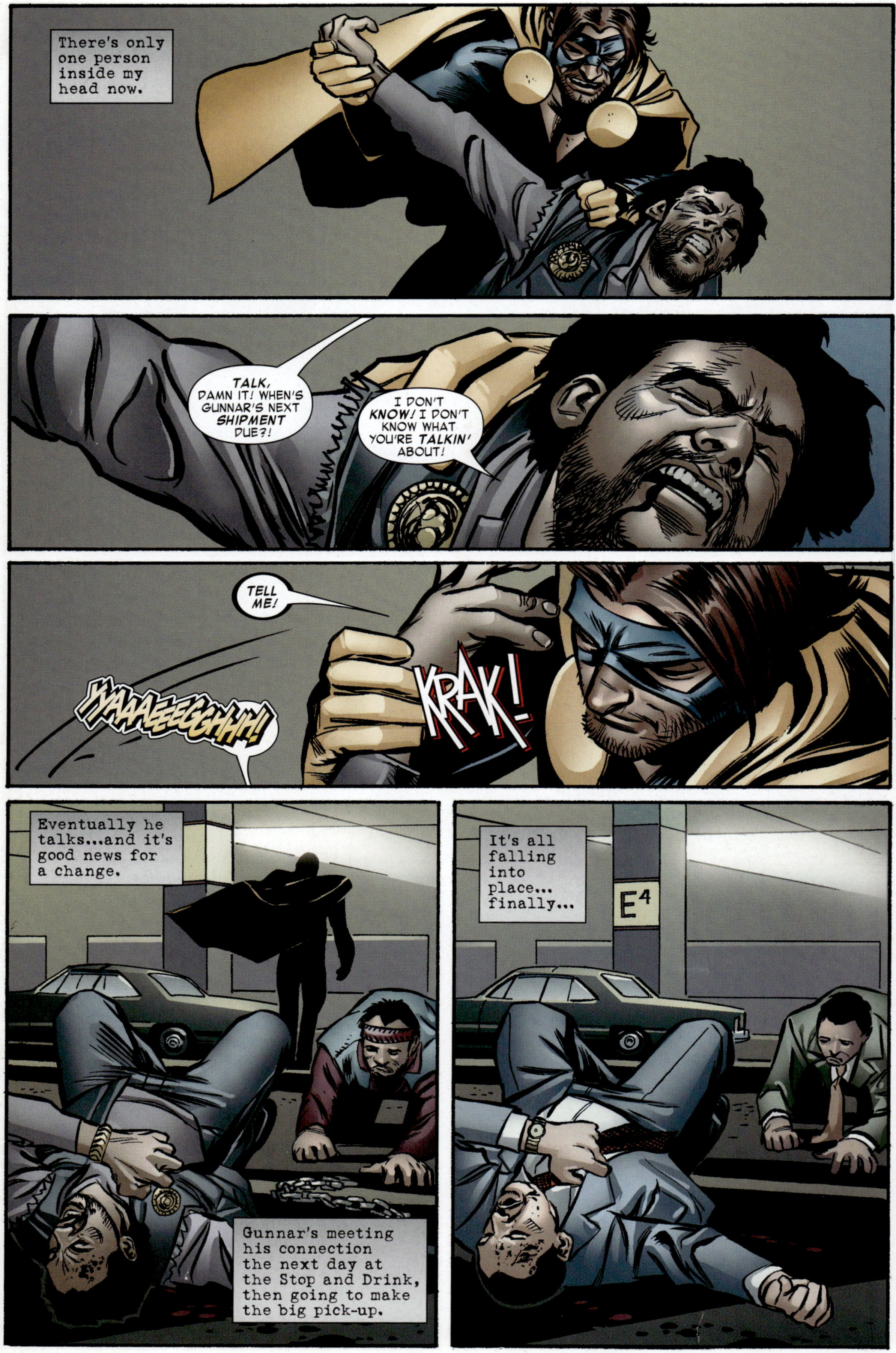
There's only one person inside my head now.
TALK, DAMN IT! WHEN'S GUNNAR'S NEXT SHIPMENT DUE?!
I DON'T KNOW! I DON'T KNOW WHAT YOU'RE TALKIN' ABOUT!
TELL ME!
YYAAAEEEGGHHH!
KRAK!
Eventually he talks...and it's good news for a change.
Gunnar's meeting his connection the next day at the Stop and Drink, then going to make the big pick-up.
It's all falling into place... finally...
E4

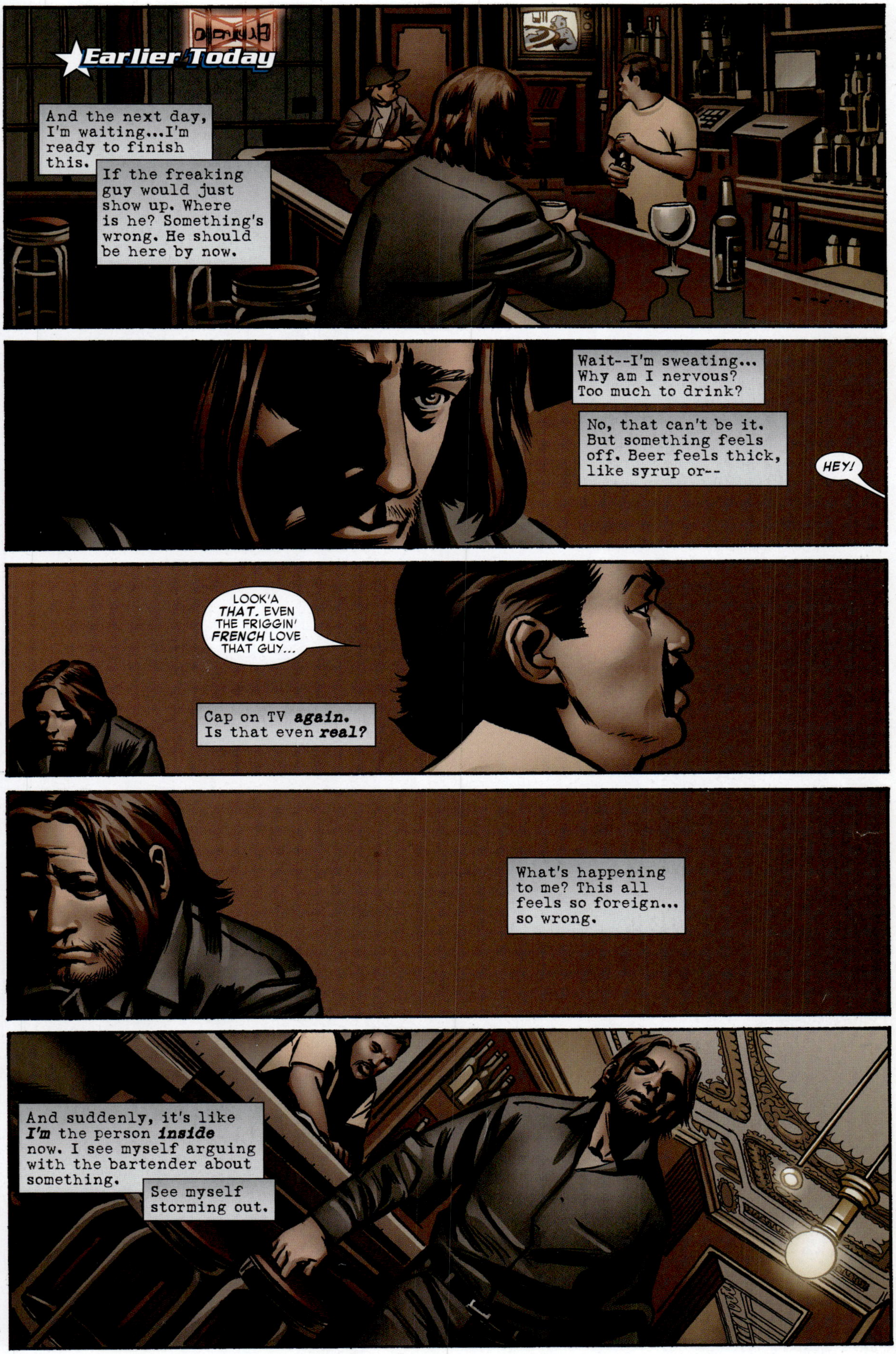
Earlier Today
And the next day, I'm waiting...I'm ready to finish this.
If the freaking guy would just show up. Where is he? Something's wrong. He should be here by now.
Wait--I'm sweating... Why am I nervous? Too much to drink?
No, that can't be it. But something feels off. Beer feels thick, like syrup or--
HEY!
LOOK'A THAT. EVEN THE FRIGGIN' FRENCH LOVE THAT GUY...
Cap on TV again. Is that even real?
What's happening to me? This all feels so foreign... so wrong.
And suddenly, it's like I'm the person inside now. I see myself arguing with the bartender about something.
See myself storming out.

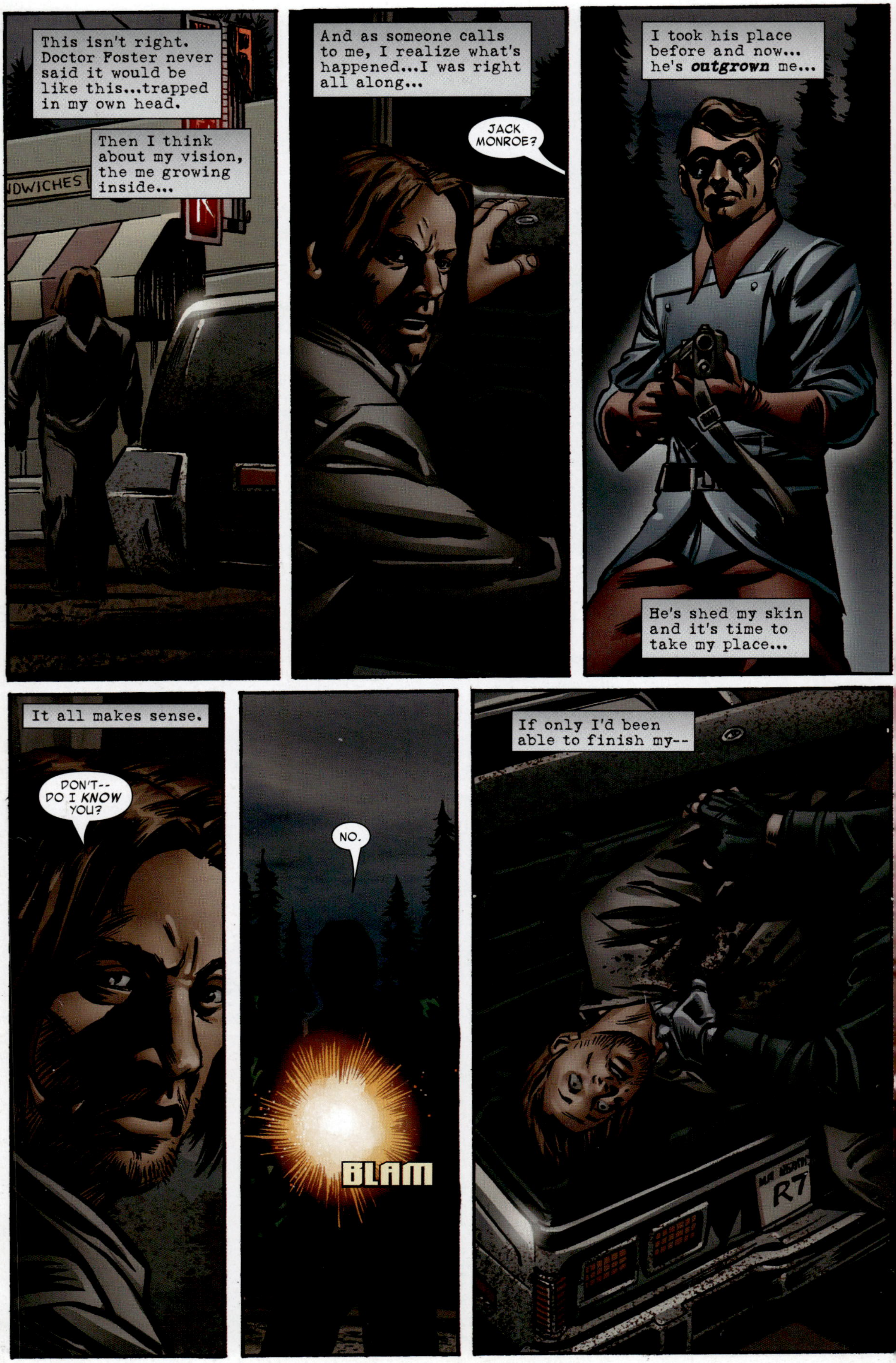
This isn't right. Doctor Foster never said it would be like this...trapped in my own head.
Then I think about my vision, the me growing inside...
NDWICHES
And as someone calls to me, I realize what's happened...I was right all along...
JACK MONROE?
I took his place before and now... he's *outgrown* me...
He's shed my skin and it's time to take my place...
It all makes sense.
DON'T-- DO I *KNOW* YOU?
NO.
BLAM
If only I'd been able to finish my--
R7

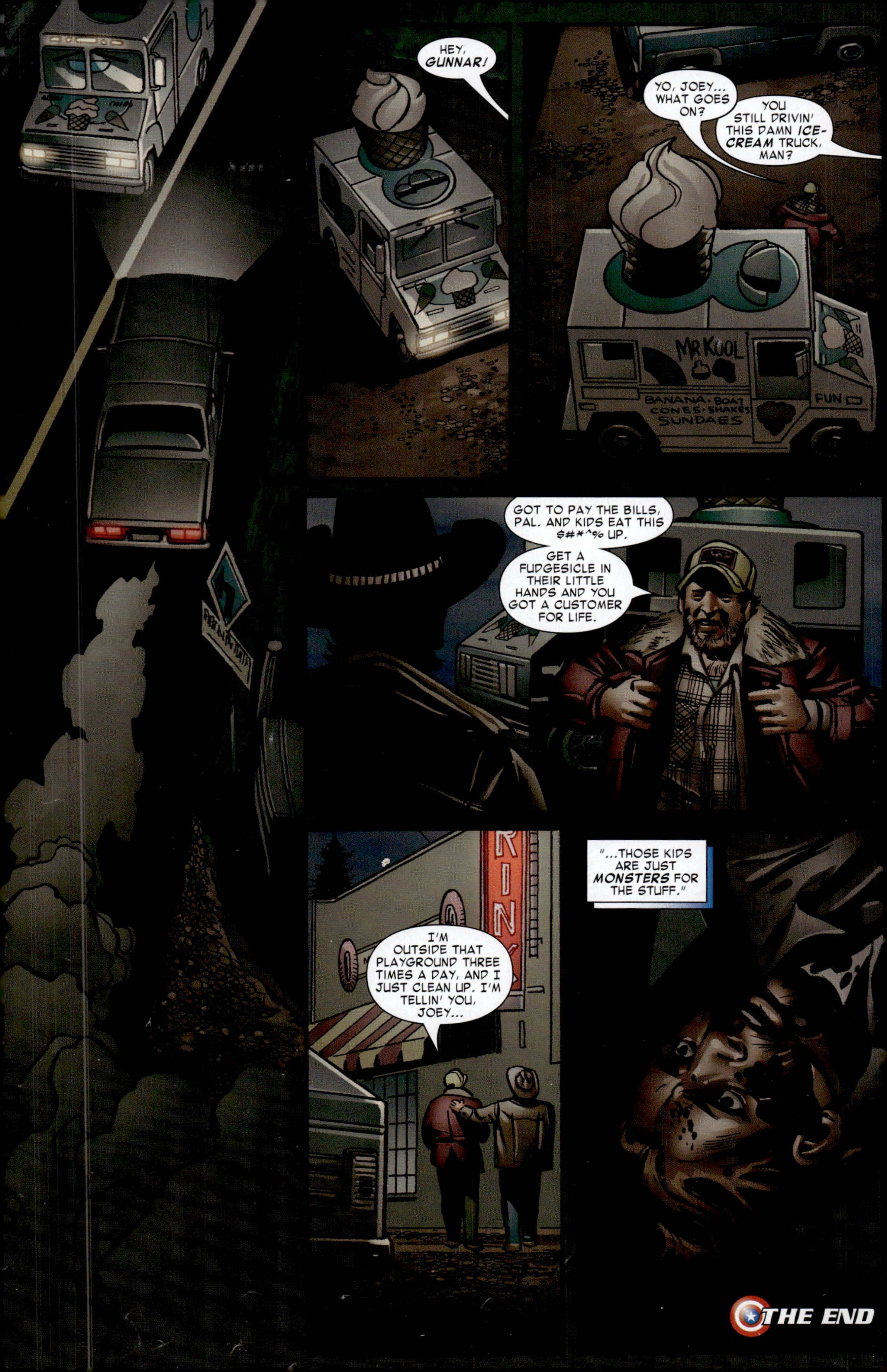
HEY, GUNNAR!
YO, JOEY... WHAT GOES ON?
YOU STILL DRIVIN' THIS DAMN ICE-CREAM TRUCK, MAN?
MR KOOL
BANANA · BOAT CONES · SHAKES SUNDAES
FUN
GOT TO PAY THE BILLS, PAL. AND KIDS EAT THIS $#*^% UP.
GET A FUDGESICLE IN THEIR LITTLE HANDS AND YOU GOT A CUSTOMER FOR LIFE.
I'M OUTSIDE THAT PLAYGROUND THREE TIMES A DAY, AND I JUST CLEAN UP. I'M TELLIN' YOU, JOEY...
"...THOSE KIDS ARE JUST MONSTERS FOR THE STUFF."
THE END

PROMOTIONAL ART FOR *CAPTAIN AMERICA* #1 BY STEVE EPTING

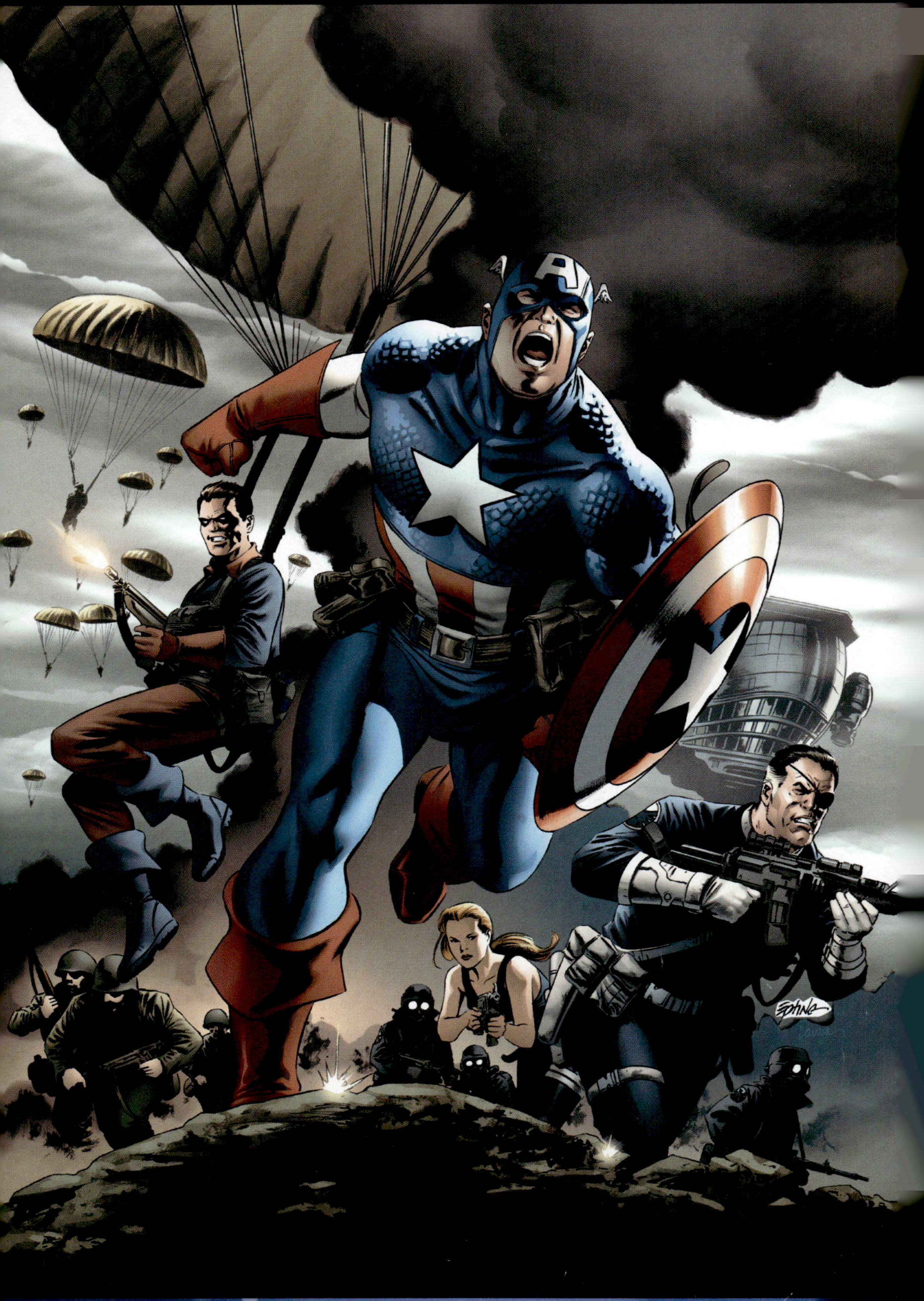

CAPTAIN AMERICA #6 VARIANT COVER BY STEVE EPTING

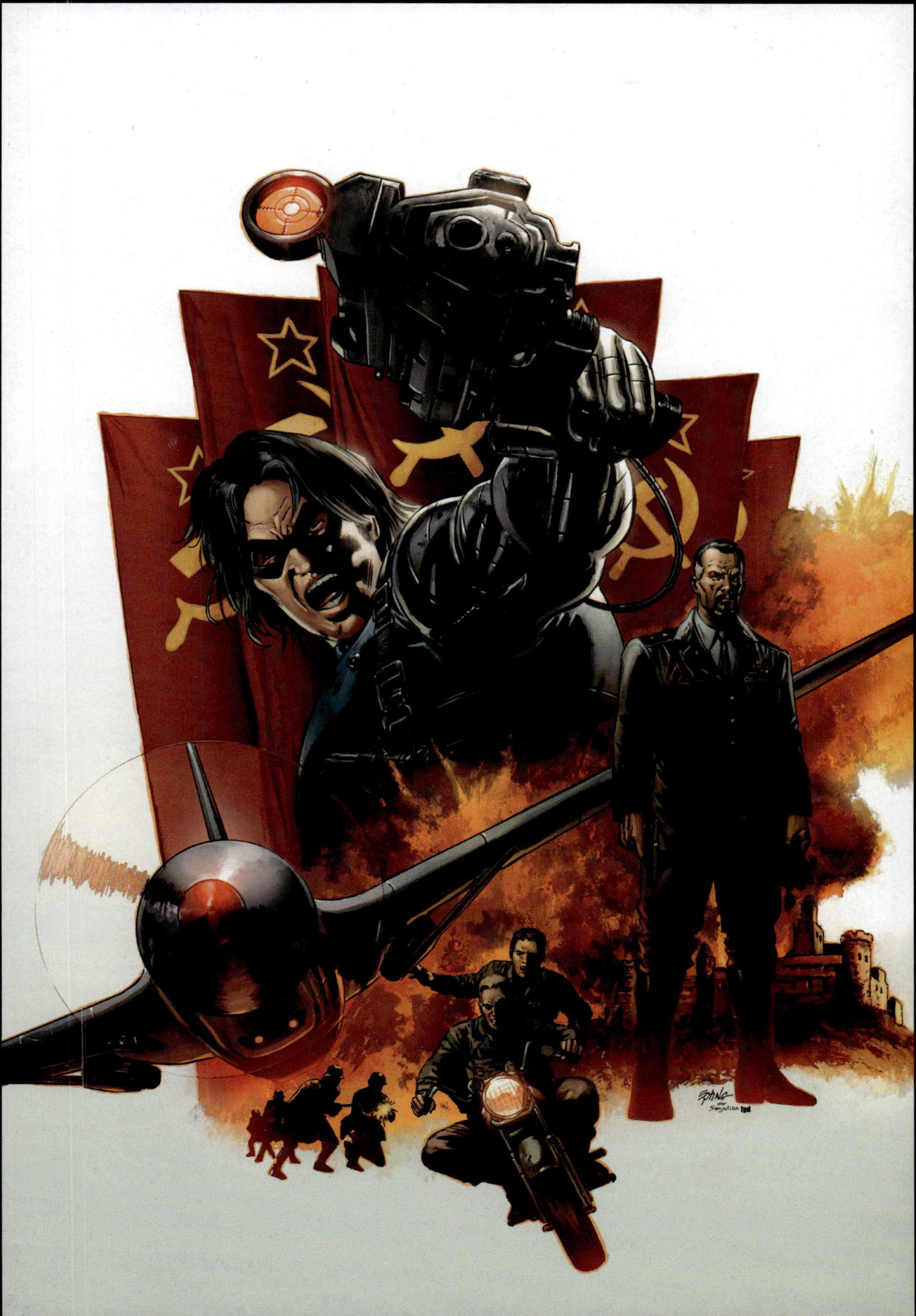

WINTER SOLDIER CONCEPT SKETCHES BY STEVE EPTING

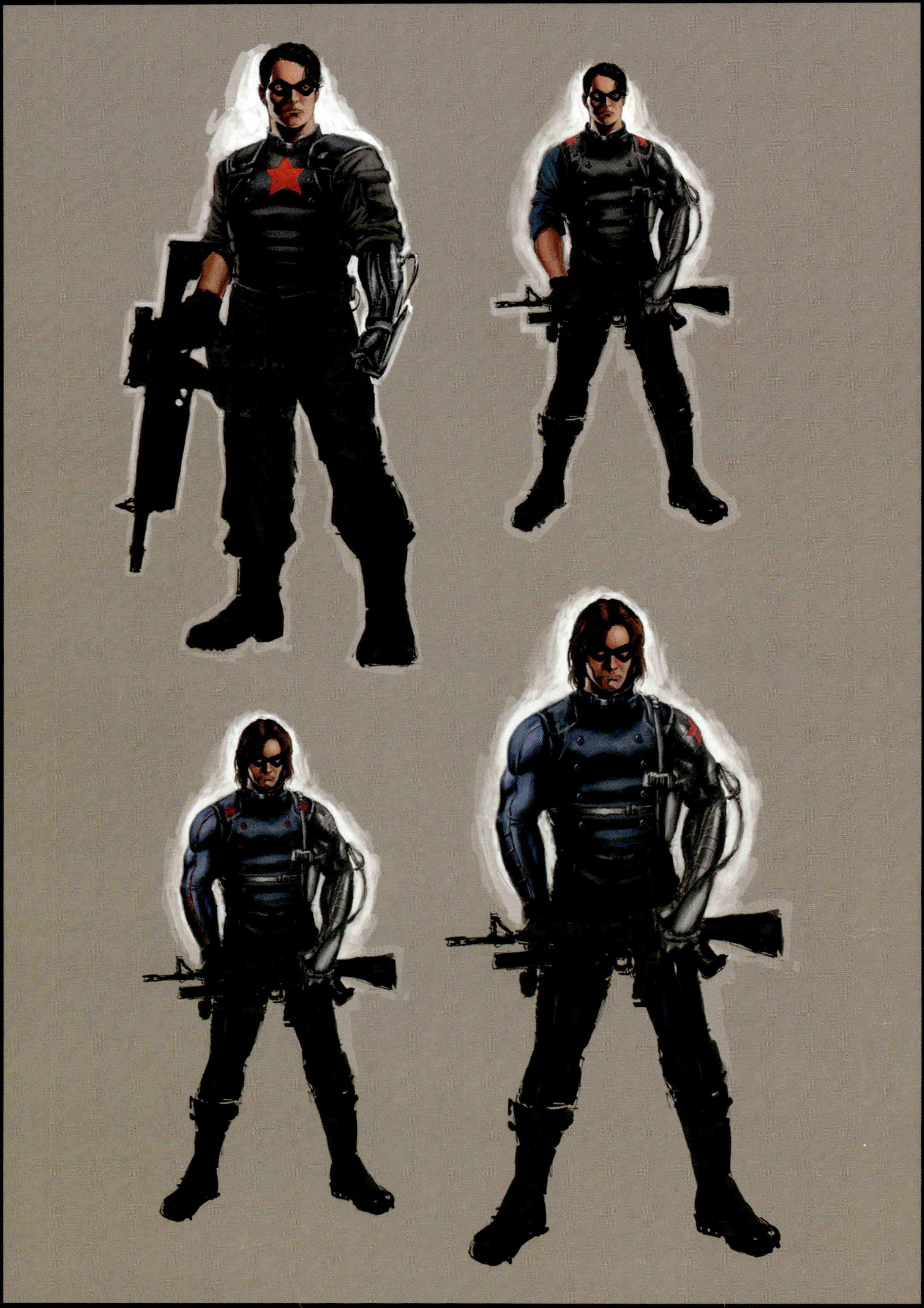